UNITED STATES
NAVAL POWER
IN A CHANGING WORLD

Other books by Edwin Bickford Hooper

Mobility, Support, Endurance: A Story of Naval Operational Logistics in the Vietnam War

The Navy Department: Evolution and Fragmentation

With Dean C. Allard and Oscar P. Fitzgerald
The United States Navy and the Vietnam Conflict: The Setting of the Stage to 1959

UNITED STATES
NAVAL POWER
IN A CHANGING WORLD

Edwin Bickford Hooper

PRAEGER

New York
Westport, Connecticut
London

Library of Congress Cataloging-in-Publication Data

Hooper, Edwin Bickford.
    United States naval power in a changing world /
Edwin Bickford Hooper.
        Bibliography: p.   cm.
        Includes index.
        ISBN 0-275-92738-5 (alk. paper)
        1. Sea-power—United States—History.   2. United
States. Navy—History.   3. United States—History, Naval.
I. Title.
VA55.H66 1988
359'.03'0973—dc19   87-29942

VA
55
.H55
.H66
1988

Library of Congress Catalog Card Number: 87-29942

ISBN: 0-275-92738-5

First published in 1988

Praeger Publishers, One Madison Avenue, New York, NY 10010
A division of Greenwood Press, Inc.

Printed in the United States of America

The paper used in this book complies with the
Permanent Paper Standard issued by the National
Information Standards Organization (Z39.48-1984).

10   9   8   7   6   5   4   3   2   1

To the memory of my beloved wife,
Elizabeth Withers Patrick Hooper,
source of joy and inspiration.

Contents

Editors' Preface   xiii

Preface   xv

1. Basic Considerations   1

PART I: THE EARLY YEARS

2. Naval Power and Winning Independence   9
   The Revolutionary War Begins   10
   Maritime Warfare   13
   The Continental Navy   14
   Privateers   15
   France Enters the War   16
   The Final Phase of the Revolutionary War   16
   Sea Control   17

3. Consequences of Neglect   19
   The Department of the Navy   21
   The Quasi-War with France   22
   The Barbary Wars   24
   Declining Readiness   27

PART II: THE TRANSITIONAL PERIOD

4. Coming of Age   31
   The War of 1812   31
   Conclusion of the Barbary Wars   34
   The Board of Navy Commissioners   35
   Naval Influence after the Barbary Wars   38

5. Advancing Technology   40
   Steam Propulsion   42
   Ordnance   44
   The Bureau System   44
   The War with Mexico   45
   Advances in Technology   48
   Peacetime Operations   49

6. The Role of Naval Power in Preserving the Union   51
   The Civil War   53
   Blockade   54
   The Navy Department   55
   Amphibious Operations   58
   Logistics Support   60
   Cruiser Warfare   61

7. Inland Waters   62
   Riverine Control   64
   Ironclads   67
   Operations in Support of the Army of the Potomac   68

8. Concluding Phases of Warfare between the States   71
   Developments in Iron-clad Ships and Torpedoes   71
   Continuing Riverine War in the West   73
   The War Ends   75

9. The Postwar Period   76
   Showing the Flag   76
   Direction of Naval Affairs   78
   Worldwide Deployments   81
   Growing Obsolescence   81

PART III: THE NEW NAVY

10. Beginnings of the New Navy   85
   Strategy   86
   The Concepts of Mahan   87

11. Warfare against a European Power   90
   The Spanish-American War   91
   Army-Navy Operations in Cuba   94

12. Prelude to Another War   96
   Naval Power Gains New Dimensions   98
   Naval Power Enters a New Era   100
   The London Naval Conference   101

Ship Characteristics 101
The Nation Becomes a Major Naval Power 102

PART IV: TWO WORLD WARS

13. The Great War 119
    Undersea Warfare 120
    The Western Pacific 121
    Maritime Warfare 121
    Fleet Actions 122
    Air Warfare 123
    The United States 123

14. America Enters the War 127
    The Naval Transportation Service 130
    Naval Operations 130
    Effects of the Blockade 131

15. Between Wars 133
    The Air Power Issue 133
    Disarmament Treaties 134
    Curtailment of Naval Construction 137
    Research and Development 139
    Amphibious Warfare 141
    An Increasingly Troubled World 142

16. Another Global War Begins 143
    Neutrality Patrol 145
    Norway 146

17. The Crucial War at Sea 149
    The Mediterranean 150
    Battle of the Atlantic 154
    Invasion of the Soviet Union 154
    The Far East 155

18. A Two-Ocean War 156
    Command of the Operating Forces 158
    The Pacific War 160
    The North Atlantic 166
    The South Pacific 167

19. Turning the Tide 168
    Antisubmarine Warfare 169
    Air Defense 171
    The Pacific Campaigns 172

The Mediterranean   175

20. World War II: The Final Phases   176
     The Central Pacific   176
     Submarine Warfare   181
     The Atomic Bomb   181

PART V: THE NUCLEAR AGE

21. The Cold War   185
     The Soviet Union   186
     Demobilization   187

22. Erosion   190
     The National Security Act   190
     Expansion of Communist Control   196

23. Limited War   198
     The Korean War   200
     Mine Warfare   203
     Naval Air Support   205

24. The New Look   208
     Strategy   210
     Southeast Asia   210
     Taiwan   214

25. Naval Influence   216
     Ballistic Missile Submarines   217
     The Suez War   218
     Deterrence   219
     The Middle East   219
     The Far East   220
     Reorganization   220
     The Cold War Continues   222

26. Flexible Response   225
     The Bay of Pigs   226
     Vietnam: The Beginning of U.S. Involvement   227
     Cuban Missile Crisis   228
     Counterinsurgency   229
     The Vietnam War   230
     Cambodia   236

27. The Shifting Balance of Sea Power   238
     The Defense Establishment   239
     The Soviet Navy   241

Soviet Strategy 242
The U.S. Navy 245

PART VI: THE FUTURE

28. The Past Is Prologue 251

29. Requisites 260

Notes 263

Bibliography 275

Index 285

About the Author 295

ILLUSTRATIONS

Maps

1.1	The Globe	2
2.1	Northern Waters	12
3.1	The Mediterranean Sea	25
6.1	Coast and Rivers of Southern States	54
14.1	European Waters	129
18.1	Ocean Hemisphere	162
23.1	East Asian Waters	199
26.1	Southeast Asia	234

Charts

3.1	Naval Organization in Early Years (1800)	23
4.1	Naval Organization with Board of Navy Commissioners (1817)	36
6.1	Naval Organization in 1862	57
13.1	Naval Organization in 1916	125
18.1	Naval Organization During World War II	159
27.1	Department of Defense Organization Chart, 1986	240

Plates

1. Alfred Thayer Mahan 105
2. Admiral S. G. Gorshkov 105
3. USS *Surprise* capturing packet 106
4. Gustavus Conynham 106

 5. Commodore John Rodgers   107
 6. Rear Admiral David Dixon Porter   107
 7. Admiral William Benson and Secretary of the Navy Josephus Daniels   108
 8. Fleet Admiral Ernest J. King   108
 9. Admiral Arleigh A. Burke   109
10. *Monitor* vs *Merrimack*   109
11. Battle of Santiago   110
12. U.S. Corvette *John Adams*   110
13. Underway replenishment during World War II   111
14. World War I convoy of U.S. merchant vessels   111
15. Confederate keg mine   112
16. South Korean minesweeper blown up   112
17. USS *Gloucester* in Battle of Santiago   113
18. Fletcher-class destroyers   113
19. Amphibious assault, Mexican War   114
20. Amphibious assault, World War II   114
21. Civil War riverine force   115
22. Vietnam riverine force   115

Editor's Preface

When Vice Admiral Edwin B. Hooper retired in December 1976 as director of naval history, he determined to take on this analysis of the role of the navy in United States' history to determine the "fundamental principles concerning the naval power needs of the nation." He knew it would be a lengthy undertaking. The manuscript had just been accepted for publication when he died suddenly in September 1986 at his 55th Naval Academy reunion.

We have acted as editors on his behalf with the goal of publishing the work in the form he would have wanted. The footnoting has taken considerable effort; his working files contained extensive quotes, but tracing the precise references was sometimes difficult. We believe that we have been successful, but apologize for any errors. The bibliography is assembled from his notes.

The maps are those he requested in the manuscript. The organization chart for World War II is from a 1946 report by the secretary of the navy, and the 1986 chart is from the Department of Defense. We could find no earlier charts and thus take responsibility for those included here. Finally, we chose the photographs to illustrate some of the history emphasized by the author; they came from the files of the Naval Historical Center.

We wish to thank Rear Admiral Raymond P. Hunter for reviewing the final manuscript. The assistance of the personnel at the Naval Historical Center and at the Naval Historical Foundation is also greatly appreciated.

We have striven to maintain both fact and the author's emphasis in all text changes. We thank Carol Stock for her expert and sensitive editing in this difficult situation.

William P. Hooper
E. Bickford Hooper, Jr.
Dean C. Allard

Preface

The cumulative effect of technological advances over the past two centuries has altered and diversified the means of applying military power. The changes have included those in overlapping capabilities of sea and land forces. Navies now include submarines of extended endurance. High performance aircraft operate from naval ships as well as from airfields on land. Satellites have been introduced capable of performing a number of military tasks such as surveillance and reconnaissance, the provision of navigational information, and relaying communications. Conventional explosives have been augmented by nuclear and thermonuclear warheads of vast destructive power. Guided missiles capable of performing a variety of tasks have been introduced, some capable of being launched from land, some from surface vessels, some from submarines, and some from aircraft.

The motivation to tackle this work came from a growing concern that many recent decisions and actions in the United States have not reflected a proper balance between the consideration of such changes and the enduring lessons of the past, a few of which have had to be learned again and again. The approach has been to conduct a selective review of naval power, the basic changes that have taken place, and the employment of that power in peace and war during the course of American history—in an attempt to reveal lessons that may be of enduring validity.

The main focus is on such matters as policies, naval capabilities and missions, the influence of naval power, determinants of that power, the direction and management of naval affairs, the exercise of command over the operating forces, aspects of naval power that are unique, and interservice relationships.

The selection of coverage and interpretations are influenced by the knowledge and experience, and perhaps biases, gained by the author in a wide variety of assignments at sea and ashore over the span of almost a half century of naval service.

Interpretations of lessons of the past in such a way as to be meaningful today and in the future must take into account enduring as well as changing factors. Therefore, a brief discussion of basic considerations precedes the main chapters.

ACKNOWLEDGMENTS

The author is highly grateful for the constructive comments of Doctors Dean Allard and George Chernowitz on an earlier draft.

1

Basic Considerations

To understand the naval element of national power, the most basic consideration of all—one that seems all too often overlooked—is that the *raison d'être* of a navy is use of the sea, nonmilitary and military. Another basic fact is that the interconnecting oceans surrounding the continents and islands—the habitat of man— cover some 70 percent of the globe. Expanses of sea separate the United States from all the other countries of the world except Canada and Mexico and also separate the 48 contiguous states from the 49th and 50th states, Alaska and Hawaii, and from Puerto Rico and other island territories. This allows the nation ready access to the sea as a result of its long coastlines, many harbors, inlets, and rivers.

Although sea-going vessels are no longer the sole means to transport persons and other cargoes between lands separated by oceans, the laws of physics require that the vast majority of the tonnages still go by such vessels. As a result of sea water's fluid properties and a density of about 64 pounds per cubic foot, with some variation from place to place, buoyancy is sufficient to support displacement vessels carrying heavy and voluminous cargoes.

Transoceanic air transport first became possible as a consequence of developments in lighter-than-air craft. There was some use of dirigibles to move individuals and items overseas. But, since buoyancy was merely the difference in weight between air and the hydrogen or helium contained in gas bags, the cargo weight was extremely restricted. On the other hand, continuing advances in airplane capabilities have resulted in spectacular increases in speed, range, and carrying capacity to the point that most travel by individuals and small groups overseas, along with mail and increasing amounts of other urgent cargoes, is now by air. Further improvements are to be expected; but since airplane lift is dependent on air thrust produced by air flow across airlift surfaces, carrying capacity is severely limited.

Meanwhile, advances in structural materials and ship propulsion systems have made possible the introduction of large carriers of liquefied natural gas, vessels

**Map 1.1
The Globe**

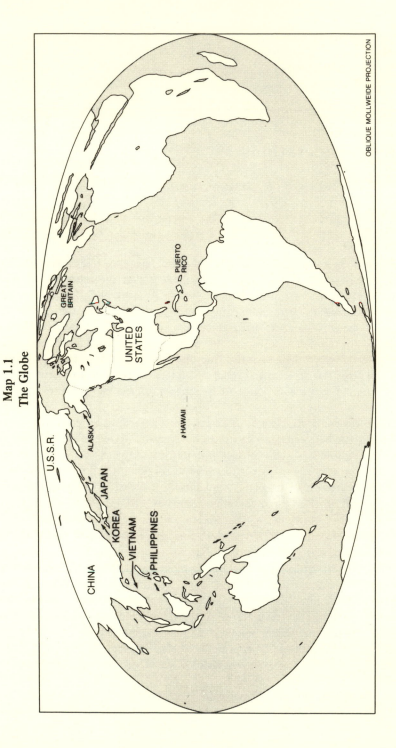

OBLIQUE MOLLWEIDE PROJECTION

U.S.S.R.

GREAT
BRITAIN

UNITED
STATES

PUERTO
RICO

ALASKA

HAWAII

CHINA

JAPAN

KOREA

VIETNAM

PHILIPPINES

Source: Drawn for the editors by the University of Maryland Geography Department, Cartography Services Laboratory, 1987.

capable of transporting as many as 1,000 24-foot containers, huge ore carriers, and supertankers displacing as much as 300,000 tons. Water's viscosity is low enough to permit ships to proceed at moderate speeds with relatively little drag. Consequently, it will always provide an extraordinarily economical means of transportation for most cargoes. Per-ton fuel consumption is but a small fraction of that for aircraft, and sources of natural crude oil are gradually being depleted. As the energy situation worsens in time, increased emphasis will be placed on means of transportation that require minimum consumption of oil and its distillates.

Many countries are becoming ever more dependent upon overseas shipments. One of these is the United States which, once largely self-sufficient, has had to rely increasingly on imported petroleum, minerals, and ores. Indicative of expanding demands was the increase in ocean-borne commercial cargoes to and from the United States in the 1970s, which totaled more than 800 million tons by the end of the decade.

There have been major increases in the use of air transport by the military since the middle of the century, although restricted in size and tonnage. Such a means of transportation is, of course, largely dependent upon the availability of secure, conveniently located, and adequate airfields. Important use was made of air transport during the Vietnam War. In this case, conditions were favorable, particularly as a result of the high priority given to the extensive airfield construction program. Nevertheless, all of the fuel, over 99 percent of the ammunition, and 96 percent of the dry-cargo tonnages were delivered by sealift.

Consequently, there is every reason to believe that future peacetime and wartime naval roles relating to sea lines of communication will be similar to those of earlier years, and fully as crucial.

As for some of the other uses of the sea, the world's oceans have always provided one of the most plentiful sources of food. In recent years the demands for catches have multiplied. Not only are a number of countries critically dependent on sea food for the protein needed by their inhabitants, but certain types of fish have become an increasingly important source of fertilizer in some parts of the globe. Throughout history fishing rights have been a recurring cause of conflict between nations, and the ability to prevent the exercise of such rights has been used at times as a means of coercion.

Modern times have seen a great expansion in efforts to extract other resources from the oceans and their bottoms. The increasing demands of developed countries for a number of critical raw materials have been depleting known land sources. Although begun only recently, the extraction of oil and gas from the sea bottom has rapidly expanded. Offshore wells already provide significant quantities of crude oil.

Appreciable amounts of tin and titanium are being extracted from continental shelves. Attempts have been underway to develop economical means of gathering manganese nodules from deep ocean bottoms. Scarcity, rising prices, and controls of critical materials will undoubtedly lead to additional underseas mining projects.

In any case, disagreements between nations concerning the rights of exploiting ocean resources indicate that competition over them can become a source of serious maritime conflict and even war.

There are other important uses or potential uses of the sea, although they do not seem to have similar implications for naval power. From early times salt has been obtained from sea water by evaporation utilizing the sun's rays or other heat sources. There are many as yet unexploited possibilities of extracting additional chemical compounds and elements. The oceans are, of course, the primary source of the fresh water deposited on land by rain after natural evaporation. Man-made evaporator-condenser systems are being employed to furnish fresh water to arid regions, and one scheme proposed from time to time is towing massive icebergs from the Antarctic Ocean to such regions. Tides and tidal basins can be used to generate electricity. As a result of major differences in temperature of surface water and that at deeper depths, the vast heat capacity of the oceans is a potential source of energy.

Recent years are one of the periods when efforts have been made to reach agreement on a body of international law pertaining to uses of the seas. The most recent agreement sought encompassed such matters as national jurisdiction over coastal fishing zones, which some countries now claim to extend 200 miles offshore; national control over the resources of the continental shelves; boundaries of exclusive economic zones between states; deep-sea mining rights; and extensions of territorial waters. A word of caution, however, is in order, for experience has demonstrated that whenever an aggressive nation possesses what it deems to be sufficient naval power, and it deems that its objectives outweigh the predicted consequences, international laws are likely to be violated.

As for military uses of the sea, naval power is unique in a number of respects. One is the ability of naval forces to exercise influence and carry out important missions while operating on or within the vast expanses of the seas generally recognized as an international domain open to all. Unlike situations in which land and air forces are operating from bases on foreign soil, naval operations need not raise questions of the sovereign rights of other nations.

There have been times when national objectives were achieved through shows of force or controlled use of power by navies, without resort to war. At other times conflicts have been resolved by maritime warfare, unaccompanied by warfare on land.

Key considerations to be taken into account regarding employment of a navy and the relationships of its operations with those of the other armed services are the unique capabilities of warships, including their high degree of self-sufficiency and operational endurance, and their ability on short notice to shift from one area of the world to another. Also, the capability of conducting sustained operations at sea has been extended by the underway replenishment rigs and techniques developed by the U.S. Navy in the twentieth century. And, as so vividly demonstrated in World War II, the dependence upon fixed bases can be reduced drastically by using special ships and craft to provide services and support at advanced anchorages.

Another important consideration is that warship capabilities typically have included—in addition to their high degree of self-sufficiency—offensive and defensive weapons, countermeasure devices, communications, and means of command and control. These contribute to the versatility and operational flexibility of the vessels and to the ease with which individual ships or groups of ships can be combined and recombined into task organizations tailored to varying situations—in peace or war.

Also to be considered are the new dimensions added to naval power by developments in submarines and their weapons. In this case, unique capabilities stem primarily from the extent to which the submarines are able to operate and carry out missions while hidden beneath the surface of the sea—an ability that varies according to the nature of the operations, underwater endurance, and silencing measures, as well as the antisubmarine capabilities of the opponent.

Projections into the future must take into account factors such as these, as well as the relevant laws of physics. For instance, not only are light and radar subject to reflections at the ocean's often turbulent interface with air, depending upon the angle of incidence, but also the energy of electromagnetic waves is rapidly attenuated by sea water.

As a consequence, efforts to detect submarines must rely considerably on underwater sound, utilizing both active and passive systems that have their own limitations. Although sound propagates well in water, the sea is not a homogeneous medium. Changes in density and layering cause refractions and in some cases channeling. Scattering and ambient noises complicate the problem. There are other means of detection that exploit the fact that a submarine presents a magnetic anomaly in the ocean, but the potential detection ranges by these means are severely limited.

As in other warfare areas, further progress is bound to be made, both in the means of detection and in countermeasures. However, there seems to be little doubt that the ability to maintain a high degree of concealment within the ocean medium will continue, depending upon the nature of the operations required to fulfill a mission.

Today one of the most important military uses of the sea is the employment of submarines to deter nuclear warfare. If properly operated, they should be able to avoid detection. Furthermore, survival probability is being enhanced by expanding operating areas by developing longer-range ballistic missiles.

Meanwhile, the predictions of so many, following the advent of the atomic age, that there would be little need for naval power in the future have proven to be unfounded. Instead, traditional roles of navies remain important, and the basic principles concerning that power and its effectiveness remain valid.

Part I

The Early Years

2

Naval Power and
Winning Independence

The exercise of naval power was a decisive factor in determining the course of history in the British colonies of North America and the outcome of the Revolutionary War.

Basic, important lessons can be derived from those years regarding naval policies, the direction and administration of naval affairs, the roles and missions of naval forces, and naval logistics.

Much of the credit for the British Royal Navy's successes in the Seven Years War (1756-63) has been accorded to the sound direction of Admiral George Anson, who became first lord of the Admiralty in 1751 and, except for one brief period, served in that capacity until his death in 1762. His understanding of the operational navy, its needs and potentials, coupled with his administrative capabilities and firmness, achieved remarkable results. Previously, individual warships built under Order-in-Council plans had been inferior in speed and in other respects to the new French ships. Anson corrected the situation by revising the system. He had experiments conducted in coppering the bottoms and instituted fleet and dockyard inspections. The Navy Discipline Act was revised and improvements in court-martials were instituted. Changes were made in tactics that permitted more flexibility in combat, and a corps of marines was formed.

As so often happens with victory after a prolonged war, British policy was influenced by wishful thinking regarding naval requirements. References to the beginning of "universal and perpetual peace"[1] bring to mind statements of President Woodrow Wilson after World War I, the insufficiencies of U.S. naval construction programs throughout most of the following interwar years, and policies adopted following the decisive defeat of Germany and Japan in World War II.

Royal Navy preparedness also suffered from the direction of naval affairs by individuals who lacked knowledge of maritime matters or were otherwise poorly qualified. Admiral Anson's successor was a civilian. Except for a four-year span, political appointees occupied the office of first lord of the Admiralty over the following two decades. The high degree of efficiency and effectiveness that had been achieved under the admiral's leadership was soon dissipated. Shipyard officials often acquired their positions as a reward for political support. Some paid money to be selected. Evidence of corruption increased. Dockyards became extremely inefficient. Naval stores were not maintained at adequate levels. The upkeep of warships, their fitness for seagoing operations, and the readiness of their crews declined. And thus it was that over-reliance on civilian control, wishful thinking, false economies, and maladministration all contributed to deficiencies in the operating forces of the Royal Navy. In any case, British warships operating off America during the early phases of the Revolutionary War were not only too few for effective sea control actions along the extended coast, but also were in poor repair. Furthermore, the ships in the North Atlantic Squadron were undermanned, and impressments of colonials were an added cause of alienation.

Another limiting factor was one that is all too often experienced at the start of a war in modern as well as earlier times—inadequacies in naval operational logistics. In this case the requirements for such support had been minimal before the rebellion began since provisions, other supplies, and services were available locally. As resistance increased, the deployed squadron had to depend increasingly upon the timely receipt of cargoes from England. The Admiralty not only failed to anticipate resupply needs, but it also underestimated the lead times required to purchase goods, charter vessels, and transit the broad and often stormy North Atlantic. Nor was sufficient allowance made for losses due to high seas or enemy actions. Vice Admiral Samuel Graves, commander of the British fleet in American waters, wrote repeatedly to the Admiralty of the shortages of food; the insufficiencies in "Musquetry" and equipment; the other supplies that he was "extremely in Want of";[2] the failure of stores ships to arrive in a timely fashion; the lack of seamen, petty officers, and warrants; and the requirement for a hospital ship.

In contrast, France had benefited from lessons learned in the Seven Years War. Among the factors that had contributed to the earlier French defeat had been the lack of a full understanding of sea warfare and its importance, as well as the determination of naval policies, administration, missions, and operations primarily on the basis of contributions to land warfare. We would do well to avoid these pitfalls today. France, under the leadership of the Duc de Choiseul, instituted corrective measures. Their Navy Department was reorganized. A group of competent and progressive designers and naval constructors was formed. Dockyards and naval arsenals were improved. Emphasis was placed on the design and manufacture of standardized naval cannon with more precise bore dimensions, thus providing greater accuracy, higher velocities, and longer ranges. Through actions such as these, France created a fleet of well-armed warships of modern design.

THE REVOLUTIONARY WAR BEGINS

The colonies were heavily dependent upon the sea. The main settlements were still along the coast and inland waters. Bays and rivers divided the country into island-like areas between which transportation was mainly by water. Fishing provided an important source of food. Whaling was a significant industry. The settlers were largely dependent upon ocean shipments for goods and equipment. More than 1,000 American merchant vessels were engaged in trade with Britain and the West Indies alone.

Following the Stamp Act, a number of key actions by the British government were maritime related. These included taxes on imported items; restrictions on trade other than with Great Britain, Ireland, and the British West Indies; and, following the Boston Tea Party in 1773, the closing of Boston harbor.

Early rebellious acts might not have expanded into united opposition by the colonies had Boston not been occupied by the British Army. As it was, sending two regiments there in 1768 was not only deeply resented in New England but also was a major factor in rallying many in the other colonies to the cause. The Quartering Act passed by Parliament in June 1774 was one of the actions that led to convening the First Continental Congress three months later. And it was the march on Lexington and Concord that triggered the ensuing war. This is but one of many examples throughout history and up to the present when the peacetime use of ground forces had unfortunate effects.

Once the war began Britain might have been able to control the rebellion early in the conflict had it moderated its political actions, had the warships it deployed across the Atlantic been in a high state of readiness and adequate in numbers, had they been properly employed to exert sea power's potential influence, and had adequate and timely operational logistic support been provided.

This was one of those times when due attention was not paid to a primary mission of naval power—on this occasion, the establishment of sea control along the coast of the colonies. King George III and his ministers underestimated what was required for decisive naval strength in North American waters. Further, in its attempt to bring the colonies into line, Britain focused its main military effort on army operations in an increasingly hostile land, and it considered the foremost role of the Royal Navy to be to support this effort. British naval power was not used more effectively, in part, because of the competing demands for Royal Navy forces and the overall low state of readiness of these forces. With a far-flung empire and worldwide shipping to be protected, other squadrons were operating out of Newfoundland, Jamaica, Antigua, and the East Indies. Confronted by the growing strength of the French Navy, powerful warships were being retained in home waters.

Furthermore, this was a war in which a government minister, remote from the scene of action, was attempting to mastermind combat operations. Vice Admiral Graves had justifiable complaints concerning over-zealous orders, counter-orders, and suggestions for diversionary operations issued by the Earl of Sandwich, first lord of the Admiralty. Problems were compounded by the very long time necessary for communications back and forth across the North Atlantic.

Map 2.1
Northern Waters

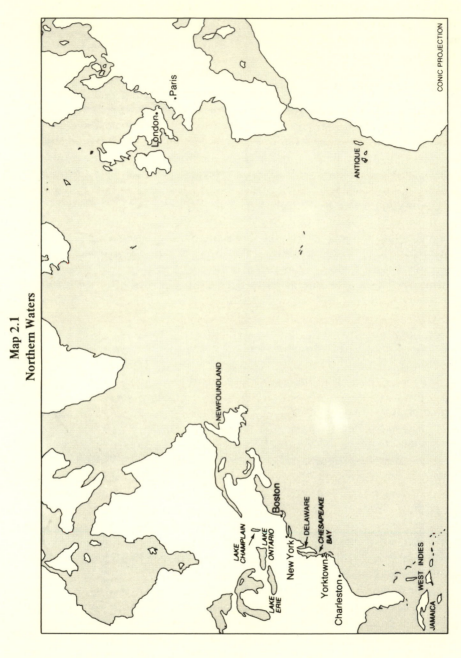

Source: Drawn for the editors by the University of Maryland Geography Department, Cartography Services Laboratory, 1987.

Naval effectiveness has been enhanced greatly in the modern era by radio communications developments. On the other hand, there have been times—a notable example being the Vietnam War—when radio capabilities have encouraged some at the seat of government to interfere, even in minute detail, with the exercise of command at the scene of action.

MARITIME WARFARE

Britain's failure to make full and proper use of its naval power potential in the war's early phases allowed piecemeal actions to be taken by quasi-naval and naval units, which permitted continuance of the armed struggle, helped influence France to enter the war, and had a profound effect on the attitude of the British people. Ultimately, the naval victory off the Virginia Capes in 1781, which decided the land battle at Yorktown, also contributed to Britain's granting of independence.

Having no naval forces, the loosely united colonies resorted to a wide variety of means in their attempts to counter Royal Navy operations and take offensive maritime actions. They took full advantage of numerous private vessels that could be armed with smaller cannon with relative ease.

The earliest actions by American armed vessels were by private citizens to prevent delivery of supplies to British military forces. In May 1775 men from the Dartmouth-Bedford area of Massachusetts, mounting small cannon on two sloops, recaptured two prizes with cattle intended for delivery in Boston to feed troops there. Soon thereafter inhabitants of Machias, Maine seized a loyalist sloop and a schooner. They then engaged and defeated His Majesty's armed schooner *Margaretta,* whose mission was to escort a small convoy laden with lumber, provisions, and wood for fuel to Boston.

The first state navy was that of Rhode Island, which chartered and fitted out two armed vessels in June 1775. The stated purpose was "for the Protection of the Trade of this Colony." However, the instructions to Commodore Abraham Whipple went further than that, ordering him to take action against those who might attempt "the Destruction, Invasion Detriment or Annoyance of the Inhabitants," not only of that colony, but others that were joined with it. Furthermore, "all Ships and Vessels carrying Soldiers, Arms, Powder, Ammunition, Horses, Provisions, Cloathing, or any thing else for the Use [of] the Armies of Enemies of the united American Colonies Shall be Seized as Prizes."[3]

During the following month the congress of representatives from the colonies resolved, "each colony, at their own expence, make such provision by armed vessels or otherwise . . . for the protection of their harbours and navigation on their sea coasts, against all unlawful invasions, attacks, and depredations, from cutters and ships of war."[4] In time, all but one of the colonies acquired a navy of one sort or another, although some lacked sea-going capabilities.

The first fittings out of armed vessels "at the Continental Expence" were arranged by General George Washington. As noted in the general's orders on

September 2, 1775 to Nicholson Broughton, who was assigned to command the lightly-armed (four 4-pounders) schooner, *Hannah,* Washington's navy had a limited purpose. Whereas Broughton was directed to proceed "immediately on a Cruize against such Vessels . . . laden with Soldiers, Arms, Ammunition, or Provisions for or from sd Army, or which you shall have good Reason to susspect are in such Service," there was a restriction: "You are particularly charged to avoid any Engagement with any armed Vessel of the Enemy."[5] Seven days later, *Hannah* captured a vessel carrying naval stores and lumber.

The colonies' ability to fight the enemy on land and at sea depended upon their obtaining ammunition. In October 1774 Parliament had forbidden the export "of Saltpetre, Gunpowder, or any Sort of Arms or Ammunition"[6] to the colonies and had taken steps to prevent delivery from other sources. The Continental Congress urgently sought ways to obtain gun powder. Many more months would pass before America would have the means to manufacture the required ammunition. Meanwhile, critical needs were filled by sending armed and unarmed vessels to such places as the West Indies, by capturing transports laden with powder, and by amphibious raids. The most notable success of Washington's tiny navy was the capture of the unescorted brig *Nancy* by *Lee,* armed with only two 2-pounders. It was said that the captured ammunition was equivalent to what the colonies could manufacture in 18 months.

THE CONTINENTAL NAVY

The steps that finally led to the birth of the Continental Navy started in October 1775 when Congress appointed a committee "to prepare a plan, for intercepting vessels coming out with stores and ammunition" and then resolved that two would be armed, manned, fitted out, and sent on a cruise with such a mission and "for such other purposes as the Congress shall direct." A Committee of Three was formed to prepare a cost estimate and to contract for the fittings out. A total estimate for "a Fleet of Ten Sail" was included in its report. To employ such a fleet, the committee proposed that the vessels "cruise, only to protect the Trade of these Colonies from the insults of Ministerial Cutters, & Shipps of Warr, & for intercepting, & seizing such Vessels as shall be employed to Transport Stores, or shall have Stores on board for the Ministerial Forces employed against these Colonies."[7] Congress approved the arming and fitting out of two more armed ships. The four men-of-war (10, 14, 20, and 36 guns) comprised the Continental Fleet over which Commodore Ezek Hopkins became commander in chief in December.

In December 1775 Congress formed the Marine Committee of 13 members, one from each colony, "to devise ways and means for furnishing these colonies with a naval armament."[8] This led to the first American naval construction program, under which yards in seven colonies were to construct 13 frigates.

The building, fitting out, arming, and manning of these proved to be far more difficult and time consuming than anticipated, and not until 1777 were the first four able to put to sea. The majority never made it, four because Britain gained control of New York and Philadelphia, and two as a result of actions in the Delaware River and Chesapeake Bay.

It should scarcely be surprising that a congressional committee proved inept at running naval affairs. Not only were they involved only part time, but also the membership was forever changing and many were not well informed of maritime matters. The large size of the body made it cumbersome, indecisive, time consuming, and inefficient. There was difficulty in getting a quorum.

The problems experienced were such that the Marine Committee sought and gained congressional approval in November 1776 for a board in Philadelphia composed of "three persons, well skilled in maritime affairs"[9] to execute the committee's business, including a new building program that now included three ships of the line, five frigates, and two other ships. Subsequently, a second board was established at Boston to supervise, under the committee, activities within the four states in New England.

PRIVATEERS

By far the most numerous of the American armed vessels were privateers. Citing the July 1775 congressional resolution, Massachusetts empowered its council on November 1 "to Commission, with Letters of Marque and reprisal, any person or persons, within this Colony, who shall at his or their own Expence fix out & equip for the defence of America any Vessell."[10]

Other colonies followed in taking similar actions, and Congress issued strict instructions to govern the procedures and conduct of the privateers and of vessels with letters of marque. There were at least 2,000 American privateers at one time or another during the war. Although not under naval control, which hindered a few attempts at combined operations, some 60 of the most formidable were commanded by officers who held or would later hold commissions in the Continental Navy.

Whereas the colonies lacked naval forces adequate for battles against powerful squadrons of the Royal Navy, "cruising warfare"[11] actions of privateers, state navies, and the Continental Navy had a far greater impact upon the war than has generally been recognized. A century later, when the United States began to build what is known as the New Navy, the potential of cruising warfare was deprecated. In World War I, however, Germany's U-boats demonstrated how effective it could be.

As for the course of the land war, the Royal Navy's ability to exercise local sea control and conduct amphibious operations gave the British a tremendous advantage. The situation of the Continental Army was indeed desperate as a result of the movement of a British fleet across the Atlantic accompanied by transports, the amphibious landings at Staten Island and Long Island in the summer of 1776, and the capture of New York. This provided a main base for naval operations, a central location for movements by sea to points along the coast or up inland waters, and sea lanes for logistics.

The importance of controlling inland waters was seen in the Battle of Valcour Island during October 1776. Benedict Arnold's tiny group of gunboats was defeated, but they so delayed the troop movements by water down Lake Champlain that the British returned to Canada to await good weather in the following year.

The occupation of Philadelphia in September 1777 by the bulk of General William Howe's troops, who had been transported by sea under Royal Navy escort from New York and up the Chesapeake to Elkton, and the harsh winter that followed made the Continental Army's situation at Valley Forge extremely desperate. If it had not been for the remarkable resolve and leadership of George Washington, the cause probably would have been lost.

FRANCE ENTERS THE WAR

As for the maritime war, Britain increasingly was feeling the effects of American actions against shipping. Increasing numbers of its merchantmen and valuable cargoes had been taken as prizes. In excess of 250 cargo vessels and transports were lost in 1776, including a third of a transport fleet carrying 1,000 Scotch Highlanders who were taken prisoner.

It is unlikely that France would have signed the Treaties of Commerce and Alliance in February 1778 had it not been for the daring 1777 raids on shipping in British home waters by the Continental Navy ships commanded by Lambert Wickes and Gustavus Conyngham, coupled with the Continental Army victory at Saratoga.

This meant that the Continental Navy would now receive full French support, such as that which made possible the spectacular successes of John Paul Jones in the British Isle area. More important, it meant that major British squadrons could no longer expect to operate unopposed.

Despite the fact that the total number of ships on the British list was greater, the French had more major warships ready for service. Britain was fortunate that optimum use was not made of French naval potential. An unduly long time elapsed before Vice Admiral the Comte d'Estaing proceeded to American waters with a powerful French squadron. Later, the admiral failed to take advantage of favorable opportunities for fleet actions, and he did not follow up on tactical victories in the western hemisphere. On the other hand, the French fleet's arrival did cause the British to evacuate Philadelphia.

THE FINAL PHASE OF THE REVOLUTIONARY WAR

It was not until France's entry into the war that the British initiated changes to correct basic ills of the Admiralty. The overwhelming credit for the improvements has been given to Captain (later Admiral) Charles Middleton who was appointed comptroller in 1778 and by the end of the American Revolution became head of the Navy Board. Dockyards were rendered highly efficient.

Long-needed repairs of warships in ordinary or in the mothball fleet were completed and all were fitted out for sea. Such actions take time. They had been started too late to affect the outcome insofar as the United States was concerned, but they would prove to be of great importance in the continuing warfare against France.

After France and its navy entered the war, Congress reduced funding for the Continental Navy. Of the five 36-gun frigates and three 74-gun ships that had been authorized in late 1776, only two of the former were finished and saw service. The only ship of the line to be completed was presented to the French to replace one of theirs lost by grounding in Boston harbor.

Congress finally decided in December 1779 to establish a Board of Admiralty of five persons to take over the Marine Committee's duties, but the powers delegated to the board were limited, as was the funding. Two of the board were members of Congress. Only two of the three other positions were filled, and thus getting a quorum was difficult. It was decided in early 1781 that the board would be superceded by a secretary of marine. He was not, however, to be charged with direction of naval movements, and no one approached would accept the job.

An agent of marine was appointed until a secretary could be found. Meanwhile, Superintendent of Finance Robert Morris, who had served on the Marine Committee, took the initiative on a number of naval matters during the period of uncertainty. By that summer the warships in commission had been reduced to three. Subsequently assigned the "duties, powers, and authority"[12] of agent of marine in addition to his other responsibilities, Morris acquired the title before the end of the year. His efforts to strengthen and make better use of the Continental Navy were frustrated.

Spain joined the war in 1779 and Holland in 1780. The Royal Navy's attempts to sever the trade of neutrals with the colonies became more difficult as a result of the "Armed Neutrality"[13] of Russia, Denmark, and Sweden. American privateers and cruising warships continued to achieve a high measure of success against British merchantmen until the final stages of the War for Independence.

SEA CONTROL

What finally decided the war was the September 1781 defeat of Admiral Thomas Graves's British fleet off the Virginia Capes by the French fleet under Rear Admiral Count de Grasse. This permitted delivery of cannons for the siege of Yorktown by the ships of Commodore Count Saint-Laurent de Barras, who had come from Newport. Further, after Graves retired from the scene of action, the French Navy was in local control of the sea. Britain could no longer reinforce or support General George Cornwallis's beleaguered troops trapped at Yorktown. Once Washington learned that de Grasse was heading for the Capes, he headed his army and that of General Comte de Rochambeau south. The ships of the French squadron ferried some of these forces down the Chesapeake from Elkton and provided gunfire assistance. Cornwallis surrendered his army on October 19, 1781.

The British Cabinet decided the next spring to recognize American independence. The final peace treaty was signed in September 1783.

Difficult times lay ahead for the as-yet but loosely United States. Regrettably, the new nation had not learned from the war of the American Revolution the fundamental lessons regarding the importance of naval power and its application.

3

Consequences of
Neglect

The importance in times of peace of naval power and roles carried out by naval forces is rarely fully recognized. In fact, a navy's ideal contributions are when it protects and advances the nation's interests without resort to war, and when it serves as a deterrent to hostile actions ranging from terrorism to the use of military force.

The period after the Revolutionary War provides an extreme example of the tendency, in the wake of a costly war, to neglect naval requirements. On this occasion the nation was indeed in dire financial straits. In debates concerning naval requirements, there were opponents who, as is so often the case, engaged in rationalization or wishful thinking. Yet, recovery from the costly war depended to a considerable degree upon the restoration of a profitable merchant marine and the renewal and expansion of oceanic trade. Some of the most lucrative commerce in colonial days had been with the West Indies. Now, Britain, seeking to increase its own merchant marine's profits, directed its possessions in that area not to engage in trade with American shipping. Expansion of trade with other areas was thus of key importance.

The last ship of the Continental Navy, frigate *Alliance,* was sold in 1785. During the following year when Henry Knox became secretary of war, a position responsible for army affairs established during the Revolutionary War, no one was occupying the office of agent of marine. Consequently, General Knox was assigned some responsibilities for naval matters.

One of the articles, proposed when Congress decided in 1776 to try to negotiate a treaty with France, was for French protection of American shipping from the Barbary corsairs operating out of North Africa. The Treaty of Amity and Commerce signed two years later went no further than to gain France's agreement to use its influence with the Barbary powers in the interest of the united colonies. Any expectations that the French Navy would provide security for American merchantmen became unrealistic after the United States signed a separate peace treaty with Britain.

The war was hardly over before the Barbary states began their depredations. In 1784 Morocco seized one U.S. merchantman, and in the next year Algiers took two. The crews of two vessels captured by Algiers were enslaved and ransom was demanded for their release.

After an Algerian cruiser took a couple more American merchantmen, this time in the Atlantic, the United States paid for a treaty of immunity with Morocco but refused to meet the exorbitant demands of Algiers. Thomas Jefferson, then in Paris and charged with the negotiations, appreciated the long-term consequences if the young nation bowed to coercion. Rather than "buy a peace," he would prefer "obtaining it by war" and advocated a fleet of 150 guns, one-half to be "in constant cruise," and also a "marine force."[1] His views were expressed in a letter to John Adams, who also sought to establish a navy.

As set forth in the preamble of the Constitution, which became effective in 1789, one of the purposes was to "provide for the common Defence." Basic differences between armies and navy were recognized. In one article Congress was assigned the power to "raise and support Armies" with a two-year limitation on appropriations. In another article the power was to "provide and maintain a Navy" with no such limitation. Moreover, the president, rather than a military officer, was designated commander in chief of the Army and Navy of the United States.

To succeed the former Board of War and Ordnance, a War Department was formed after the Constitution went into effect in 1789, but the reestablishment of a navy continued to be deferred. A Senate committee did conclude that U.S. trade in the Mediterranean would not be safe without a navy, but it did not advocate taking corrective measures until "the state of the public finances will admit."[2]

U.S. merchantmen were able to sail with convoys of Portugal and Spain during the period of hostilities between Portugal and Algiers. However, the situation changed after the revolutionary government of France declared war against Spain and the British arranged a treaty between Algiers and Portugal.

Piratical actions were expanded in the fall of 1793 when a fleet of North African corsairs captured ten U.S. merchant vessels in the Atlantic. Over 100 seamen were held for ransom. Congress, after receipt of a message from President Washington, finally passed a resolution to provide a naval force for protection against such attacks. But there was a proviso. To gain the votes necessary for passage of the Naval Act of 1794, an amendment was added stipulating that there would be "no farther proceeding" under the act in case of peace with Algiers. Recognizing that preventing acts of piracy would not suffice in itself to safeguard U.S. maritime interests, the president wisely directed that the warships be built of "live oak and cedar" and combine "such qualities of strength, durability, swiftness of sailing, and force, as to render them equal, if not superior, to any . . . of the European Powers."[3]

Later that year a British Order in Council directed the seizure of vessels carrying goods to or from the West Indies colonies of France, then at war with

Britain. U.S. private ships in the Caribbean were taken as prizes, sometimes in a ruthless fashion. A large percentage of the cargoes was condemned. Although the treaty negotiated by John Jay in 1794 led to Britain revoking her order, there was no mention in that treaty of Britain's illegal impressment of U.S. seamen. Further, the United States appeared to acquiesce to the British doctrine concerning neutral rights and contraband.

Two years later the United States ignominiously obtained a treaty of peace and amity with Algiers by paying cash and agreeing to transfer a 36-gun frigate to the Barbary power. Rather than cancel the naval construction program, the president wisely reached a compromise that permitted completion of three of the frigates.

THE DEPARTMENT OF THE NAVY

Meanwhile, it was becoming ever more apparent that the department responsible for army affairs was ill-suited to carry out the tasks of constructing and fitting out warships. Steps to implement the program were diffuse, poorly coordinated, and inefficient. Some of the critical actions were carried out by the Treasury Department, including renting shipyards in six ports (Portsmouth, New Hampshire; Boston; New York; Philadelphia; Baltimore; and Norfolk). The Treasury acquired timber from the three most southern states and recruited cutting crews and carpenters from four other states. The contracts for sails were with a Boston company; those for cannon balls with New Jersey and Pennsylvania firms. In view of the experiences in the Revolutionary War, it scarcely should have been surprising that when the slowly-building ships were desperately needed in the spring of 1798, the most serious deficiencies were the lack of naval cannon and their inadequate proofing.

The crisis at that time resulted from the actions of France, which viewed Jay's treaty as having violated the rights of neutral or "free ships"[4] to carry noncontraband unhindered, under the provisions of its own treaty with the United States. In retaliation, by the summer of 1797 the French had captured more than 300 U.S. vessels. In the following January the Directory of France declared that ships carrying even small amounts of merchandise from England or her possessions could be taken as prizes and condemned along with entire cargoes.

As the maritime situation became ever more desperate, the need for a separate organization to direct and handle naval affairs became increasingly apparent. Recognizing the need for corrective action, Secretary of War James McHenry advised Congress early in 1798:

If the United States contemplate an arrangement for gradually providing a naval protection to their commerce, suitable to the resources of the country, and its relative situation with foreign Powers, the marine business, in such a case, ought to be separated from the Department of War, or the Department of War enabled, by proper institutions, to conduct it in a manner more conformable to the practice of other nations.[5]

On April 30 Congress directed that a new executive agency, the Department of the Navy, be established. Its secretary was to be responsible for carrying out "such orders as he shall receive from the President of the United States, relative to the procurement of naval stores and materials and the construction, armament, equipment and employment of vessels of war, as well as all other matters connected with the naval establishment of the United States."[6]

The scope of the authority assigned was commensurate with the responsibilities. This is worthy of special note in present days, when the superimposition of the Department of Defense over the military departments has been followed by extensive diffusion of authority through such means as creating specialized Defense Department agencies.

THE QUASI-WAR WITH FRANCE

On May 28, 1798, Congress authorized President John Adams to order warship commanders to seize any French armed vessels attacking U.S. merchant ships. When the president directed that the navy "seize, take and bring into any Port of the United States"[7] French armed vessels, the three frigates launched in 1797 were not yet ready for service, since Congress had until then withheld the funds for fitting out and manning them. Exercising initiative to the fullest, the prospective commanding officers performed remarkable feats to get their warships ready for action in less than two months. The first to put to sea was the USS *Constellation.* Since she had not been armed, Captain Thomas Truxtun acted on his own to acquire cannon from a fort.

On May 23 leading merchants of Newburyport, Massachusetts resolved to open a subscription to build a 20-gun warship in 90 days for loan to the United States. The keel was laid in July. *Merrimack* was launched three months later and put to sea in December. Congress passed a bill on June 14 whereby the president could accept a maximum of 12 such ships "on terms, in his opinion, advantageous . . . for the public service."[8]

By then, merchants of Philadelphia, Baltimore, and New York had begun their own programs. They were soon followed by Boston, Charleston, several Virginia cities, and Salem. Nine warships were built under the subscription program. Five saw action in the Quasi-War.

Meanwhile, Congress, beginning to take long-overdue action, appropriated funds to complete the other three frigates, and authorized construction of 12 more warships and acquisition of ten or more smaller vessels.

Responsibilities for naval affairs were soon transferred to the new department. Benjamin Stoddert was a wise selection as the first secretary of the navy. Not only was he highly knowledgeable about maritime affairs, but also he was a sound executive and competent administrator.

His direct responsibilities to the president and Congress and membership in the cabinet meant that naval power would receive more meaningful consideration in the formulation of national policy. Constructing, preparing, and maintaining naval forces would now receive the specialized direction so urgently required. The new department could devote its efforts to achieving the goals of sea power; providing naval influence in peace; and fulfilling, if necessary, wartime missions without these efforts having to compete within a single department with the needs of the army. This would reduce the danger of naval operations being unnecessarily diverted from primary missions.

In his first report Stoddert urged approval of a major construction program that would include 74-gun ships of the line. He sought also the purchase of islands off Georgia or at least the purchase of their live oak timber, and the construction of docks at convenient and safe locations for warship repair. In time Congress provided funds toward construction of the 74s, building two dry docks, and buying timber. The secretary used some of the ship construction funds for the purchase of sites for navy yards.

The nation soon was benefitting from the reestablishment and expansion of a navy. U.S. warships patrolled the western Atlantic and the Caribbean, escorting merchant vessels engaged in the West Indies trade. They distinguished themselves in engagements against warships of the French Navy. One such engagement resulted in the defeat and capture of the celebrated frigate *Insurgente*. Highly successful operations by both the U.S. Navy and the Revenue Cutter Service were conducted against enemy pirates. Once again, as had been the case in the Revolutionary War, cruising warfare had its impact upon the enemy, as

Chart 3.1
Naval Organization in Early Years (1800)

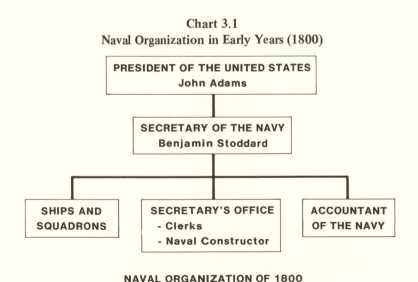

NAVAL ORGANIZATION OF 1800

Source: By the editors, based on information in Charles O. Paullin, *Paullin's History of Naval Administration, 1775-1911* (Annapolis, MD: U.S. Naval Institute, 1968).

privateers carrying letters of marque captured many French merchantmen. The end of the undeclared war with France came with the signing of the Convention of Peace in Paris in September 1800, which, after negotiation of changes, was ratified ten months later.

Successful as the new department had been, a potentially serious deficiency was recognized by Secretary Stoddert, namely the lack of participation of experienced naval officers in the direction of naval affairs. He urged the creation of a board of three to five officers who "should retain their rank in the navy." It would be their responsibility "to superintend, in subordination to the Head of the Department, such parts of the duties as nautical men are best qualified to understand and to direct." Stating that "the business of the Navy Department embraces too many objects for the superintendence of one person, however gifted," he reported that "the public interest, I am very sensible, has already suffered from this cause."[9] It was not until the need was clearly demonstrated by experiences in the War of 1812 that such a board was established.

Stoddert's recommendation was in the annual report he submitted as the administration of John Adams was coming to a close and a new administration was coming into office. This was to be one of those times when the nation would suffer from false economy. Stressing the importance of diminishing expenditures, newly elected Thomas Jefferson wrote, "this may be done in the Navy Department." The new Congress passed an act "providing for a Naval peace establishment."[10] This was in March 1801.

THE BARBARY WARS

Only four months after passage of that act the nation was engaged in another maritime war. By then the construction of ships of the line had been terminated and work suspended on dry docks and other navy yard facilities. Six frigates were to be maintained in service, seven in ordinary. The rest of the warships were to be stripped and sold, although later it was decided to retain one schooner, *Enterprise.*

Two months after taking office, President Jefferson ordered a squadron of three frigates and the schooner to the Mediterranean. The plan was to rotate it with one composed of the other three frigates, thus maintaining a naval presence to deter the Barbary powers from demanding increased tribute and to protect American commerce in case of war.

Upon his arrival at Gibraltar in early July the commodore of this squadron, Richard Dale, learned that war had been declared two months before by the pasha of Tripoli. He headed east to blockade Tripoli.

Had the squadron been able to maintain a fully effective blockade, there might have been an early peace. But, as was the case of Britain at the beginning of the American Revolution, the warships deployed were too few, and they suffered from inadequacies in operational logistics. In this case, since the scene

Map 3.1
The Mediterranean Sea

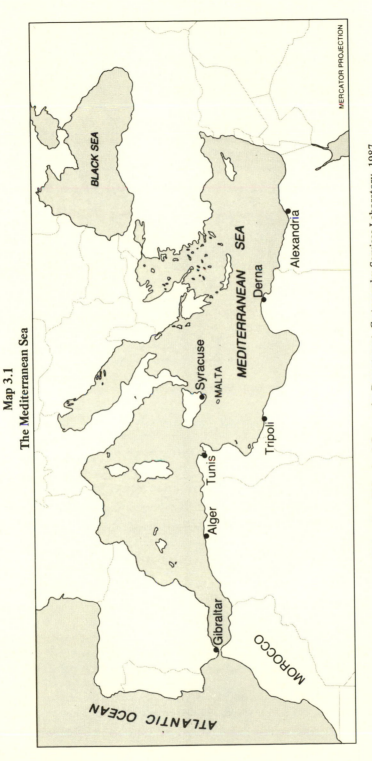

Source: Drawn for the editors by the University of Maryland Geography Department, Cartography Services Laboratory, 1987.

of action was almost 6,000 miles from the United States and about 1,500 from Gibraltar, the squadron had no replenishment or other supporting vessels.

When the warships began to run out of fresh water, the commodore sent *Enterprise* to Malta to obtain some. Since her capacity was very limited, the blockade was weakened, as frigates had to go to that port from time to time. They had much greater endurance with regard to other supplies but, sooner or later, extensive replenishments would be required.

One measure often recommended to save money in times of peace is to cut back on auxiliary ships of the navy by using chartered vessels. Problems encountered in the war against Tripoli provide examples of the hazard of placing undue reliance on private vessels for resupply. For example, a merchant vessel chartered by the Navy Department was to leave the United States during the first week of August with provisions and supplies for the deployed squadron, but its departure was delayed by a private adventure. Upon receiving Commodore Dale's letter reporting that he had "to give up the Blockade . . . for want of Provisions,"[11] Secretary of the Navy Robert Smith issued orders on October 14 directly to the merchantman's captain to proceed with the cargo. Meanwhile, Dale was forced to purchase naval stores from the British at Gibraltar.

Later in the war there was one instance in which the master of a chartered ship with stores for the squadron had to be paid an excessive fee before he would head from Gibraltar to Syracuse, which Dale's successor, Edward Preble, was being allowed to use for "provisions & Stores and the general rendezvous of the Squadron."[12]

In another case, involving a chartered ship loading at Norfolk, the secretary of the navy did his best to counter the crew's fears of capture. Although the vessel was insured for unescorted passage to Malta, her captain did not wish to go beyond Gibraltar. Then, after he had gotten to Malta, he refused to comply with Preble's instruction to proceed to Syracuse until escort was provided. Difficulties with vessels manned by civilian crews are not unique to that period of time. For instance, some would be experienced in the two world wars and even in the Vietnam War.

USS *John Adams* might be considered in some respects a forerunner of the U.S. Navy's service force ships of recent times. It was decided that, "armed *en Flute,*" she would be employed as a transport ship. During Mediterranean operations she was often referred to as a "Stores Ship."[13] After removing all but eight of her gun carriages, she made her passage, heavily laden, across the Atlantic to join the Mediterranean Squadron.

Benefiting from steadily improving operational logistics, Preble maintained a high tempo of operations after he took command of the Mediterranean Squadron in 1803. During his year in command he applied a continuous and increasingly effective blockade, captured vessels at sea carrying supplies destined for the beleaguered city, conducted bombardments day and night, and attacked ships within the harbor. The pasha of Tripoli began to offer terms of peace.

In response to Moroccan actions against U.S. commerce, the commodore led a group of warships into the harbor of Tangier and cleared decks for action. The sultan then reaffirmed the former treaty with the United States.

To tighten the blockade of Tripoli still further, Preble sought gunboats to employ in shoal waters east of the city through which shallow draft craft were delivering enemy supplies. Rather than wait for the delivery of gunboats being constructed in the United States, he sought and obtained the loan of eight from the Neapolitan government. All were fully manned and complete with cannon, mortars, powder, shot, shells, and gunner's stores.

During the period of intense action against Tripoli from August 3 to September 10, 1804, ammunition, stores, fresh water, vegetables, and other provisions were transferred on station to the warships, large and small. Had the blockading and other naval action been continued at a comparably high tempo and effectiveness, as undoubtably would have occurred had Preble remained in charge, victory soon would have been realized. Instead, in accordance with the navy secretary's decision, command of the squadron was passed to the much more senior Captain Samuel Barron when he arrived in the frigate *President.*

In 1805 William Eaton, who had come over with Barron to serve as navy agent, began an expedition from Egypt. He was accompanied by Hamet Caramanli, deposed brother of the dey of Tripoli. That April three warships bombarded the coastal town of Derna and its harbor some 750 miles east of the capital. The improvised army, which included Lieutenant Presley O'Bannon, U.S. Marine Corps, one midshipman, and seven enlisted marines from USS *Argus,* captured the town. In June the peace treaty was signed, and the war ended when the Senate granted its consent ten months later.

DECLINING READINESS

Had the nation maintained a reasonably strong presence in the Mediterranean, the Barbary wars might have been over. Instead, once again with the coming of peace the strength of the sea-going fleet was drastically reduced. Influenced to a considerable extent by financial and political considerations, the administration began to place major reliance on the type of gunboats used off Tripoli, which were inexpensive to build and operate. Politics was also a factor since they could be constructed by small private yards and thus provide employment and profits in many areas of the country.

Congress authorized 25 gunboats in 1805 and 50 more the following year. Some mounted one long gun (32-pounder); others had two. Stability was marginal, and even in relatively mild seas the guns had to be stored below. Intended for harbor defense, the gunboats lacked the ability to protect even coastal shipping. This would not be the last time when the desire to reduce the cost of naval forces would lead to assumptions or claims that the nation's needs could be fulfilled by smaller, less expensive warships.

Whatever the rationale, gunboats were of no use in deterring or countering infringements of U.S. rights at sea, which had been increasing since the renewal of warfare between Britain and France in 1803 and the issuance of Orders in Council and retaliatory decrees. Exhibiting disdain for the weak U.S. Navy, the Royal Navy once again began impressing seamen from U.S. merchant vessels. Two British frigates even went so far as to impose what amounted to a blockade of New York harbor in 1806, stopping and searching ships, some of which were sent to Halifax for condemnation. Further, more restrictive Orders in Council were forthcoming. Then, in the spring of 1807 the United States was subjected to humiliation: Off the Virginia Capes, USS *Chesapeake* was hailed by the captain of HMS *Leopold* who demanded the delivery of three men who he claimed were deserters. When Commodore James Barron refused, *Chesapeake,* which was not prepared for action, received three broadsides and Barron lowered the frigate's flag.

Not only did this fail to result in actions to increase the strength of the U.S. Navy, but three of the largest warships in service were placed in ordinary. As Jefferson requested, Congress passed the Embargo Act, which did more harm than good. The president ordered the building of 188 more of the pitiful gunboats.

Warships were returned to home waters. After the last left the Mediterranean in 1807, Algiers resumed its piratical acts. As the year ended there were only two frigates and four smaller seagoing men-of-war in service. Then, in January 1809 an act of Congress restricted their use to home waters.

In June 1809, after James Madison had become President, his secretary of the navy, Paul Hamilton, pointed out the need for "well armed, fast sailing, frigates, and smaller cruisers."[14] Instead of following his advice, Congress reduced funds for ship maintenance and repairs. By 1810 almost 1,000 U.S. vessels had been taken by Britain, 500 by France, and 300 by other powers.

Whereas Madison's State of the Union message in November 1811 proposed strengthening the nation's defenses, his recommendations concerning the navy were confined to improving existing warships and enlarging naval stockpiles.

In response to questions posed by the House Naval Committee, Hamilton advised that in case of fighting with either belligerent, Britain or France, an adequate naval force would be 12 ships of the line and 20 frigates, five of which were already in service and five in ordinary, and the smaller vessels already in service. In the forthcoming "Act concerning the Naval Establishment,"[15] the money appropriated was merely for repair, fitting out, and manning three frigates and stockpiling timber.

On April 4, 1812, Madison imposed a 90-day embargo on vessels in U.S. harbors. He sent his war message to Congress on June 1.

Part II

The Transitional Period

4

Coming of Age

President Madison's June 1, 1812 message to Congress referred to actions of Great Britain in which "the conduct of her Government presents a series of acts, hostile to the United States as an Independent and neutral nation." These included impressment of crews from vessels on the high seas; cruiser violations of rights along the coast, within territorial waters, and even within harbors, harassing entering and departing commerce; imposition of "pretended blockades, without the presence of an adequate force . . ."; and "the Orders in Council."[1]

In spite of the maritime nature of the reasons for Congress's declaration of war, the United States had no plans or strategic concept for employing naval forces. The War Department, the administration, and many in Congress naively thought the conflict would soon be resolved by land campaigns into Canada. This was far from the last time in U.S. history that neglect of the nation's naval power would be rationalized on the supposition that a war would be decided too soon for maritime actions to influence the outcome.

Although there was considerable opposition in Congress, the act resulting in the declaration of war was passed and signed by the president on June 18.

THE WAR OF 1812

In June 1812 there were only 16 seagoing warships in commission, and the War Department consisted of only the secretary and clerks. Naval officers in command of ships, squadrons, and shore stations took the initiative in preparing ships for action as best they could.

The secretary of the navy was Paul Hamilton, a politician who had served with irregular land forces in the Revolutionary War and who lacked experience in maritime affairs. His concept was that major warships should either be laid up or used as floating batteries in harbor defense. On the other hand, senior naval officers urged offensive sea actions against the Royal Navy. When the commander-in-chief, the president, agreed, Hamilton wrote to Commodore John

Rodgers in late May asking for "a plan of operation, which, in your judgment, will enable our little navy to annoy in the utmost extent, the Trade of Gt Britain while it least exposes it to the immense naval force of that Government."[2]

Rogers' plan, submitted on June 3, went into considerable detail. The initial employment, for at least the first six months of war with Great Britain, was to operate the navy's small vessels against "all the avenues leading to & from her West India Islands, Surinam, Berbice, & Denamara"; to employ "a small squadron of two, or three of our fastest sailing frigates & a single sloop of War, to cruise on the coasts of England, Ireland, & Scotland"; to utilize "the residue of our frigates to act separately, or in squadron on our own coasts . . . cruising in the tract of his ships trading between him & his colonies of Canada, Nova Scotia, & Newfoundland; and occasionally to unite *all* our Frigates & attack his East India convoys."[3]

The secretary then asked Commodore Stephan Decatur for his opinion. Decatur proposed employment "distant from our coast, & singly, of not more than two Frigates in company, without giving them any specific instructions as to the place of cruising."[4]

Commodore Rodgers had not yet received word of the declaration of war when he wrote to Hamilton informing him of intelligence concerning British naval forces in the western Atlantic. He stressed the importance of getting warships at sea in squadron as soon as war was declared, and he stated that one of his frigates and a 16-gun ship were ready and another frigate would be ready in ten days.

By the time the secretary issued him orders, Rodgers had his squadron at sea on a cruise lasting until September. Only then did the commodore receive the letter.

The congressional declaration of war was not followed by an appropriation of funds for badly needed warship repairs or by enactment of a naval construction program. Nor were funds provided for the woefully deficient shore establishment. Yet at the time only one navy yard, at Washington, was manned and active.

Although lacking the strength to engage major squadrons of the Royal Navy, the U.S. Navy was able to achieve successes in naval engagements that made highly significant contributions to American morale and public support of the war. In the final analysis these contributions were to prove crucial because of adverse reactions to reverses suffered in the land war. The first campaign ended with General Hull's surrender in August 1812 and the loss of Detroit and Fort Dearborn (at the site that later became Chicago).

In the same month USS *Essex* captured British sloop *Alert,* and USS *Constitution* obtained the surrender of HMS *Guerrière.* The October victories of USS *Wasp* over HMS *Frolic* and USS *United States* over HMS *Macedonian* followed by only a few days the army's severe defeat at Queenstown Heights.

Congress finally appropriated sorely needed ship repair funds, and in January 1813 it approved the construction of four ships of the line and six heavy frigates.

In addition to continuing actions against Royal Navy warships, the U.S. Navy, as in the revolution, engaged in cruiser warfare. Sloop *Wasp* (a different ship than cited above) operated for a time in the British Channel. In addition to sinking merchant ships there, she even attacked a convoy being escorted by a ship of the line. As time went on, Britain's loss of ships and valuable cargoes, most of them taken by U.S. privateers, had a serious impact on its finances and the willingness of its people to continue the war. The Royal Navy finally succeeded in reducing shipping losses to a tolerable level, but not before the U.S. anti-shipping campaign had exerted a major influence upon the outcome.

As was true also in the Revolutionary War, naval operations played pivotal roles on inland waters. At the beginning of the war the United States had but one warship on the Great Lakes, a 16-gun brig that while operating on Lake Ontario had captured a schooner for violating the embargo. Further east, control of Lake Champlain, between the Adirondacks of New York and the Green Mountains of Vermont, would be decisive in case of a British campaign south of the St. Lawrence. The navy had constructed two gunboats there, but they were grounded and not fit for service.

The commanding officer of the Lake Ontario brig, Lieutenant Sidney Smith, took the initiative in arming two prize schooners with six cannon and a 32 pounder originally intended for the brig. Other vessels were fitted out as more guns became available. Offensive actions that summer damaged British armed vessels.

Commodore Issac Chauncey was ordered north from the New York Navy Yard to gain control of Lakes Ontario and Erie. He was authorized to obtain weapons, munitions, and crews from the New York yard and to acquire, build, and fit out vessels at his discretion.

Gaining control of Lake Erie in 1813 saved the northwest. What made this possible was the remarkable success under naval officer direction in constructing and outfitting armed vessels under the primitive conditions at Presque Isle, Maine during four months of harsh winter and spring, and Oliver Hazard Perry's able command of his small squadron.

In the fall of 1812 Lieutenant Thomas Macdonough was assigned command of the two gunboats and six vessels that had been purchased by the army on Lake Champlain. In 1814 his tiny inland fleet of small, locally built, armed vessels won the action off Plattsburg that turned back the British Army's campaign down Lake Champlain toward the Hudson River.

Meanwhile, vastly superior British naval forces operating in the western Atlantic were able to impose an increasingly effective blockade and to conduct amphibious raids almost at will. One such raid culminated in the burning of Washington in 1814. The U.S. naval force assigned to defend Chesapeake Bay was merely a flotilla of 15 tiny Jeffersonian gunboats under the command of Commodore Joshua Barney. Any attempt to engage the powerful warships of the Royal Navy would have been disastrous. It was ashore that the commodore and his forces, including about 400 seamen, five cannon from the gunboats, and about 100 marines from the Washington Navy Yard, distinguished themselves in action against the enemy. Nonetheless, their brave stand at Bladensburg did not halt the British advance on Washington.

As for the direction of naval affairs and management of the department, Hamilton had resigned early in the war. His successor, William Jones, was far better qualified. Not only had he owned a ship for a considerable time, but he had served in a privateer during the Revolutionary War. Since there were no officers assigned to the Navy Department, the new secretary had sought the ad hoc professional advice of individual officers experienced in command. While he received a variety of recommendations, Jones's uncertainties were such that there were occasions when captains left port without sailing orders.

In 1814 Secretary Jones reported, "the multifarious concerns of the naval establishment, . . . the absence of wholesome regulations in its civil administration, and the imperfect execution of duties due to want of professional experience, lead to confusion and abuses." The Senate requested his recommendations concerning a better organization for the department. Reminiscent of the advice given by Stoddert, the first secretary, Jones proposed nine months later to create "a board of inspectors of the navy" to whom the president would delegate powers for the "general superintendence and direction of the affairs of the navy."[5]

Word of the signing of the Treaty of Ghent in December 1814 had not yet been received when the Battle of New Orleans was fought. The defense of the city by Andrew Jackson's troops might not have succeeded if it had not been for the heroic actions of Commodore Daniel T. Patterson's small squadron that delayed the movement of British naval forces up from the Gulf of Mexico. Other naval contributions included schooner gunfire against enemy troops and effective actions of naval cannon and crews from the squadron after landing on the flanks of British troops.

The treaty of peace left much to be desired. However, the United States had proven that it would, if necessary, fight for the protection of its ships and their crews on the high seas. What some have called the Second War of Independence was formally concluded with Congress's ratification of the treaty in February 1815.

CONCLUSION OF THE BARBARY WARS

By this time the U.S. Navy was being strengthened by frigates and ships of the line that had been authorized in 1813. Since war with Britain now was over, Congress authorized the use of force to protect U.S. commerce against the continuing actions of Algerian warships.

Two squadrons, one under the command of William Bainbridge, the other under Stephen Decatur, were fitted out for operations in the Mediterranean. Decatur's squadron, which included three frigates, was the first to get to sea. The commodore stopped in Gibraltar just long enough to communicate with the U.S.

consul. Enroute to Algiers, he fought a one-sided engagement on June 17, 1815. Damage inflicted on the Algerian flagship, a 44-gun frigate, resulted in her surrender, and an Algerian brig was driven ashore a couple of days later.

Upon his arrival at Algiers, Decatur sent ashore his terms of peace. Along with other stipulations, it was to be agreed that no further tribute would be paid, Americans held captive would be released immediately, U.S. property would be restored, and $10,000 would be paid for a brig that had been captured prior to the War of 1812. If not ratified at once, every Algerian ship that tried to enter port would be captured.

The capture of a cruiser led to the dey's prompt acceptance of the terms. Decatur then proceeded with his squadron to Tunis and Tripoli where he extracted payments for the value of the U.S. ships that these states had permitted the British to recapture within their territorial waters during the War of 1812.

Thereafter, the Barbary powers respected the United States' rights at sea.

THE BOARD OF NAVY COMMISSIONERS

The nation, for a time at least, had gained an appreciation of the importance of possessing a navy capable of earning the respect of others and employing it in the nation's interests. Furthermore, the nation was about to benefit, at long last, from the assignment of naval officers to positions of authority in the Navy Department.

In February 1815 Congress, after obtaining written views from senior naval officers, authorized a Board of Navy Commissioners. The members were to be three officers not below the rank of "post captain"[6] (there being at that time no statutory rank above captain in the U.S. Navy).

Under the secretary of the navy, the board was to "discharge all the ministerial duties of said office, relative to the procurement of naval stores and materials, and the construction, armament, equipment, and employment, of vessels of war, as well as all other matters connected with the naval establishment of the United States." It was empowered to prepare rules and regulations to secure "uniformity in the several classes of vessels and their equipments, and for repairing and refitting them, and for securing responsibility in the subordinate officers and agents."[7] It was to furnish estimates of expenditures for the different branches of the naval service and, on the request of the secretary of the navy, provide other information.

The officer chosen as president of the board, Commodore John Rodgers, proved an ideal choice. Not only was he to serve in this capacity during two almost equal periods totaling 19 years, interrupted only by a three-year tour in command of the Mediterranean Squadron, but also turned down the offers of appointment as secretary of the navy by Presidents Madison and Monroe. The other members were Commodores Isaac Hull and David Porter who were chosen by Rodgers and were also extremely well qualified.

Chart 4.1
Naval Organization with Board of Navy Commissioners (1817)

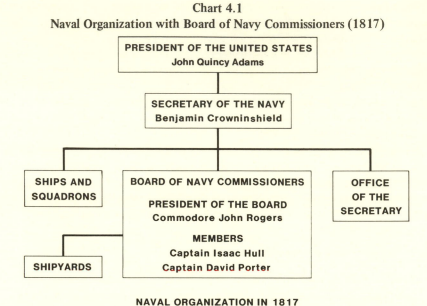

NAVAL ORGANIZATION IN 1817

Source: By the editors, based on information in *Paullin's History of Naval Administration.*

Considering the command experience of the commissioners, it was surprising that the one area in which they were not permitted to carry out their statutory responsibilities was the employment of vessels of war. Not only did the new secretary, Benjamin W. Crowninshield, a prominent shipowner and former merchant vessel captain, insist on exercising that authority himself, but he even refused to provide the board with information on ship movements—information that could be crucial for providing timely and adequate logistics support. Nevertheless, when President Madison ruled in Crowninshield's favor, the commissioners tackled their jobs with remarkable zeal.

The commissioners' first efforts were to acquire information on the naval establishment and its activities, as a result of which they became convinced of "the absolute necessity of a reorganization and reform of the Navy." They concluded that not enough attention had been paid to expenses and that there was a need to adopt "at once a general system of economy." They instituted sound procedures for estimating and accounting and took steps "to insure responsibility in the subordinate agents of the [Navy] Department, by means of a quick accountability; and in the event of failure by inflicting upon the delinquent the immediate punishment of his offense in heavy penalties."[8]

Estimating that "by a reduction of the number of navy yards alone, there would arise an annual saving of a sum nearly equal to the expense of building four frigates of the first class,"[9] they unanimously concluded that only three yards were needed. Political considerations, however, prevented congressional action on this particular advice.

There are inflationary tendencies in the expansion of the naval shore establishment in times of war and a reluctance to reduce its manning level with the coming of peace. Concerning naval personnel, over whom the secretary of the navy retained direct control, the commissioners expressed alarm over the number of officers in the expanded naval establishment who were inexperienced, incompetent, or lacked a desire for responsibility. Many were said to be occupying positions in navy yards. A specific recommendation was that "unsuitable" officers be pruned from the navy. This was another case in which actions were not forthcoming but would be found badly needed in later years. Another recommendation on personnel upon which no action was forthcoming was that, "with a view to remedy the want of professional skill," a "naval college"[10] for midshipmen be created.

One of the most critical problem areas, both in the Revolutionary War days and thereafter, had been the production of the armament and ammunition upon which the combat capabilities of warships depend. The sound recommendation of the board was to establish "a national foundry, and of an Ordnance Department, for the Navy—the want of which has been long and severely felt; and the consequences has been the introduction into our ships of a variety of ordnance, some of a nature calculated to endanger the lives of those employed in serving the pieces, and to render the success of our arms very doubtful."[11] Experiences over the following years would repeatedly demonstrate the validity of this recommendation, but almost two decades would pass before actions to correct the grave deficiencies were initiated.

In response to the commissioners' recommendation that new construction commence on "one ship of the line, two frigates of the first class, and two sloops of war of the first class,"[12] Congress had the wisdom to go beyond that. In 1816 it authorized an orderly, long-range building program that was to survive into the 1820s.

In view of the obvious merits of multi-year naval construction programs, it is regrettable that presidential budgets and congressional authorizations and funding are so often on a piecemeal basis. Not only do long-range programs facilitate planning and minimize lead times involved in obtaining approval and in designing, constructing, and fitting out, but they promote the economical use of funds, encourage standardization, take better advantage of lessons learned, and facilitate training, manning, and logistics. And, with the passage of time, these benefits have become even greater as a result of the increasing complexity of warships, their armaments, and systems.

The Board of Navy Commissioners system was to continue for 27 years. During this period there were, in addition to Crowninshield, eight other secretaries. All were lawyers and politicians. One was absent from his office for almost eight months. All but two lacked experience in maritime matters. This would have had extremely unfortunate consequences had not all, including Crowninshield, relied greatly on the advice of the board concerning the employment of naval forces as well as other matters.

NAVAL INFLUENCE AFTER THE
BARBARY WARS

A U.S. naval presence was maintained in the Mediterranean after the last of the Barbary wars in 1816. With logistics support facilitated by leasing facilities at Port Mahon, Minorca, the visits of U.S. warships exerted a beneficial influence on political as well as commercial relations. At the time of much piracy in the eastern Mediterranean during the Greek revolt against Turkey, the Mediterranean Squadron provided protection to U.S. merchantmen by attacking pirate vessels and by convoying.

This also was a time of instability in the western hemisphere. Spanish colonies fought for independence and then engaged in local wars. Revolts and issuance of letters of marque by the revolutionary regimes contributed to the spread of piratical actions from the mouth of the Mississippi to the Bahamas, and in the Caribbean. Almost 3,000 cases of piracy in those areas were recorded during the period 1815-23. The navy took many successful actions against the pirates. It was not until after the formation of a strong West India Squadron, however, that the depredations were essentially eliminated.

An early cruise of great importance was that of USS *Ontario*, which left New York in October 1817 to sail around Cape Horn and up the Pacific coast of South America. The sloop of war arrived at Chile during that colony's war for independence from Spain. The ship's commanding officer, Captain James Biddle, negotiated the release of U.S. ships that had been captured by the Spanish. In accordance with his secret orders, Biddle then proceeded to the Columbia River and laid claim to the territory on both sides of the river in the name of the United States.

Formed in 1821, a Pacific Squadron operated primarily along the west coast of South America. To protect whalers, merchant ships, and citizens ashore, periodic visits were made to the Sandwich (Hawaiian), Society, and Marquesa islands. Warships were sent also to the Far East, where U.S. trade was rapidly expanding.

The principles that would become known as the Monroe Doctrine were announced in the president's annual address of December 1823. Concerned that the European governments that comprised the Holy Alliance might attempt to regain Spanish colonies in South America, Britain had asked the United States if it would join in warning France not to intervene in that continent. Instead, Monroe took the unilateral action of stating that the Americas were "not to be considered as subjects for further colonization by any European power" and that the United States would view any such attempts as "dangerous to our peace and safety."[13]

Warfare between Brazil and Argentina, the institution of Brazilian and French blockades, and seizures of whalers in the Falkland Islands area led to the deployment of U.S. naval forces to the east coast of South America, and to the formation of a Brazil Squadron in 1826. Operations during the previous year had included protection of vessels fishing in the Newfoundland area. Following the selection of a site in Africa for the American Colonization Society by a U.S. Navy ship, occasional visits were made to Liberia and operations were conducted off the African coast in efforts to suppress the slave trade.

This period, after a board with senior naval officers was established, demonstrates the importance of sea power to the United States during times of peace.

The navy was now entering a period of accelerating progress in technology, advancing capabilities, and added complexities.

5

Advancing Technology

Most technologically-based changes in warships and their armaments were incremental, step-by-step improvements of existing capabilities. The most notable exception was the introduction of steam propulsion. The breakthrough, however, did not have an immediate revolutionary impact upon naval power and its application because of the inevitably low performance throughout early development stages.

The world's first steam-powered warship was the wood-burning vessel designed by Robert Fulton and constructed under a navy contract during the War of 1812. Although a long time would pass before the state of the art would permit extended operations by a ship powered only by steam, independence from the wind would be particularly valuable in restricted waters. Intended as a blockship or floating battery to be employed in such duties as harbor protection, the warship had a unique design, employing a single paddle wheel in the race between catamaran hulls below gun and spar decks. The war was over by the time the pioneering ship *Fulton* (*Demologos*) finished her successful trials, and she was placed in ordinary.

Congress authorized three more steam batteries in 1816. Some machinery was purchased, but because of accelerating improvements being introduced, it was soon obsolete.

The first steam-powered warship to see service in the U.S. Navy was *Sea Gull*, a side-wheel river steamer converted into a gunboat with sails. She was used against pirates in the shallow coastal waters of the Caribbean.

Despite constant improvements, the latest plants of the time still consumed fuel—first wood and later coal—at prodigious rates and were unreliable. For most missions, warship capabilities would have been degraded instead of enhanced by equipping them with steam plants until major advances were made in cruising radii.

In this connection, the strategic situation of the United States was far different from that of the European powers in close proximity to one another. The Board of Navy Commissioners, which was keeping apprised of progress abroad in steam propulsion, requested funding in 1826 for experiments in warship propulsion by steam, but no money was appropriated for this purpose. A lesson yet to be learned was the value of research and development, particularly in times of severe budget limitations. The nation was then suffering from an economic depression, which led to placing the most powerful warships in ordinary and to curtailing the long-range ship-building program.

Problems in introducing steam and technological advances in other areas added to the growing complexity of the management of departmental affairs. The position of chief constructor was established that year on the recommendation of the board. The commissioners were experienced in the problems of seagoing operations, including in distant areas, and understood the relationships of ship characteristics to combat effectiveness under varying conditions. The chief constructor's interactions with them made valuable contributions to decisions on warship design in these times of change.

Concluding that their collective responsibilities resulted in "too great a variety of duties to be performed . . . by the Board itself, collectively acting upon each case," the commissioners recommended in 1829 that their "Ministerial" responsibilities be subdivided "so that each member, giving particular attention to the branch confided to him, might perform his own part in the most satisfactory manner." Under their concept, each of the three would become "chief" of a "department" and would execute his duties in conformity with decisions of the board, which would "decide upon general principles, and upon all new principles and improvements."[1]

One department, which would include "a Naval architect, . . . an ordnance officer," other officers, and clerks, would be for "building, repair, and equipment."[2]

Another, "the Department of Docks, Navy Yards, &c.," would require a "civil engineer," and a special officer in charge of nautical instruments and charts who was to "attend particularly to the time-pieces, or chronometers, to ascertain precisely their character, such as their rate of deviation from true time, [and] whether they are affected by changes of weather."[3]

The third department would be "victualling and clothing."[4] A staff surgeon would assist in procuring and distributing medicines, hospital stores, and surgical instruments.

As for "financial" duties, the commissioners reported that Congress's principle of applying appropriations only to particular objects had proven impracticable and thus was frequently violated. They proposed establishing five appropriations, three of which would be aligned with departmental chief responsibilities. Under their concept money requisitions would be subject to a "special examination of the branch under which they are to be expended; . . . and, if found correct, . . . submit it . . . to the Secretary of the Navy." Another of their recommendations was that "the power of transferring from one appropriation to another, as the exigencies of the service may render necessary, be committed to the President."[5]

Secretary John Branch agreed with changes along the recommended lines, but Congress took no action beyond approving creation of the Depot of Charts and Instruments.

We would do well today to pay heed to the sound principles by which the commissioners arrived at their recommendations. If put into effect, the authority delegated to individuals would have been commensurate with their responsibilities. The benefits of having a policy-level body of senior naval officers would have been retained. Sufficient flexibility in the use of funds would have permitted efficient management in meeting changing needs while maintaining full accountability.

STEAM PROPULSION

By 1830 technological progress warranted construction of warships with steam-powered plants. Funds were requested in 1831 for two of the three that had been authorized 15 years earlier, but none were forthcoming. In his annual report for 1834, Secretary Mahlon Dickerson expressed the desirability of steam-powered "floating batteries" to aid in defending rivers, bays, coasts, and harbors. Liquidation of the national debt and an accumulating surplus made this a favorable time for progressive action. Nevertheless, it was not until the secretary took the initiative by laying down a keel of such a warship that funds were appropriated. What followed provides an example of the sorts of actions involved in achieving new capabilities made possible by advances in technology.

There were as of then no steam engineering experts within the Navy Department. In preparing plans for the man-of-war to be constructed, the Board of Navy Commissioners obtained the advice of outside experts. After submitting these plans to the president, the secretary took it on his own to advertise for bids on the propulsion plant. Concerned that the contract might go to the wrong bidder, the commissioners expressed doubts as to "whether the advertisement gives the necessary information to enable persons to make proper offers."[6] Theirs was a justifiable concern. In following years there would be all too many instances in which awarding a contract for an advanced system to the lowest bidder resulted in an inferior product or even failure and higher expenditures in the long run.

There are always grave dangers in having to place undue reliance on contractors and consultants. On this occasion, the commissioners sought permission to employ someone "to advise them upon this subject, and to superintend and inspect the engines during their progress, and until they shall be satisfactorily tested." When they renewed the request a month later they cited the need for such an expert, not only during installation of the boiler and the rest of the system, but afterward, "to work them in the vessel."[7] Mr. C. H. Haswell, chosen for this assignment, was first appointed for two months, and then his tour was extended. In July 1836 he was assigned the duties of chief engineer of the second *Fulton.* Under the contract awarded six months later, the engines were produced according to Haswell's design, while an engineer of the contractor designed the boilers.

One of the most crucial problems was how to integrate into the ship's complement new personnel qualified to operate and maintain the steam propulsion plant. During the fitting-out period Captain Matthew Calbraith Perry, prospective commanding officer, sent the Board of Navy Commissioners a long letter on the subject in which he made recommendations that included details on qualifications, duties, pay, and status of naval engineers. The board's letter dated four days later on the subjects of engineers, assistant engineers, firemen, and coal heavers was promulgated as a secretary of the navy order.

The commissioners now sought "a considerable number of steam vessels"[8] for the navy. Eighteen thirty-seven, however, was a difficult year. The highly respected Commodore Rodgers, president of the board during two terms totaling 19 years and for a time acting secretary of the navy, retired due to poor health. His successor was not a proponent of change. It was a period of financial panic and budgetary reductions. The new president, Martin Van Buren, minimized the requirements for naval forces and their modernization.

On the other hand, *Fulton,* commissioned in December 1837, was soon giving convincing evidence of the technological progress already achieved, such as the besting of Britain's well-publicized commercial steamer *Great Western* in a speed contest off New York. Armed with only four 32-pounders, the combat capabilities of the side-wheel steamer warship, with her tall stacks for good draft and three masts for sails, were limited. But valuable experience was being gained.

Mahlon Dickerson continued as secretary of the navy until the summer of 1838. His successor, James K. Paulding, a writer who had served as the commissioners' first secretary and was the navy agent at New York, was opposed to transforming the navy into a steam fleet. This time the initiative was taken by Congress as it authorized building two or more steam-propelled warships. Not only did the performance of the two, completed in three years, prove to be superior to similar types of European navies, but experimental knowledge was gained by using a different design for each ship's engines.

There were, however, still grave limitations. Perhaps the most serious one was the need for side paddle wheels. Not only were they ill-suited for operating in even moderately rough seas, but the paddle wheels were highly vulnerable to gunfire and took up much space that otherwise could have accommodated broadside batteries. Another possibility was being incorporated in the design for the next warship to be constructed. The result was *Princeton,* the world's first screw-propelled warship, which was commissioned in 1843. A further improvement incorporated in this vessel was to place the machinery below the waterline where it was less likely to receive battle damage.

ORDNANCE

Almost 20 years had passed since the commissioners had reported on the sad state of naval ordnance and had made recommendations that had gone unheeded. Now the need to improve naval guns was stressed in the annual report for 1835. A "series of experiments"[9] was proposed, as was establishment of a national foundry.

After the Stevens brothers invented an explosive-shell gun in the United States in 1814, further developments by a French artillery officer, Henri-Joseph Paixhans, had resulted in a gun that was in use in the French Navy. Captain Perrry, the commanding officer of *Fulton*, was assigned the task of conducting tests to compare conventional cannon with Paixhans guns firing explosive shells. His tests, which began in 1839, employed several types of shells and fuzes, solid shot, grape, and canister. Shell gun fire was found to be far more destructive than solid shot. Moreover, the tests showed the cannon fire to be less accurate than expected. Attributing this to rusty cannon balls, Perry recommended application of a preservative during manufacture. Two results of the tests were adoption of the new gun by the U.S. Navy and retention of long-range cannon because of the restricted range of the Paixhans.

Meanwhile, the United States continued to deploy naval forces to distant areas to protect shipping and citizens ashore, and for the advancement of commercial interests. An East Indies Squadron was formed in 1835 with responsibilities ranging all the way to Arabia. In 1842 the squadron's commodore, Lawrence Kearny, laid the groundwork for a treaty on trade with China. The United States Exploring Expedition, commanded by Lieutenant Charles Wilkes, began a four-year cruise in 1838, which was to provide information of basic value on the ocean hemisphere, the Pacific. It also conducted surveys on the west coast of North America.

In 1841, during the troubled period between the United States and Britain highlighted by controversies over the Oregon Territory and the boundary of Maine with Canada, the U.S. Navy's West India Squadron was dissolved and warships in ordinary were fitted out to form a strong Home Squadron.

THE BUREAU SYSTEM

Collective management of departmental affairs was becoming ever more difficult, and the board system was being criticized more and more. Changes along the lines recommended by the commissioners in 1829 were becoming ever more imperative.

In 1842 Congress passed the Reorganization Act establishing five bureaus. Many adjustments would be required in future years but the basic system would prove its worth over a century and a quarter. There was, however, a potentially very serious deficiency in the initial arrangement as a result of the failure either to retain a board of senior naval officers, as the commissioners had recommended, or to assign such an officer as advisor to the secretary of the navy, as proposed by Lieutenant Matthew Fontaine Maury.

Congress unfortunately accepted the assurances of Secretary A. P. Upshur that "these bureaus should be conducted in harmony with the others," and "when necessary" the heads of the bureaus would "form a council for the Secretary."[10] In the following years temporary boards would indeed be formed to furnish professional advice and assistance, but, as revealed time and again, such ad hoc arrangements would be far from adequate.

As for the transition from one system to the other, it was fortunate that close coordination and continuity in the conduct of naval affairs were assured by assigning the three commissioners to head the Bureaus of Ordnance and Hydrography, Construction and Repair, and Navy Yards and Docks, with the board's secretary being assigned to the Bureau of Provisions and Clothing. A naval surgeon became chief of the Bureau of Medicine and Surgery.

Not only were the next four secretaries of the navy political appointees, devoid of experience in maritime affairs, but also their tours averaged only six months. Commodore Lewis Warrington, a former commissioner who had become chief of the Bureau of Yards and Docks, was made acting secretary for a time after the death of Secretary Thomas W. Gilmer.

During this period Congress authorized an Engineer Corps and an engineer in chief, as had been recommended earlier by the Board of Navy Commissioners. To help obtain better ships and make contributions to improvements in machinery, an experimental facility was established.

Bureau Chief Commodore W. M. Crane initiated actions to improve the reliability and safety of naval ordnance. He obtained funds for a laboratory to be established in the Washington Navy Yard for testing metals and explosives. Funds were also obtained to establish the Naval Observatory and Hydrographic Office.

Preparation of officers for duty in an ever more complex navy was enhanced by starting a navy school, which in 1850 became the Naval Academy. The future would benefit from the inclusion in the academy's curriculum of courses in steam propulsion and engineering. This was done at the insistence of Lieutenant J. H. Ward, officer in charge of the academy's Ordnance Department, who taught the first course and published a book on the subject.

THE WAR WITH MEXICO

In 1845 the navy was fulfilling its missions in scattered areas of the globe when a joint resolution passed Congress annexing Texas. Due to the risk of war with Mexico, President James K. Polk ordered the Home Squadron to Veracruz. In the following conflict valuable lessons could have been learned on command relationships during major amphibious operations, but they were not recognized until the disastrous Gallipoli campaign of World War I was analyzed.

Instructed to protect U.S. citizens and property while maintaining friendly relations, Commodore David Connor maintained a naval presence in the Veracruz area for six months. Then, at the request of Mexico upon agreeing to receive a commission in an effort to settle the Texas dispute, he temporarily withdrew his warships.

Nevertheless, war broke out between Mexico and the United States in May 1846. The U.S. Army crossed the Rio Grande and, expecting an early victory, headed for Mexico City. Connor was instructed to impose a blockade so that war contraband being delivered by neutral vessels would be subject to condemnation. This provides an example of naval power's ability to apply a discriminating form of sea control. There have been many instances in history in which the desired results have been obtained by a conditional blockade, sometimes in war and sometimes in peace, as for example in the Cuban missile crisis of the latter part of the twentieth century.

This was also an occasion when naval effectiveness suffered from operational logistics deficiencies during the early months of a war. The U.S. Navy now had stores ships but none was assigned to the Home Squadron, even though these forces were operating in the western portion of the Gulf of Mexico about 1,200 miles from Pensacola, the nearest naval base.

Connor sent some of the warships to Pensacola for water and topping off of other supplies prior to taking up blockading stations. He subsequently gained control of streams for fresh water. On the other hand, inability to obtain fresh fruit from the hostile shore resulted in an outbreak of scurvy that reached epidemic proportions that summer. The maintenance of a tight blockade was hindered by the frequent shuttling of warships to Pensacola.

Unlike earlier wars, the navy was now confronted with the need for frequent refuelings of the steam-powered ships, which expended coal according to the type and tempo of operations. Operations were complicated further by the very limited endurance of shallow-draft steamers that were employed near the shore and in restricted waters. Commodore Connor asked the Navy Department to send him a coal hulk to provide replenishment at an anchorage inside a chain of shoals, reefs, and barren islands. Prior to its arrival, boats from the larger warships were used to transfer coal to a depot on a low-lying island in the area. In time, the squadron was augmented by stores ships, USS *Relief* arriving first. The next two were converted merchantmen *Fredonia* and *Supply,* which arrived in February 1847. Issues from these stores ships included ammunition and ordnance spares. A later arrival was ordnance ship *Electra,* another conversion. Additional naval stores were delivered by chartered merchant vessels.

On the other side of Mexico, the Pacific Squadron not only carried out blockade actions but also conducted operations that led to the seizure of Monterey, San Francisco, and San Diego from Mexico. Further, it delivered a force that contributed to the capture of Los Angeles. The small squadron's area of operations was 12,000 to 15,000 miles by sea around South America from the ports and navy yards of the United States. Its logistics support, therefore, was provided by its two stores ships, which, being armed with cannon, served as more than auxiliary vessels.

After the land campaign bogged down, the capture of Mexico City was made possible by moving troops, arms, equipment, and supplies by sea; a large amphibious operation; naval gunfire support; and sea lines of logistics support for the forces that had been landed.

The command relations in effect during the amphibious operations, which were similar to those adopted just prior to World War II, are of special interest. Commodore Connor proposed that he, as naval commander, should exercise overall command of the landing. Lieutenant General Winfield Scott, the land commander, concurred. Joined by Scott and members of his staff, Connor reconnoitered the coastline and selected a landing site to which the general agreed. In conformity with Connor's plan, troops were transferred to warships, and with 65 surf boats in tow they made their way to positions off the beach. These warships plus seven light gunboats were stationed near the landing site in positions favorable for providing gunfire support. With a steamer stationed to mark a line of departure, a navy captain directed the ship-to-shore movement. The landing craft, coxswained and rowed by sailors, were organized into divisions, each commanded by a navy lieutenant. The craft beached and landed their troops, then returned to pick up those to be put ashore in succeeding waves.

Simply stated, the principle that should be followed, as would be the case in World War II, is that the navy should exercise overall command until the ground forces are securely established ashore. Not only does this reduce the likelihood of a poorly coordinated operation (all too often experienced under dual command arrangements), but also allows full advantage to be taken of the naval commander's knowledge and experience in such matters as the effects of sea conditions, depths of water, tides and currents, and the capabilities and limitations of ships and landing craft. The assignment of authority, of course, is particularly important when there is a possibility of encountering naval opposition en route or in the objective area. Regrettably, there have been tendencies in recent years to compromise that fundamental principle, with adverse results.

In the March 9, 1847 joint operation, the Home Fleet landed 10,000 troops and carried out combat supporting operations. During the subsequent attack on Veracruz, the sea wall and fort were bombarded by a flotilla of two steamers and five gunboats. The fire of a landed battery of six large naval cannon breached the city wall on the land side.

After the capture of Veracruz, the ground forces, supplied by sea, fought their way step by step to Mexico City. The war ended with the Treaty of 1848, by which the conquest of Texas was confirmed, as was the acquisition of territories that were to become California, New Mexico, Nevada, Utah, and parts of Wyoming and Colorado.

ADVANCES IN TECHNOLOGY

One area experiencing accelerated progress was naval weapons. Commodore Crane, chief of the Bureau of Ordnance, had been seeking to standardize guns, reduce the number of different calibers employed by the navy's warships, and improve procurement and storage. Officers were sent abroad to study similar actions by Britain and France. Following an ordnance board's recommendation, the great variety of U.S. naval guns was reduced to six models of 32-pounders and two of the 8-inch shell gun. Most ships in service had changed to the new system of armaments by 1847. Important advances were made in naval ordnance inspection, proofing, and preservation.

After the bureau assigned a pyrotechnist to the Washington Navy Yard laboratory, rights to Hales rocket were acquired. The officer in charge of its production, Lieutenant John A. Dahlgren, obtained a workshop in 1847 and by the end of the year was directing all of the ordnance work at the yard.

Gunsights and range scales were provided for the recently-approved standard guns. A firing range with a test battery was established. Dahlgren designed what became the standard boat-howitzer. The first casting of the famous Dahlgren gun was in 1850.

New dimensions were being added to naval warfare, among which underwater weapons developments were especially significant. Such weapons would play important roles in the future because of the high vulnerability of ships to hull damage below the waterline. The tamping effects of the surrounding mass of water means that a large percentage of the energy of an explosion against the side or bottom of a vessel is directed to opening a hole and inflicting blast damage inside the ship. Before the days of increased watertight compartmentalization and adoption in the twentieth century of scientifically arranged voids and fluid-filled spaces, even the largest ship could be sunk by a single underwater explosion. As so often happens with the introduction of a new means of warfare, countermeasures received insufficient attention until desperately needed.

The development of underwater weapons, of course, was not new. David Bushnell had designed his one-man turtle during the Revolutionary War. Its purpose was to attach a cask of powder to the underwater hull of a ship at anchor. A clock-work exploder permitted the manned submersible to escape before the explosion. Another development during that war was George Fleming's keg torpedo (mine) with its flintlock firing mechanism. Subsequently, Robert Fulton had conducted experiments in underwater ordnance and diving vessels.

No notable successes were achieved until after the development of galvanic torpedoes. An abortive project from which lessons should have been learned was that of Samuel Colt, who sought funds in 1841 to develop a submarine battery of electrically actuated mines controlled from a tower ashore. (Others in the United States and abroad had already used electrical currents to detonate explosives.) After telling Senator Samuel L. Southard, a former navy secretary, of his idea, he tried unsuccessfully to obtain money from President John Tyler, from Secretary George E. Badger, and from the House Naval Committee for a demonstration or trials. A working advance provided later in the year by the new secretary of the navy helped Colt get private funds for a speculative venture. Government officials and the public were invited to spectacular exhibitions over the next three years in which no complete system was ever employed. Colt would not permit naval ordnance experts as observers, refused to provide them with information on the system, and would not inform members of the scientific community. The government would have to agree to buy the unknown system before any details would be provided.

The Prussians were the first to employ a minefield controlled by wiring from ashore. In 1848 they employed such a field to deter the Danes from carrying out a naval bombardment during the Schleswig-Holstein War.

While mining would not supplant other forms of naval warfare, it would play important roles, offensive as well as defensive, in future wars. As with other naval weapons, there would be continual advances, and the full story would be one of measures and countermeasures.

These years witnessed continual progress in hull construction and propulsion. The first iron-hulled steamer, USS *Michigan* (renamed *Wolverine* in 1905), was launched at Lake Erie in 1843, built of parts manufactured in Pittsburgh. A board of four commodores, three naval constructors, the engineer in chief, a chief engineer, and a civil engineer determined the characteristics of four war-steamers for which funds were appropriated in 1847. Noting that screw vessels consumed less coal, Secretary Dobbin in his 1853 report recommended the construction of "six first-class steam-frigates [with] propellers."[11] When completed, their performance proved superior to that of foreign warships. Under the 1857 act, five large sloops of war were built, and a year later Congress provided funds for seven screw-sloops (one with twin screws geared to the engines) and a side-wheel war steamer designed for shallow-water operations. A couple of years later, in response to a congressional directive that consideration be given to converting all the navy's sailing ships into steamers, a board of naval officers concluded this was not expedient for brigs, sloops, and frigates. They did recommend that ships of the line be razeed and converted into first-class frigates.

As the U.N. Navy continued its peacetime operations in the nation's interests, warships with steam power as well as sail increasingly were being deployed to distant areas. The impressive steam-powered warships of Commodore Matthew Calbraith Perry's squadron helped in the negotiations that culminated in the Treaty of Kanagawa of 1854 and the opening of Japan.

PEACETIME OPERATIONS

Naval cruises during these years collected geographic, hydrographic, and other scientific information from portions of the Arctic, North Pacific, China Sea, and the Amazon and Plate rivers. During their oceanic transits, the U.S. Navy's ships collected data for Matthew Fontaine Maury, from which he derived his famous wind and current charts. The *American Nautical Almanac* was compiled. The navy's deep-sea soundings and bottom samples helped establish the practicality of a transatlantic cable, which was laid later by U.S. and British vessels.

Notable as the contributions of the navy had been since the War of 1812, the United States was entering a time of declining readiness, which would seriously delay the effective use of naval power in the next war. The decline began in 1858, and by 1861 warships badly needed repairs. Only 42 were in commission, and all but 12 of these were on foreign station.

On December 20, 1860, a state convention of the South Carolina legislature declared that its union with the other states was dissolved.

6

The Role of Naval Power
in Preserving the Union

Events leading up to and during the Civil War, especially in the early phases, demonstrated the adverse consequences of not appointing a naval officer as advisor to the navy secretary and the president. He would be responsible for the readiness and employment of naval operating forces and deal with the general in command of the U.S. Armies on such matters as strategy and the planning and conduct of joint and supporting operations. At one point in the Civil War, Congress considered forming a board of admiralty comprised of naval officers but took no action.

On December 26, 1860, six days after South Carolina seceded, the federal garrison abandoned Fort Moultrie and manned Fort Sumter on its island at the entrance to Charleston. After President James Buchanan refused to comply with South Carolina's demand that troops be withdrawn from the harbor, the War Department employed a merchant steamer to deliver reinforcements.

The effort might have succeeded if the relief vessel had been escorted by steam-powered warships armed with ordnance capable of effective shore bombardment. As it was, the relief vessel returned to New York after encountering fire from Fort Moultrie and Morris Island upon its entry into the channel on January 9, 1861. By then, Alabama had seized Fort Morgan at the entrance to Mobile Bay. The secession of Mississippi, Florida, Alabama, Georgia, Louisiana, and Texas was followed by formation of the Confederate States of America on February 8.

It was not until after Abraham Lincoln became president that another attempt was made to provide relief to Fort Sumter, which by then desperately needed supplies. It was an ad hoc operation along lines proposed to General Winfield Scott at the end of January by former naval officer Gustavus Vasa Fox, with the help of his brother-in-law, Montgomery Blair (who was to be the next postmaster general). Fox's plan was that he would proceed to the scene in a large steamer carrying troops and "two powerful light draft . . . tug boats, having the necessary stores on board."[1] He requested that his ships be accompanied by the only steam-powered warship then available, *Pawnee,* and revenue cutter *Harriet Lane.* He planned to operate outside the bar to counter any opposition by armed craft. Any hostile ships that came downstream would be engaged by the fort.

When such an operation was authorized, Fox wrote to Blair advising him that "Com° Stringham is the person for the Sec'y to consult"[2] with regard to naval preparations for the operation. Because of problems created by the resignations of Southern officers, Stringham had been assigned to the Navy Department to head the Office of Detail.

On March 29 the president directed Gideon Welles to "cooperate with the Secretary of War" in planning the expedition, which was to be ready as early as April 9. Secretary of War Simon Cameron informed Fox that he was to "take charge of the transports . . . and endeavor, in the first instance, to deliver the substance."[3] On April 1 the commandant of the Brooklyn Navy Yard received two telegrams directing him to fit out screw-steamer USS *Powahatan* to go to sea at the earliest practical moment. One telegram was from the secretary of the navy, the other from the president; each had in mind a different operation.

The secretary issued orders on the Fort Sumter operation. He assigned *Powahatan*'s commanding officer, Captain Samuel Mercer, command of a squadron that included his ship and another screw-steamer, *Pocahontas,* and ordered him to furnish protection for "the transports or boats of the expedition in the object of their mission . . . repelling by force, if necessary, all obstructions toward provisioning the fort and reenforcing it." Mercer was advised that "these purposes will be under the supervision of the War Department, which has charge of the expedition . . . intrusted to Captain G. V. Fox, with whom you will put yourself in communication, and cooperate with him to accomplish and carry into effect its object."[4] Fox's rank in the navy had been lieutenant.

On the following day the president directed Lieutenant David Dixon Porter to take command of *Powahatan* and to reinforce Fort Pickens off Pensacola. No one had bothered to inform Welles when Secretary of State William H. Seward, Lieutenant Porter, and Army Captain M. C. Meigs recommended to Lincoln that the warship be sent on such a mission.

Meanwhile, Welles had sent oral instructions via an officer to the senior captain of warships in the Gulf of Mexico to land embarked troops immediately. And so it was that army troops and marines reinforced Fort Pickens on the night of April 12, five days before the arrival of *Powahatan.*

Also on April 12 Fox, along with his relief vessels *Pawnee* and the revenue cutter, reached the entrance to Charleston where they witnessed the bombardment of Fort Sumter, which surrendered on April 13.

This marked the point of no return for finding a peaceful solution to the problems of the nation. On April 16 state troops of North Carolina, which had not yet seceded, captured two U.S. forts. On April 17 Virginia passed its ordinance of secession, and President of the Confederacy Jefferson Davis invited all interested parties to apply for letters of marque and reprisal.

President Lincoln's declaration two days later of a coastal blockade from South Carolina to the Rio Grande, soon extended to the Virginia Capes, was viewed by other nations as equivalent to a declaration of war.

THE CIVIL WAR

Despite the fact that the conflict was between adjoining groups of states on the North American continent, naval power was a decisive factor. While the exercise of that power was unique in many respects, insights and lessons of enduring importance, if properly interpreted, can be derived from the Civil War.

It was a war in which there were no engagements between opposing fleets. The South lacked a navy capable of contesting actions such as Union control of the sea, the projection of military power by sea, seizure of sites for naval bases along the coast of the Confederacy, and provision of logistics support. The maritime war, as a consequence, was confined essentially to Northern blockading operations and Southern cruising warfare actions in distant waters.

The war also was unique with regard to the extent of naval power projection into bays, sounds, and rivers, and employment of riverine forces along the Mississippi and tributaries crucial to army campaigns.

Basic lessons on command relationships, which somehow have had to be relearned time and again, can be derived from the many Civil War amphibious assaults and from naval operations conducted jointly with or in support of the land war.

The Civil War was fought in the early stages of the Industrial Revolution, a time of rapidly advancing technology. Innovations in the means of carrying out naval missions and the related interplay of measures and countermeasures went beyond that of previous wars. The National Academy of Sciences, which would serve the nation so well in peace and war in the coming years, was established during the Civil War.

As the war went on, the Confederate Navy employed mines (or torpedoes) far more extensively than ever before in history. Mining proved to be a highly innovative form of naval warfare, its effectiveness largely determined by the interplay of measures and countermeasures. In the years to follow there would be many times when mine warfare, often neglected in peace, would play important roles.

The war was also the first one in which steam-powered warships were extensively employed. Their ability to operate relatively independently of the wind's force and direction provided the seagoing forces with what was in many respects a new range of capabilities for offshore operations and for the extension of naval power into sounds and up navigable rivers. And nowhere was the impact of this means of propulsion more vividly demonstrated than on the Mississippi and its tributaries, where the exercise of riverine control and combat support of the army was crucial to the success of land campaigns.

Map 6.1
Coast and Rivers of Southern States

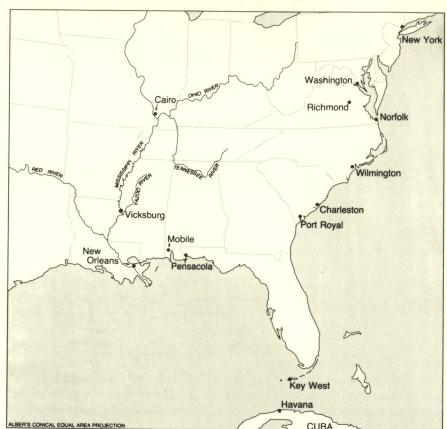

Source: Drawn for the editors by the University of Maryland Geography Department, Cartography Services Laboratory, 1987.

BLOCKADE

The military capabilities of the South were greatly enhanced by the large quantities of cannon, arms, and ammunition acquired by gaining control over five army arsenals and the Pensacola and Norfolk navy yards, and by the capabilities of the Richmond naval ordnance facility. On the other hand, the Confederacy's overall industrial capacity was so severely limited and its economy so highly dependent upon foreign cotton purchases that it was susceptible to being gravely weakened by a prolonged interruption in the flow of cargoes to and from its ports.

According to the 1856 Declaration of Paris, "Blockades, in order to be binding, must be effective."[5] As it was, the U.S. Navy had far too few ships in service to provide even token coverage along a coast that stretched some 3,500 miles and was indented by almost 200 inlets to harbors, bays, sounds, and rivers. Readiness had been degraded by the departure of experienced officers to the Confederacy, with 171 leaving the service by the end of May 1861. By the end of that year the navy lost 24 percent of its line officers and 17 percent of its engineering officers.

There were other demands for naval operations. Concern over the army's ability to defend Washington led to the ordering of warships to the Potomac River. *Pawnee* arrived at the capital on April 23 and was not assigned to blockading duties until August. During this period other men-of-war were employed to run down privateers that had many early successes against shipping off the southern coast.

Moreover, in view of the low state of U.S. readiness, Britain might engage in unneutral acts or even become an ally of the Confederacy. There also was concern over what France might do. While the British did not enter the war, they provided the South with vessels and bases for blockade running and cruiser warfare.

THE NAVY DEPARTMENT

It was fortunate that there were two departments of military affairs so the navy could cope with the immense problems of building up the fleet and meeting its rapidly expanding needs while the army was engaged in mobilizing large numbers of troops, and providing them with arms, ammunition, and logistics support. During the months that followed, the Navy Department proved to be highly effective in responding to the requirements of the operating forces. Extensive use was made of industry as well as navy yards for overhauling, constructing, and fitting out warships, and for converting merchantmen into men-of-war.

Urgent actions were initiated to repair, equip, and prepare for service all "vessels that were dismantled and in ordinary at the several [navy] yards." A program was begun for the construction of eight steam-powered warships. To determine which merchant vessels should be purchased and outfitted as warships, boards, each consisting of an experienced constructor, an engineer officer, and an ordnance officer, were convened at key cities to evaluate the "adaptation" and "capacity" of such ships "by alteration . . . to perform the particular service."[6] Other private vessels were chartered to serve as transports and assist in providing logistics support.

As reported by Secretary Welles, "one of the most embarrassing difficulties" at the start of the war was "procuring . . . ordnance . . . rapidly." Many guns were needed to arm the rapidly expanding fleet; yet these were in short supply as a result of the heavy losses of ordnance stores and cannon, particularly Dahlgrens, when the Confederates gained control of the Pensacola and Norfolk navy yards. As a consequence, "old artillery" had to be installed in many ships until more adequate weapons could be produced; yet one of the nation's three foundries capable of casting modern guns was in Confederate hands. Shot, shell, grapnel, grape, and canister for cannon and projectiles for rifled guns were manufactured by navy yards and contractors. Great quantities of gunpowder were urgently required. According to the Bureau of Ordnance's interim chief, Lieutenant H. A. Wise, the "most serious embarrassment" was the "want of suitable depots for the safe storage of the vast amount of material required."[7]

About one-half of that bureau's officers, including the chief, had departed to join the Confederate cause. Nevertheless, the depleted organization's performance was such that Wise would be able to report, "not a single ship or squadron has ever been delayed in its movements for the want of ordnance."[8]

The department's ability to meet expanding requirements was further advanced by a congressional act in the summer of 1862 that increased the number of bureaus to eight. The formation of a separate Bureau of Steam Engineering proved to be a sound decision. Fulfillment of the navy's manning requirements was facilitated by establishing the Bureau of Equipment and Recruiting. With a Bureau of Navigation, the responsibilities of which included those for the Hydrographic Office, the Nautical Almanac Office, and the Naval Academy, the Bureaus of Ordnance and Construction and Repair could now give full attention to their primary responsibilities.

On the other hand, effectiveness and efficiency of naval power were handicapped by the lack of an officer charged with strategic planning, the exercise of overall command over the operating forces, and the direction of logistics support. Two blockading squadrons were formed early in the war, one to cover the east coast, the other the Gulf of Mexico. South of Hampton Roads, the sheltered anchorages that were relatively secure and suitable for use as squadron bases were at Key West and the Fort Pickens area off Pensacola. Since the operational ranges of warships proceeding under steam power were still very limited, the ability to impose a tight blockade was contingent upon establishing additional conveniently located bases for frequent refueling and for providing other forms of logistics support, including repairs.

After the declaration of the blockade, two months passed before planning began for seizing base locations; in late June 1861 Welles convened a committee charged with selecting two sites to be captured for use as coal depots, one on the coast of South Carolina, the other in a location suitable for supporting blockaders off Georgia and Florida. The members were Captain Samuel F. Du Pont as chairman, the superintendent of the U.S. Coastal Survey, and an army engineer.

Submitting analyses and recommendations to Secretary Welles in a series of memoirs, Captain Du Pont went beyond the selection of sites. One of his proposals was to form three squadrons, the first to be responsible for Virginia and North Carolina, the second for the Atlantic seaboard to the south, and the third for operations in the Gulf of Mexico.

Chart 6.1
Naval Organization in 1862

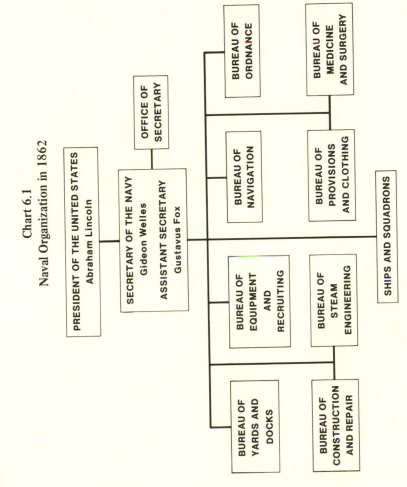

PRESIDENT OF THE UNITED STATES
Abraham Lincoln

OFFICE OF SECRETARY

SECRETARY OF THE NAVY
Gideon Welles
ASSISTANT SECRETARY
Gustavus Fox

BUREAU OF ORDNANCE

BUREAU OF MEDICINE AND SURGERY

BUREAU OF NAVIGATION

BUREAU OF PROVISIONS AND CLOTHING

BUREAU OF EQUIPMENT AND RECRUITING

BUREAU OF STEAM ENGINEERING

SHIPS AND SQUADRONS

BUREAU OF YARDS AND DOCKS

BUREAU OF CONSTRUCTION AND REPAIR

NAVAL ORGANIZATION IN 1862

Source: By the editors, based on information in *Paullin's History of Naval Administration.*

As long as Norfolk and its navy yard remained in Confederate hands, Hampton Roads would serve as an anchorage supporting the North Atlantic Blockading Squadron. Three locations suitable for the South Atlantic Squadron's bases were identified along the coast of South Carolina. Either Bull's Bay or Saint Helena Sound was deemed preferable to Port Royal because they would be easier to capture. For support of operations further south, it was recommended to take Fernandia, at the Georgia-Florida border.

Another key position, the first that should be seized, was Hatteras Inlet, one of the two main passages into the extensive sounds, rivers, and waterways of North Carolina; the other was Ocracoke. Along with other suggestions, the committee advised that one way to interrupt Southern trade could be to put down "material obstructions," such as old vessels laden with ballast, "in the appropriate places."[9] One of the reports submitted by Du Pont to the secretary of the navy went so far as to discuss the Mississippi River, its tributaries, and the approaches to New Orleans.

Meanwhile, the administration and management of departmental affairs were benefiting from Welles' understanding of naval operations that he had gained as the son of a man who had been both a shipbuilder and a West Indies merchant, and knowledge he acquired while serving as civilian chief of the Bureau of Provisions and Clothing.

The secretary's understanding of naval operations, however, was limited. It was thus fortunate that Gustavus Fox was brought into the department, first as chief clerk and then, on August 1, 1861, as the first assistant secretary of the navy. Focusing his primary attention upon the employment of the operating forces, Fox, to some extent, filled the gap resulting from the absence of a naval officer in the role of chief of naval operations.

One of the assistant secretary's early actions was to direct preparations for an operation in which two groups of schooners laden with stones, each towed by a schooner, were to be moored and then sunk in the inlets to Hatteras Sound. They arrived on the scene but swells and currents prevented the operation from being carried out. Actually, this proved fortunate for the Union because it was to benefit greatly from subsequent inland water naval operations and the transportation of troops and supplies by sea into these waters.

AMPHIBIOUS OPERATIONS

In the operation to gain control of Hatteras Inlet, unlike that at Veracruz, the army was to carry out its own landing. The attack began with the highly effective bombardments of Forts Hatteras and Clark on August 28 by warships of Flag Officer Silas H. Stringham, then commanding the North Atlantic Squadron. Major General B. F. Butler's attempt to land troops from his transports, however, was not successful. As those experienced in beaching craft on an exposed shore have so often noted, the surf proved to be far more severe than it appeared from offshore. Some army troops and marines did reach the low-lying island, along with a few artillery pieces, but losses and damage to landing craft were such that follow-on reinforcements and supplies could not be delivered.

Fortunately, on this occasion naval gunfire was sufficient to gain the surrender of both forts. Then, three weeks later, USS *Pawnee* and her landing force captured lightly-defended Ocracoke.

The next amphibious objectives were Bull's Bay and Fernandia. The ships chartered by the army to transport the landing force were scheduled to put to sea on September 17, 1861, but when the time came no troops were provided due to the seemingly insatiable demands of Major General George B. McClellan for more and more forces for his Army of the Potomac.

On the following day Du Pont was appointed commander of the South Blockading Squadron—one time when the authority delegated was fully commensurate with operational responsibilities. Instead of Bull's Bay, Flag Officer Du Pont, after considerable thought, now chose to attack the more heavily defended but better suited Port Royal and to delay the assault of Fernandia so that all available forces could be concentrated against the South Carolina objective. On his request, the squadron was assigned a battalion of marines.

Seeking to benefit from the Veracruz experience, Du Pont studied reports of the War with Mexico. One of his conclusions was that the available boats were not suitable for the assault landing. After obtaining advice from naval constructors, he selected a design for a new type of whale boat, broad-beamed and of shallow draft. Once the landing craft had been constructed, he carried out an exercise making practice landings of Brigadier General Sherman's troops in Hampton Roads.

Although preparations for the assault phase were sound, the combined operation had to be abandoned because of a sudden violent storm on November 1. This was long before the days when transports carrying army forces to the objective area were under naval command. For the naval ships under his command, Du Pont had provided for such a contingency by issuing sealed orders to each captain. Although the squadron became widely scattered as individual ships altered courses and speeds to avoid damage from high seas, the squadron reassembled promptly off Port Royal after the storm.

This was in sharp contrast with what happened to General Sherman's ships. Among those lost were the ship carrying most of the landing craft and another containing the army's ordnance stores, much of the artillery, and the bulk of the small arms.

Upon being informed in a conference with the general that army forces would be unable to take part in a joint amphibious assault, Du Pont altered the plan, and on November 7 he led his warships into Port Royal Sound, the entrance to which was guarded by forts on both sides. He focused the major warship bombardment on the stronger of the two, Fort Walker on Hilton Head Island, and subjected it to prolonged naval gunfire. Sailors and marines were landed. By the time they reached the beach the fort had been abandoned. The Confederate Army evacuated Fort Beauregard, north of the channel, later in the day.

The army did not provide troops for an amphibious operation to take Fernandia until March 1862. This time the Confederates withdrew their cannon and offered only token resistance when the Union warships and transports appeared. In praising Brigadier General Horatio G. Wright, Du Pont reported, "Our plans of action have been matured by mutual consultation, and have been carried into execution by mutual help."[10]

LOGISTICS SUPPORT

As anchorages for basing ships were occupied, the blockade became increasingly effective. One reason, of course, was the remarkable progress made in converting and arming steamers, in constructing steam-powered warships, and in manning and preparing the various men-of-war for service. Another was the expanding resupply and repair capabilities of logistics vessels deployed to the advance base locations along the coast. The latter, in some respects, were precursors of the establishment of service force mobile bases, which were to make extremely important contributions to the trans-Pacific campaigns of World War II.

As is invariably the case at the start of war, the adequacy and timeliness of logistics support were limiting factors. These problems were compounded by the fact that propulsion systems were still quite elementary. Frequent refuelings were necessary, and there were many demands for in-port maintenance and repairs. Moreover, the weight of large steam plants and the space they occupied on ships greatly restricted the fuel, ammunition, and other supplies that could be carried.

The magnitude of the demands at Port Royal were well beyond those anticipated by the bureaus. Indicative of the resupply problems was Du Pont's complaint to the secretary of the navy that, although he had reason to believe requisitions for "general stores" were being "immediately attended to by the bureaus, . . . there seem to be unaccountable obstacles to our receiving them." It had been necessary to purchase oil for machinery "from transports, or wherever it could be found, two or three barrels at a time." As for provisions, "important parts of the ration, such as sugar, coffee, flower, butter, beans, and dry fruit," had been "exhausted on the storeships of this squadron."[11]

It was decided in January 1862 to employ a second squadron for the Gulf of Mexico. Based on Key West, the Eastern Squadron would cover the Bahamas, Cuba, and the coast of Florida from Cape Canaveral on the Atlantic around to the mouth of the Choctawatchee River in the Gulf of Mexico. Ordered to command the Western Gulf Squadron, Flag Officer David D. Farragut proceeded to Ship Island where, in late February, the force was transferred to his control. That island off Mississippi had been occupied five months earlier by the landing party of a Union warship to gain a location for an afloat base until Pensacola could be recaptured.

CRUISER WARFARE

The maritime warfare efforts of the Confederate privateers were quite successful in the early months of the war, but the actions of the expanding Union Navy soon brought the situation under control. At the same time, the Confederate Navy was employing cruisers, some built in British yards, with considerable success in distant areas of the globe. Although raiders were few, tracking them down was very difficult before transoceanic cable or radio communications.

Successful *guerre de course* actions against shipping brought a sharp rise in insurance rates, many transfers of U.S. merchantmen to foreign flags, and a higher percentage of cargoes being transported in ships of other nations. Five Confederate cruisers were particularly successful and required a disproportionate amount of the Union Navy's effort before their careers were ended. The most renowned was CSS *Alabama,* a sloop of war constructed in a British dockyard for the Confederacy. Commissioned in August 1862, she continued her famed exploits until June 1864 when she was engaged and sunk by USS *Kearsage* off Cherbourg, France.

Throughout this period maritime warfare actions of the Union Navy were accompanied by inland naval operations far more extensive than at any other time in world history.

7

Inland Waters

While the Civil War naval operations on inland waters were unique in many respects, valuable insights can be gained from them regarding such matters as interservice relationships and the impact of advancing technology. As for the latter, this was the first time mines were extensively employed, and valuable lessons can be derived from examining the dynamic interplay of mine warfare measures and countermeasures.

The most basic naval roles on the waterways were similar to those offshore, and many were, in essence, projections of power from the sea by the Union Navy. For instance, control of the body of water inside the Virginia Capes was crucial for the North. This area included Hampton Roads, Chesapeake Bay, and the navigable portion of the Potomac River extending from the bay to the capital at Washington. These waters not only separated much of Virginia from the North but, along with the tidewater rivers of that state, provided important routes for moving military forces and their support. Ships at anchor in Hampton Roads, the main base of the North Atlantic Squadron, had to be protected from possible attacks down the Suffolk River from the Confederate-held Norfolk Navy Yard and from assaults out of the James River. Moreover, the Suffolk River was connected by the Dismal Swamp Canal to the waterway system of North Carolina.

The Mississippi and its tributaries, another water system of extreme importance, was not only the normal route for transporting large quantities of produce and manufactured products from midwestern states to the Gulf of Mexico, but it divided the southwestern states from the rest of the Confederacy. Furthermore, main routes for campaigns of the Union Army would be along the Tennessee and Cumberland rivers.

Army officers promptly recognized the desirability of gunboats that could carry out operations in such campaigns. The Navy Department should have been assigned responsibility for creating, maintaining, and operating a riverine force of gunboats and providing for its logistics. Instead, Secretary Welles, who was confronted by the imposing problem of rapidly augmenting the seagoing squadrons, preferred that the responsibilities be assumed by the War Department. In May 1861 Commander John Rodgers was ordered to the War Department, which assigned him to the Army of the West commanded by John C. Fremont.

Rodgers faced many difficult challenges to create the riverine force. He failed to obtain money from the navy for the purchase and conversion of three river steamers, but funds were then acquired from the War Department. Manning the force was one of the most critical problems. Except for the naval officers assigned to his command, no crews were provided by either the navy or the army. To do his own recruiting, Rodgers traveled all the way from Buffalo to Chicago.

When ready for service, the three wooden gunboats proceeded to Cairo at the juncture of the Ohio and Mississippi rivers, arriving there on August 2. Cairo was to become the main base for the expanding flotilla. Rodgers began gunboat operations, exercising control of waterways, conducting reconnaissance, and carrying out bombardments that contributed to army successes. Yet Fremont (who fortunately would soon be replaced by Major General H. H. Halleck) objected to this exercise of initiative.

When the War Department contracted for the construction of seven lightly-armored gunboats at St. Louis, Naval Constructor Samuel M. Pook was detailed to the program. The War Department then complicated matters, overloading the yard by contracting for two more gunboats, 38 mortar rafts, and other vessels. The gunboats were found to have excessive drafts and were down by the stern. Funds provided at that time for alterations were insufficient for completing more than four of the vessels.

Once again, crew acquisition was a major problem. The War Department authorized the transfer of soldiers with appropriate experience, but these were not provided. Captain Andrew H. Foote, who relieved Rodgers on September 5, recruited men to serve in his force but Halleck transferred them to an artillery company. Foote then requested 1,000 from the navy. The demands of the expanding blockading squadrons were such that only 500 seamen were sent. Meanwhile, the local recruiting problem became even more difficult when some of the men went for two months without pay because of a lack of money. When the first seven additional gunboats were ready, only three could be provided with minimal crews.

Fortunately, Foote sought the assistance of General Ulysses S. Grant. Temporary personnel were detailed to complete the gunboats' manning just in time for the bombardment and capture of Fort Henry on the Tennessee River on February 6, 1862 and for the operation with the army that gained control of Fort Danelson ten days later. After these actions by green crews, Foote conducted special training to reduce the waste of ammunition due to poor gunnery.

Ammunition had been one of the most critical factors in those early days of the war. According to Lieutenant Wise, acting chief of the Bureau of Ordnance and Hydrography, President Lincoln fired a general when apprised of the situation. Upon receipt of a telegram from Captain Foote, the bureau sent badly needed powder and primers that the army had not provided.

The problems that Captain Foote encountered when he first took command had been made worse by colonels and generals who frequently pulled rank across service lines and expected compliance with orders they issued to units of the flotilla. Yet, not only did Captain Foote hold the highest statutory rank in the U.S. Navy, but he was directly responsible to the general in command of the Army of the West. On one occasion a brigadier general even attempted to take from the flotilla the supply barge of the Cairo afloat base. This war was far from the last time that an army officer issued orders bypassing the naval chain of command as a result of assumptions concerning the comparability of ranks. All too often these officers lacked an appreciation of the basic differences between land and naval forces. In this case, Foote's command problems were greatly eased when Secretary Welles designated him flag officer, U.S. Naval Forces, western waters.

The expanding flotilla was engaged in a continuing high tempo of combat operations. These included patrols; captures of Confederate vessels; actions against enemy naval forces; bombardments of forts, batteries, and concentrations of troops; gunfire support of the Union Army; transporting and convoying troops movements by water; amphibious operations; and the capture of shore installations. While Foote exercised operational command at the scene of action, his fleet captain at Cairo administered the force, directed supporting measures, brought additional vessels into service, and exercised control over naval units not under the direct operational command of the flag officer. Commander Alexander M. Pennock, later a captain, continued to serve in this important capacity under subsequent commanders of the flotilla and its successor, the Mississippi Squadron. Time and again, Grant and other generals requested the navy to exercise control of a river section, convoy troops, provide combat support or other naval operations only to learn that Pennock had already issued orders anticipating the need.

RIVERINE CONTROL

One naval objective beyond that of making contributions to army campaigns was to establish control along the entire length of the Mississippi. Not only was it desirable to open the waterway from midwestern states to the sea, but such control would, in effect, extend the blockade of the Confederate states in the east.

To that end, in addition to riverine flotilla operations, it would be necessary to project sea-going naval power up the river. When Farragut took command of the new Western Gulf Squadron in February 1862 his instructions from Secretary Welles were to "proceed up the Mississippi River and reduce the defenses which guard the approaches to New Orleans, when you will appear off that city and take possession of it under the guns of your squadron, and hoist the American flag thereon, keeping possession until troops can be sent to you."[1]

Reconnaissance of the delta revealed that passage was blocked by a chain supported by anchored hulks spanning the river just below two forts, one on each bank. Transports with army troops, under the command of Major General Benjamin F. Butler, arrived at Ship Island in late March. The plan agreed to by the general was that the transports would follow in the squadron's wake. The army would then hold whatever Farragut was able to take.

By then the squadron had been augmented by mortar boats organized into a flotilla under Commander D. D. Porter. Porter began his bombardment of Fort Jackson on April 18. Damage from the prolonged firing, however, was limited since the floor of the fort had recently been flooded and the mud absorbed the explosions of the mortar shells, which were fired at high angles.

Farragut soon changed his plan, but awaiting the reduction of the forts before proceeding upstream. The transports would not be subjected to cannon fire from the forts. Instead, Butler's force was to land above the forts from the sound on the east side of the delta. Under cannon fire at night, two squadron gunboats succeeded in breaking a narrow gap through the Confederate chain barrier. Exchanging gunfire with the forts as the mortar boats stepped up their bombardment, the squadron made through the opening before dawn on April 24. Warships sustained damage but none was put out of action. Opposition above the barrier by a Confederate naval force was eliminated and batteries ashore were silenced. Farragut obtained the surrender of New Orleans the next day and the city was occupied by Butler three days later.

By now Foote had begun actions to extend Union Navy control down the Mississippi. The first obstacle to overcome had been island number ten at a sharp S-turn of the river 60 miles below Cairo. There were many cannon on the island, and there were batteries on the Tennessee shore where, because of swamps, they were not vulnerable to attack by land. After three weeks of bombardment by gunboats and mortar boats, the island surrendered on April 7, 1862. Fort Pillow was subjected to naval gunfire a week later. Then on May 9 Foote, physically deteriorating from a wound suffered three months before, delegated command to Captain Charles H. Davis. During a bombardment of Fort Pillow the next day, the riverine force was attacked by nine Confederate rams. Two Union ironclad gunboats were holed; one was sunk, the other intentionally grounded. Both were later refloated and repaired.

Fort Pillow, subjected to prolonged bombardments by Davis's gunboats, was abandoned on the night of June 4. Except for one ram, the Confederate Defense Fleet was sunk in a naval battle the next day. Memphis soon surrendered to Captain Davis. Later that month, after a joint operation with the army opened communications up the White River into Arkansas, Davis was designated flag officer in command of his flotilla.

The lack of mobile logistics, especially coal supplies, hindered the initial movement of Farragut's warships above New Orleans. Farragut's main objective was Vicksburg, where key railroads connecting the western and eastern sections of the Confederacy terminated on opposite shores of the river, overlooked by powerful gun batteries.

Farragut in USS *Hartford,* two other screw-sloops, eight gunboats, and transports carrying Butler's troops reached Vicksburg on May 23, 1862. It was hoped that the show of force might result in the abandonment of defenses, but this did not happen. Reconnaissance by the flag officer and general revealed Confederate batteries mounted on terraces as high as 250 feet. Butler gauged his force insufficient for an attack by land, so Farragut headed back down the river, leaving his gunboats to carry out blockading actions and harassing bombardments.

In June, urged by Washington, Farragut again headed north on the *Hartford,* despite the declining summer flow of the river system. This time his force included supply vessels and coal barges, six steamers of the mortar flotilla, and 16 mortar boats. *Hartford* grounded, and she was refloated only after a major, prolonged effort. Farragut later passed Vicksburg under the cover of darkness, and after making contact with Captain Davis's riverine force, he returned south.

Shortly thereafter, Congress directed the transfer of responsibilities for the western gunboat fleet to the Navy Department. The second long-overdue congressional action that day established the ranks of rear admiral and commodore.

If General Halleck could have been induced to join in a coordinated attack on Vicksburg an early victory might have been achieved. This was, however, not the case and the defenses there were greatly strengthened before such an attempt would be made. By the time of the attack, difficult, costly, and prolonged army and navy operations were required. Thus, the Confederates remained, until the next summer, in control of the position blocking the flow of Union cargoes up and down the Mississippi and the point of crossing for supplies and troops from Arkansas, Louisiana, and Texas to the eastern states of the South.

In the meantime, operations by the Union Navy on other inland waters connecting with the sea were making crucial contributions to the North's overall war effort. Here, too, a prerequisite of success was to exercise control over waterways. Military actions into North Carolina were wholly dependent upon sea and inland water lines of communications. Such lines also were crucial in the early army offensives into southern Virginia. Furthermore, the effectiveness of the North Atlantic Squadron hinged to a large extent on the security of this anchorage at Hampton Roads.

The seizure of the two passages into Pamlico Sound in the summer of 1861 had opened the way to operations on the interconnecting sounds that stretch from the Virginia border to Cape Lookout. Important rivers flow into these sounds, one of which connected by canal to Norfolk. Union control of these waterways would hinder Confederate efforts in that area and would permit the projection and support of military offensives by the Union.

Establishing such control, however, took considerable time because of the limited number of warships available in the early stages, and the competing demands of the blockade mission that were necessary to fulfill while also carrying out actions against Southern privateers and cruisers. Moreover, Roanoke Island would have to be taken before the squadron could extend its operations into Albermarle Sound and beyond. Three small Confederate men-of-war captured the unescorted steamer carrying troops from Hatteras Inlet when the first effort to occupy the island was made on October 1, 1861. In February 1862 the island, now fortified, was taken by an amphibious operation that began with a bombardment by Flag Officer L. M. Goldsborough's squadron and continued with the landing of Brigadier General Burnside's force.

As for Hampton Roads, its security was a major concern since the Confederates possessed the Norfolk Navy Yard. This had been completely equipped with wharves, docks, ship-houses, workshops, and store houses. Although the defenders had put the torch to flammable structures upon leaving the scene, the Southerners saved some buildings and extinguished the fire that was intended to destroy the dry dock. Among the naval stores and materials lost by the Union were about 1,200 cannon. The trunnions of many had been knocked off, but efforts to damage the Dahlgren guns did not succeed. One of the warships set on fire and sunk upon evacuation of the yard had been USS *Merrimack*. That screw-frigate soon was raised by the Confederates, who renamed her CSS *Virginia*.

IRONCLADS

As early as February 1861 Commander Dahlgren, who was on duty at the Washington Navy Yard where the Ordnance Bureau was developing armor, recommended that Congress approve the construction of an "iron-cased" ship. This was discussed in the Navy Department that May but deferred because of other pressing problems. The lack of a sense of urgency was overcome when the Union learned of Confederate actions to shield *Merrimack* with sloping armor (four-inch iron) "to render her ball-proof" and "to arm her with the heaviest ordnance"[2] so that she might drive Union ships from Hampton Roads and the ports of Virginia.

On August 4 Congress, on the recommendation of Secretary Welles, authorized a board of naval officers to examine plans and specifications that might be submitted for ironclad vessels. Funds were appropriated for their construction. Advertising for proposals led to a large number being received by the Navy Department. The Ironclad Board's report of September 16 recommended letting contracts "for the construction of one or more iron-clad vessels or batteries of as light a draught of water as practicable consistent with their weight of armor." Summarizing evaluations of the 16 most promising proposals, the board recommended letting contracts with three firms: Merrick and Sons (*New Ironsides*), Bushnell and Co. (*Galena*), and John Ericsson (*Monitor*). Another of the board's recommendations was "the construction, in our own dock-yards, of one or more"[3] armored warships.

The construction of *Monitor*, with all of her innovative features, was truly a remarkable feat. Ericsson prepared many sketches and detailed plans, arranged for the participation of several firms, and directed and coordinated their work. One of the companies built the hull; one furnished the plates, bars, and rivets; one made the turret; another provided port stoppers; and yet another manufactured the propulsion plant and machinery for the turret. Some work, such as rolling the first plates, was underway by the time the contract was signed on October 4.

Launched on January 30, 1862, the cheese-box on a raft was then towed to the New York Navy Yard for completion, arming, and fitting out under the prospective commanding officer, Lieutenant John L. Worden. When the first trials revealed a serious problem with the steering system that resulted in the ship ramming a dock, Ericsson's alterations minimized the time necessary for corrective measures. The shakedown period was begun on February 27, only two days after commissioning. A misunderstanding concerning gun-carriage braking devices resulted in both guns being disabled during firing tests. Nevertheless, towing the *Monitor* south began on March 5, the day after successful firings of the repaired guns.

On March 8, 1862 CSS *Virginia* made her first sortie from the Suffolk River and sank two Union Navy warships. When the Confederate ironclad returned the next day, she was confronted by USS *Monitor*, which had just arrived in the area. Although neither warship was sunk during the inland water slugging match that followed, the solid shot from *Monitor* cracked the iron plates that clad *Virginia* and fractured some of the wooden backing. Damage to the superstructure and hull required extensive repairs in drydock. At the time of this Battle of Hampton Roads, the *Monitor's* new 11-inch gun was restricted to 15-pound charges, although up to 30-pound charges were authorized after later tests. If such weights had been used during this dual, the Confederate ironclad probably would have been destroyed. Nonetheless, the action had a very beneficial effect on Union morale and proved to be the turning point of the war in the Norfolk area.

OPERATIONS IN SUPPORT OF
THE ARMY OF THE POTOMAC

The long-awaited Union Army campaign toward Richmond was about to begin. Early in March 1862 it had been decided that the Army of the Potomac would be transported by water from Alexandria to Chesapeake and then to the Rappahannock River city of Urbanna. From there they would advance toward the Confederate capital by way of West Point where the Pamunkey joins the York River. Major General George B. McClellan characteristically went to the extreme of requesting that a part of Du Pont's South Atlantic Blockading

Squadron be sent north to be employed with the army on the York or Rappahannock rivers. It was hardly surprising that Secretary Welles did not agree.

By March 17, when transports with the first element of the army left Alexandria, the army's destination had been changed to Fort Monroe on the north side
of Hampton Roads. According to the plan finally adopted by General McClellan,
the main force was to be assembled there preparatory to an advance up the peninsula. A corps transported via the Potomac, the bay, and up the York River
would establish a base at West Point. It would be joined there by the main force
and head for Richmond.

McClellan pronounced that "the Navy should at once throw its whole available force, its most powerful vessels, against Yorktown."[4] Yet the fortification
guarding the river there was only about 25 miles from Fort Monroe. The general
tried to get the North Atlantic Squadron placed under his command, but Flag
Officer Goldsborough did not concur. His warships would assist the land campaign, but not to the extent of jeopardizing the mission of protecting Hampton
Roads, which was still threatened by *Virginia* and other Confederate warships
that might emerge from the navy yard and the James River. Furthermore, the
troops who were to advance north from Fort Monroe would be dependent on
resupply operations via Hampton Roads.

For operations on the York, Goldsborough sent a small group of gunboats
and later other warships. It was not until April 5 that McClellan ordered up a
siege train, and a month more passed before he employed it. Upon its arrival in
the Yorktown area the Confederate Army withdrew. Army transports reached
West Point two days later. The screw-sloop of war and gunboats that had protected them during the movement up the river assisted in the landing and conducted counter-battery fire. Another Union warship captured two enemy vessels in a tributary of the York.

These were but the first of a rapid sequence of events involving naval power.
Indications were that the Confederates might be withdrawing their forces from
the Norfolk area. Lincoln, then visiting Hampton Roads, ordered the naval bombardment of Sewell's Point. The action revealed reductions in the fire power of
the batteries ashore.

Another of the president's orders was that *Galena* and two gunboats, if not
needed for protection against CSS *Virginia*, be sent into the James River. This
small force engaged two shore batteries and caused two Confederate gunboats
to retire. *Galena*, the second warship of the Ironclad Board's program to see
service, had reached Hampton Roads on April 24.

Virginia made limited sorties into the roads on May 7 and 8 but escaped before Goldsborough could carry out his plan to ram her. Three days later the last
of the Southern forces left Norfolk and, after highly effective destruction of
facilities, left the navy yard at Suffolk. The Confederate iron-clad's draft was too
great for passage up the James, and she was destroyed by her crew off Craney
Island the next day.

Under Commander John Rodgers, who commanded *Galena,* the James River flotilla, now including *Monitor,* reached Drewry's Bluff on May 15. There, at the narrow sharp turn in the river about eight miles below Richmond, they encountered strong lines of obstacles filled with submersive batteries and guns up on the bluff just downstream from the barrier. By then the few Confederate Army cannon available had been augmented by naval guns, including heavy ones from *Virginia,* manned by sailors and marines. Lightly-armored *Galena* suffered casualties from hits that penetrated her iron-clad sides. The flotilla retired. Rodgers concluded that the battery could be reduced only by a land attack from the rear, but no such attack was attempted. Throughout the remainder of the war the flotilla controlled the river below there.

As for the peninsular campaign, the Army of the Potomac had advanced to the point that its outposts were within four miles of Richmond when, on June 26, General Robert E. Lee launched his famed seven-day offensive. McClellan sent word to Flag Officer Goldsborough that it was "a matter of vital importance and may involve the existence of the army" that the provision transports be brought safely to the James. By the next day the land communications line from the supply base at White House on the Pamunkey River (above West Point) had been severed. In a June 30 meeting on board *Galena,* Rodgers, now a captain, pointed out to the general the dangers to the transports if they came to the narrow portion of the James River. He recommended that the flotilla halt at Harrison's Landing. Here the river was much wider and so situated that the navy could protect both flanks and command the approaches from Richmond. McClellan agreed. The navy gave effective gunfire support when the Confederates attacked that evening, and the general wrote, "The gunboats rendered most efficient aid at this time, and helped drive back the enemy."[5]

The flotilla, by now strengthened, covered the army's retreat to Harrison Landing. Its warships bombarded Lee's advancing columns and reserve forces and provided close gunfire support when McClellan's troops were engaged. Lee informed Confederate President Davis on July 4 that he did not "wish to expose the men to the destructive missiles" of the flotilla. Two days later he wrote, "The great obstacle to operations here is the presence of the enemy's gunboats, which protect our approaches to him, and should we even force him from his positions on his land front, would prevent us from reaping any of the fruits of victory and expose our men to great destruction."[6]

Although the Army of the Potomac was withdrawn from the peninsula during the following month, the navy continued to exercise its power on the James River and on other inland waters in the Virginia-North Carolina area.

Here, as on the western rivers and in the maritime war, experience demonstrated the importance of employing warships and their supporting vessels in a way that avoided undue diversions from the primary mission of controlling the sea and inland waters, and of taking full advantage of the mobility, flexibility, and versatility of naval forces.

8

Concluding Phases of Warfare
between the States

The failure of the Union Army's peninsular campaign to capture Richmond meant that a prolonged war would be required. As time went on, the naval blockade exerted pervasive and increasingly decisive effects on the outcome. After the withdrawal of the Army of the Potomac in August 1862, naval forces continued to exercise control of the James River and render assistance to land campaigns in southern Virginia. One step taken by the Confederacy to counter Union use of the river was the construction of Fort Powahatan. Rear Admiral S. F. Lee, commander of the North Atlantic Squadron, exercised direct command over the naval force that captured the fort in July 1863.

The attack on Fort Sumter that April was one of those cases in which an appointed official in Washington issued direction to the naval commander on the scene of action as to how he was to employ his forces to achieve an objective. The orders issued by Assistant Secretary Fox to Rear Admiral Du Pont, which included several restrictions, contrasted with the full authority granted him at the time of the capture of Port Royal.

DEVELOPMENTS IN IRON-CLAD
SHIPS AND TORPEDOES

A contributing factor, as happened many times, was the over-enthusiasm resulting from a spectacular advance in military capabilities. The breakthrough in this case was the development of the turret. This led to ignoring or underestimating the limitations of the cheese box on a raft.

Soon after the loss of *Monitor* in a storm off Cape Hatteras on December 31, 1862, other ships of this type came into service. They were of the *Passaic* class, for which contracts had been let shortly after the Battle of Hampton Roads. Although still not capable of fighting in even moderately rough seas, their ability to survive storms was enhanced by greater length, wider beam, and better hull form. On the other hand, their top speed was even less than the *Monitor*'s, for despite increased displacement the power plant was of the same design.

Du Pont opposed using them against the fort because of an extremely low rate of fire (one round every six or seven minutes), poor maneuverability, and a speed that scarcely exceeded the maximum tidal flow past Sumter. Fox overruled the admiral.

During the assault in April 1863, six of the seven monitors were put out of action and an iron-clad steamer was sunk. In contrast, the flagship—the 230-foot, 3,500-ton *New Ironsides* with broadside batteries of 14 11-inch smooth bores, two rifle guns, and equipped also with sail—carried out her bombardment well. In any case, neither this nor a subsequent effort succeeded.

Due to the threat of *New Ironsides,* the Confederacy considered a variety of proposals for attacking the formidable warship, including gunboats, a fireship, and torpedo rams. A $10,000 reward was offered for her destruction. An attempt with a torpedo by gunboat *Torch* failed. In August 1863 gunboat *David,* low in the water, exploded a torpedo rigged on a ten-foot spar against the anchored ship's hull. The damage, however, was soon repaired and *New Ironsides* resumed her operations.

The most notable successes with spar torpedoes were the sinking of USS *Housatonic* by partly submerged man-powered submarine *H. L. Hunley,* and the sinking of iron-clad CSS *Albermarle* by Lieutenant William Barker Cushing's steam picket launch. Both ships were at anchor when attacked.

Meanwhile, operations by naval forces in rivers, sounds, and bays were having to cope more and more with Confederate mines. Two floating mines had been recovered in the Potomac in July 1861. Seven months later others were discovered in the Tennessee River where, after having been planted, they were broken loose by floodwaters. A battery of moored tin cans with wires to the banks for electrical firing was found in the Savannah River.

The Confederates established a Torpedo Bureau and Service in October 1862. Two months later USS *Cairo* was sunk by a demijohn exploded by a friction primer from a pit ashore. All in all, some 40 Union vessels were sent to the bottom by torpedoes during the course of the war. If it had not been for the various means devised for sweeping and clearance and the adoption of protective measures for ships at anchor, the losses would have been far higher.

As it was, operations on inland waters had to be planned so as to minimize the probability of damage by mines. At the end of the war Secretary Welles reported that torpedoes had been "always formidable in harbors and internal waters, and . . . have been more destructive to our naval vessels than all other means combined."[1]

The abortive attack on Fort Sumter in the spring of 1863 was followed by the design of the greatly improved *Canonius* class of monitors, the construction of which began that fall. Five of nine planned monitors in this class saw service later in the war.

Other seagoing monitors, some with one turret, others with two, were under construction at navy yards. The most advanced were of the iron-clad *Miantonomoh* class. After the war she and *Monadnock,* the only one of the four in the program to see action during the war, would gain respect for the U.S. Navy during long cruises to foreign ports.

A program to produce monitors for service on the western rivers failed. After the assistant secretary had plans drafted for such a class by Ericsson, he bypassed the bureaus and assigned the program to an iron-clad office in New York. Chief Engineer Alban C. Stimers, who had worked with Ericsson during the construction of *Monitor* and then served as her engineer officer, made extensive alterations to the plans. Chief Constructor John Lenthall and Chief Engineer Benjamin F. Isherwood, who headed the Bureaus of Construction and Repair and Steam Engineering, essentially boycotted the iron-clad office. Neither reviewed the plans or provided assistance.

When the first hulls were launched in May 1864 their freeboard was so marginal that they could not have remained afloat after being fitted out. While Fox accepted blame for the failure, Secretary Welles took Lenthall to task for not having provided advice.

CONTINUING RIVERINE WAR IN THE WEST

In the fall of 1862 the gunboat fleet on western waters had been assigned to the Navy Department. By then the ranks of commodore and rear admiral had been established. Appointed acting rear admiral, David Dixon Porter succeeded Charles H. Davis as the force's commander. Porter formed two divisions, one to patrol the Mississippi, the other to cover the Ohio, Tennessee, and Cumberland rivers.

The Army of the Tennessee, now operating in Mississippi, was under the command of Grant, now a major general. Neither he nor General Halleck was informed that the president had commissioned his political friend, John A. McClernand, a major general, and directed him to recruit and organize an Army of the Mississippi for joint operations against Vicksburg "to clear the Mississippi River and open navigation to New Orleans."[2]

Porter headed south from Cairo in December 1862 for a joint operation with Grant's forces, in order to land troops to conduct a flanking movement and assault the fortifications at Vicksburg. Vessels of the enlarged squadron swept the heavily-mined lower portion of the Yazoo River, cleared obstacles, and escorted troop-carrying steamers to the landing area. During this operation *Cairo* was sunk by a Confederate mine. After being landed, the soldiers suffered heavy casualties and were reembarked.

Troops commanded by Major General W. T. Sherman were landed to assault Chickasaw Bluffs above Vicksburg, but they encountered adverse conditions due to rain and enemy reinforcements. Although well supported by naval gunfire, the casualties forced Sherman to reembark. Command relationships during these joint operations led Admiral Porter to write Assistant Secretary Fox that "there is a delightful concert here between the Army and the Navy. . . . we agree in everything, and . . . they are both able men."[3]

The Chickasaw operation was still in progress when McClernand sought the participation of Porter's squadron in a campaign into Arkansas. Here, the gunboat bombardment of Fort Hindman led to its capture along with 6,500 prisoners. But Grant informed the general of his disapproval of diverting effort from Vicksburg, and Lincoln revoked the special commission. When Grant was informed that he could either take direct command of the Vicksburg operation or assign it to the next in rank, Grant chose the former. Vicksburg's surrender was finally achieved on July 4, 1863.

The Confederates had developed another formidable strong point where heavy batteries on a high bluff at Port Hudson, about 100 miles below Vicksburg, were capable of engaging vessels trying to pass. Upon being informed by Major General Nathaniel P. Banks that he was ready to assault the position, Rear Admiral Farragut headed up the river to engage the fortifications. Bucking a strong current, the warships sustained many hits. Only flagship *Hartford* made her way past the batteries.

Banks did not begin his attack until May 1863. Naval guns and mortars provided support but, in view of the casualties, the general withdrew his forces to seize other positions and did not try another assault until after the fall of Vicksburg. Port Hudson finally surrendered on July 9. Soon thereafter, Porter was assigned responsibilities along the entire river system down to New Orleans.

Shortly after his capture of New Orleans, Farragut had sought permission to attack Mobile. More than two years passed before the operation was approved, but by then the narrow channel past the forts and into the bay was heavily mined. After the lead ship, monitor *Tecumseh* was sunk by a mine, the admiral "damned the torpedoes," ordered full speed ahead, and then engaged Confederate warships in his famed victory at the Battle of Mobile Bay in August 1864.

In the following months naval operations in the area had to contend with many mines, particularly in the Blakely River. Something like 100 were swept by the Union Navy. Six warships were sent to the bottom as a result of mining before the army, aided by naval bombardments, finally occupied Mobile in April 1865.

Meanwhile, the riverine force was carrying out operations to exercise control of the Mississippi, protect vessels carrying cargoes, and prevent crossings of the river by forces and supplies of the Confederacy. Other operations were on the Tennessee, Cumberland, Ohio, Yazoo, and White rivers.

The Red River campaign, in which Nathanial P. Banks was the army commander, failed. Porter had been concerned about low water but, instead of insisting on waiting for the coming of the spring tide, he agreed to the proposed operation. Gunboats ascended the river at the end of February 1864 on a six-day reconnaissance mission. Despite falling water levels and hits received during exchanges of fire with batteries ashore, they were sent upstream a week later to prepare the way for transports carrying the troops of Brigadier General A. J. Smith, with the navy providing escorts.

Banks selected a road well away from the river for his overland advance. Not only did he lack the support of gunboats, but he encountered trouble in moving his long baggage train through dense woods. Meeting heavy Confederate resistance half way to the objective, he retreated.

The navy encountered great difficulties as a result of the low water, problems in crossing the rapids at Alexandria, and enemy actions. After the decision to withdraw, there were major difficulties in getting back over the rapids. Whether or not a campaign at that time of year had a reasonable chance of success, the combined operation provides an example of poor planning and coordination.

THE WAR ENDS

In the eastern theater, the Union Navy continued to maintain control of the lower portion of the James River in order to assist army operations in southern Virginia. Following the Union capture of Fort Powahatan in July 1863, there were many engagements with batteries ashore. Minesweeping was required in these and other operations. The threat of underwater weapons became so great that a special "torpedo and picket division"[4] was established in May 1864.

Grant, promoted to Lieutenant General, now had overall command of the Union Army. Taking personal command of the Army of the Potomac, he launched his offensive south against the Confederate Army of Northern Virginia. The navy furnished gunfire support for one of his flanking operations, an advance up the south bank of the James. Other naval operations prevented Confederate gunboats from coming down the river. By the end of 1864 General W. T. Sherman had completed his march through Georgia to the sea and was soon heading north. On the last day of January 1865 General Robert E. Lee was assigned command of all of the armies of the South. By then the Confederacy, gravely weakened by the naval blockade and suffering reverses in the land war, was in desperate straits.

In February 1865, shortly after taking Wilmington, North Carolina, and Charleston, Secretary Welles directed Rear Admiral Dahlgren, commander of the South Atlantic Squadron, to return vessels he no longer needed, especially the least efficient. Rear Admiral H. K. Thatcher, who commanded the West Gulf Squadron, was ordered to "send North such purchased vessels as appear by surveys to require very extensive repairs . . . and all those no longer required. These will probably be sold or laid up. . . . any stores that are not required"[5] should be sent home.

The bulk of the logistics used by Grant's forces was by water to the main base at City Point, where the Appomattox joins the James. This support was essential during the final operations that led to Lee's surrender on April 9. Hence, from the first to last, the navy played an essential role in preserving the Union.

9

The Postwar Period

Concerned with the situation south of the border and the possibility of violations of the Monroe Doctrine by European powers, the United States maintained two major naval squadrons in service. An ultimatum presented to Napoleon III in February 1866 led France to agree to withdraw soldiers from Mexico, and the last left early the next year. After Mexican forces occupied the capital Emperor Maximilian, who was supported by Napoleon III, was captured, court martialed, and executed in June 1867.

As was the case after the War of 1812, the United States emerged from the Civil War with an inflated shore establishment. Peacetime politics were again a major factor. In addition to seeking funds for restoring the Norfolk and Pensacola navy yards, the Secretary of the Navy noted in his report at the end of 1866 that the Portsmouth, New York, and Washington yards were being enlarged. Secretary Welles advocated the construction of additional dry-docks, ship-houses over building ways, more shops, and increased facilities for manufacturing and repairing steam machinery. Stating that the supply of timber was exhausted, he reported, "it will be true economy to provide an abundance"[1] for use in a future emergency.

The secretary made only one reference to ship construction programs—a future requirement for major warships built of iron—but this was to justify a proposal for a navy yard at League Island, Philadelphia. In his next annual report Welles stated that the "ships and men in service" were "vastly inferior in numbers to other maritime powers." However, instead of suggesting any increase in the fleet or replacement of obsolescent warships, he expressed pride in maintaining "the smallest number of steamers compatible with the requirements."[2]

SHOWING THE FLAG

The nation emerged from the Civil War with certain types of warships that were the most advanced in the world. The most impressive were those of the class of iron-clad monitors with two turrets and twin screws. One of these, USS

Monadnock, began her cruise around South America in October 1865. One early leg of the voyage—from Salute Island, French Guinea to Ciarar, Brazil—took nine days and consumed 86 percent of the coal. The captain reported that the weight of her turrets caused the warship to work when the bunkers were not full. The engines, which often raced as propellers broke water in heavy seas, needed overhaul. Temporary repairs also were made on the boilers.

Later in the trip the commanding officer made it a practice to maintain 60 revolutions per minute. Not only was this found to be the most fuel efficient speed, but it reduced the wear and tear on machinery. The ship coaled at 12 ports enroute from Hampton Roads to San Francisco, and during several of the stops the steam plant was overhauled. Distances covered per day ranged from 19 to 196 miles. The entire voyage, including port visits, took more than a year. When it was completed on June 21, 1866, the captain reported the machinery and boilers to be in good condition, but the blow and feed pipes were "worn out."[3] Nine days later *Monadnock* was decommissioned.

Assistant Secretary Fox had departed that May on a triumphant cruise to Europe in *Monadnock*'s sister ship, *Miantonomoh.* After coaling first at Nova Scotia and then at Newfoundland, the next leg was to Ireland. Consuming "a fair portion of [her] coal," the warship was towed "a great portion of the way" by *Augusta* as "a matter of convenience and precaution."[4] Understandably, the accomplishments were highlighted rather than the logistical limitations of the 17,767-mile cruise, during which calls were made at 38 ports. In any case, the two monitors so impressed foreign powers that they soon began construction of similar types.

The nation took justifiable pride in these achievements. However, the transition from sail, begun a half century earlier, was not yet completed, at least insofar as worldwide operations were concerned.

Lessons of continuing relevance can be derived from the history of another ship that made a spectacular demonstration of the progress made by the U.S. Navy in steam propulsion. She was the 355-foot steamer *Wampanoag.* Naval Engineer B. F. Isherwood, chief of the Bureau of Steam Engineering, designed the propulsion plant and specified the basic configuration of the hull, which was designed by clipper-ship architect B. F. Delano. Laid down in 1863, she was built under an act authorizing a class of screw-frigates for use in commerce destruction and raiding ports in case of a war with Britain.

Commissioned in September 1867, the steamer averaged 16.6 knots for 38 hours during a trial run down the coast. While she may have been aided by the southerly Labrador current, this was truly a notable achievement.

Overwhelming emphasis had been placed on attaining maximum speed. Four very tall stacks provided draft for the fires of the coal-burning furnaces under each of the eight fire-tube boilers, four forward and four aft of two horizontal geared engines with cylinders 100 inches in diameter and surface condensers. There were two small superheating boilers in the engine room.

The engines were connected by an extraordinarily long shaft to a four-bladed propeller that was 19 feet in diameter.

As for her suitability for cruising warfare missions in remote areas, she also had a bark rig, but sails were small and so proportioned and distributed that her sailing characteristics were poor. The propulsion plant filled the underwater portion of the slim hull from the stern to far forward, thus greatly reducing the capacity for storing coal, water, ammunition, and supplies. The size of engineering spaces meant the ship would be highly vulnerable to battle damage. There were complaints concerning the violent rolling of the vessel, undoubtably the result of the low center of gravity and the slimness of the hull.

After serving a month and a half as flagship of the North Atlantic Squadron, *Wampanoag* was decommissioned, laid up, and renamed *Florida*. A board of line officers, convened in 1868, was highly critical of the ship's characteristics. This was followed by the appointment of a Board on Steam Engineering Afloat to "examine the steam engines afloat in our national vessels," and "to state which are, and which are not fit, for service."[5] The members were Rear Admiral L. M. Goldsborough, Commodore C. S. Boggs, and Engineers E. D. Robie, J. W. Moore, and Issac Newton.

Eleven of the 64 pages of the board's 1869 report were devoted to *Wampanoag* (now named *Florida*). After describing the frigate in some detail and commenting on some features as the large machinery spaces, cramped quarters for the crew, the need to store over one-fourth of the coal on the berth deck, heavy consumption of coal, the rolling, and poor maneuverability, the board judged the warship "utterly unfit to be retained in the service."[6] The board also condemned sister ship *Ammonoosuc,* which had been laid up after completing her trials. Isherwood and Lenthall took heated public issue with the report. After being maintained in ordinary for five years, *Florida* served as a receiving and stores ship at New London until 1885.

This case illustrates the importance of balancing the judgment of officers well experienced in naval operations with that of experts concerning what is realistically achievable in the design of warships. There is much to be said, however, for occasionally building experimental ships or craft.

Tests were also conducted in 1867 on the use of petroleum instead of coal. Benjamin Isherwood acknowledged the technological practicality of using oil, but he opposed this measure on the grounds of "convenience, comfort, health, and safety."[7] He also acknowledged that the use of fuel oil would result in some reductions in the bulk and weight of fuel required. Other advantages, such as those realized in refuelings, were not identified.

DIRECTION OF NAVAL AFFAIRS

Once again, U.S. naval power was suffering from the lack of a senior officer experienced in command at sea with responsibilities and authority comparable to those of the chief of naval operations at the end of World War II. Assistant Secretary Fox had filled the gap in some respects, but he had been away from the department since the spring of 1866 and upon his return retired. The successor to the former naval officer was the wartime chief clerk of the department, William Faxon, a former newspaper friend of Welles. Faxon's eldest son became the new chief clerk. Meanwhile, adverse effects were resulting from placing emphasis on the shore establishment, management inefficiencies, reductions in the number of ships in service, declining readiness, and a relaxation of standards.

After winning the presidential election in 1868, Grant's preference for secretary of the navy was Vice Admiral Porter, who had impressed the general so favorably during the western river campaigns. However, political considerations led to a compromise. In appointing A. E. Borie to the position of secretary, Grant also designated Porter the new secretary's adviser. As directed by the president, Borie ordered that "all matters relating to the Navy coming under the cognizance of the different bureaus will be transmitted to Vice-Admiral Porter before being transmitted to the Secretary of the Navy."[8]

In carrying out his additional responsibilities, the vice admiral commuted from Annapolis where he was serving as superintendent of the Naval Academy. One of the first actions he took was to terminate Isherwood's long tour as chief of the Bureau of Steam Engineering.

The prompt issuance of many secretary of the navy general orders, 25 of which were forthcoming during Borie's first term in office, revealed that Porter had been giving considerable thought to corrective measures that should be taken to overcome what he viewed as maladministration since the coming of peace. All in all, more than 40 such orders were promulgated in the two and a half months prior to Borie's resignation following an embarrassing personal incident.

In view of the extent to which the many general orders have been criticized, they deserve examination. Most were very brief. Some directed that fleet officers have no authority beyond that conferred by the regulations of the navy, clarified the status of executive officers (second in command), and specified that they took precedence over staff officers. The offices in navy yards were not to be considered as branches of bureaus, but as departments under the direction of the commandant of the yard. Copies of all communications concerning conflicts of authority were to be sent to the Navy Department. Orders and directions to the yards were to go to the commandants, who would see that they were executed.

There also were general orders covering such wide-ranging topics as providing for the ship's examination by a board of three line officers prior to an officer taking command of a vessel; reorganizing the naval forces in the Pacific; setting the length of officer tours at sea and ashore; directing that applications for duty be sent through proper channels; promulgating rules concerning sea pay, including compliance with the law; stipulating that travel allowances be in accordance with a congressional act; barring suspension of an officer and his return to active duty by a commanding officer without a court of inquiry; requiring that midshipmen be examined prior to promotion; forbidding the shellacking of berth decks (probably because of the dangers of slippery surfaces at sea); directing that the painting of spars be in accordance with previous custom; providing that the only officers to be saluted by tossing oars would be those commanding squadrons, naval stations, or vessels; and specifying that communications to bureaus on matters under their cognizance be sent directly to the bureau concerned.

A number of the general orders promulated actions taken by the secretary of the navy on court martial cases. Others had to do with following the law in such cases as corrections to the regulations that governed the proceedings of these courts. Several orders pertained to uniforms, including the wearing of proper insignia.

It could be debated as to whether or not the less important of these instructions might have been covered more appropriately than by general orders issued in piecemeal fashion. Issue could be taken with some of the specifics. Nevertheless, the overall effect was beneficial in the long run.

The most telling criticisms pertained to two orders concerning steam-powered warships. One, recognizing limitations of cruising ranges under steam, directed that all ships of the navy except tugs and dispatch vessels thereafter be fitted with full sail power. Specific exercises were required in using this mode of propulsion. The other order covered actions to be taken to ensure strict economy in coal consumption. As for the contention that Porter hated steam engines, this certainly was not the case when he commanded naval forces on inland and coastal waters. Moreover, as superintendent of the Naval Academy, he had established a Department of Steam Engineering.

It is pertinent to note that U.S. warships were once again being deployed to remote areas of the globe. The ability of ships powered solely by steam to carry out missions and tasks depended on the availability and convenience of recoaling and, despite continuing advances, operational radii under steam were still very limited.

Porter, who was advanced to the rank of admiral of the navy after Farragut died in 1870, became an outspoken and very influential advocate for constructing modern steam-propelled warships following further advances in efficiency and reliability. At the same time, he believed that cruisers equipped with sail as well as steam might still play important roles in commerce destruction.

During the tours of the next three secretaries of the navy there was a grave decline in fleet capabilities. Borie's successor, G. M. Robeson, served for the remainder of President Grant's two terms. A lawyer who had been attorney general of New Jersey, he was a lax administrator and was poorly qualified for the post. Congress considered but failed to pass a bill that would have resulted in a permanent board of officers directly under the secretary—in some respects similar to the earlier Board of Navy Commissioners. As it was, the Robeson era was a time of patronage, inefficiency, corruption, high costs, declining readiness, and growing obsolescence. Moreover, the number of officers on active duty exceeded by far the needs of the dwindling fleet, and promotions were pitifully slow.

The next secretary, R. W. Thompson, was extremely ignorant of maritime affairs. Contracts were canceled, and an economy-minded Congress reduced appropriations to less than 50 percent of the annual average during Grant's regime. Thompson was forced to resign as a result of his acceptance of money to serve on an "advisory council"[9] to a French firm that planned to build a canal across the Isthmus of Panama. The tour of Secretary Nathan Goff lasted only the final three months of Rutherford Hayes' administration.

Only ten new vessels were authorized during Robeson's tour of almost eight years. One was a wooden-hull screw-frigate. Seven were gunboats, four with wooden and three with iron hulls. The other two were iron-plated torpedo boats for use in experiments by the Bureau of Ordnance. Since the bureau's tests in 1867 of the Whitehead self-propelled torpedo, a hydraulic depth regulator had been added to these weapons. A decade later the Russians were to employ such torpedoes in combat, but more developments were required before these revolutionary weapons had a major impact upon naval warfare.

WORLDWIDE DEPLOYMENTS

Following the French departure from Mexico, U.S. naval forces were employed in tasks similar to those prior to the Civil War. Small squadrons were deployed to distant areas, with their foremost mission the promotion and protection of commerce. One warship was sent on a world cruise, visiting many ports in an effort to foster trade.

A coaling station was established at Midway Island in 1867. A show of force resulted in the opening of two more ports in Japan. Sailors were landed on Formosa in retaliation for actions against wrecked U.S. merchantmen crews. There were actions undertaken, highlighted by an attack on Inchon, that brought about the opening of trade with Korea. There were landings in Uruguay and Panama. Agreements were extracted in the Fijis for the protection of seamen, traders, and missionaries. Negotiations took place at Samoa. The flag was shown at the Hawaiian Islands, and actions were taken together with British and French naval forces at the time of riots in Canton, China.

GROWING OBSOLESCENCE

The failure to provide the U.S. Navy with modern warships contrasted with steps being taken by European powers, which were achieving major progress in steam propulsion, naval ordnance, armor, and hull design. At least two South American countries—Brazil and Chile—had warships superior to those of the United States.

The extremely low state of the nation's forces, other than those on foreign station, was revealed by events following a Spanish gunboat's seizure in 1873 of U.S. merchant steamer *Virginius* and the execution of her captain for attempting to deliver munitions to Cuban rebels. During the following crisis only a weak, unready, and obsolescent group of U.S. Navy ships could be assembled at Key West to conduct maneuvers in the Caribbean. Although hostilities were avoided at this time, the opposing interests of the United States and Spain in the Caribbean were to provide a continuing source of potential conflict.

In the meantime, Germany was employing its naval forces to acquire colonies. In the Pacific, it gained possession of New Guinea, the Bismark Archipelago, the northern Solomon Islands, and the Marshall Islands. The conflicting interests of Germany and the United States in Samoa, where each desired to establish at least a coaling station, would lead in 1889 to a naval confrontation that would be defused by a neutral typhoon, which grounded most of the warships.

The need to modernize and strengthen the U.S. Navy and to maintain a high state of operational readiness was becoming more urgent.

Part III

The New Navy

10

Beginnings of the New Navy

Steps to modernize the U.S. Navy were begun during the secretaryship of William H. Hunt, 1881–82. The time was ripe, since this was one of those rare occasions when the nation's treasury had a surplus. The world trade of the United States had been undergoing a remarkable expansion. Exports had tripled during the preceding decade. There was strong advocacy of increasing the size of the merchant marine.

Admiral Porter, now head of the Board of Inspection, urged that Hunt form a group of "naval assistants"[1] to provide advice on the needs of the fleet. The members of the Naval Advisory Board convened by the secretary were Rear Admiral John Rodgers (president), Chief Constructor Lenthall and two other naval constructors, Chief Engineer Isherwood and two other naval engineers, and nine line officers, including naval ordnance experts. The board was charged with making recommendations on the numbers of vessels to be built; their classes, sizes, and displacements; the material and form of construction; the nature and sizes of engines and machinery; ordnance and armaments; equipment and rigging; and internal arrangements.

The board's November 1881 report recommended the construction of 8 first-rate cruisers (4,560 and 5,873 tons), 10 second raters (3,043 tons), 20 fourth raters (793 tons), 5 rams, and 25 torpedo boats. The cruisers were to be armed with guns of increased accuracy, rapidity of fire, and range.

The report also recommended that the first and second raters be built of steel. A minority report submitted by Lenthall, Isherwood, and two of the other staff officers proposed that instead of steel ships a lesser number of large wooden-hulled iron-clads be built. Secretary Hunt strongly supported the majority report before Congress.

The subsequent act authorized six cruisers, one ram, eight torpedo boats, and a "Naval Board of Advice and Survey" to supervise and design the building of the vessels. The appropriations bill that followed barred spending Construction and Repair Bureau funds on wooden ships when the estimated cost of repairs was in excess of 30 percent of that for a new ship of the same size and material. It was stipulated that any money saved could be spent toward construction of "two steam cruising vessels of war"[2] built of domestically manufactured steel.

Another of Hunt's actions was to assign the Bureau of Navigation responsibility for intelligence. One result of this was the gathering of more complete knowledge on foreign navies and their progress.

Hunt's successor, W. E. Chandler, formed a second advisory board composed of Commodore R. F. Shufeldt, a chief engineer, a naval constructor, an assistant naval constructor, two line officers, and two civilians (one a naval architect, the other a marine engineer). The chief of the bureaus of Construction and Repair and of Steam Engineering refused to furnish blueprints. Nevertheless, the board recommended the construction of three steel protected cruisers and an iron dispatch boat. The 1883 Naval Appropriation Act provided funds for such a program, but the problems to be overcome were formidable. No U.S. mills had as yet rolled plates suitable for the hulls of the cruisers, and the navy yards lacked capabilities for building vessels of this material. In view of the problems with the two bureau chiefs, it is understandable why the secretary advertised for bids by private firms. Chandler awarded all four contracts to John Roach of Chester, Pennsylvania, the lowest bidder on each.

Despite their limitations, these vessels marked the beginning of the new navy of the United States. The final breakaway from the age of wooden ships and sail was underway. Experience with these steel warships led to major improvements in the characteristics of those that followed. Two more steel cruisers were authorized in 1885, together with two armored cruisers, a cruiser, and another dynamite-gun ship (never built) in 1886, and two cruisers the next year.

STRATEGY

It was during this period, at long last, that ship movements began to be directed by a naval officer, when Secretary Chandler assigned the responsibility to the chief of the Bureau of Navigation in 1884.

Another of the secretary's important contributions that year was the establishment of the Naval War College. To that end, he appointed Commodore Stephen Luce president of a board, the other members of which were Commander W. T. Sampson and Lieutenant C. F. Goodrich. Luce had been a leader among intellectual naval officers who had been expressing ideas on sea warfare, as in the Naval Institute, which had its beginnings in the 1870s. The establishment of the college was timely. The means of exercising naval power was entering a major transitional period. Teachings of the past deserved reevaluation in light of the changes taking place.

Despite the increasing likelihood of a naval confrontation with another nation, such as Spain or Germany, policies used as a basis for determining U.S. naval power programs were very restrictive. According to the next secretary of the navy, W. C. Whitney, strategy would be limited essentially to coastal defense and protection of commerce. This was not the first time, nor would it be the last, that holding naval expenditures to a minimum was rationalized by preconceived and limited assumptions as to the nature of future wars involving the United States. Despite their assignment, which was to produce plans for coastal defense, a board of naval officers concluded that the larger warships also should have offensive missions.

THE CONCEPTS OF MAHAN

Captain Alfred Thayer Mahan's work, *The Influence of Sea Power upon History, 1660–1783,* was to have a major influence on the naval policies and programs of the future. It had been on Luce's recommendation that Mahan was detailed to the War College where he reported in 1885. His book, published five years later, was based on the lectures he had been delivering and thus were tailored to what he thought were the current intellectual needs of line officers. Ranging across a wide spectrum, its coverage embraced naval policy, strategy, tactics, battles, campaigns, wars, peacetime naval operations, and maritime trade—often going into considerable detail. He attempted to bring out causes and effects related to "general history."[3]

At the time Mahan was delivering his lectures and writing his work there were, as is so often the case in times of dramatic advances in the means of waging war, tendencies especially among the younger naval officers to view the study of history to be of little value in solving future problems. As Mahan phrased it, there was "a vague feeling of contempt for the past, supposed to be obsolete." He thus assessed his main challenge at the college to be "how to view the lessons of the past so as to mould them into lessons for the future, under such differing conditions." He pointed out that there would be "continual change in the manner of fighting." Cautioning against being carried away by his "analogy until it has been thoroughly tested," he stressed "broad strategic considerations" that he felt would have "comparative permanence."[4]

There have been tendencies since World War II to depreciate or even ridicule the continuing applicability of the teachings of his seminal work. We would, however, do well to consider his interpretations of the special nature of sea power as well as the more fundamental of his concepts, as evaluated in light of the modern age.

Mahan concluded about the span of history he covered that navies had influenced the destiny of nations to an extent not commonly recognized. Often this influence had been the decisive factor in wartime and peacetime struggles for power and prosperity.

He stressed that a nation must maintain the oceanic flow of materials, food, and goods to its ports. Wealth was gained by sea commerce and control of the entrepots of trade. The final determining factor in many conflicts between nations had been the denial of ocean-borne supplies to an adversary over a prolonged period.

The ideal situation was to achieve such a level of supremacy at sea that a navy, "controlling the great common, closes the highways by which commerce moves to and from the enemy's shores." Mahan stressed that "This overbearing power can only be exercised by great navies." Although he wrote, "naval control . . . is only a means, not an object,"[5] there were historical examples when gaining such control had caused an enemy to recognize the inevitable consequences and come to terms. In some cases, the exercise of sea control achieved end objectives without resort to war.

Wars arising from other than maritime causes were "modified in their conduct and issue by the control of the sea." Mahan drew attention to the subtleties of naval warfare by concluding, "In a war undertaken for any object, even if that object be the possession of a particular territory or position, an attack directly upon the place coveted may not be . . . the best means of obtaining it." He highlighted the dependence of armies on sea lines of communications. As for the projection of military power by sea onto the land, he observed, "Of any maritime expedition two points only are fixed, the point of departure and that of arrival. The latter may be unknown to the enemy."[6]

The struggles examined by Mahan had sometimes been decided by naval battles or campaigns. In other conflicts, the final outcome of a prolonged war had been determined by pervasive effects described by him as "the noiseless, steady, exhausting pressure with which sea power acts, cutting off the resources of the enemy while maintaining its own, supporting war in scenes where it does not appear itself, or appears only in the background, and striking open blows at rare intervals." In his opinion, few had recognized these effects of naval supremacy, since "from its very greatness its action, by escaping opposition, escapes attention."[7]

If the objective of naval warfare "is to break up the enemy's power on the sea, cutting off his communications with the rest of his possessions, drying up the sources of his wealth in his commerce, and making possible a closure of his ports, then the object of attack must be his organized military forces afloat; in short, his navy."[8] It is pertinent to note, particularly with regard to underseas as well as surface forces, the occasions noted by Mahan in which decisive results were achieved when an enemy fleet was prevented access to the high seas.

Furthermore, one of the means of stemming the flow of cargoes had been the control of narrow passages along trade routes. Imposition of blockades had been particularly efficient; moreover, in a blockade recognized as effective, neutral ships attempting ingress or egress were also subject to capture and confiscation.

Mahan's historical narratives provide examples in which neglect of navies had led to disastrous consequences for the countries concerned. The provision and maintenance of warships adequate in numbers, in performance, and in armament were essential. But this was only part of the story. He showed that time and again naval successes had depended on far more than the relative capabilities of warships and their numbers. Success had often hinged on the experience and professional qualifications of officers in command of fleets, squadrons, and ships; on their understanding of the unique and varying conditions that affect the operation of vessels and the conduct of sea warfare; on physical and moral courage; on decisiveness and reactions under stress; on leadership; and on other qualities that, although differing from one individual to another, were so combined as to form a successful naval commander. Mahan emphasized the importance of professional pride, a sense of military honor and ésprit de corps of the officers, and the training and discipline of the crews.

But, more than that, success in the long run had depended upon the proper employment of operating forces. Eventual failure was a usual consequence when a navy was controlled by those who did not truly understand the special nature of naval warfare, its potentials and limitations, and the operating environment. In some cases, failure had been caused by restricting naval operations to what Mahan called "ulterior objects."[9]

Such points were reaffirmed in *The Influence of Sea Power upon the French Revolution and Empire 1793-1812.* This second major work was published in 1892, only two years after the first.

Mahan's work highlighted engagements between opposing fleets or major squadrons. This is understandable both because of the decisive effects of many of these battles on the war at sea and because the teaching at the War College embraced tactics as well as strategy. Moreover, the recent focus of U.S. naval policies and programs on cruising warfare and coastal defense meant that the navy lacked the capabilities for major actions.

Comparable attention was not given to cruiser warfare in his first sea-power book. While recognizing that it could make valuable contributions, particularly when other means might not be available to an inferior navy, he cautioned about reliance on "purely cruising warfare," since "evidence seems to show that even for its own special ends such a mode of war is inconclusive, worrying, but not deadly."[10]

It is pertinent to note that Mahan put these matters in better perspective with regard to the Revolutionary War in a later book, *The Major Operations of the Navies in the War of American Independence,* published in 1913. Furthermore, he had concluded in the third of his sea-power works, *Sea Power in Its Relations to the War of 1812,* published in 1905, that American privateers had produced "an effect upon British commerce, which though inconclusive singly, doubtless co-operated powerfully with other motives to dispose the enemy to liberal terms of peace."[11]

In any case, the applicability of some of the sea-power concepts to wars involving new navies was put to the test soon after the publication of Mahan's first works.

11

Warfare against a
European Power

Among the continuing advances in naval capabilities, none would have a greater impact than the progress in automotive torpedoes. The major breakthrough had been the addition of gyroscopic steering controls, an American invention, in 1885. Together with increases in range and speed provided by improved propulsion systems, this meant that the weapon could be employed effectively not only against ships at anchor but also in actions at sea. Congress authorized the first modern torpedo boat of the U.S. Navy in 1886. Built of domestic steel, it went into service four years later.

The awesome potential of the improved torpedo was demonstrated in the Chilean Civil War of 1891 when a torpedo gunboat squadron achieved a hit that sank an armored iron-clad. Two years later, during the Brazilian Revolution, an attack by a torpedo boat sent a turret ship to the bottom. Then, in 1895, in the Sino-Japanese War, a battleship and cruiser of the Chinese Navy were sunk by night torpedo attacks.

There have been times in history when a spectacular advance in weaponry has caused some to conclude that former means of waging war are being outmoded. This was one of those occasions, and assertions were made that large expensive warships would no longer be needed. France did decide temporarily to suspend construction of battleships. The decision, however, was reversed after severe limitations of torpedo boats, such as their sea keeping capabilities, were revealed in an exercise against iron-clads at anchor.

The full story, as usual, would be that of a dynamic series of measures and countermeasures. The protection of ships at anchor could be aided by using nets. Those at sea could maneuver to reduce the probability of hits. Britain was the first to build high-speed, well-armed torpedo boat destroyers designed to intercept attacking craft as well as for offensive missions employing their own torpedoes. In time large warships would be provided with greatly improved watertight compartmentalization and special voids and liquid-filled spaces. Secondary batteries of improved accuracy and higher rates of fire would be added for defense against attacking craft. Yet far-reaching as the effects of self-propelled torpedoes would become, armored warships were still to play important roles, such as in actions against enemy naval forces and in-shore bombardment.

A new type of warship far more radical than either the torpedo boat or torpedo boat destroyer was soon to be added—the sea-going submarine. The "submarine torpedo boat"[1] authorized by the U.S. Congress in 1893 was never completed. The act three years later that authorized two others specified that they be of the Holland type. The first to be commissioned would be the privately built *Holland*, purchased in 1900.

There were other significant advances in naval capabilities. Triple-expansion engines were providing increasingly higher efficiencies and thus greatly extended cruising ranges. Improvements in naval guns, gun mounts, and projectiles were resulting in increased ranges and more effective damage. Rangefinding devices were being invented. Progress was being made in the manufacture of better armor.

In 1886 Congress had authorized "two sea-going double-bottomed armored vessels." These were first classified as armored cruisers and then as second-class battleships. Four years later "three sea-going coast-line battle ships designed to carry the heaviest armor and the most powerful ordnance" were authorized. An "endurance of about five thousand knots on the total coal capacity at the most economical rate of speed"[2] was specified. Others would follow. One of the first actions as secretary of the navy of Benjamin F. Tracy, who served from 1889 to 1893, was the appointment of a policy board of officers to recommend plans for the buildup of the new navy.

THE SPANISH-AMERICAN WAR

The probability of warfare with a European nation was increasing. As the Cuban rebellion against Spanish rule began, the Naval War College submitted recommendations in 1895 to the chief of the Bureau of Navigation concerning strategy in case of war with Spain. Hopefully to resolve issues without the need to invade Cuba, the imposition of a blockade and other actions were proposed to sever the delivery of supplies to Spanish forces on the island. These operations would be accompanied by one against Manila. The Office of Naval Intelligence drew up a plan implementing these concepts.

Later Secretary H. A. Herbert appointed a planning body of senior officers chaired by Rear Admiral F. A. Ramsey, the bureau chief. It also recommended severing lines of communication to Cuba. But the board's members advocated that, instead of the Asiatic Squadron being employed against Manila, it join forces with the European Squadron and battleships from the North Atlantic Squadron to seize the Canary Islands and conduct operations off Spain. When the board reconvened in the summer of 1897 with changed membership by the new secretary, J. D. Long, it brought forth a plan that once again included actions in the Philippine area rather than in the eastern Atlantic.

After the explosion that sent USS *Maine* to the bottom on February 15, 1898, ailing Rear Admiral M. Sicard was relieved as commander of the North Atlantic Squadron by W. T. Sampson and was ordered to head a newly-formed

Naval War Board. The other members were the chief of the Bureau of Navigation, the head of the Office of Naval Intelligence, and a captain from the secretary's office. Assistant Secretary Theodore Roosevelt attended meetings until Sicard reported. And thus it was that for the first time the U.S. Navy had a strategic plan before the beginning of a war.

President McKinley issued his war message on April 21, 1898, declared the blockade the next day, and approved the naval war plan on April 24. Mahan was recalled from Europe to serve on the board. After his arrival in Washington on May 9, he sent a letter to Secretary Long recommending abolishing the board, appointing an officer to perform its functions, and assigning assistants to that individual. Nevertheless, Long retained the board and invariably followed its advice while continuing to rely on the chief of the Bureau of Navigation's advice on directions for employing the operating forces.

During the Spanish-American War, success in naval battles against enemy squadrons was the decisive factor in achieving victory in a remarkably short time and with a minimum of casualties.

Prior to the outbreak of war, the Far East Squadron had proceeded to Hong Kong, which is only about 700 miles from Manila. There Commodore George Dewey, who had been its commander since January, brought his warships to a high state of preparedness for action, purchased two steamers to provide mobile logistics support for coal and provisions, and took steps to gain up-to-date information on the Spanish Squadron and fortifications in the Philippines.

It was on April 25 (west of the date line)—the day the president approved the war plan—that the commodore received cabled directions to proceed to the Philippines and to "commence operations at once, particularly against the Spanish fleet. You must capture vessels or destroy. Use utmost endeavors."[3] Dewey first checked to see if the enemy's warships were in Subic Bay and then entered Manila Bay under cover of darkness to fight the famous battle of May 1, which eliminated the Spanish Squadron and captured the naval base at Cavite.

The victory was achieved in less than a week after the declaration of war. Following a strategy along the lines of the principles espoused by Mahan, the objective had been the defeat of the enemy navy. So long as the U.S. Navy encountered no other naval opposition, other actions could be taken that would take more time, including those employing land forces, to achieve national objectives.

On the other side of the globe, an unwarranted scare, stimulated by rumors and the press, of attacks on the U.S. east coast led to some compromising of the naval war plan, at least concerning the initial employment of forces. As was to be true in World War I, this resulted in a diversion of the U.S. Navy from its primary mission. In 1898 concern grew when news was received of Admiral Pascual Cervera y Topete's departure from Spain with a squadron of warships. Due to political pressures in the United States, a Northern Patrol Squadron was formed to cover coastal waters down to the Delaware Capes. Fortunately, little harm was done since the vessels assigned were obsolete and lesser men-of-war, and some were later sent south to participate in the blockade of Cuba.

Far more dangerous was the division of the North Atlantic Squadron into two forces, one of which, the Flying Squadron under Commodore Schley, was based at Hampton Roads and assigned the mission of protecting the Atlantic seaboard. Worried over keeping these ships "in the Chesapeake, instead of Cuban waters,"[4] Mahan advised the Naval War Board:

This was perhaps inevitable, owing to popular nervousness; and the result, though mortifying, is not vital. But if the enemy succeed, not only in entering Porto Rico, but quitting it, coaled and ready, with the Cape Verde and Cadiz division united, our perplexity will become extreme, and may lead to a vital misstep. The enemy would be stronger than either of our divisions, . . . if either division of ours be met and singly and badly beaten, they will have control of the sea till we get new ships out.[5]

Another possible diversion from the primary mission of the naval war plan was a decision to assign priority to an operation with the army against Havana. Rear Admiral Sampson himself proposed early in April a naval bombardment followed by the landing of army troops. Navy Secretary Long, undoubtedly on the advice of the Naval War Board, did not wish to endanger warships that might be required for a naval battle. Major General N. A. Miles, commanding general of the army, also opposed such an operation. One of his reasons was the low state of preparedness of his forces. Nevertheless, President McKinley, after conferring with the secretaries of war and navy, decided on May 2 that 40,000 to 50,000 troops should be landed near Havana for an assault on the capital. What led to reconsideration of the operation was news that the Spanish Squadron had reached the Caribbean.

Meanwhile, the portion of the North Atlantic Squadron directly under Sampson's command was engaged in blockading actions and in carrying out the primary mission of locating Cervera's squadron and then engaging it in western waters. Fully appreciating his forces' dependence upon adequate and timely logistics support at and from the Key West base, Sampson wisely assigned responsibility for providing such support to Commodore G. C. Remey.

The Spanish Squadron would be short of fuel by the time it reached the Caribbean. When it was learned that Cervera's squadron had left Cape Verdes, it was assumed that coal would be taken on at San Juan, Puerto Rico—another Caribbean possession of Spain. Sampson headed for Puerto Rico with two battleships, an armored cruiser, a torpedo boat, and two monitors. Slowed by the need to tow the monitors, when Sampson arrived and found no sign of enemy ships, he conducted a shore bombardment and then turned back west. He left the monitors to make their slow way by themselves.

Concerned that the Spanish Squadron might attempt to deliver ammunition to Havana, Sampson left his other warships off that harbor to strengthen the blockading forces while he proceeded to Key West in the flagship to obtain the latest information on enemy movements.

Cervera, who had arrived off Martinique on the same day that Sampson reached San Juan, actually was proceeding to the southern Cuban port of Santiago. In the meantime, Schley was ordered to Key West, while fast scouts were sent to try to locate the enemy force. Shortly thereafter, Sampson arrived at Key West. He ordered Schley, who had just gotten there, to proceed with his division augmented by a first-class battleship to blockade Cienfuegos in order to prevent supplies from being delivered there for rail shipment to Havana. Follow-up orders, sent by dispatch boat, directed that if Spanish ships were not located there, the commodore was to look for them at Santiago. Schley arrived off that port on May 28 and discovered the enemy.

Sampson was on the scene four days later. Since the harbor's narrow, twisting channel was mined and flanked by shore batteries, he employed the combined force to bottle up the Spanish warships in the harbor while conducting frequent bombardments of the forts. An attempt to block the channel by sinking a collier was frustrated by hits from guns ashore, which caused the vessel to go down in a location where she could easily be passed.

To secure an advanced naval base close to the scene of action, warships landed some 600 marines at Guantanamo Bay under cover of naval gunfire. The base was securely established after a week of fighting ashore.

ARMY-NAVY OPERATIONS IN CUBA

As for the planning and conduct of coordinated and joint operations of the army and navy, lessons that should have been learned from the Civil War were ignored. Major General W. R. Shafter, under whom 16,000 troops were hastily assembled at Tampa, received War Department orders on May 31 to "proceed under convoy of the Navy to the vicinity of Santiago de Cuba, [and] land your force at such place east or west of that point as your judgement may dictate."[6]

Inadequate provision for joint planning at both the Washington and command levels was revealed by these orders and by the instructions that "under the protection of the Navy," Shafter was to move his troops "onto the high ground and bluffs overlooking the harbor or into the interior, as shall best enable you to capture or destroy the garrison there; and cover the Navy as it sends its men in small boats to remove torpedoes, or with the aid of the Navy capture or destroy the Spanish fleet."[7]

Enroute to the objective area, the civilian ships being employed as transports were inept at station keeping and slow. Not only were they not properly loaded for an amphibious assault, but they were insufficiently equipped for feeding the troops that were embarked.

After a conference between General Shafter, Admiral Sampson, and some Cuban officers on June 20, the army conducted its landing at Daiquiri. Warships were prepared to give gunfire support. Fortunately, no opposition was encountered. There had been no sound planning of the ship-to-shore movement of men and supplies. Boats from the transports encountered trouble in landing through the surf. The navy helped with boats from its warships. Beach clearance was poorly handled, and it took four days before the landing was completed.

Sampson had come away from the conference believing that the general had agreed to assault the shore batteries guarding the entrance into the harbor. Instead, as the admiral belatedly learned, the army's plan was to advance inland and then to the west of the city, which was five miles from the head of the body of water that formed the harbor. By the time the troops had fought their way to the outskirts of the city they had suffered such heavy casualties that Shafter was urging the navy to "make effort immediately to force the entrance to avoid future losses among my men."[8]

Sampson was proceeding in his flagship to a position east of the harbor to confer with Shafter when Cervera sortied on July 3 in an attempt to escape. In the ensuing naval battle all of the Spanish ships were sunk, beached, or forced to surrender. Not only was the U.S. Navy now in full control of the waters around Cuba, but a Spanish squadron that had reached the Red Sea enroute to the Far East was recalled because of the possibility that the U.S. fleet might be deployed to European waters.

Later that month Spain sought terms of peace. By the proper employment of its navy the United States had achieved victory in a remarkably short time and had gained respect as a world power. As had been true at the end of the War of 1812, the nation emerged from the Spanish-American War with a fuller appreciation of the importance of naval power to its destiny.

12

Prelude to
Another War

At the turn of the century navies were on the verge of advances that would not only enhance existing capabilities but would also introduce new modes of naval warfare. These capabilities would have major impacts upon the conduct of warfare at sea, increase the need for strategic planning in times of peace and war, make the direction of naval forces by experienced officers ever more urgent, and result in added complexities in the relationships of navies and armies.

As had been the case at the end of the War of 1812, actions by Congress reflected an increased awareness of the importance of naval power to the nation, and lessons derived from the conflict resulted in organizational changes within the Navy Department. With the coming of peace, the Navy War Board was dissolved. Recognizing the value of its contributions, Secretary of the Navy Long sought the advice of the chief of the Bureau of Navigation, Captain (later Rear Admiral) Henry C. Taylor, concerning the continuing need for planning to ensure the navy's readiness to meet the challenges of the future. Early in 1900, after receiving Taylor's recommendation that a permanent board be formed directly under the secretary, Long issued a general order creating the General Board. Its initial responsibilities were to devise plans for the employment of naval forces, organize coastal defense, provide for the use of naval reserves and the merchant marine, advise the secretary on the disposition of the fleet under various war conditions, deduce the war plans of foreign navies, prepare campaign plans for the U.S. Navy, and fix strategy for naval bases. The board also was charged with achieving, by consultation with army leaders, full and cordial cooperation of the two services in case of war. The board was later assigned responsibilities for recommending methods to execute the plans, determine the military characteristics of ships, and devise measures and plans to prepare the fleet for war. Highly respected Admiral of the Navy George Dewey became the board's head. With specific duties changing from time to time, the General Board was to continue for more than a half century.

As a result of experience gained in the Spanish-American War, the Joint Board of the Army and Navy was created in 1903 by Secretary of the Army

Elihu Root (whose predecessor had resigned because of criticisms of War Department actions during the conflict) and Secretary of the Navy W. H. Moody. Except for a time when its meetings were suspended by President Wilson, this body of high-ranking officers performed valuable service until World War II, when the Joint Chiefs of Staff was formed.

Upon becoming president, Theodore Roosevelt advocated that the U.S. Navy, which was then fifth among the world powers, should become superior to all navies except that of Britain. In response to a request from the secretary, the General Board submitted a proposal for a long-range construction program. Its recommendations for this and subsequent programs were highly respected by Congress.

Convinced that actions were needed beyond establishing an advisory body, a number of naval officers advocated assigning to line officers, working under the secretary, authority over the operating forces and the naval establishment upon which their effectiveness depended. When Root gained congressional approval for an Army General Staff, some of the naval officers proposed a staff of this nature for the navy. Not only was this recommended by Moody, but Roosevelt advocated it in his annual message to Congress.

However beneficial the general staff may have been for the War Department, the differences between armies with their units and naval forces with their warships, and the supporting requirements of each, made the general staff system illsuited for the navy. The bureau system, with its direct assignments of responsibility together with commensurate authority, was highly decentralized and thus prompt-acting and efficient. The bureaus had proven effective in exploiting the potential of advancing technology and were flexible in adapting to changing needs.

While the bureau system ensures neither that the efforts are focused upon achieving the end objective—namely the readiness and effectiveness of the operating forces—nor that close cooperation takes place between the bureaus, the bureau system avoided unnecessary overhead. The superimposition of a staff creates its own problems. In general, staffs tend to grow, with staff size becoming more important than accomplishments. Large staffs are typically accompanied by the diffusion of accountability, delays, unnecessary compromises, and involvement of individuals in the decision process who do not understand the basic operational considerations. Not only is coordination least effective when imposed from above, but it restricts the coordination that is needed at all levels.

In any case, the bill actually proposed by Moody would have made the General Board a statutory body of seven officers who would be assigned duties by the secretary of the navy. Some of the bureau chiefs were opposed. Congress took no action.

A subsequent secretary, C. J. Bonaparte, recommended in 1906 the assignment of two flag officers to the Navy Department. One would be responsible for operating forces, with authority beyond that granted the chief of the Bureau of Navigation; the other would direct the four material bureaus—Construction and Repair, Steam Engineering, Ordnance, Equipment, and Yards and Docks. The assistant secretary of the navy would be responsible for the Hydrographic Office and the Naval Observatory. The Office of Naval Intelligence and the judge advocate general would report directly to the secretary.

It was becoming ever more important that a senior line officer exercise the authority of a chief of naval operations (CNO). One of the reasons was the advances in communications. In the not very distant past the only way of exchanging information with ships at sea and those deployed to distant areas was by sea-going vessels. This meant long delays such as had plagued the British in the American Revolution.

The introduction of telegraph lines and transoceanic cables in the nineteenth century had greatly reduced the time lags involved. It had been by cable to Hong Kong that Dewey had received his orders promptly from Washington. There were, however, severe limitations. Important cables were under foreign control, dispatch vessels were still needed to provide links between cable stations and remotely-located ships, and communications between warships at sea were restricted to visual contact.

American warships had conducted tests of the Marconi system of radio telegraph in 1899, and these had been followed by tests comparing other European and American equipment. The U.S. Navy constructed naval radio stations and began to install radios in warships in 1903.

Over the years that followed advances overcame the low performance of early shipboard transmitting and receiving systems. Information, guidance, and directions could then be sent directly to units and forces at sea. Operations out of sight of one another could be coordinated. Warships could be regrouped as the situation changed.

In time improvements would result in major changes in the efficiency of employing units of the fleet, in strategy, and in tactics. Enemy transmissions could be intercepted. An additional parameter would be introduced by radio direction finders, ashore and afloat, for the location of enemy forces and merchant vessels. Cruising warfare by surface ships of an inferior navy became ever more difficult.

NAVAL POWER GAINS NEW DIMENSIONS

An additional mode of maritime warfare would soon become possible by developments of sea-going submarines of ever increasing capabilities. Seven gasoline-electric ones, basically of the Holland design but larger, were commissioned in the U.S. Navy in 1903. Because of their vulnerability on the surface, submarines were ill-suited for control of sea missions, but their ability to lie hidden and approach a target undetected, combined with the hull-damaging potential of self-propelled torpedoes, added an awesome new capability for sinking ships.

However, before they could have a major effect on naval warfare, early deficiencies had to be overcome. The first submarines were small, of limited endurance, and slow. When totally submerged they were blind. A grave deficiency was the uncertainty of underwater navigation, for within a steel hull magnetic compasses were useless.

Subsequent construction programs produced bigger submarines with improved performance. Periscopes were added. Underwater endurance was increased by advances in air purification and oxygen replacement. Steady progress was made in propulsion. The gyroscopic compass was perfected by Elmer A. Sperry and tested in an American battleship in 1911. The first of the diesel boats of the U.S. Navy were laid down that same year. The shift from gasoline engines for surface operations and the recharging of batteries resulted in greater cruising ranges and improved safety.

Naval power gained yet another dimension as a result of advances in aircraft. Gas balloons had been employed for military purposes in the nineteenth century, for example tethered to Union balloon boats for observation of installations and movements ashore during the Civil War. A major advance toward the end of the century was the development of airships powered by internal combustion engines. Naval use of lighter-than-air ships in such roles as reconnaissance, scouting, and antisubmarine warfare would continue until after World War II. The overall impact on sea power, however, could not be classified as revolutionary.

In 1903 the Wright brothers achieved the first successful flights, short as they were, of a manned heavier-than-air craft. Whether or not truly basic principles of warfare would be altered by this, continuing advances in aircraft would in time introduce changes in the exercise of naval power. The overlapping capabilities of land- and sea-based planes would not only add further complications, but they would be a source of conflicting interests and controversies.

American naval aviation had its modest beginnings shortly after the Wrights' success. In the years to come it would be developed and operated as an integral part of the fleet and would prove to be vitally important later in the century.

The ability to take off and land on an improvised flight deck was demonstrated by the U.S. Navy in 1910. During the next year Glenn H. Curtiss developed the first practical seaplane. In 1915 the armored cruiser USS *North Carolina* was the first ship to launch aircraft at sea by catapult.

Advances were also being made in naval gunnery, the most revolutionary of which were in fire control. One of the inventions of Bradley A. Fiske, then a lieutenant, had been a form of rangefinder tested on a U.S. warship eight years before the war with Spain. This consisted of two remotely-located sighting stations and a Wheatstone bridge that solved the triangulation problem electrically and indicated the distance to the target. The low percentage of confirmed hits in the 1898 battle off Santiago had been a source of concern. One of Sampson's complaints was the lack of rangefinders. Fiske's device had been superseded by optical types, and by this time longer ones of greater accuracy were being designed.

Major breakthroughs came with the development of a director system by which an entire battery of a warship could be controlled as one unit with corrections for parallax, and with the development of a U.S. Navy analog computer, called a rangekeeper, that would determine gun elevations and corrections in train from the director's line of sight on the basis of ranges, of courses and speed of firing ship and target, and of ballistic data. The power drives of turrets and mounts were being improved. Effective naval gunfire was possible at ever greater ranges.

Step-by-step improvements also were being achieved in guns. Weapons of greater lengths and calibers were being manufactured. A type of smokeless powder had been adopted. Armor-piercing projectiles with steadily improving penetration capabilities were being developed.

A never-ending series of advances was occurring in other warship characteristics as well, such as in the efficiency of propulsion plants, hull design, watertight compartmentalization, armor, electrical systems, and interior communications. At long last, oil burning boilers were being designed. The use of oil fuel increased mobility due to faster refuelings and from the development in later years of underway replenishment.

NAVAL POWER ENTERS A NEW ERA

The Russo-Japanese war soon after the turn of the century, while providing examples of the increasing impact of underwater weapons, confirmed once again the basic principles of Mahan. The start of that war is of special interest in view of what was to happen on December 7, 1941. Hostilities commenced in 1904 with a surprise night torpedo attack that damaged two Russian battleships and a cruiser anchored in the outer roadstead off Port Arthur. In various actions that followed, Russia's East Asian naval forces were decimated during the remainder of 1904. Warships of both sides were sunk by mines. One sunk battleship resulted in the loss of the newly assigned, competent, inspiring, and aggressive commander of Russia's Far East Squadron, Vice Admiral Stephan O. Makarov. What determined the war's final outcome, of course, was the decisive victory of Vice Admiral Heihachiro Togo's fleet in the 1905 Battle of Tsushima.

That was the year Mahan's third work based on his War College lectures, *Sea Power in Its Relations to the War of 1812,* was published. By then his principles were being followed to a large extent in the United States. Perhaps this is one reason why he gave increased credit to the contributions of cruising warfare. We might do well today to heed Mahan's advice concerning the objective of using military force:

War now is never waged for the sake of mere fighting, simply to see who is the better at killing people. The warfare of civilized nations is for the purpose of accomplishing an object, obtaining a concession of alleged right from an enemy who has proved implacable to an argument. He is to be made to yield to force what he has refused to reason; and to do that, hold is laid upon what is his, either by taking actual possession, or by preventing his utilizing what he may still retain.[1]

THE LONDON NAVAL CONFERENCE

The publication of his work was timely, since an attempt was being made to codify laws of war, including those related to sea power. Through usage and agreements over the centuries, gradual progress had been made toward the avoidance of ruthless carnage and the protection of neutral property.

Since its beginnings, the United States had insisted on the rights of neutral ships and private cargoes, the limitation of contraband lists, and a reduction of the prerogatives of belligerents. The Declaration of Paris of 1856 had defined the conditions of a legal blockade. It also protected from capture noncontraband goods owned by a neutral or in a neutral ship. Believing the statement had not gone far enough and not wishing to give up the option of privateering, which the declaration abolished, the United States had not ratified it.

Eight of the conventions adopted by the Second International Peace Conference at the Hague in 1907 pertained to naval warfare. These dealt with rules concerning enemy merchant ships at the start of hostilities, conversion of merchantmen into warships, mines, naval bombardment, adaption of the Geneva Convention to naval war (hospital ships, etc.), restrictions on the rights of capture in naval war, creation of an international prize court, and the rights and duties of neutrals.

Continuing differences among major nations on these issues led to convening the London Naval Conference in 1909, which was attended by representatives of Great Britain, Germany, the United States, Austria-Hungary, Spain, France, Italy, Japan, the Netherlands, and Russia. The result was a code covering blockade, contraband, nonneutral service, destruction of neutral prizes, transfer of ships to a neutral flag, enemy character of ships and goods, convoy, and resistance to search. Although the various reservations of the many individual nations were such that the London convention was not ratified, the overall code was generally accepted. The extent to which it would govern the application of naval power under the stress of a major war remained to be seen.

SHIP CHARACTERISTICS

Until the steam age battlelines were composed of ships of the line. After the advent of new navies, the capital ships became known as battleships. Significant progress continued to be made in major caliber guns, ammunition, projectiles, and armor. The forerunner of the modern battleships was the British all-big-gun warship *Dreadnought,* commissioned in 1906. The two U.S. first-class battleships laid down that year followed the principle of having only two gun batteries. They had 12-inch guns for the main battery that were mounted in centerline turrets, and a secondary battery of rapid firing 3-inch guns for close defense, such as against torpedo boat attacks.

Advances were made in more than technology during this period. Merging the Engineering Corps into the line was one progressive step taken soon after the Spanish-American War from which the U.S. Navy would greatly benefit in years to come. Whereas since the Civil War separate courses of instruction had been conducted at the Naval Academy, all future graduates would now prepare to become qualified to carry out the duties of both deck and engineering officers.

A recurring issue was whether or not the officers who operated and commanded the ships would be permitted to pass judgment on bureau-drafted plans upon which construction was based. The issue was brought to a head by a magazine article in 1908 that criticized the organization of the Navy Department, directing attention to alleged errors in design that degraded combat capabilities such as improper locations of armor belts, insufficient freeboard, excessive sizes of gunports and their exposure to seas as a result of being too close to the water line. There was also a report from one prospective commanding officer of a battleship nearing completion that identified five apparent design faults. The plans of four such warships were examined by a conference of the General Board, the staff of the Naval War College, and other officers. Discovering mistakes, the conference concluded that all future plans should be reviewed by a board of seagoing line officers and an organization, known as the Board on Construction, was established by Secretary V. A. Metcalf.

In addition, President Roosevelt convened the Commission on Naval Reorganization composed of former Secretaries W. H. Moody and Paul Morton, a former member of the House Naval Affairs Committee, and five admirals, among them Mahan. Their recommendation was that the department be reorganized into five divisions. One would be the Division of Operations, the chief of which, a flag officer, would be the secretary's principal adviser. He would serve also as ex-officio head of both the General Board and the Board on Construction. The naval officer chiefs of the Personnel and Inspection Divisions would join the operations chief in forming the Military Council. The Material Division also would be headed by a naval officer. Under the assistant secretary of the navy, the fifth division would be composed of the Bureaus of Supplies, Yards and Docks, and Medicine and Surgery. The five division chiefs would form the General Council. By now, however, the term of the Roosevelt administration was almost over. Congress took no action.

THE NATION BECOMES A MAJOR NAVAL POWER

U.S. naval power was benefiting from the acquisition of sites suitable for naval bases and coaling stations. The nation now possessed the Hawaiian Islands,

Wake Island, and Tutuila, Samoa. Spain had ceded Puerto Rico, Guam, and the Philippines. Guantanamo and Bahia Rondo had been leased from Cuba. Panama had become a republic. The canal, to be controlled by the United States, was under construction. Its opening in 1914 would mean that ships no longer had to make the long trip around the South American continent to move between the North Atlantic or Caribbean and the Pacific.

Since the end of the Spanish-American War, the U.S. Navy had been conducting operations in the Philippines, many jointly with the army, to help put down the insurrection in those islands. In 1903 the demands of the Boxer Rebellion in China led to the deployment of a second U.S. squadron to the Asiatic Station.

In the western hemisphere Britain, Italy, and Germany had instituted a blockade of Venezuela in 1902 following its default on its foreign debts, and fears of an invasion were heightened when German warships bombarded a fort. As the United States sought a diplomatic solution to the crisis, the U.S. Navy formed a fleet under Admiral Dewey composed of the North Altantic, South Atlantic, and Mediterranean Squadrons. Admiral Taylor was assigned as Dewey's chief of staff.

Britain indicated that it would comply with the Monroe Doctrine. Germany finally agreed to submit the Venezuelan issue to the International Court at the Hague but insisted on its right to intervene in Latin America when European interests were involved. The deterrence influence of U.S. naval power thus would still be needed. Subsequent operations of the navy in this hemisphere included the protection of the nation's interests in Nicaragua and Honduras.

The Great White Fleet began its cruise around the world, first announced as a voyage to San Francisco, in 1907. After steaming some 46,000 nautical miles, it ended with a review in Hampton Roads 14 months later. In addition to the respect and good will gained from visits to the ports of many countries, valuable experience was acquired in sustaining prolonged operations by a modern fleet. One lesson learned was not to rely on chartering civilian colliers for refueling remote from coaling stations. The fleet did include two stores ships, a torpedo flotilla support ship, a tender, and a repair ship. The ability of warship crews assisted by this small support force to accomplish maintenance and essential repairs was a remarkable achievement.

The fleet returned less than two months after Roosevelt's tour as president ended. Under his successor, President William Howard Taft, long-overdue improvements were made in the direction and coordination of the Navy Department. Instead of first seeking congressional approval, Secretary George Von Lengerke Meyer obtained legal advice and then, on December 1, 1909, shortly before Congress convened, detailed four line officers as "aides."[2] One was aide for operations, and the responsibilities of the others were for personnel, material, and inspections. He terminated the Board on Construction, transferring its functions to the General Board. His recommendation that the Bureau of Equipment be dissolved and its functions transferred to other bureaus received congressional approval. Other reforms followed.

On the other hand, the four years of the Taft administration witnessed a severe decline in the rate of warship construction as a result of congressional opposition, particularly after the Republican party lost control of the House of Representatives. Not only were fewer capital ships authorized, but also the building of other types, such as destroyers, was neglected.

The extent of pork barrel politics was revealed by the naval appropriations bill passed after the election of Woodrow Wilson. Despite a reduction in funds for warship construction, the total amount appropriated for the Department of the Navy was higher than ever before.

Archduke Franz Ferdinand was assassinated on June 28, 1914. Austria-Hungary declared war on Serbia a month later. The armed conflict was expected to be of short duration, but this was not to be the case. Instead, World War I was a prolonged war in which the struggle at sea was pivotal.

Alfred Thayer Mahan authored the important book on naval strategy, *The Influence of Sea Power upon History,* and was second president of the Naval War College.

S. G. Gorshkov, who was admiral of the fleet in the Soviet Union and commander in chief of the Soviet Navy, presided over the Soviet Navy during its rise to become a major naval force.

The USS *Surprise* commanded by Gustavus Conyngham captures the "Harwich Packet" in 1778 within sight of the English coast. Artist: Edward Tufnell.

Gustavus Conyngham's daring raids into British home waters influenced France to recognize the United States' independence. Original miniature attributed to Lewis M. Sicard. Redrawn by V. Zveg.

Commodore John Rodgers was president of the Navy Board of Commissioners from 1815 to 1824 and from 1827 to 1837. He also turned down offers from two presidents to be secretary of the navy. Artist: Orlando Lagman.

Rear Admiral David Dixon Porter, photographed in 1863. During the Civil War he was commander of the gunboat fleet in western waters and, during Grant's administration, special adviser to the secretary of the navy.

Josephus Daniels, secretary of the
navy during World War I, and Admiral William S. Benson, the first
chief of naval operations, photographed together in Paris.

Fleet Admiral Ernest J. King
was commander of the U.S.
Fleet from 1941 to 1945 and
chief of naval operations from
1942 to 1945.

Admiral Arleigh A. Burke, with Rear Admiral Smedly (at right rear) and other staff. As chief of naval operations, Admoral Burke was instrumental in setting up the navy's ballistic missile submarine program.

Monitor fights against *Merrimac* in the first battle of iron-clad vessels on March 9, 1862. Line engraving by J. Rogers, 1862.

The Battle of Santiago during the Spanish-American War, painted by Dr. Alfonso Saenz, a Spanish surgeon.

U.S. Corvette *John Adams,* the first U.S. stores ship, was used in the Barbary Wars. Copied from "Piracy and West Indies."

The USS *Guadalupe* refuels the destroyer USS *Maury* and the carrier USS *Lexington* during the Gilbert Campaign, November 25, 1943.

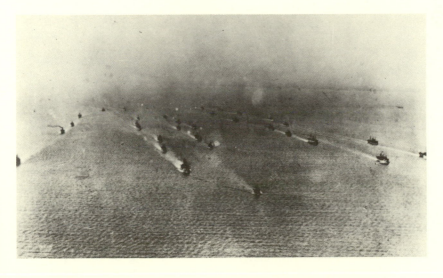

A convoy of U.S. merchant vessels nears the English coast during World War I.

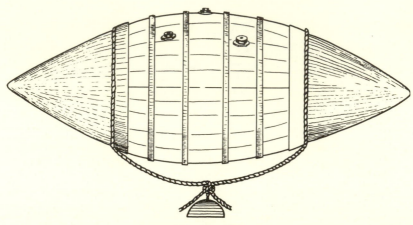

CONFEDERATE KEG TORPEDO - Civil War

A Confederate keg mine developed by their Torpedo Bureau and Service. Redrawn by the Naval Historical Center from J. Thomas Scharf's "History of C. S. Navy."

The Republic of Korea minesweeper (YMS-516) is blown up by a mine during the Wonsan Operation, October 18, 1950.

The USS *Gloucester* closes in on a Spanish destroyer during the Battle of Santiago, July 3, 1898. Painting by Howard F. Sprague. Copied from *Century Illustrated Monthly Magazine,* May 1899.

Fletcher-class destroyers bombard the coast in World War II possibly during the Saipan Campaign, June 1944.

A lithograph of the Mexican War shows barges being towed by US steamers *Scorpion, Spitfire,* and *Scourge* during the assault on Tobasco River, Mexico. Designed and drawn on stone by Lt. H. Walke, USN.

The initial wave of landing craft heading for Iwo Jima's southeast coast, February 19, 1945. The battleship *Tennessee* is at lower left.

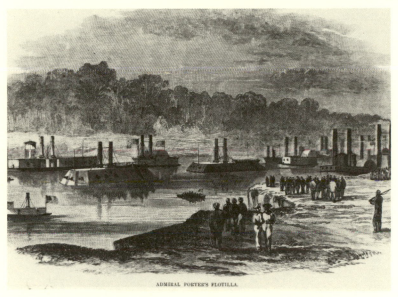

ADMIRAL PORTER'S FLOTILLA.

An engraving of Rear Admiral Porter's flotilla assembled at the start of the Red River Campaign, March 1864. Engraving copied from *Harper's Weekly,* 1864.

A U.S. Navy monitor leads two armored troop carriers on a patrol in November 1967 during the Vietnam War.

Part IV

Two World Wars

13

The Great War

During the early days of the republic belligerent countries engaged in European wars had seized U.S. ships and cargoes, and the United States found it necessary to employ naval forces to bring the depredations to a halt. Now, a century after the War of 1812, another conflict was beginning in which actions against neutral shipping would lead to the United States' entry into the war.

As in some of the wars examined by Mahan, and as in the case of World War II, the fighting that began as army campaigns on the European continent resulted in a crucial maritime struggle. Hoping to achieve an early victory, as in the Franco-Prussian War of 1870-71, Germany declared war on Russia on August 1, 1914 and on France two days later, and it set in motion a modified Schieffen plan. Under that scheme, a powerful wide sweep would be made through and past Belgium to envelope the French Army while holding operations were conducted against the Russians. Germany's failure to respect the neutrality of Belgium brought Great Britain into the Great War on August 4.

The Grand Fleet of the Royal Navy was positioned in the North Sea ready to engage the German High Seas Fleet, should it emerge. Britain also formed a Channel Fleet that included second-line battleships to seal off both entrances into the British Channel, with the help of British and French patrol vessels. Shuttled across by transports, an expeditionary force of five divisions was in France by August 22. Within three months the fighting on the western front had bogged down along lines of trenches.

Taking prompt action to stem the flow of oceanic cargoes destined for the enemy, Britain stated that only with modifications and limitations would it comply with the Treaty of London. Rather than following the provision that "a blockade must not extend beyond the ports and coasts belonging to or occupied by the enemy," British naval power imposed a long-range blockade. Ships heading for neutral as well as enemy ports were diverted to harbors of the allies. Not only was "absolute contraband" (arms, for example) condemned, but the doctrine of "continuous voyage" was extended to cargoes classified as "conditional contraband,"[1] and even more items soon were added to the list. The United States protested the violations of her neutral rights and the interruption and curtailment of trade with ports of other neutrals.

UNDERSEA WARFARE

The first submarine success was the torpedoing of a British cruiser that was sunk on September 5, 1914. Another U-boat sank three more later that month. These were ideal targets, obsolescent warships with inadequate underwater compartmentalization, which were patrolling a fixed pattern at constant speed. When the first went down, the others slowed to rescue survivors.

One feature of the maritime war that differed at least in degree from prior conflicts was the extent to which Germany employed mining offensively against shipping, a preview of what would happen in World War II. Only a day after Britain declared war a German minelayer planted about 150 of the underwater weapons off England's coast. Other such operations would follow, first by surface ships and then by specially-fitted submarines.

As would be the case in later years in the United States, Britain was not properly prepared for mine warfare. The Royal Navy had no minesweepers. Yawls were first hired for the job. Equipment was crude and techniques primitive. Initially one yawl was sunk for every two mines swept.

As ship losses mounted, corrective measures were initiated. Additional types of vessels were employed in mine clearance, and minesweeping forces were formed to clear channels for sorties by the Grand Fleet. Serrated sweep wires were developed for cutting the cables of moored mines. Major warships and then merchantmen were fitted with another new device—the paravane—that diverted mines from the ship's side and cut the cables. However, considerable time elapsed before ship losses were reduced to an acceptable level. During the course of the war more than 250 merchant vessels of Britain alone were sunk by mines.

Another location where mines played a crucial and even decisive role, insofar as the future of Russia was concerned, was the Turkish Straits. The full potential of the tsar's army could not be developed unless additional munitions and military equipment were delivered. By the end of 1914 Russian ammunition had been gravely depleted in combat and through losses such as in the Battle of Tannenburg. Production capacity was insufficient to provide adequate stocks for the future. Deliveries via Vladivostok were severely limited by the single track and poor condition of the Siberian railroad. Land transportation from Arctic ports also posed grave limitations. In view of the ease with which the German Navy could shift from the North Sea through the Kiel Canal, the Baltic was hardly a practical route. Persia was neutral.

Britain concluded that deliveries should be made by way of the Mediterranean and Black Sea. The treaty denying passage through the straits by belligerents was no longer applicable in view of Turkey's entry into the war on the side of the Central Powers in October 1914.

Prompt actions to open the straits might have succeeded. As it was, by the time the naval effort to gain passage to the Sea of Marmora began in February 1915, the Dardenelles was well mined, and heavy guns augmented by field artillery had been mounted in forts on both sides. The craft assigned to the British and French naval forces for mine clearance were merely some wooden craft manned initially by fishermen. Further, warships of the force were not employed properly for protection of the sweepers. The minesweepers and their gear sustained severe damage. Then, as a result of taking a retirement course through an unexpected, recently-laid minefield, two battleships and two battle cruisers ended up on the bottom.

The abandoned attempt was followed by amphibious assaults at or near the tip of the Gallipoli peninsula in late April, by which time Turkish troops had arrived and were well positioned. Among the many reasons for the very heavy casualties were faulty planning in London; the lack of sound doctrine for preparation, execution, and support of amphibious assaults and subsequent operations ashore; inadequate command relationships; and poor choice of initial objectives. The subsequent failure to make satisfactory progress in the land campaign led to withdrawal in December.

One result of the costly affair was a common belief that major amphibious assaults would not be practical in the modern era. Instead, studies of the Gallipoli affair by U.S. naval and marine offices made major contributions to the doctrine adopted for joint amphibious operations with so much success in World War II. Not surprisingly, the basic principles were along the lines of those that should have been learned long ago from U.S. experiences.

THE WESTERN PACIFIC

There was long-term significance in what was happening on the other side of the globe. Japan, which had an alliance with Britain, declared war on Germany on August 23, 1914. Exploiting its naval superiority in the western Pacific, Japan blockaded Tsingtao and later, in an operation in which a few British units participated, landed troops and obtained the surrender of the German forces there. Taking advantage of the wartime opportunity, Nippon employed its naval power promptly to capture the German-held Marshall, Caroline, and Mariana islands. Japan would continue to control these strategically-located groups north of the equator and west of the date line after the war under a League of Nations mandate. These acquisitions, in accordance with secret British commitments, altered the balance of sea power in the Pacific.

MARITIME WARFARE

Some of the effects of the introduction of radio communications on naval warfare became apparent as soon as hostilities commenced. For instance, its use facilitated the tracking down of enemy warships in distant areas. Germany's

Pacific Ocean Squadron was engaged off Chile and subsequently defeated in the South Atlantic Battle of the Falkland Islands in December 1914. A few months later, as a result of naval actions and internments, German surface raiders had been practically eliminated. In these days of radio a country with an inferior navy could no longer hope that cruising warfare by surface vessels could significantly affect the outcome of an armed struggle.

What made the maritime war this time so different from the past was, of course, the employment of U-boats against merchantmen. One difference stemmed from the difficulties of detecting and destroying underwater vessels. The other, with far-reaching implications, was the vulnerability of submarines on the surface. The end effects of this would be unrestricted warfare by submarines in violation of internationally recognized principles of visit and search, failure to provide for the safety of passengers and crews before sinking noncombatant ships, and the loss rather than confiscation of ships and cargoes.

In February 1915 Germany warned neutral shipping to steer clear of a war zone consisting of the English Channel and waters around the British Isles. The reason given was retaliation for breaches of international law by the Allied Powers. Britain responded with a retaliatory order in council. Everything was now on her list of contraband. Once again, the United States, which hoped to continue its neutral trade with Europe, protested to no avail. Some of the U.S. press advocated war against Britain.

That May a U-Boat torpedoed and sank a U.S. tanker without warning. Six days later the British liner *Lusitania* suffered the same fate, with more than 100 American passengers losing their lives. It was not until after other American lives were lost that summer that U.S. protests led to an agreement with Germany that provision would be made for the safety of noncombatants in liners that did not resist or try to escape.

Germany continued to sink armed merchantmen without warning and the United States threatened to break off relations. In 1916 Germany agreed that its actions would conform to prize law. For a time the U-boat campaign shifted back to an offensive against British warships.

FLEET ACTIONS

Although absolute control of the sea was not possible as long as U-boats were able to make their transits to operating areas, it was still crucially important to Britain to exercise control insofar as vessels on the surface were concerned. To that end, the Grand Fleet operated out of Scapa Flow and ports on the east coast of Scotland, ready to engage enemy warships that ventured into the North Sea and to prevent their reaching the Atlantic by way of the Norwegian Sea.

Limited naval actions, including Heligoland Bight and Dogger Bank in 1915, were followed by the engagement between the Grand and High Seas Fleets in the 1916 Battle of Jutland. Neither side pressed the action to a decisive conclusion.

Nevertheless, the presence of the powerful fleet of the Royal Navy deterred the Germans from seeking another major battle. And thus it was that the High Seas Fleet was contained. On the other hand, the continuing threat of the fleet meant that warships, personnel, and resources that might have been applied to other naval tasks were committed to the Grand Fleet.

AIR WARFARE

Although fixed-wing aircraft were still in an elementary stage of development, they were employed by both sides, along with lighter-than-air craft, to aid naval operations in the North Sea. Aviation also had roles to play in the approaches to the British Isles and Europe.

In addition to the wars on land and sea, Germany was employing aircraft in a mode of warfare that was counter to a declaration at the Hague Conference of 1907 (not signed by the Germans) whereby the contracting powers agreed to prohibit "the discharge of projectiles and explosives from balloons or by other new methods of a similar nature."[2] The bombing raids against England had started in December 1914. Later in the war Zeppelins, as many as 11 in a group, carried out such raids. Attacks by a specially-equipped squadron of fixed-wing bombers were carried out by the Germans late in the war. Although the bombing of installations and cities did not affect the outcome of the conflict, the use of this form of destruction had profound implications for the future.

THE UNITED STATES

Back in America, there were no increases in the modest naval construction program enacted by Congress in March 1915, despite the outbreak of a major war between European powers in the summer of 1914, the employment of British naval power to control the shipping of the United States and other neutrals, the seizure of Pacific islands by Japan, and Germany's declaration of a maritime war zone.

There were, however, other congressional actions that year that would enhance the naval readiness of the nation. One—the establishment of a naval reserve—proved its value when rapid expansion was required at the start of three wars. Another combined the revenue cutter and life guard services to form the U.S. Coast Guard. A key provision was that the Coast Guard "shall constitute a part of the military forces of the United States . . . and operate as a part of the Navy, subject to the orders of the Secretary of the Navy, in time of war or when the President shall so direct."[3] Revenue cutters had captured prizes in the Quasi-War with France and in the War of 1812; engaged in actions against pirates; participated in the Seminole, Indian, Mexican, and Civil wars; and fought together with the navy in the Spanish-American War. Cooperation between the two services had been excellent. The provision of the act was timely in view of the added complexities of modern naval warfare. The relationship would prove to be particularly valuable in meeting the needs of antisubmarine warfare in the two world wars.

The act of greatest significance was establishing the position of chief of naval operations (CNO). This long overdue action was a result of a rider to the appropriations bill submitted by Congressman Raymond P. Hobson, a naval officer hero of the Spanish-American War. In opposing the amendment, Secretary Josephus Daniels submitted another proposal. The resultant act establishing the position stipulated that it was to be filled by a line officer on the active list "who shall, under the direction of the Secretary of the Navy, be charged with the operations of the fleet, and with the preparations and readiness of plans for its use in war."[4] During the absence of both the secretary and assistant secretary, he would be acting secretary of the navy.

Instead of choosing Rear Admiral Fiske or some other flag officer, Daniels decided that William S. Benson, then a senior captain, would be detailed to the job. The act of March 3 had specified "that if an officer of the grade of captain be appointed Chief of Naval Operations, he shall have the rank, title, and emoluments of a rear admiral while holding that position."[5]

Bradley Fiske's position as aide for operations was discontinued. That of aide for materiel was not, but a successor was not appointed when the incumbent, a rear admiral, completed his tour.

Soon after taking office Benson recommended the creation of advisory council consisting of the CNO, the assistant secretary, the bureau chiefs, the commandant of the marine corps, and the judge advocate general. Approved by Daniels, the council held weekly meetings. Another recommendation approved by the secretary was that an assistant to the CNO perform the functions of the materiel aid. One of Benson's major achievements was establishing good relationships with the bureau chiefs who followed his guidance and cooperated fully with him throughout his tour.

The Bureau of Navigation's Division of Naval Militia (created by congressional act in February 1914) and the Naval Communications Service were transferred to the CNO. An aeronautics office was added.

As recommended by Benson, the Joint Army and Navy Board—meetings of which had been suspended by President Wilson two years earlier—was reconvened.

By 1916 the United States had become worried that the U-boat successes might cause Britain to reach some sort of accommodation as a result of which German naval power then might be employed against U.S. interests, such as in the western hemisphere. This possibility and the indecisive results of the Battle of Jutland were among the factors that determined the final contents of the Naval Act of 1916, which provided for a major multi-year construction program of battleships, battle cruisers, scout cruisers, destroyers, submarines, and other naval vessels. A naval flying corps was established and substantial funds were appropriated for the further development of naval aviation.

Chart 13.1
Naval Organization in 1916

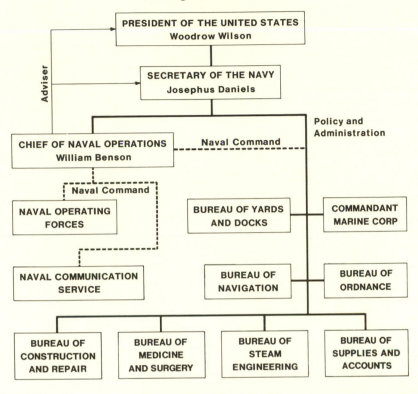

NAVAL ORGANIZATION IN 1916

Source: By the editors, based on information in *Annual Report of the Secretary of the Navy, 1916.*

One important provision of the 1916 act strengthened the powers of the CNO. Congress raised his rank to admiral and specified that "all orders issued by the Chief of Naval Operations in performing the duties assigned him shall be performed under the authority of the Secretary of the Navy, and his orders shall be considered as emanating from the Secretary, and shall have full force and effect as such."[6]

Yet another congressional action that year authorized the Naval Auxiliary Reserve. At that time the colliers, supply ships, and transports that comprised the auxiliary service were all manned by civilian crews. Enrollments into the newly established reserve began in January 1917, mainly from the officers and crews of the auxiliary ships, all of which would be placed in full naval status soon after the United States' entry into the war.

Germany was suffering increasingly from the effects of Britain's blockading-type actions. The German Army was making no progress on the western front and was suffering heavy casualties, as were troops of the Allied Powers.

In an attempt to break the deadlock, Germany resumed unrestricted submarine warfare early in 1917 in two extensive war zones. One encompassed the waters around the British Isles and off the coast of Europe from the Netherlands to the Spanish border. The other was in the Mediterranean Sea east of Spain and Morocco. The Germans recognized that this action probably would result in a U.S. declaration of war. Their conclusion, however, was that Britain could be forced to come to terms before the power of the United States could affect the outcome. And they were very nearly right.

14

America Enters
the War

The course of events moved rapidly. On February 3, 1917, three days after the German declaration that unrestricted submarine warfare was being resumed, a U-boat gave warning and then sank the U.S. steamship *Housatonic*. Later that month President Wilson sought congressional approval to arm merchantmen destined for the war zone. Because of a filibuster, Congress adjourned without acting on his request. The arming of merchantmen was authorized by an executive order on March 12, the same day that a U.S. ship was sunk without warning. Other sinkings followed.

On April 2 the president asked a special session of Congress for a declaration of war. The resolution passed the Senate two days later, opposed by only six senators, and the House concurred by an overwhelming vote in the early hours of the 6th.

Leaders in the United States were shocked by the closely guarded information as to the full extent of shipping losses revealed by the British when Rear Admiral William S. Sims, assigned as the Navy Department's liaison officer with the Admiralty, arrived in England. Sinkings had risen rapidly since the first of the year. In April 875,000 gross tons had been sent to the bottom. English grain supplies declined to an amount sufficient for only three weeks. Britain could not long continue her war efforts unless greater quantities of food and other supplies were delivered across the Atlantic.

Not only was it essential that the rate of sinkings be drastically reduced, but also many new cargo ships were required to replace those lost. U.S. shipping totaled only a million tons. On the other hand, truly remarkable results were achieved in a very short time by the response of U.S. industry and labor to the program organized by the Shipping Board.

Even more remarkable were the achievements of the Navy Department, the chief of naval operations, and the bureaus in rapidly expanding the operating forces, preparing for fulfillment of their missions, and providing logistics support.

The most profitable hunting ground for the U-boats, which were very limited in underwater speeds and endurance, was in the shipping approaches to England. General purpose destroyers provided the most effective antisubmarine capabilities. Few British modern destroyers were available since the vast majority were committed to the Grand Fleet.

To meet these urgent needs the U.S. Navy, unlike the Royal Navy, suspended building capital ships in order to provide resources and capabilities for mass construction of destroyers. Newly-designed submarine chasers also were soon sliding down the ways. Many of these relatively small ships made the difficult crossing to Europe and the Mediterranean; Italy had joined the Allied Powers in 1915.

The first division of U.S. destroyers arrived at Queenstown, Ireland four weeks after the declaration of war. By the end of June 34 more had arrived. Although Admiral Sims, in the temporary rank of vice admiral, was designated commander United States Naval Forces operating in European waters, the Royal Navy exercised operational command of the warships deployed to the area of the British Isles.

Sims concurred in the British request that U.S. Army troops and marines and their supplies be transported to England. Instead, the United States decided to deliver them directly to France. This step avoided the need for transshipments, and the routes taken avoided the high-risk, narrow British Channel, which was close to U-boat bases.

Vice Admiral H. B. Wilson was sent to France. There he was to exercise command directly under the chief of naval operations. In addition to the destroyers sent to operate under the British Navy, others were deployed to French waters where they operated out of a U.S. naval base at Brest, convenient to both the English Channel and the Bay of Biscay.

The first U.S. military forces to arrive on the continent were naval aviation units. Operating out of air stations established along the west coast of France, their patrols were to provide valuable service in locating U-boats and passing information on them to U.S. destroyers. There were no depth bombs in those days, but bombing runs could cause the enemy submarines to submerge and as a result fail to achieve favorable positions for torpedoing ships.

In some earlier wars, including the American Revolution and the War of 1812, Britain had found it necessary to convoy merchantmen to protect them from surface raiders. Such a decision was always reached reluctantly, for it prevented optimum use of the available ships. After loading they had to wait until a sufficient number was available. Transit times were increased because speed was limited to that of the slowest vessel. The simultaneous arrival of the merchantmen clogged ports and delayed off-loading. Demurrage costs increased.

The problems, of course, were now vastly compounded by the ability of submerged submarines to approach their targets and attack. Suitable sea-going antisubmarine escorts would be needed. Prior to the U.S. entry into the war, allied escort ships were in short supply because of the requirements of the Grand Fleet and demands for patrols off the British Isles.

Map 14.1
European Waters

Source: Drawn for the editors by the University of Maryland Geography Department, Cartography Service Laboratory, 1987.

One argument against using convoys in World War I was that individual ships steaming different routes would be more difficult for U-boats to intercept. Such reasoning did not take fully into account the fact that the majority of submarine operations would be where traffic was converging at the approaches to the ports of destination. Moreover, whereas zigzagging high-speed liners had a significant probability of avoiding attacks, U-boats on the surface well beyond gun range could gain favorable positions ahead of slow ships before submerging. The speed differential would then be insufficient for safety unless radical course changes were made. Even then, an attacker might achieve a favorable position when the victim resumed course toward her destination.

Despite the convoy problems, allied convoying of merchantmen began in June 1917. Thereafter, losses to German U-boats steadily declined.

THE NAVAL TRANSPORTATION SERVICE

As would be the case in World War II, poor discipline among some of the civilian crews endangered ships. Of particular concern was showing lights in the war zone. Regarding troop ships, the secretary of war requested that "in order to procure entire harmony in the operation of such vessels" and to "provide the greatest possible security and safe convoy, . . . the Navy should be called upon to furnish the necessary personnel." He requested also that all ships carrying animals, cargoes, and munitions for the army have "complete Naval personnel for the manning and operation of all such vessels." He deemed it "desirable for the safety of the vessels and their safe convoy that the Navy, as hitherto, shall have complete control of these vessels at sea."[1] That July President Wilson approved a joint recommendation of the War and Navy Departments that ships taken over for use as transports be commissioned in the navy.

During the course of World War I, the chief of naval operations separately directed U.S. convoys transporting the American Expeditionary Force to France. Not a single eastbound ship was lost. Moreover, the vast majority of the supplies for the troops were delivered by vessels of the Naval Overseas Transportation Service organized under the CNO in January 1918.

The appearance of six long-range U-boats off the United States that year, the sinking of a few coastal craft and fishing vessels, and the laying of a few mines stimulated inflated alarm among the citizenry and demands for the diversion of additional naval forces for coastal defense. Fortunately, the flow of supplies to Europe was not interrupted.

NAVAL OPERATIONS

A division of five battleships had been sent to join the Grand Fleet. Later, others were deployed to Bantry Bay, Ireland to oppose any German warships that might reach the Atlantic and endanger convoys.

CNO Admiral Benson from the start had urged offensive actions to contain or destroy the German submarine fleet. In addition to helping patrol nearby waters and assisting in the protection of convoys, U.S. Navy aircraft in France bombed U-boat bases. An American submarine flotilla was sent to the Azores. Another was deployed to the British Isles where it joined submarines of the Royal Navy in conducting patrols. The British attempted in April 1918 to block the entrances of the German submarine bases in Flanders but failed at Ostend. The British did succeed in sinking two vessels in the inner channel at Zeebrugge, but a passage was soon dredged around the scuttled hulks.

Mine fields became increasingly effective against submarines transiting to the open sea. A notable U.S. achievement was the rapid development and manufacture of a new type of antenna-triggered, moored mine by the Bureau of Ordnance. Assembled at U.S. facilities in the British Isles, some 70,000 of these were planted across the North Sea, mostly by the U.S. Navy.

The war ended before laying the fields was entirely completed. Gaps left by the British to facilitate movement of their own warships were transited by the Germans. Some U-boats, however, were damaged or sunk and the danger was having an adverse effect upon the morale of German crews.

EFFECTS OF THE BLOCKADE

The cumulative effect of the prolonged long-range blockade made it ever more difficult for Germany to sustain its war effort. Deprivations were creating hardships and malnutrition on the home front. Spirit and hope were declining. Food rationing was one of the causes of a strike by workers in munition plants in February 1918.

There were signs of a loss of discipline after the High Seas Fleet made its last sortie on April 23. Mutinies in four battleships were followed by other outbreaks that summer. The situation was reminiscent of that described by Mahan in his second major work wherein he pointed out that the French policy of avoiding fleet action and adopting a naval strategy of commerce destruction had resulted in "demoralization of their navy, the loss of the control of the sea and their own external commerce . . . and the fall of the Empire."[2]

In the land war, German troops freed from the eastern front by a truce with the Soviet communist leaders and the treaties of Brest Litovsk had reinforced those in France. With the coming of spring the first of a series of German Army offensives began.

As U.S. Navy convoys transported army and marine forces to Europe at an ever increasing rate, the Kaiser launched the fourth phase of the desperate 1918 offensive in mid-July. Germany could no longer replace all the guns that were wearing out nor the ammunition being expended. With the beginning of the allied counter-offensive during August the tide of the land war had shifted.

The final breakdown of German resolve commenced with a naval mutiny at the end of October 1918. This was followed by revolutionary actions in several cities. Yet, the German Army was still intact and continued to control large portions of enemy territory when the armistice was signed on November 11.

The Great War just concluded demonstrated the impact on naval warfare of the introduction of sea-going submarines and their advancing capabilities. In many respects, it provided a preview of the battle of the Atlantic of World War II.

The outcome of the land war had hinged upon the concurrent war at sea. The most basic lessons on the functions of naval power in a major conflict, the pervasive effects of that power, and the necessary prerequisites for its success should have been learned from repeated experiences of the past.

Of the additional dimensions introduced into naval power, that with the most profound impacts in this war had been the developments in submarines and their employment against merchantmen as well as warships. The underseas vessels had one disadvantage—their vulnerability on the surface prevented exercising selective control over shipping, capturing prizes, and providing for the safety of noncombatants. On the other hand, it appeared for a time as if Britain might be influenced to withdraw from the war as a result of U-boat successes in unrestricted warfare.

The best solution for the Allies, of course, would have been to prevent their reaching the open sea by one sort of action or another. Given time, the mine fields nearing completion at the war's end might have achieved such a result.

Yet, crucial as the mode of warfare involving submarines and antisubmarine warfare forces was, control of the sea surface had proven to be as potentially decisive as ever before. It was through actions against German warships and the containment of the German High Seas Fleet that shipping was controlled. Not only was the enemy denied desperately needed materials, but the Allies benefited from the condemnation of cargoes and the acquisition of ships taken as prizes.

As another added dimension, the accelerating advances in military aircraft had profound implications for the future. The increase in numbers of aircraft and aviators in the U.S. Navy was nothing short of remarkable. The first U.S. forces to land in France had been the naval aviators. By the end of the war the navy had 18 seaplanes and three dirigibles operating out of France, together with planes based on five U.S. naval bombing stations. The most important contributions were in antisubmarine warfare, particularly in reconnaissance. U-boat locations were passed on to surface ships and the naval aircraft helped guide destroyers into position for depth charge attacks.

In the future benefits would be reaped from improved aircraft performance and their ability to operate from ships. On the other hand, the increasing overlap of army and navy aircraft capabilities was to lead to controversies, the solutions to which would be critically important for naval power in the future.

One of the lessons of World War I, which somehow has to be learned again and again through bitter experience, is the danger of concentrating on one major mode of naval warfare to the neglect of other modes. The need for multipurpose naval forces would continue to increase as time went on.

15

Between Wars

The United States emerged from the war keenly aware of the consequences of another power holding control of the sea. Once again the nation experienced British naval interference with its freedom to use the seas. Before hostilities were over Great Britain had taken steps to enhance its position in post-war competition for trade, gaining control of major sources of increasingly important crude oil. There was growing concern over Japanese actions in the Far East and over its ability to exercise naval power in that area and in the western Pacific as a result of gaining control over mandated islands and an aggressive warship building program.

The construction of U.S. destroyers understandably was terminated soon after the war, since over 300 were already commissioned and being completed. On the other hand, construction resumed of large warships of the 1916 program. As a result of gaining congressional approval for increases in ship sizes, the newest incorporated improvements gained from war experiences, including hull design and compartmentalization to minimize the effects of underwater damage from torpedoes or mines and adding horizontal armor to resist bombs.

THE AIR POWER ISSUE

The period between the two world wars was a time when air-power extremists downgraded and even ridiculed the need for a major navy—as would be the case after 1945. Furthermore, there was a strong and persistent campaign in the United States, as in other countries, to assign authority over all military aviation to a separate department or agency. It would prove fortunate that the campaign failed.

Both U.S. and Japanese experiences would demonstrate the importance of retaining naval aviation as an integral part of their navies. These experiences contrasted sharply with Britain's, which soon after World War I formed the Royal Air Force and gave it extensive authority over naval aviation. Italy also suffered the consequences of such action.

Immediately after signing the armistice, citing "the great advantages given to a fleet by an efficient air service," Admiral H. T. Mayo, commander-in-chief U.S. Atlantic Fleet, recommended such a service "sufficient in all respects for reconnaissance, spotting, carrying torpedoes, antisubmarine patrols and escort duties."[1] A fleet exercise in January 1919 employed naval aircraft to scout, intercept an enemy fleet, and strike it with simulated bombing attacks.

The General Board conducted a study shortly concluding that "fleet aviation . . . must become an essential arm of the fleet . . . capable of accompanying and operating with the fleet in all waters of the globe." Such an air arm's purpose was "to insure air supremacy, to enable the United States Navy to meet on at least equal terms any possible enemy, and to put the United States in its proper place as a naval power."[2]

The first airplane flight across the Atlantic was by flying boat NC-4 in May 1919. Two months later Congress authorized conversion of collier *Jupiter*, the navy's first surface ship with an electrical propulsion system, into an "aeroplane carrier."[3] Renamed *Langley* and commissioned in 1922, she was equipped with the world's first arresting gear permitting aircraft to land back on board. By now the Navy Department's Bureau of Aeronautics had been established.

Soon, however, a variety of influences and the absence of an immediate threat led to a period deemphasizing sea power objectives. The armistice and terms of the subsequent peace treaty, which seemed to provide a guarantee against further German aggression, encouraged the natural tendency to shift from all-out war to all-out peace. Military expenditures were soon drastically reduced.

DISARMAMENT TREATIES

Freedom of the seas was one of the 14 points set forth as a basis for peace by President Wilson in January 1918, along with disarmament and establishment of the League of Nations. The covenant of such a league was included in the Treaty of Versailles, which was not approved by the U.S. Senate, although it was signed by all the other allies. In any case, the hopes of many that major wars might be forestalled by the league's actions were not realized.

U.S. efforts to achieve lasting peace through international agreement would continue into the 1930s. But later events would demonstrate that military power and the will to use it were still the controlling factors.

With the coming of peace, many pre-war isolationists and pacifists reappeared, and their numbers expanded. Some insisted that the war had been caused primarily by arms competition, the main culprits being the munitions industries. There were many, as in earlier times, who believed that the nation's need for a navy did not extend beyond the protection of the continental United States. Others rationalized that the strength of the British Navy provided safeguards that minimized U.S. naval requirements. A group of congressmen advocated curtailment of the navy program and shifting funds to social improvements. A Senate resolution requesting the president to negotiate a treaty on naval limitations received strong public support.

The 1921 Washington Conference had two objectives. In one section, nine nations met on questions involving the Far East. Early in World War I Japan, backed by its sea power, had presented China with the 21 demands. Although the Japanese, after much negotiating, agreed to the Nine Power Treaty respecting the integrity of China and the Open Door policy, they still retained positions in Manchuria and Mongolia and controlled economic resources in Shantung.

The other section of the conference addressed the question of arms limitations. Although attempts to restrict land forces were soon abandoned, the five powers agreed on capital ship limitations. This was scarcely surprising since the United States, which was constructing modern battleships and battle cruisers that would give the U.S. Navy superiority in these types, agreed to scrap all but two of those not completed except for two battleships that were nearing completion and two battle cruiser hulls being converted into aircraft carriers. The conference also agreed to limit overall carrier tonnage. But the United States failed to limit cruisers, flotilla leaders, destroyers, and submarines.

There were grave strategic implications for U.S. interests in the Pacific. The United States agreed not to erect new fortifications, establish naval bases, increase naval repair and maintenance facilities, or strengthen insular defenses in the Pacific other than in mainland Alaska, the Panama Canal Zone, and the Hawaiian Islands. Japan and Britain made similar agreements, but only pertaining to certain specified locations.

This and subsequent naval disarmament treaties curtailed U.S. construction programs in certain types of warships while permitting other nations—most notably Japan—to increase naval power by building more warships incorporating the latest advances. Moreover, the United States refrained from constructing to treaty limits in some types, including aircraft carriers. The two hulls laid down as battle cruisers would become *Lexington* and *Saratoga* (each 33,000 tons). The Five Power Treaty permitted a total of 135,000 tons, yet none designed from the keel up was authorized by Congress until 1929 when it authorized the *Ranger*, displacing a mere 14,500 tons.

Soon after the war was over the Navy Department began planning test bombings of ships to obtain data and information on damage for determining design changes that would enhance the abilities of warships to survive and maintain combat effectiveness. When tests were conducted in 1921 the targets were ex-German and obsolete U.S. battleships deficient in watertight integrity. They were dead in the water and, of course, had no crews for air defense or damage control.

The Army Air Service was invited to participate. In the phase in which naval aircraft conducted the bombings, technical observers boarded targets after each hit to examine the damage. A similar procedure was planned for joint bombings.

However, the army participants ignored the agreed emergency signals for suspending attacks whenever examination of damage was warranted. When the time came for attacks by the air service alone, runs were continued without suspension and at favorable altitudes until the target was sunk.

When the Joint Army-Navy Board evaluated results it concluded that the maximum possible development of naval aviation was imperative for national defense and recommended creation of an adequate aviation force integral with the fleet. The board also recommended building aircraft carriers of maximum size and speed. On the other hand, there were extreme air force enthusiasts who interpreted and exploited results of the tests in a way that bolstered exaggerated claims regarding the vulnerability of naval ships to air attack.

In a 1922–23 conference at the Hague, the United States, Britain, France, Italy, Japan, and the Netherlands drafted rules for aircraft use in war. Under these rules, bombing would only be legitimate when directed at "military forces; military works; military establishments or depots; factories constituting important and well-known centres engaged in the manufacture of arms, ammunition, or distinctly military supplies; lines of communication or transportation used for military purposes."[4] The rules included provisions to minimize danger to civilians and to protect buildings dedicated to public worship, art, science, and charity; historic monuments; hospitals; and so forth.

Observance of such rules would be quite another matter. Disciples of Italian Colonel Guilo Douhet insisted that existing methods and even the nature of warfare were being revolutionized. Their basic contention was that wars would be decided by massive land-based aircraft attacks to destroy the enemy's resources in their primary form and bring about a national collapse of material and morale resistance. The result, it was claimed, would be rapid victory. To the air power extremist, warfare meant all-out or absolute war. Forms of influence, such as those traditionally exerted by sea power, and the possibilities of limited wars seemed to be ignored.

According to U.S. advocates of these views, all military aviation should be transferred to a newly created service, separate from the army and the navy. They maintained that all armed forces should be under a single department of defense, a supreme military commander, and a general staff. The military commander would determine the relative portion of resources to be allocated to land, sea, and air forces. Based on the assumed decisiveness of the bombing of targets in the enemy homeland, there would be a new and higher concept of strategic operations and a thoroughly integrated doctrine for conducting war, one encompassing all of the services. Army and navy operations could no longer be considered separately.

The extreme nature of some of the arguments being advanced can be seen from a sampling of statements scattered through Brigadier General Billy Mitchell's book, *Winged Defense,* published in 1925. He wrote that one bomb "hitting a battleship will completely destroy it. . . . imagine how much easier it is to sink all other vessels and merchant craft; . . . surface sea craft cannot hide; . . . the superior fleet menaced by submarines and long distance aircraft could not long exist on the high seas; . . . the surface ship, as a means of making war, will gradually disappear, to be replaced by submarines that will act as transports for air forces and destroyers of commerce; . . . [seacraft] will again revert to being an auxiliary of armies and air forces."[5]

Mitchell maintained that aircraft "are not dependent on the water as a means of sustentation; . . . strings of island bases will be seized by the strong powers as strategic points so that their aircraft may fly successively from one to the other and as aircraft themselves can hold these islands against seacraft, comparatively small detachments of troops on the ground will be required for their maintenance; . . . [small islands] can be supplied by other aircraft or by submarines, with everything that is necessary."[6]

According to him, "a superior air power will dominate all sea areas when they act from land bases . . . no seacraft, whether carrying aircraft or not, is able to contest their aerial supremacy; . . . aircraft carriers cannot compete with aircraft acting from land bases; . . . as airplane carrying vessels are of no use against hostile air forces with bases on shore, and as they can only be of use against other vessels or hostile fleets that are on the surface of the water, and as these fleets will be supplanted by submarines, there is little use for the retention of airplane carriers in the general scheme of armaments."[7]

Mitchell asserted that "control of sea communications . . . can be done by aircraft within their radius of action"; in the case of an insular power dependent on maritime commerce, an air siege "would starve it into submission in a short time; . . . an attempt to transport large bodies of troops, munitions, and supplies across a great stretch of ocean, by seacraft, as was done during the World War from the United States to Europe, would be an impossibility; . . . to gain a lasting victory in war, the hostile nation's power to make war must be destroyed"; and aircraft "will accomplish this object in an incredibly short space of time."[8]

During the year the book was published there was a bill before Congress for the creation of a department of defense to replace the Departments of War and Navy. Under the bill, an undersecretary for air would be assigned authority over all military aviation, including that for naval purposes and also civil aviation. Two other undersecretaries were proposed—one for land, one for sea. Fortunately, the bill was not passed.

CURTAILMENT OF NAVAL CONSTRUCTION

These were indeed lean times for the naval programs of the United States. Appropriations were but a small fraction of those that would have permitted building to treaty limits. The number of warships completed, those under construction, and the ones that had been both authorized and funded by Congress during the five years following the Washington Conference totaled only 16. The comparable number for Japan was 116 and for Britain 37. Furthermore, each had initiated major shipbuilding programs in types not limited by the Five Power Treaty.

When representatives of these three foremost naval powers met in the 1927 disarmament conference, no agreement was reached on limitations for additional categories of warships. The London Treaty three years later did reach a compromise agreement. However, the allowed tonnages imposed little or no restraint on the ambitious program of Nippon.

The long period of very low military budgets continued into the early 1930s. An area in which notable progress was made during these years was aviation. One reason was the National Advisory Committee for Aeronautics [the predecessor to the National Aeronautics and Space Administration (NASA)], which, with army and navy representation, had the purpose of advancing research and development in both civilian and military aviation.

With full control of its own aviation programs, the U.S. Navy developed and produced planes of ever increasing performance, including features required for operations at sea. Not only were seaplanes unique, but those designed to operate from land were unsuited for handling, launching, and recovery on rolling, pitching, and heaving decks. In addition to providing the necessary structural and landing gear characteristics, emphasis was placed on the development of air-cooled engines. This was in contrast with the Army Air Corps, which sought only those cooled by liquids.

Another important factor was that commissioned aviators in the U.S. Navy were of the line, unlike those in Britain. Moreover, some given flight training at this time were officers experienced in command at sea. After the commissioning of *Lexington* and *Saratoga* in 1927, further rapid progress was achieved in carrier aircraft, techniques of carrier operations, fighter protection against enemy aircraft, and new methods such as dive bombing.

Not only were operations conducted in combination with and in support of other fleet forces, but task force concepts were developed to exploit the high speed mobility of carriers and to permit more flexible employment of their aircraft in offensive and defensive missions. In addition to training in operations against enemy naval forces, capabilities against land targets, including neutralization of airfields, were being explored. One example was the 1929 fleet exercise in which carriers attacked targets in the Panama Canal Zone and inflicted heavy simulated damage without encountering opposition.

The severe depression that began that year in the United States brought about further cutbacks on the already frugal navy budget. Early in 1932 the Scouting Force, homeported on the Atlantic Coast, joined the Battle Force in the Pacific for a fleet exercise. There it remained, the reason being Japan's aggression in the Far East. The incursion of the Kwangtung Army into Manchuria culminated in the establishment of a puppet state and, in response to a Chinese boycott, the landing of forces by the Japanese Navy in Shanghai to retaliate by military actions before withdrawing. Nippon's move toward hegemony in the Far East had begun.

The only truly up-to-date warships in the U.S. Navy were the two large carriers, eight 10,000-ton treaty cruisers, and six modern submarines. The quality of officers and enlisted men was high, but in those depression years the fleet was only partly manned.

One of the construction programs begun by the Japanese in the 1920s had been that of the *Fubaki*-class destroyers, which were vastly more powerful than the U.S. four-stackers. It was not until 1932 that the United States started to lay keels for eight modern destroyers of the *Farragut*-class. Then, after passage of the National Industrial Recovery Act of 1933, President Franklin D. Roosevelt authorized using some of its funds to start construction of more destroyers, submarines, and other types, including two carriers.

RESEARCH AND DEVELOPMENT

It was to prove extremely fortunate that, despite the very low level of funding, the navy was making highly significant progress in developments that would enhance combat capabilities. What made this possible during these lean years was the flexibility permitted in the use of appropriated funds in carrying out assigned responsibilities—a situation in sharp contrast to that in recent years. Delegation of such authority in present times has been severely eroded, increasingly large layers of staff have been imposed both above and within the Navy Department, budgets have been compartmentalized and projectized, and program approval has been subjected to a seemingly unending series of reviews, including those by expanded congressional staffs.

Some of the most important advances in the 1930s were kept so highly secret they have received scant recognition. One area in which the U.S. Navy led the world by the middle of the 1930s was in gunnery fire control, the extent of which would be revealed when the warship in which this author was serving operated with the British Home Fleet in 1942. There were key innovations in what we now know as computers. Before the veil of secrecy descended, the American Ford Rangekeeper, an analog computer, was patented in 1918. It and equipment coupled with it were greatly improved over the years. Most significant was the addition in the 1930s of the gyroscopic stable vertical and associated computing elements whereby guns could be kept pointed accurately in space regardless of the rolling and pitching of the warship. Other secret achievements were in servos (automatic controls), also in the 1930s. This resulted in automatic fire control systems for gun batteries being installed whereby directors mounts and guns with automatic drives followed the signals being received from the rangekeepers or computers of the battery concerned.

Crucial progress also was being made in naval antiaircraft (AA) capabilities. AA guns of 3"/50 caliber, the installation of which had begun in 1912, continued to be employed in small men-of-war and auxiliaries throughout World War II. The 1920s saw the introduction of the 5"/25 guns controlled by directors incorporating gyroscopic rate-solving computers in the larger warships. Now, a new generation of destroyers was about to introduce the 5"/38 gun. Whereas the old destroyers had 4"/50 guns for surface engagements and a couple of pitiful 3"/23 guns for AA, new ones would have dual-purpose batteries of automatically driven 5"/38 guns and mounts controlled by an advanced system consisting of a director with an automatic drive and a computer with a gyroscopic stable element.

Similar batteries were being incorporated into the designs of other types of new construction warships. But the date was late. As of December 7, 1941, the only ships, other than destroyers, with such batteries were one cruiser and the first two of the fast battleships. More vessels, including four AA cruisers, would soon be joining the fleet. A serious limitation was the dependence on mechanical time fuzes. With this in mind, the Bureau of Ordnance was experimenting with proximity fuzes using infrared technology. The development of the radar proximity (VT) fuze was underway before the U.S. entry into the war.

The most significant breakthrough of all was radar. The fact that ships could be detected by electromagnetic waves had been discovered accidentally in 1922 during an experiment by two engineers of the U.S. Navy's Aircraft Radio Laboratory exploring the possible use of high-frequency communications. The publication of their paper stimulated further investigations leading to independent development of radar by the United States and Britain.

In 1924, using equipment constructed by the Naval Research Laboratory (NRL), the Carnegie Institute employed radio pulses to measure the height of the ionosphere. Six years later the NRL discovered that airplanes reflected enough radio energy for long-range detection. Finally, in 1938 an experimental air search radar was installed on board USS *New York* and, following successful tests, production models were installed on other large warships.

Thereafter, naval forces properly equipped would be able to detect enemy aircraft at long distances and provide the intercept direction to fighter planes. Antiaircraft batteries could be alerted and helped to pick up attackers. Fire control radars being developed, as a result of their even higher frequencies, could track accurately enough for gunfire. Mounted on directors, these made it possible to engage air or surface targets obscured by darkness, clouds, or fog. Moreover, since radar ranges were far more precise than those obtained by optical rangefinders, gunnery effectiveness was vastly improved.

It was unfortunate that the notable progress in the capabilities of the navy's heavy antiaircraft batteries and dive bombing was not accompanied by major improvements in close-in AA batteries. However, research and development began in 1940 on what would become lead computing sights.

In one class of naval weapon the U.S. Navy did not match the progress of a future enemy—the torpedo. For instance, the air-launched variety, upon entering the water, underwent large transient depth oscillations, preventing their use against ships in shallow water. Torpedo nets, which could have helped protect warships in Pearl Harbor, were believed unnecessary. Only through disaster did the Americans learn that Japanese developments had reduced the oscillation amplitude.

As for the surface ship variety, the United States would belatedly discover that the Japanese Navy had developed torpedoes of larger size, explosive weight, range, and speed than those of the United States.

The exploder mechanism was a serious deficiency of submarine torpedoes that was not discovered until the Pacific war was well underway. The lesson is that, despite the costs involved, it is imperative that weapons and their warheads be employed in destructive tests against targets they are intended to destroy. Thus, while torpedoes—a form of guided missile—were relatively expensive, more realistic testing could have revealed the deficiency. It is important that this lesson be heeded in the modern age of sophisticated weapons.

AMPHIBIOUS WARFARE

Progress of another sort during the interwar years contributed later to campaigns in the Pacific. In World War I the vast majority of marines were engaged in the land war in France. After the war, consideration of the situation in the Pacific focused more U.S. Marine Corps attention on its potential role in major amphibious assaults. A 1921 plan, "Advanced Base Operations in Micronesia" by Lieutenant E. H. Ellis, was in some respects a forecast of events two decades later. In 1927 the Joint Army-Navy Board recognized the landing force role of the marines. In 1933 the Fleet Marine Force, to operate as a part of the United States Fleet, was established. Before long the U.S. Pacific Fleet's Amphibious and Fleet Marine Forces would be engaged in extremely difficult and crucial assault operations.

Studying past experience—especially the disastrous 1915 Gallipoli landings—and conducting exercises, the U.S. Navy and Marine Corps formulated standard doctrines and procedures to plan and conduct amphibious operations. Later, these were also adopted by the U.S. Army.

The need for standard doctrine, demonstrated long ago by operations in the Mexican, Civil, and Spanish-American Wars, particularly with regard to joint amphibious assaults, had become increasingly urgent because of warfare's growing complexities. The new policies resolved the control problem so often encountered in the past by assigning the navy overall authority to control movements by sea to the objective area, preparatory actions there, ship-to-shore movements, and joint actions during the amphibious phase and until the beachhead had been secured. The standard procedures adopted encompassed all phases of operations including combat loading of amphibious ships, preparatory bombardments, landings, air and gunfire support, and logistical operations to and across the beach. Meanwhile, advances were being made in techniques, landing craft, and amphibious vehicles.

AN INCREASINGLY TROUBLED WORLD

Passage of the Vinson-Trammel Act in 1934 authorizing a substantial long-range warship construction program signaled a growing recognition of the naval requirements of the nation in an increasingly troubled world. However, as in all such authorizations, program implementation would depend both on subsequent appropriations bills and presidential decisions. Construction of some of the ships did not begin until 1941.

In 1934 Japan gave its two-year notice of renunciation of the Washington Treaty of 1922 and the London Treaty of 1930. In the next year Japan withdrew from a new arms limitation conference in London. Yet, the other major powers not only continued to abide by earlier restrictions but agreed to other limitations as well.

Disputes over the Somali border, which Benito Mussolini refused to submit for arbitration, were used as an excuse for Italy's invasion of Ethiopia in October 1925. When the League of Nations condemned the action, Britain considered employing naval forces to sever the water line of communications upon which the invading army depended, but no such action was taken. The League of Nations invoked limited economic sanctions, but these failed to prevent annexation.

In 1936 Hitler's troops reoccupied the Rhineland in violation of the Versailles Treaty. Germany and Italy were aiding fascist forces in the Spanish Civil War. Japan invaded China in 1937 "to preserve the peace of East Asia."[9] The U.S. river gunboat USS *Panay* was sunk by Japanese bombs in the same year.

In 1938 Congress authorized a 20 percent increase in total naval tonnage and replacement of overage warships. At the same time Adolf Hitler began the series of actions in Europe that would lead to World War II.

16

Another Global
War Begins

The plan of conquest initiated by Hitler was precisely along the lines set forth in his two-volume *Mein Kampf,* published in 1933, the year he came to power. The memory of the terrible effects of the naval blockade of Germany had been vivid when he started that book in prison in 1924. Urging avoidance of war with Britain and her sea power, at least initially, he wrote, "The correct road would, even then [referring to World War I], have been . . . *strengthening of continental power by the winning of new soil and territory in Europe.*"[1] (Emphasis in original.)

To that end, he proposed to *"terminate the endless German drive to the south and west of Europe, and direct our gaze towards the lands in the east."* (Emphasis in original.) The defeat of France, however, might be necessary as "a means of subsequently and finally giving our nation a chance to expand elsewhere." Once France was conquered, "not only do English population centers constitute a worthwhile goal for aircraft and long-distance batteries, but British commercial traffic lines would also be most unfavorably exposed to submarine activity. A U-boat war, based on the long Atlantic coast as well as on the no less extensive stretch of French frontier region on the Mediterranean coasts of Europe and North Africa, would have ravaging effects."[2]

Placing overwhelming emphasis on land warfare in his military preparations, Hitler chose a long-range plan for naval construction rather than one that, assuming the imminence of war at sea, would have given priority to capabilities for destroying commerce. His confidence as to the time available before having to cope with Britain's sea power would prove to be a grave miscalculation.

Having been allowed to occupy the Rhineland in 1936, he sent the German Army rolling into Austria in 1938. Accepting a peace declaration, Britain and France acceded to German demands for Czechoslovakia's Sudetenland. Other portions of Czech territory were soon transferred to Hungary and Poland. The Republic of Czechoslovakia was dissolved in March 1939. Germany occupied Bohemia and Moravia, with Hungary seizing Carpatho-Ukraine. Germany annexed Memel.

After Italy invaded Albania, Hitler signed a military pact with Mussolini. When Germany entered into a nonaggression treaty with the Soviet Union on August 23, the Admiralty began to control British shipping in anticipation of a possible war.

The fuehrer launched his blitzkrieg into Poland eight days later. France and Britain declared war on September 3. Poland fell in a mere 35 days. The Soviets shared in its partition.

War with France was consistent with Hitler's expectation that it might be a prerequisite to realization of territorial ambitions to the east. On the other hand, apparently he had not anticipated that the British would so promptly reverse their policy of caution and concession. With British sea power involved, it no longer would be enough to gain victories in continental warfare.

As for the British, their ability to carry out a distant blockade and participate in the war on the western front once again would depend upon receipt of ocean-borne supplies. Two German pocket battleships, at sea when the war began, sank a few ships. One made her way back to the homeland. The other, the *Graf Spee,* conducted raiding operations in the south Atlantic and Indian Ocean, was damaged in battle with ships of the Royal Navy, and entered neutral waters in South America where her crew destroyed her in December 1939.

The most ominous threat to Britain was the same as in World War I. Despite the fact that Hitler's Third Reich had agreed to the provisions of the 1936 London Protocol requiring submarines to adhere to the same rules of international law that applied to surface warships when they attacked merchant ships, Germany resorted immediately to unrestricted U-boat warfare. Less than 50 of the submarines were available, and more than half were small, short-range boats, yet they sank 150,000 tons of allied and neutral shipping and a British aircraft carrier during the first month of war.

Soon minefields were laid across the Dover Strait and they had considerable success against ships using that route. The convoying of merchantmen began, but many still steamed independently. Britain possessed far too few antisubmarine warships to fulfill all missions such as screening warships, escorting merchantmen, and patrolling coastal waters. In any case, the tonnage sunk by U-boats continued at about the same average rate for the next eight months.

Again, as in World War I, shipping in waters around the British Isles suffered many losses to mines. The threat was even more ominous this time because of a new type of German mine, one triggered by changes in the earth's magnetic field when a steel ship passed over it. Laid on the bottom at harbor entrances, in estuaries, and in shallow coastal waters by aircraft, surface ships, and submarines, the mine was devastatingly effective. Venting its explosive force against the vulnerable bottom of the victim, this new type was far more destructive than a mine detonated upon contact with a ship's side. Magnetic mines could not be swept by conventional methods. Sinkings in the first four months of the war by this weapon totaled more than 260,000 tons.

Britain's situation was becoming truly critical but, as in the case of other innovations in naval weapons, countermeasures would be devised to reduce the new mines' effectiveness. Recovery of a mine in November 1939 revealed the nature of the influence mechanism. The British engaged in an all-out research and development effort, accompanied by a similar effort by the U.S. Navy. As a result, deperming and degaussing systems were developed to neutralize ships' permanent and induced magnetic fields. New sweeping methods also were devised. As is invariably the case, the Germans responded with changes, and the dynamic contest between measure and countermeasure was on.

NEUTRALITY PATROL

In September 1939 President Roosevelt directed the navy to commence a "Neutrality Patrol,"[3] with instructions to report and track belligerent air, surface, and underwater units approaching the coast of the United States or the West Indies. Later in 1939 other American countries joined in a declaration to keep the war from the western hemisphere. This patrol extended approximately two-thirds of the way from New York to London and three-quarters of the distance to Gibraltar.

Other maritime routes of critical importance to Great Britain were between the Indian Ocean and the Atlantic. Control of the Suez Canal was crucial because movements from the east into the Mediterranean were via that waterway, as were those from Italy to its forces in Ethiopia. Australian and New Zealand troops were transported to Egypt early in 1940. In anticipation of Italy's entry into the war, Britain augmented its Mediterranean Fleet that spring. Operating out of Alexandria, it was in a position to exercise control over the eastern portion of that long sea. Then merchantmen were ordered to proceed all the way around the African continent.

In this theater, as in the North and Norwegian seas, Britain suffered severely from the inadequacies of its naval aviation. After creation of a separate Air Ministry with responsibilities including naval aircraft, the ministry's policies and actions were greatly influenced by the concepts of those who believed that strategic air power was now the decisive means of waging war and that navies and armies were only of secondary importance.

Concerning the design of new aircraft, production, manning, and training, the overwhelming emphasis was on the capabilities of the Bomber and Fighter Command. Programs sought by the Admiralty concerning aircraft carriers, their sizes and numbers, and numbers of naval airplanes were opposed by the Air Ministry. A case in point was in 1932 when the ministry sought "a more drastic limitation of ship-borne aircraft" and proposed that aircraft carrier tonnage be reduced "to the lowest possible limit."[4]

There were shortages of volunteers to serve in naval aircraft, questions of terms of service for Royal Air Force officers with the fleet, and promotion problems. Recurring issues were control of the Fleet Air Arm (aircraft operating from ships of the Royal Navy), the extent to which maritime planes of the Coastal Area Command would be placed under naval "operational disposal,"[5] and whether or not the flying boats of that command would form a part of the fleet.

It was not until 1937, after years of bitter debate, that the British government accepted a conclusion of an inquiry that "the Admiralty should be responsible for selecting and training the personnel, and generally for the organisation of the Fleet Air Arm."[6] Although the Fleet Air Arm was subsequently transferred to the Admiralty, intermediate flight training was conducted by Royal Air Force schools and the navy was still dependent upon the Air Ministry for the design and construction of planes and for much of the required support. The Coastal Command and its flying boats remained under the air force.

The performance characteristics of Britain's carrier, battleship, and cruiser aircraft were far inferior to those of the U.S. and Japanese navies. Their naval fighter planes lacked the speed to overtake enemy bombers. The maximum size of bombs that their dive bombers could deliver was only half that dropped by U.S. Navy counterparts.

British carriers were very limited in the number and sizes of aircraft they could accommodate. Handling, launching, and recovery of the planes were very slow and inefficient. The elevators were not large enough to transfer the higher-performance airplanes of the U.S. carriers between hanger and flight decks. HMS *Illustrious,* completed in May 1940, had a complement of only 33 obsolescent planes. In contrast, USS *Enterprise,* already in service, operated 76 modern aircraft. Moreover, the Royal Navy's concepts and tactics for carrier operations were far behind those developed by the U.S. and Japanese navies.

NORWAY

On April 7, 1940, a seaplane of the Royal Air Force's Coastal Command on a patrol mission over Heligoland Bight sighted a group of German warships headed north. The British naval force that departed home waters a few hours later had no aircraft carrier. On the next day the fleet commander was unable to get assistance to locate the enemy from a coastal flying boat on patrol from the Shetland Islands. Only one German ship—a cruiser—was located due to the inadequacies of air searches.

On April 9 German forces landed at five locations in Norway, including Oslo, where they secured the airport so that additional forces could be brought in. Two locations for amphibious landings—Arendal and Kristiansand—were along the Skaggerak; another was at Bergen, across from the Shetlands; and the fourth was at Trondheim, almost 300 miles further up the coast and into the fjord there. The northernmost was above the Arctic Circle at Narvik, some 1,100 nautical miles from Germany. The German invasion of Denmark that same day included two amphibious operations, one at Copenhagen.

A British Army detachment headed for Narvik three days later in ships that were not combat-loaded. Harstad, the objective, was located on the other side of the large, snow-covered peninsula north of the fjord into Narvik. A destroyer engagement in the approaches to that port resulted in losses to both sides. A British destroyer blew up a German ammunition ship. A larger British naval force, including a battleship and a carrier, sank the surviving eight German destroyers. Nevertheless, the initial objective of the British Army was not altered.

In the Narvik campaign there was little hope that the British Army could make its way to the port, at least in the near future. As should have been apparent from the start, what was needed was a navy-commanded joint operation culminating in the establishment of a beachhead near Narvik itself. After assignment of overall command to Admiral of the Fleet Lord Cork and Orrey, troops were transported safely up the fjord and landed only a few miles from the objective. Air strips were constructed nearby and air force fighters were flown from the decks of two carriers that had ferried the planes from the British Isles.

Another objective was Trondheim. The first landings were 80 miles north and 100 miles south of that point. The amphibious assault planned for April 22 was canceled by London in favor of a two-pronged attack by land from the secondary landing sites. Not only were no carrier strikes planned against airfields, but fighters from the carriers proved incapable of countering the German planes, which dominated the air over the beachheads and interdicted ships bringing in reinforcements and supplies.

Concern over Scandivavia was soon overwhelmed by more startling events. Led by air-supported Panzer divisions, the German Army began its sweep through the Low Countries north of the Maginot Line.

British forces engaged in the Narvik operation were directed to take the port, destroy installations, and prepare for evacuation. During withdrawal of forces from the Trondheim area, German battle cruisers *Scharnhorst* and *Gneisenau* sank carrier *Glorious* with its planes on deck, an antisubmarine trawler, and two merchantmen.

Unlike the situation in World War I, Hitler's warships and submarines could now operate from fjords and other sheltered waters beyond the North Sea all the way to the North Cape of Norway over 1,000 miles northeast of Scapa Flow. Operating from fields in Denmark and Norway, planes could conduct reconnaissance, support naval operations, and attack enemy ships within range. Another reason why control of Norway was important to Germany was that three-fourths of its iron ore was obtained from northern Sweden. The route in the winter, when the Gulf of Bothnia froze, was by rail to nearby Narvik and then by ship. Ore carriers' ability to hug the coast and proceed inside offshore islands would minimize the chances of interception by the British.

As Germany's European offensive quickly overwhelmed the defenses in the Netherlands and Belgium, the British Expeditionary Force retreated to Dunkirk. There, as they and French forces prepared to evacuate to England, heavy attacks by the Luftwaffe began. Arms and equipment were left behind while destroyers, transports, and numerous civilian craft of all sizes returned the troops across the channel and fighter planes fought overhead. Local control of the sea made possible the success of the desperate operation.

On May 23 the Royal Navy began to stop Italian ships in the Mediterranean and search them for contraband. Italy's long-awaited declaration of war against Britain and France came on June 10. The presence of Italian destroyers in the Red Sea caused a convoy headed for Egypt from New Zealand to be diverted around the Cape of Good Hope to England.

Following Dunkirk, the German campaign into the rest of France moved with spectacular rapidity. Paris began evacuation. Verdun was captured. A new French government signed terms of armistice on June 22, 1940. Hitler had achieved one of the goals set forth in *Mein Kampf*—France's defeat, and thus the acquisition of airfields for bombing England and Atlantic coast bases for intensifying U-boat operations.

On the day that the German Army entered Paris, the U.S. Congress passed a bill authorizing about 25 percent more carrier, submarine, and cruiser tonnages. The request of Admiral Harold R. Stark, chief of naval operations, that $4 billion be appropriated to start building a two-ocean navy was promptly approved. Until then, construction of many of the warships authorized in 1934 and 1938 had been unfunded.

One argument often advanced in modern times by those minimizing U.S. naval requirements is that any European war will be brief. The fighting on the continent between Germany and the western allies had lasted only a few months—too short a time for sea power's cumulative effects to influence the outcome. The war at sea, however, would continue for another five years.

17

The Crucial War
at Sea

World War II now entered its second phase. Victorious over France, Hitler initiated actions to eliminate English opposition by launching air attacks against it while intensifying the U-boat campaign.

He also directed preparations for a cross-channel invasion. German air-borne troops might achieve some limited objectives, but to gain control of southern England large-scale amphibious operations were necessary, followed by the delivery of supplies and reinforcements across the British Channel. Deterring or defeating such operations was crucial to Britain. For, once beachheads were established, the invasion could probably overcome any opposition by the British Army, gravely weakened by abandoning its heavy arms, vehicles, munitions, and equipment during the retreat and evacuation from Dunkirk.

In the summer of 1940 the Germans judged the means available for a major attack from across the channel insufficient to ensure a high probability of success, particularly in view of the naval opposition that would be encountered. After Germany lost the air Battle of Britain, the prospects grew even dimmer. By the next spring the fuehrer had committed forces to other objectives.

World War I had demonstrated the high demand for versatile destroyers in modern warfare. Whether or not the lesson had been learned, British funding of naval programs had been austere and the Royal Navy had far too few of the type. The number in service had been further reduced by losses and damages in the Norwegian campaign and by the needs for long-overdue overhauls.

In June 1940 alone, the British lost almost 600,000 tons of merchant vessels from U-boat attacks. Early the next month the United States agreed to activate 50 World War I-class destroyers from the Reserve Fleet and transfer them to Britain in exchange for 99-year sovereign rights over naval base sites in the western Atlantic and Caribbean. Although not suited for many modern warfare tasks, the obsolescent four-pipers had antisubmarine potentials, as did ten coast guard cutters subsequently provided.

Early in the Battle of Britain in June the Luftwaffe supported the planned German invasion across the channel by attacking coastal defenses and ships. This was followed a couple months later by attacks on fighter plane bases and aircraft factories.

The threat of such bombings was one reason for sending a British mission to the United States in August to exchange technical information on weapons and military devices. Each learned the other had succeeded in developing radars, and both benefited from exchanges on this subject. Especially valuable to the Americans was information on resonant, multicavity magnetrons, which would be of great value in providing ships and aircraft with high-resolution microwave radars with greater power outputs than had been achieved in the United States.

Correctly anticipating that day raids would be followed by night attacks, the British sought assistance in the mass production of radars for fighter planes. These were coming off the line in a remarkably short time and made crucial contributions to defending England against air attacks.

Germany began night bombing of London in early September. Heavy raids against cities continued into October. By the end of the month the Battle of Britain tapered off. Attacks were made for a time again against coastal targets. Then, starting with the large and heavily destructive raid on Coventry in November, an all-out offensive against cities began, climaxing in the terrifying incendiary attack on London at the end of December. Despite the destruction and high casualties, Britain held on. Germany had lost many planes without achieving decisive results. The raids diminished and then ended entirely in the spring of 1941.

In the meantime, the fate of Britain continued to hinge upon the outcome of the Battle of the Atlantic. Many U-boat operations were now beyond effective ranges of coastal command air patrols, and thus the submarines could proceed much of the time on the surface. The monthly tonnages they sank during the last half of 1940 were about double the average of the first five months of the year. In order to support Britain, President Roosevelt gained congressional approval of the Lend Lease Act in January 1941.

THE MEDITERRANEAN

The problems confronting British naval power were compounded by Italy's entry into the war in June 1940. Operating out of Alexandria, the British Mediterranean Fleet was in position to exercise control in the eastern portion of the 2,000 nautical mile-long sea and to ensure the defense of the Suez Canal. Recently-formed Force H, based at Gibraltar, controlled the western sea and traffic through the strait. Within two days after declaring war Italy had lost 130,000 tons of merchant shipping—seized, scuttled, or interned.

As Mahan would have advocated, the foremost Mediterranean objective of the British Navy now was to defeat or contain opposing naval forces. Concerned, rightly or not, over the possibility that Vichy French warships might serve the Axis Powers, the Royal Navy's Force H was ordered to Mirs el-Kebir, Algeria where, after issuing an ultimatum, the warships there were engaged. Only one French battleship escaped. Other French Navy ships were at Alexandria. By agreement, they became effectively interned.

Sea lines of communications were crucially important in the Mediterranean war.

Italy was able to ship the oil and other important cargoes upon which her military effort depended from the Black Sea via the Dardenelles, the Aegean, the Corinth Canal, and the Ionian Sea.

British use of the central portion of the Mediterranean was contested by the Italian Fleet and land-based aircraft, including those operating from Sicily, Sardinia, and North Africa. Conversely, the British naval base and airfields on Malta were alongside communication lines between Italy and Africa and in position to support British naval forces and convoys in that area.

The bombings of that island, which began when Italy entered the war in June 1940, continued with varying intensity during the following months. The Royal Navy was hard pressed to protect delivery of fuel, ammunition, essentials, and personnel to beleaguered Malta. From time to time fighter planes were transported by carriers to the region and flown off. However, very few could be accommodated each trip.

Fortunately for Britain, Italy's navy was suffering from the loss of its own air arm as a result of creating a single air force. Preoccupied with strategic concepts of air power, pilots had little or no training in naval missions or operations with the fleet. Except for some reconnaissance units, the Italian Navy lacked operational control of aircraft. Air support had to be requested, and this meant delays and poor coordination. The requests often competed with other missions and were not always granted. From time to time British ships were subjected to horizontal bombing attacks, but the percentage of hits was extremely low.

The first British–Italian naval engagement was off the sole of Italy and thus near its airfields. Italian Air Force heavy bombers attacked in many sorties both before and after the battle. The result was only a couple of hits and a few near misses. Planes from a British carrier launched torpedoes at cruisers without success. A brief exchange of long-range gunfire was indecisive.

The Italian warships were returning after escorting a convoy to Benghazi, Libya, when the land offensive began there in September 1940. As Mussolini's army initially made rapid progress into Egypt, the British Mediterranean Fleet bombarded Benghazi and locations further east along the invasion route. Submarines attacked Italy's sea lines of communications to the Libyan port, but they had little success for the next three months, since the vessels stayed close to shallow water.

As for Britain's sea lanes of communications, the Italians earlier had invaded British Somaliland and the Horn of Africa. Except for small Vichy-controlled

Somaliland, the southern coast of the Gulf of Aden and the Red Sea were in Axis hands. Nevertheless, westbound ships carrying military forces and supplies to Egypt transited safely in convoys with escorts that came through the canal. The Royal Navy also got a few convoys across the Mediterranean from the Atlantic, permitting the British counteroffensive in North Africa that began in December. Soon thereafter the Italian Army was retreating into western Libya.

The ambitious fascist dictator had begun what amounted to another war as he invaded Greece in late October 1940. In this case, the sea lane of communications of the Italian Army was across the narrow Adriatic.

Britain, allied with Greece, shipped munitions from Egypt and deployed a small Royal Air Force contingent of fighters and bombers. The Royal Navy was allowed use of Suda Bay, Crete, to refuel.

The British, using torpedo planes, attacked Italian warships at anchor off Taranto on the night of November 11. Two carriers were intended to launch the strike. Although one was not available, three of the six battleships there were damaged A light naval force sank four Italian merchantmen convoying to Albania.

The Greeks repulsed the land offensive and were soon fighting on Albanian soil. A month later British warships bombarded Valona. But there were heavy commitments elsewhere, and the flow of Italian troops and supplies across the narrow sea was never completely severed.

Now that the British Navy could use Suda Bay, Italy could no longer be assured of shipments from the Black Sea. Despite Hitler's earlier judgments against a diversion of military effort to the south, he decided to employ German forces to help his Axis partner in North Africa and the Balkans.

Fliegerkorps X, specially trained in attacking ships, was deployed to Sicily and Sardinia from icy Norway—where even in the south there was little winter daylight. Their operations in January 1941 against a British naval force covering an eastern-bound convoy revealed the seriousness of the German dive bomber threat. German troops, arms, ammunition, equipment, and supplies began moving across to North Africa a month later.

German planes, refueling on the island of Rhodes, laid magnetic mines in the Suez Canal. These operations, repeated in months to follow, sank some ships and closed the canal for long periods.

Bulgaria joined the Axis powers in 1941. In view of the increased threat against Greece, British troops were on their way from Egypt in naval ships and merchantmen four days later. The Mediterranean Fleet intercepted an Italian Naval force sent to oppose such movements. Carrier planes hit a battleship and a cruiser, which were later sunk by gunfire. In the following night the British, aided by the radar now installed on one of their battleships, defeated the Italians in the March 28 Battle of Matapan.

Since the Axis troops were making progress toward Egypt, the victorious fleet then focused its main efforts against the sea-borne traffic from Italy to Libya.

At the same time, Germany declared war on Yugoslavia and Greece. An air attack on Piraeus that included dropping magnetic mines effectively closed that important port. The Mediterranean Fleet bombarded Tripoli and then headed for the Aegean. The rapid German advance into Greece caused Britain to withdraw its army. Ships of the fleet extracted forces from scattered beaches on seven consecutive nights. As at Dunkirk, only small arms and a few special items accompanied the soldiers, many of whom were taken to nearby Crete.

German planes, including 168 dive-bombers from Sicily and Sardinia, were soon operating from Greek airports. As had been the case off Norway, British carriers and aircraft lacked the capabilities to conduct effective strikes against the fields.

Following air bombings and landing air-borne forces, Crete's airfields were soon in German hands. Only one British carrier with but a fraction of her low-performance fighters operational was available, since the other was aiding the passage of an urgent convoy to Egypt from the western Mediterranean. Fleet warships succeeded in turning back vessels carrying German troops to Crete and then began withdrawing forces from the island on the night of May 28. Many merchantmen and warships engaged in the evacuation were damaged or sunk by dive bombing attacks.

British ships, in contrast to the U.S. Navy, were very deficient in heavy antiaircraft fire control. One result of experiences in the Mediterranean was the installation of impressive numbers of antiaircraft pom-pom machine gun mounts on warships throughout the Royal Navy.

This was an area in which the U.S. Navy lagged. The chief of naval operations' Antiaircraft Defense Board had reported at the end of 1940 that "the lack of adequate close range antiaircraft gun defense of existing ships of the Fleet constitutes the most serious weakness in the readiness of the Navy for war."[1] Most ships had only .50- and .30-caliber machine gun mounts. The Bureau of Ordnance had developed a 1.10-inch rapid fire gun and mount that was being redesigned to correct difficulties and that year had been testing the Bofors 40-mm and Oerlikon 20-mm machine guns. However, close-in antiaircraft gunnery was still seriously deficient at the time of Pearl Harbor.

Sea lanes of communication to forces in North Africa remained crucial to both sides. From the start of warfare there the effectiveness of the Royal Navy had been hindered by inadequate responsiveness and scope of maritime air search operations. It was not until October 1941 that the Royal Air Force formed the Naval Cooperation Group.

Britain by now had eliminated naval opposition in the Red Sea, and Roosevelt declared that sea open to U.S. shipping. Desperately needed military items began moving from the United States to the hard-pressed forces in the Middle East.

BATTLE OF THE ATLANTIC

As for the vital Battle of the Atlantic, the tonnages sent to the bottom by U-boats in the early months of 1941 were even higher than before. The March total was nearly 700,000 tons. One reason was the wolf pack tactics adopted in attacks on convoys. The situation was becoming truly desperate.

During the following month the Royal Navy, at long last, was assigned operational control of the coastal command. This led to far closer coordination of air and surface antisubmarine warfare forces, with some antisubmarine planes stationed in Iceland. Sinkings decreased sharply until December when, with the U.S. entry into the declared war, U-boats commenced their operations off the American continent and in the Caribbean.

Many factors were influencing the Battle of the Atlantic. One was radio communications intelligence. The Germans easily deciphered hand-encoded messages to convoys, and gaining prompt knowledge of routings and reroutings permitted optimum employment of U-boats. Britain's reliance on such an insecure system seems particularly strange in view of its sophisticated efforts (similar to those by which the United States was able to break Japanese machine-encoded messages) to read the encoded message of Germany's Enigma device. The U.S. Navy had begun using advanced systems for encrypting in the early 1930s, at least for the most sensitive messages. Nevertheless, the primitive British merchant ship code continued to be employed by the Allies until the summer of 1943.

The British ability to read U-boat traffic was achieved in the summer of 1941. Changes by the Germans secured their messages from time to time but, sooner or later, there was always a breakthrough.

INVASION OF THE SOVIET UNION

Hitler's attempt to gain control of the heartland began with the invasion of the Soviet Union on June 22, 1941. Emboldened by the rapidity of previous successes on the continent, he expected blitzkrieg tactics to achieve victory in about four months.

U.S. lend-lease was extended to the Soviet Union and munitions were soon being delivered by British-escorted convoys to North Russia. Other cargoes went across the Pacific to Vladivostok for delivery west via the low-capacity Siberian railroad. There were deliveries also through the Middle East.

In July the U.S. Navy transported marines to Iceland to relieve British troops and commenced antisubmarine patrol flights from the island. The United States agreed to build 100 destroyer escorts of U.S. design and transfer them to Britain. During the following month the president announced that airplanes would be ferried via the Red Sea for delivery to British forces.

In September, following the engagement between USS *Greer* and a German submarine, Roosevelt ordered the navy to shoot on sight in American waters. The United States assumed responsibility for escorting merchant convoys from

Newfoundland to the meridian of Iceland, and the Neutrality Act was amended in November to allow arming U.S. merchant ships and their entry into the war zone. U.S. warships and transports, in which a British Army division was embarked, left Halifax and headed south to go around Africa to the Middle East.

The German offensive had achieved rapid progress in Eastern Europe. Further progress was made in the drive launched by Hitler in October to end the war against the Soviet Union. However, with the coming of winter the German Army began to pull back. In this theater, too, a long war was in prospect.

THE FAR EAST

Japan had been employing its growing naval power to extend its influence and control in the Far East. After announcing in 1938 its intention to establish a "New Order in East Asia,"[2] Japan conducted amphibious operations along the southern coast of China. President Roosevelt, under the Neutrality Act, could have stopped the flow of strategic materials to China in this undeclared war, but he did not. Japanese forces occupied Hainan and the Spratly Islands in 1939. That July the United States gave the required six months' notice to Japan that the commercial treaty of 1911 was being terminated, laying a basis for applying economic sanctions against that country.

Following congressional passage of an act for licensing exports, the president forbade the sale of aircraft and aviation gasoline to Japan. With the acquiescence of Vichy France, Nippon landed troops in northern Indochina in August 1940. In the Tripartite Pact, Japan recognized the New Order in Europe, and Germany and Italy acknowledged Japanese leadership in greater Asia. The export of U.S. iron and steel to Japan was prohibited that fall.

In the summer of 1941 Japan demanded and gained from France rights to use certain Indochinese ports and to occupy airfields in the southern portion of the colony. Roosevelt responded by issuing an executive order freezing Japanese assets, thus cutting off trade, including the export of oil. Similar action by Great Britain and the Netherlands restricted Japanese petroleum procurement from the East Indies.

In late November Washington learned that a large amphibious force was moving south from Shanghai. The war in the Pacific was about to begin.

A Two-Ocean War

During the fleet problem of 1938 a U.S. Navy task force reached its launch area off Oahu undetected by army air corps patrols. The carrier planes conducted their unintercepted exercise attack of Pearl Harbor and, after recovering the planes, the group retired. At dawn on Sunday, December 7, 1941, the appearance of carrier aircraft was "NO DRILL."[1]

Along the lines of Mahan's precept, Japan's first war objective, once again, was destruction of the opposing fleet. With control of the sea, at least in the western Pacific, it could project its military power, sustain its operations to achieve a "New Order in East Asia,"[2] and protect the sea lanes along which oil and other crucial supplies were delivered to the home islands. One advantage of naval forces stressed by Mahan was an enemy's uncertainty as to the destination of an attack. Preoccupied with evidence of Japanese movements south into the South China Sea, thousands of miles away, the United States had not reacted promptly or suitably to intelligence information. As in 1904, the Japanese began the war with a surprise attack on warships at a major base prior to a declaration of war.

Japanese naval aviation was an integral part of its navy. Japanese pilots were of the highest quality, well trained in sea operations and in the conduct of precise and well coordinated strikes against ships. High performance carrier aircraft had been developed. Carriers were capable of operating a maximum number of planes efficiently. Concepts and tactics of carrier operations were sound.

Preceded by an advance submarine force, the striking force, which included six of Japan's ten carriers, had made its way undetected to a launching position about 275 miles north of Pearl Harbor. Unalerted and with portions of the crews ashore, the U.S. warships were struck by an initial wave of 190 planes. Also attacked were airfields where a large percentage of army, navy, and marine aircraft were destroyed by strafing fighters. The first devastating damage was inflicted by torpedo planes, which launched their weapons modified for the shallow harbor water. The first wave was immediately followed by dive bombing attacks. In the striking force, planes from the hangar decks were brought up as soon as the initial deck load had become airborne. The result was follow-up strikes by dive bombers and fighters.

The balance of naval power in the Pacific had been changed dramatically by one blow. Two of the older U.S. battleships were lost, while others required salvage and extensive repairs. It was truly fortunate the three carriers of the Pacific Fleet were not in port that weekend.

Long lead times are required for building and fitting out major warships. Men-of-war funded in the late 1930s were just beginning to come off the ways. The first two fast, modern battleships were in the Atlantic, having just completed their post-shakedown overhauls. The navy had a total of only seven carriers. One, only recently commissioned, had not yet joined the fleet. The United States was forced into a basically defensive strategy in the Pacific.

The same day as the Pearl Harbor attack, after the sun rose west of the date line, Japanese carrier and land-based aircraft commenced a series of strikes against airfields and naval ships in the Philippines. Hong Kong was bombarded and subjected to a blockade. Aircraft struck Singapore. Troops invaded Thailand. Amphibious forces were steaming south. Japan's offensive into Southeast Asia was underway.

The gravely weakened U.S. Navy was engaged in a two-ocean war. Whereas the conflict in the Pacific was basically a naval war upon which all else depended, the Battle of the Atlantic was crucial to the defeat of the European Axis powers. As in World War I, an adequate flow of cargoes was a vital necessity for the British Isles and essential for military operations—defensive and offensive. The Soviet Union's munitions had been seriously depleted, and the delivery of lend-lease cargoes was urgently needed. The sea lanes of logistics remained critical to both sides in the North African struggle. U.S. military contributions to the land war, including the bombing campaign against Germany and Italy, would require munitions and supplies delivered by sea. The projection of major army forces ashore would have to be by amphibious operations.

Allied ship losses had risen sharply soon after the U.S. declaration of war. This was mainly a result of U-boat deployments to the western Altantic, the coastal waters of North America, the Gulf of Mexico, the Caribbean, and the ocean off South America. The toll of tankers was particularly high. In view of the commitment of escorts to trans-Atlantic convoys and the shortages of other antisubmarine forces, it took time before adequate measures, including establishing an interlocking convoy system, were effective.

The Department of the Navy, its bureaus, and shore establishment responded to the emergency in remarkably effective fashion. Warships damaged at Pearl Harbor were not only repaired rapidly, but also improvements were made, such as in antiaircraft capabilities. The naval construction program was greatly accelerated. The additional officers and enlisted men to meet demands of the world-wide war at sea were obtained and trained promptly.

All in all, the responsiveness in achieving rapid expansion of operating forces, preparing them for action, and providing for their maintenance and support was truly remarkable. One reason was that the nature of wartime operations of the U.S. Navy were in many respects extensions of those in peace. Thus, the basic divisions of departmental responsibilities that had evolved over the years—responsibilities specially tailored to requirements unique to naval forces—was suitable to meet the expanding demands of warfare.

Another reason was the extraordinarily extensive delegation of authority—commensurate with responsibilities. Fundamentally different from a hierarchical system or one that exercises authority via a general staff, the organization functioned essentially along the lines later described in the secretary of the navy's annual report for 1945:

a. "Naval Command"[3] over the operating forces, the bureaus, and the shore establishment was exercised by the chief of naval operations (during World War II by the commander in chief, United States Fleet).

b. The authority of the CNO over the bureau chiefs extended to "logistic control related to determining requirements" and "coordination [of the shore establishment] with operating forces."[4]

c. The bureau chiefs had authority over the short establishment with regard to "management and technical control"[5] in areas under their cognizance.

d. There was but one under secretary of the navy and only two assistant secretaries of the navy. Their authority over the bureaus and marine commandant encompassed "business administration" and "logistic control relating to procurement, production, research and related matters."[6]

e. The secretary of the navy exercised direct "policy control"[7] over the chief of naval operations, the under and assistant secretaries, the chiefs of the bureaus, and the commandant of the marine corps.

Thus, the tremendous challenges of World War II were met with only a very small fraction of the bureaucratic structure of recent times.

The coast guard was assigned to the navy for the duration of the war. The Navy Department wisely refrained from becoming involved in administrative matters.

COMMAND OF THE OPERATING FORCES

Following the damage to the fleet inflicted by the Japanese at Pearl Harbor, avoiding defeat in both oceans would depend on extraordinarily flexible and efficient use of the U.S. naval operating forces. Faced with this critical situation, President Franklin D. Roosevelt assigned "supreme command of the operating forces comprising the several fleets, seagoing forces, and sea frontier forces"[8] to a commander in chief, U.S. Fleet, to be headquartered at the nation's capital.

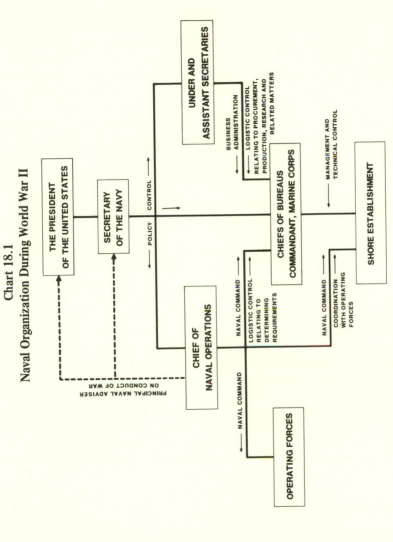

Chart 18.1
Naval Organization During World War II

THE PRESIDENT
OF THE UNITED STATES

SECRETARY
OF THE NAVY

POLICY — CONTROL —

CONTROL —

UNDER AND
ASSISTANT SECRETARIES

BUSINESS
ADMINISTRATION

LOGISTIC CONTROL
RELATING TO PROCUREMENT,
PRODUCTION, RESEARCH AND
RELATED MATTERS

CHIEFS OF BUREAUS
COMMANDANT, MARINE CORPS

MANAGEMENT AND
TECHNICAL CONTROL

SHORE ESTABLISHMENT

CHIEF OF
NAVAL OPERATIONS

PRINCIPAL NAVAL ADVISER
ON CONDUCT OF WAR

NAVAL COMMAND

LOGISTIC CONTROL
RELATING TO
DETERMINING
REQUIREMENTS

NAVAL COMMAND

COORDINATION
WITH OPERATING
FORCES

NAVAL COMMAND

NAVAL COMMAND

OPERATING FORCES

Source: Redrawn from a chart in *Annual Report of the Secretary of the Navy, 1945* (Washington DC: Government Printing Office, 1945).

Earlier there had been a commander in chief, U.S. Fleet who exercised command from his flagship in the Pacific over assigned forces, while other commanders of naval operating forces, such as in the Atlantic and Far East, reported directly to the chief of naval operations. The title had been changed to commander in chief, U.S. Pacific Fleet when Admiral J. O. Richardson had been relieved by H. E. Kimmel earlier in the year.

Now the newly established fleet commander in chief was to be the "principal Naval Adviser to the President on the conduct of the war" and, "under the general direction of the Secretary of the Navy,"[9] directly responsible to the constitutional commander in chief of the army and navy. Admiral Ernest J. King was assigned to the position.

The importance of King's relationship with the president was demonstrated time and again over the next four years. It assured prompt decisions in meeting the highly dynamic and widely scattered needs of the wars at sea and provided a safeguard against naval considerations being overlooked at the highest level. The discussions with Roosevelt helped avoid unnecessary diversions of the nation's naval power from its primary missions.

Overall joint strategic planning and direction in World War II were achieved without interfering with army and navy chains of command by forming the Joint Chiefs of Staff (JCS), successor to the Joint Board. Together with their British counterparts, they addressed the problems of coalition strategy as members of the Combined Chiefs of Staff. Admiral King's designation as JCS executive agent for the Pacific Ocean areas unified command appropriately complemented his authority over the fleets and other naval operating forces.

Under a different arrangement, adequate provisions might not have been made for reversing the course of events in the conflict with Japan. With top priority assigned to the war with Germany, allocation of even minimal additions to the depleted naval forces in the Pacific was complicated by British augmentation requests and by the efforts of the U.S. Army chief of staff, who believed the overwhelming military emphasis should be on a land offensive in northern France. Whereas General George C. Marshall urged beginning such an offensive in 1942, the experienced British were convinced that the chances of success were then too low. In any case, there was to be no quick end to the European war. The armies of Britain and the United States would not be projected across the English Channel until June 1944, and it would be almost another year before Germany surrendered.

THE PACIFIC WAR

An appreciation of the enormous distances involved in the ocean hemisphere of the globe is basic to understanding the problems faced by the United States in fighting a war against Japan and its aggressions in the Far East. The great circle course from San Francisco to Yokohama is some 4,550 nautical miles.

Much of the time severe weather and extraordinarily high seas in the North Pacific force shipping to use considerably longer routes. Pearl Harbor is 2,200 miles from San Pedro, California, and more than 5,000 from Panama. It is then 5,500 miles further to the Philippines. The distance from the Panama Canal to Australia is almost 8,000 miles. The problems of naval strategy had been further compounded by the Versailles Treaty, which mandated to Japan Germany's Pacific islands north of the equator. These included the Marshall Islands, the Carolines, and, except for Guam, the Marianas.

Ever since the Spanish-American and Russo-Japanese wars, the U.S. Navy had been giving much thought to problems that would be encountered in case Japanese aggressions led to war with the United States. Consideration of the great distances involved was an important factor in determining performance characteristics upon which the design of warships was based. As a result, the fuel capacity and design of propulsion plants provided very long cruising ranges, much greater, for example, than those of Britain, which had more conveniently located bases. This was true of undersea as well as surface vessels. The 1924–25 acts authorizing the first "fleet submarines" specified that they were to have the "greatest desirable radius of action."[10]

A U.S. naval development during the interwar years that would prove of great importance was that of refueling while underway at sea. Improvements in techniques and rigs continued at an accelerated pace after the Pacific war began. Other unique advances were in operational logistics, particularly in the form of service squadrons employed as mobile afloat bases.

Within a couple of days after the strike at Pearl Harbor Guam was captured. The Japanese gained a foothold in the Gilberts, south of the Marshall and toward the Fiji and Samoan islands. Establishing bases there posed threats to shipping routes from the eastern Pacific to New Zealand and Australia. Wake Island was soon taken.

Allied naval forces in the western Pacific were far too few to provide major opposition to the powerful Japanese naval forces operating in the South China Sea. The surface warships of the U.S. Asiatic Fleet consisted of only one heavy and two light cruisers, some World War I-class destroyers, submarines, and a few gunboats. These and the other allied naval forces suffered losses as Japanese amphibious groups projected troops ashore promptly into the Philippines and Malaya, and before long into Borneo and other islands in the area.

Submarines in the Asiatic Fleet totaled 29, six of which were the old S-boats and the remainder fleet-types. When the war began, patrols were being conducted off Takao, the Pescadores, Hainan, French Indochina, and Cochin China. Eight submarines in Manila Bay formed a strike force. Knowing that a Japanese invasion force was headed south, the priority for submarine attacks had been set in case of war: major warships, loaded transports, light warships, supply vessels, and unloaded transports.

Map 18.1
Ocean Hemisphere

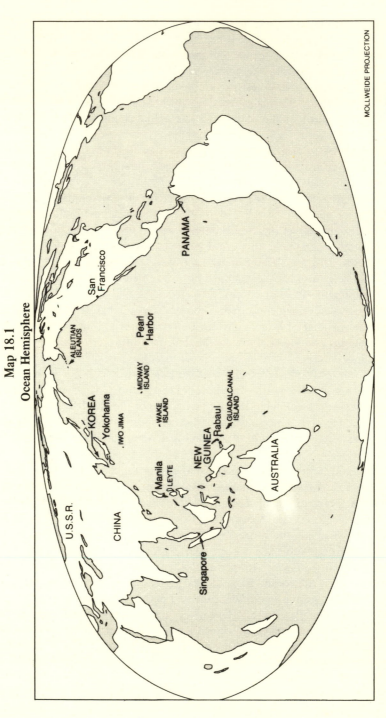

MOLLWEIDE PROJECTION

Source: Drawn for the editors by the University of Maryland Geography Department, Cartography Services Laboratory, 1987.

Warships of the enemy fleet, of course, would continue to be primary objectives throughout the war. As for the conduct of warfare against Japanese shipping, orders went out to naval forces immediately after hostilities began to carry out "unrestricted submarine and air warfare."[11]

Submarines of the Asiatic Fleet were employed initially against the Japanese offensive into the Philippines and then the Netherlands East Indies. They undoubtedly would have had more success had it not been for the torpedo difficulties, such as depth control being too deep when warheads rather than exercise heads were used, and malfunctions of exploders in torpedoes of fleet-type submarines. But even if everything had gone well, the Japanese campaigns in that area would have achieved their goals.

After the defeat of the combined naval force under Admiral K. W. F. M. Doorman (two Dutch, one U.S., one British, and one Australian cruiser, plus destroyers) in the Battle of the Java Sea and actions in the Sunda Strait at the end of February 1942, Japan was in complete control of the sea in that area. Singapore had already fallen and the Netherlands East Indies soon followed. The Japanese had acquired sources of vital oil and other strategic materials. For a long time thereafter actions in the Far East against Japanese naval power and shipping were confined to U.S. submarines, some operating out of Fremantle, Australia and others out of Pearl Harbor.

Meanwhile, Japan launched an offensive south of the excellent harbor at Truk in the Carolines toward the east coast of Australia. The first objective was the harbor of Rabaul on New Britain Island at the head of the Coral Sea. Rabaul had fallen late in January following carrier air attacks by Chuichi Nagumo's strike force—the force that had struck Pearl Harbor.

When Admiral Chester Nimitz took command of the Pacific Fleet on December 31, 1941, the tasks assigned by Admiral King were, first, to cover and hold the Hawaii-Midway line and maintain communications with the west coast of the United States; and, second, to maintain communications between the U.S. west coast and Australia, chiefly by covering, securing, and holding the Hawaii-Samoa line, which should be extended to include Fiji at the earliest practicable date.

Operations of Pacific Fleet carrier task groups in the following months provide examples of the flexibility with which naval forces can be employed if not committed to what Mahan called "ulterior objects"[12] or unnecessarily subdivided among geographic military commands. After *Saratoga* was damaged southwest of Oahu by a submarine torpedo in January 1942, there were but two carriers available in the Pacific.

Yorktown was on her way from the Atlantic. Proceeding directly from Panama, she was joined by *Enterprise,* which had come with destroyers from Pearl Harbor. After covering the movement of transports carrying marines to Samoa, the carriers formed the basis of two task groups. On February 1 the *Enterprise* group (Rear Admiral W. F. Halsey, Jr.) carried out attacks on three atolls in the Marshalls, one of which was important Kwajalein. The *Yorktown* group (Rear Admiral F. J. Fletcher) struck Makin in the Gilberts on February 1 and two atolls in the eastern chain of the Marshalls.

These offensive actions bolstered U.S. morale. Japan reacted by detaching the two most modern carriers from Nagumo's force and bringing them north to conduct defensive patrols off the home islands. Moreover, official histories written in Japan after the war reveal that these attacks west of the date line had a far greater impact on the leaders of that nation than had been realized by the United States.

The third carrier, *Lexington,* was in a task group (Vice Admiral Wilson Brown) that covered the advance of two convoys en route west from the Panama Canal— one with men and equipment for construction of a fuel station at Bora Bora, the other with troops destined for Christmas Island, Canton Island, and Noumea, New Caledonia.

On the orders of Admiral King, *Lexington* and her screen, all navy patrol planes and such army bombers as were available were sent to the Fiji–New Caledonia area to operate with Australian and New Zealand forces in the Anzac Force established under the command of Vice Admiral H. F. Leary, USN. The carrier task group headed for a strike against Rabaul. But, after being detected by Japanese planes that the group engaged with great cost to the enemy, *Lexington* was forced to retire.

To divert attention away from the South Pacific, King ordered a raid on Wake. After striking the island on February 24, Halsey proceeded further west with his group to hit Marcus Island only about 1,000 miles from Tokyo.

Desiring an even more spectacular operation, King and his operations officer conceived one against Tokyo by medium bombers launched from carriers. The commanding general of the army air forces, H. H. Arnold, agreed to the proposal. In the subsequent operation that April, Halsey's force, which included newly arrived *Hornet* as well as *Enterprise,* proceeded to a position off Honshu where the specially equipped 16 B-25s of Lieutenant Colonel James H. Doolittle were launched. The navy's role in this surprise raid was a well kept secret.

In the meantime, bombings of Tulagi in the southern Solomon Islands and points on New Guinea had resulted in *Yorktown* being sent to join Admiral Brown's force for a strike against the rapidly developing naval and air base at Rabaul. When reports were received on March 8 of landings near the eastern tip of New Guinea, the force went to that area instead. Carrier aircraft attacked a few ships but by then most had departed. The Japanese established a seaplane base at Tulagi.

Here, as in other areas of the ocean hemisphere, the outcome would hinge upon the war at sea. The first Japanese advance turned back was an invasion force headed for Port Moresby, New Guinea. The naval Battle of the Coral Sea was not a clear-cut victory for either side, since both sides suffered losses and sustained damages in the exchange of carrier air attacks on May 7 and 8. Nevertheless, the Japanese invasion force was recalled.

Lexington did not survive the damage received in the Coral Sea action. The damaged *Yorktown* was ordered back at high speed to Pearl Harbor.

Before the month was out Japanese forces were steaming east for two concurrent offensives. One was into the North Pacific, where storms and low visibility often hindered sea and air operations. Its objective was to capture positions in the Aleutians. The other offensive, aimed at seizing Midway, was based on the hope that remnants of the U.S. Pacific Fleet would be drawn to the scene and destroyed in a decisive battle with Japanese submarines, carrier aircraft, and surface warships.

The Japanese succeeded in the less important of the two operations—that into the Aleutians, where they occupied Attu and Kiska. But they were repulsed in the Battle of Midway on June 4, 1942. This was a clear-cut U.S. victory in which carrier planes sank four Japanese carriers. The United States lost one, *Yorktown*, which had been able to join the Carrier Striking Force as a result of extraordinarily rapid navy yard repairs. She was slowed by a submarine torpedo attack and later sunk by Japanese carrier aircraft.

A remarkable feature of the actions in these early months was the rapidity with which Pacific Fleet warships were shifted from one area to another and regrouped into task organizations to meet changing situations. What made this possible was the exercise of command by the fleet commander in chief, Admiral Nimitz, who reported directly to Commander in Chief, United States Fleet, Admiral King. When Nimitz was also assigned command of all Allied forces in the Pacific Ocean area, except the land defenses of New Zealand, the chain of command was the same, since King was executive agent for the Joint Chiefs of Staff.

Now, in proposing an assault on Rabaul, General Douglas MacArthur sought the transfer of naval forces, including two carriers, to his Southwest Pacific area command. The Joint Chiefs of Staff executive agent for that command was the chief of staff of the army. It was indeed fortunate that the transfer and the specific operations were not approved. Naval forces suitable for support of an advance up the coast of New Guinea were assigned to MacArthur's operational control, but the carriers and the bulk of the fleet were retained under Nimitz's command. Had it been otherwise, it is hardly conceivable that the naval forces available would have been able to anticipate and respond promptly to changing needs and be employed efficiently and effectively throughout the vast Pacific. The pivotal oceanwide struggle for control of the sea might have had a different outcome.

Warships badly needed in the Pacific had been retained in the Atlantic because of the higher priority accorded to the European war. For example, the first two fast battleships were in the Atlantic when Pearl Harbor was attacked, having completed their post-shakedown overhauls and joined the fleet.

One impending requirement resulted from the discovery by British intelligence early in 1942 that Japan was seeking German approval to take over Madagascar.

Japan had projected its naval power into the Indian Ocean, sinking four British warships and 135,000 tons of merchant shipping. Bases in Ceylon had been struck by carrier aircraft. The strategic location of the island off the east coast of Africa in relationship to maritime lanes of communications led the British to decide to occupy Madagascar in the name of the Free French. To release Royal Navy warships for the operation, Winston Churchill asked Roosevelt "to send say two battleships, an aircraft carrier, some cruisers and destroyers"[13] to take the place temporarily of their Force H in the eastern Mediterranean.

THE NORTH ATLANTIC

Admiral King urged that the U.S. Navy send instead a task force to operate with the British Home Fleet, which was operating out of Scapa Flow to block egress of German warships from the Norwegian Sea into the Atlantic and to serve as a covering force for Murmansk convoys. The Royal Navy had been escorting these formations on the run from Iceland past the North Cape of Norway to northern Russia since August 1941. U.S. destroyers as well as those of the British by now were accompanying the convoys. Germany deployed her only remaining battleship, *Tirpitz,* to Norway in January 1942 along with destroyers. Over the next four months the Germans would reinforce them with two pocket battleships, a heavy cruiser, and more destroyers.

Thus it was that a task force consisting of the new battleship *Washington,* carrier *Wasp,* two heavy cruisers, and a squadron of destroyers was sent across the Atlantic. With the coming of spring and passage of the midnight sun, the Germans began to extract a heavy toll on the convoys. Aided by air reconnaissance, their U-boats and destroyers became increasingly effective, as did aircraft operating out of nearby fields. The planes of USS *Wasp* were sorely needed, but her capabilities were so greatly superior to those of British carriers that she had been sent into the Mediterranean with a load of *Spitfire* fighters, which, after launching, flew to besieged Malta. *Wasp* returned to the British Isles and was carrying out another such mission at the time of the Coral Sea action. Then, the carrier was recalled to the United States and departed for the Pacific in a task force on June 6.

Meanwhile, high-performance Royal Air Force fighter planes had been taken on board British carriers assigned to the Home Fleet. Carrier elevators were too small to transport them to and from the hangar decks and the flight decks could accommodate very few. Not only were these planes ill-suited for carrier operations, but maintenance and repairs on the weather deck were difficult.

German search planes trailed the covering force. By the time the liquid-cooled engines had been warmed up and fighters launched, the enemy aircraft had withdrawn, later to reappear. No British strikes were conducted against airfields in Norway.

On July 4, 1942, the Admiralty injudiciously scattered Convoy PQ-17 and withdrew the screen and covering force with disastrous results. USS *Washington* was recalled to the United States and, after a brief time in the New York Navy Yard where a surface search radar was added to augment the air-search and fire-control ones already installed, she headed at high speed to the South Pacific.

Meanwhile, the Allied navies were having great difficulties in ensuring an adequate cargo flow to England, where forces were being built up for a return to the continent and the air force had shifted from raids against industrial targets to massive bombings of cities. Sinkings by U-boats were continuing at an ominous rate. Throughout 1942 they were to average almost 650,000 tons per month.

THE SOUTH PACIFIC

In the Pacific, threats increased against shipments to Australia, and preparations began for occupying the Santa Cruz Islands and an amphibious assault of Tulagi. When it was learned that Japan was constructing an airfield on Guadalcanal, the planned August 1942 operation expanded to include an amphibious assault of that island in addition to Tulagi.

The marines soon overran the airstrip, but more than six months of valiant fighting were required before the island was secured. In addition to the battles ashore, the outcome depended upon each side's ability to supply and reinforce its troops, despite naval and air opposition. A series of night actions was fought by surface ships, there were two engagements between carrier forces, and Japanese submarines damaged and sank U.S. warships, including the carrier *Wasp.* Operating in strategic areas, such as off the key naval base at Truk, U.S. submarines had their own successes.

Losses and damages to Pacific Fleet ships made the situation critical for the remainder of the year. Nevertheless, actions against Japanese vessels, including those by aircraft from the improved Guadalcanal airfield now in U.S. possession, made Japanese reinforcement and resupply efforts ever more difficult. The areas of the island controlled by Japanese troops were being steadily reduced, and in January 1943 Japan decided to withdraw the remnants.

Not only did the struggle for control of the sea in the Solomons and the attrition of Japanese warships pave the way for the subsequent advance up the island chain, but also it minimized Japanese naval opposition to MacArthur's New Guinea campaign.

In November 1942 a large U.S. Navy task force, which included naval transports and cargo ships of the Atlantic Fleet Amphibious Force, made its way safely across the Atlantic to conduct assault landings of army troops at three locations on the coast of Morocco while providing naval gunfire and carrier air support. At the same time the Royal Navy delivered British and U.S. troops from England to the Mediterranean and carried out successful amphibious landings at two Algerian locations.

Thus, as the year ended, some progress by the United States and its allies was evident, but the outcome of the world war would still depend upon the two-ocean war, which continued in grave doubt.

19

Turning the Tide

As the United States entered its second year of war the fleet was expanding ever more rapidly and becoming far better balanced to meet the challenges both in the Atlantic and the vast Pacific. Capabilities were greatly enhanced by new systems made possible by intensive and imaginative research and development, by adopting measures and countermeasures in anticipation and response to dynamically changing demands, and by adjustments in both strategy and tactics.

Much credit is due the Navy Department's bilinear organization, which was extraordinarily efficient in providing and maintaining the fleet. One significant change was that Admiral King now headed "the combined offices"[1] of commander in chief, United States Fleet (COMINCH) and chief of naval operations (CNO). After becoming COMINCH, King had sought clarification of his relationship with the CNO, who had statutory responsibility for fleet operations. These uncertainties were resolved when President Roosevelt appointed King as Admiral Harold R. Stark's successor in March 1942. The executive order directed that "Duties as Chief of Naval Operations shall be contributory to the discharge of the paramount duties of Commander in Chief, United States Fleet." King was to be "principal Naval Advisor to the President on the conduct of the war and the principal Naval Advisor and Executive to the Secretary of the Navy on the conduct of the Naval Establishment." As CNO he was "charged . . . with the preparation, readiness, and logistic support of the operating forces . . . and with the coordination and direction . . . to this end of the bureaus and offices of the Navy Department except such offices (other than bureaus) as the Secretary of the Navy may specifically exempt."[2]

By this order the president had added the final touches to the system that proved so successful throughout World War II. He had made it clear that the overriding goal of the department was the readiness of the operating forces. An ideally-qualified officer commanded these forces and was responsible for their performance. For the first time the chief of naval operations was assigned authority fully adequate for and appropriate to his responsibilities. The efficiency of the bureau system had been preserved. Admiral King and his assistants did not have to devote major attention and effort to departmental management and administrative details since the bureau chiefs were directly responsible to the secretary of the navy for such matters. Regrettably, these sound relationships would be eroded in the post-war years.

Not only were the bureaus highly responsive to COMINCH and OPNAV (Office of the Chief of Naval Operations), but needs were often anticipated through close contact with operating forces and continuing exchange of information and ideas. The system proved well-suited to provide rapid transition from concept to development, production, installation, maintenance, and improvement. The material bureaus and their laboratories were also greatly strengthened by adding highly-qualified engineers and scientists, in and out of uniform. Another important factor in the development of naval capabilities was contributions of the scientific and engineering talent of universities. A proposal in June 1940—the month that marked the fall of France—had been promptly approved by the president, and the National Defense Research Committee was formed. Meanwhile, the National Advisory Committee for Aeronautics continued to fulfill its responsibilities for "scientific study of the problems of flight."[3] Academic talent was extensively mobilized by the Office of Scientific Research and Development, which had its beginning a few days after Germany invaded the Soviet Union. Its sections collaborated closely with the armed services in many projects. These organizations thus complemented the bureaus' progress, facilities, and contractors.

ANTISUBMARINE WARFARE

As of 1943 no area more urgently needed major advances in combat capabilities than antisubmarine warfare. In the desperate Atlantic war, the ideal objective was still containment or defeat of the enemy fleet, in this case the fleet of U-boats, which could make their way to French ports via the North and Norwegian Seas. With Germany in control of Norway, the route could not be blocked by laying mine barrages such as the one nearing completion at the end of World War I. Moreover, protection against air attacks at French coastal bases was being provided by thick reinforced concrete structures over submarine pens. It was thus necessary to fight an offensive and defensive war of attrition against U-boats in transit, on patrol stations, during efforts to attack ships, and when replenishing munitions, fuel, and supplies at sea.

The problems of detection, localization, and destruction demanded a variety of means, their close orchestration, and their effective employment even under the adverse and taxing conditions so often encountered in the North Atlantic. Destroyers provided both antisubmarine and anti-air protection for naval task groups. They escorted convoys, but this duty increasingly was taken over by ASW escort types as the war went on because of the high demands on versatile, multipurpose modern destroyers for many other kinds of operations in both oceans.

Flying boats and land-based aircraft fitted and armed for antisubmarine tasks conducted patrols such as over the Bay of Biscay, at focal shipping points, and ahead of convoys. They conducted attacks against detected U-boats, sometimes alone and at other times in coordination with ASW warships.

A key step was increasing the number of U.S. escort carriers. Not only did they add the capabilities of their planes to the abilities of surface escorts, but they conducted operations in areas of the North Atlantic that were beyond the effective ranges of flying boats and land-based ASW aircraft. Hunter-killer task groups of fast, light carriers and destroyers had notable successes, especially against replenishment concentrations of U-boats.

Minefields and underwater detection systems were employed, such as at the approaches to harbors. Small antisubmarine vessels patrolled coastal waters.

After a decline of Allied vessel sinkings by Axis submarines in the first two months of 1943, losses of merchantmen rose sharply. More effective control of antisubmarine forces and shipping was required.

Faced with this critical situation, Admiral King recognized the need for an overall U.S. Navy command responsible solely for the campaign against the U-boats. The establishment of such a command, along with other U.S. and British actions, marked the turning point of the war at sea in the Atlantic. King considered forming the new command under the commander in chief, U.S. Atlantic Fleet. However, important reasons for placing it at the highest level, which later proved valid, resulted in his organizing what was known as the "Tenth Fleet"[4] at his Washington headquarters.

One reason was that the vital importance, urgency, and complexity of the antisubmarine effort demanded avoiding interference, staff layering, and unnecessary unified levels of coordination and direction. Another key consideration was the need to combine and direct the oceanwide operations of all antisubmarine forces on and below the surface and in the air.

This objective was complicated by the army air force's Antisubmarine Command, which preferred to conduct its own operations without control by another service. Only after heated debate was a decision reached in July 1943 to transfer ASW-equipped *Liberators* to the navy. A third factor was the necessity to make prompt and appropriate use of information from various sources on U-boat locations and movements, sources that included intelligence, contact reports, and bearings from naval shore-based radio direction finders. Particularly sensitive was the fact that enemy messages using the sophisticated German coding device were sometimes decrypted in time for tactical use. Knowledge of this had to be restricted to an absolute minimum, and extracted information had to be used in a manner that would not arouse German suspicions. Aided by operational analyses, the combined information from the various sources helped to direct convoys, redistribute forces, locate air and surface patrols, and employ hunter-killer task groups. And, as previously noted, it was not until the spring of 1943 that a more secure encoding system was adopted for messages to Allied convoys.

Along with fitting out escort carriers to augment convoy protection and mass construction of destroyer escorts, such measures and advances in sensors, weapons, and tactics reduced sinkings by U-boats to a more tolerable level within a few months.

One of the advanced weapons was a depth charge developed by the Bureau of Ordnance. Hydrodynamically shaped for rapid descent, it was loaded with a new explosive that produced a pressure pulse maximizing hull damage. Specially designed depth bombs enhanced the effectiveness of aircraft attacks.

Destroyers and destroyer escorts were armed with a British developed system, the hedgehog, that projected ahead a pattern of contact fuzed weapons. A rocket-propelled U.S. system was installed on smaller ASW vessels.

Airborne rockets with warheads designed to penetrate hulls were introduced. The United States developed an antisubmarine home-torpedo for use by both aircraft and warships. Aircraft sonobuoys and an aircraft magnetic detector were developed.

Sonars were improved and, together with intense training of operators, they resulted in major advances in the detection and classification of echoes. Germany soon compounded the problems by introducing a decoy device that released clouds of small bubbles into the water.

Thus the dynamic contest of measure and countermeasure continued. When the Germans introduced an acoustic torpedo that homed in on the pitch of escort propellers, a U.S. countermeasure device was promptly provided. When high frequencies were introduced for U-boat communications, the United States constructed special shore-based direction finder nets to locate the sources of transmission. U-boats were equipped late in the war with "snorkles"[5] whereby batteries could be recharged without surfacing. Detection capabilities had by then benefited from microwave radars installed on ASW ships and aircraft. The Germans equipped submarines with radar detectors and radar decoys to be released, as the never-ending contest continued.

AIR DEFENSE

As for countering the air threat, no advance was of greater importance than the electromagnetic proximity (VT) fuze secretly developed for antiaircraft projectiles of the navy's 5"/38 guns. As the United States entered its second year of war, the first production line fuzes were flown out to the South Pacific by Commander W. S. Parsons. He was accompanied by other scientists associated with the project, who went on board the ships to witness the fuzes' performance in action. Soon mass production was delivering vast quantities to the Pacific Fleet and improvements were being made.

The close-in air defenses (such as against dive bombers) of individual warships, amphibious vessels, and auxiliaries were greatly improved by installing many 20-mm machine guns that soon would be equipped with the newly developed gyroscopic lead-computing Mark 14 sight. Many ships' antiaircraft capabilities had the benefit of 40 mms, in single, double, and quadruple mounts. The latter were provided with automatic drives and directors for which another version of lead-computing sight was developed. A radar was added later.

Heavy antiaircraft gunnery became ever more effective by installing improved fire control radars on ships with 5"/38 batteries. Advances in carrier fighter plane performance, their weapon systems, ship air search radars, and aircraft radars improved interception capabilities. Not only were more carriers joining the fleet, but also higher-performance aircraft were enhancing effectiveness against enemy carriers and the ability to neutralize airfields.

THE PACIFIC CAMPAIGNS

Despite the top priority accorded to the war against Germany, the resolute Admiral King was permitted to deploy more adequate numbers of warships and amphibious vessels to the Pacific. By the spring of 1943 the Pacific Fleet was gaining sufficient strength to expand the sea areas under its control.

Strategic planning now called for three campaigns in the war against Japan. Understandably, the first of these was for forces in the North Pacific to eject the Japanese from the Aleutians. The islands that had been captured there were not only the closest to the United States but also lay along the great circle route from Japan. Another of the campaigns was for the South Pacific and Southwest Pacific forces to cooperate in a drive on Rabaul. The latter were then to advance up the north coast of New Guinea. The third campaign—the main offensive—was to be an advance westward from Hawaii by Central Pacific forces. The Southwest Pacific area forces were under the command of General MacArthur. The other three areas were parts of the Pacific Ocean areas command of Admiral Nimitz.

A key to the success of the Aleutian campaign was severing the flow of Japanese supplies to the occupied islands. An early success had been the sinking of a resupply merchant ship by a submarine in October 1942. U.S. troops and construction forces were landed on Adak where an airstrip was prepared. Although grounded much of the time by adverse weather, including hurricane-force winds, army air force planes succeeded from time to time in sinking or damaging Japanese freighters achored at Kiska and Attu. After bombarding Kiska in February 1943, the cruiser-destroyer task force assigned to the North Pacific sent a Japanese ammunition ship to the bottom and caused two transports to retire. The Japanese did succeed in delivering supplies to Attu in a convoy escorted by their navy's North Area Force early in March. Later that month another was forced to retire as a result of the indecisive naval Battle of Kormandorskis.

A planned amphibious assault of Kiska was bypassed in favor of Attu, which was not only nearer to Japan but also less heavily defended. An army division that was landed on May 11 had the island under control by the end of the month. When troops were landed after preparatory naval gunfire on Kiska in August, it was found that cruisers and destroyers had withdrawn the defenders under the cover of fog. The Aleutian campaign was now over.

Some 4,000 miles to the south, the South Pacific forces of Admiral Halsey were advancing their areas of control to the northwest up the chain of islands toward Rabaul. This campaign was highlighted by naval actions between cruisers and destroyers of Halsey's Third Fleet and comparable forces of the Japanese Navy. Landings of army forces in the middle of the Solomons led to the capture of the Japanese airfield at Munda on New Georgia Island in August and then the construction of a U.S. airstrip on Vella Lavella.

Rather than conducting a costly operation to capture heavily defended Rabaul, Admiral King recommended that it be neutralized and bypassed. His proposal was approved by the combined chiefs in August.

To that end, forces would capture a portion of Bougainville Island where airfields could be established only about 200 miles from the naval base and airfields at Rabaul. To help support the operation, Admiral Nimitz formed a task group consisting of an attack carrier (CV), a light carrier (CVL), and other ships from the Central Pacific's Third Fleet and placed it under Halsey's command.

A landing force consisting of a marine division, an army division, and a New Zealand brigade group was put ashore at Empress Augusta Bay by the Third Amphibious Force on November 1, 1943. When a Japanese cruiser-destroyer force from Rabaul arrived that night, it was soundly defeated by Rear Admiral S. Merrill's Task Force 39.

Vice Admiral Takeo Kurita was sent down from Truk with a stronger force and 173 carrier planes were flown into Rabaul airfields. But Admiral Halsey's carrier group conducted dive bombing and torpedo attacks that so damaged the recently arrived warships that they could not fulfill their mission. Augmented by two CVs and a CVL of another group from Pearl Harbor, the Third Fleet's strike force carried out a second attack. Kurita had by then departed but a few ships were still there. A cruiser lost her stern, a destroyer was sunk, and another badly damaged. There were hits also on transports and cargo vessels. One of the Japanese carrier groups was located, resulting in the destruction of 35 of its planes. Their tasks accomplished, both U.S. carrier groups were soon on their way back to the Central Pacific.

Forces assigned to the Southwest Pacific were designated the Seventh Fleet. MacArthur began his New Guinea offensive on June 30 to coincide with the South Pacific operation to capture Munda airfield. The Seventh Amphibious Force landed troops on two islands in the Solomon Sea and transported others on four successive nights by PT boats and landing craft from Buna, which had been under Allied control since February, to Nassau Bay only 17 miles east of Salamua. That Japanese-held position was bypassed, as the amphibious force landed 8,000 Australian troops near Lae on the night of September 3–4. The seizure of an airstrip by U.S. paratroopers permitted other Australians to be brought in by air.

Seventh Fleet destroyers played an important role in the capture of Lae. In September its amphibious force transported a brigade around the tip of the Huon Peninsula, across the Vitiaz Strait from New Britain. They were landed before dawn on the other side of Finschhafen, which was occupied on October 2.

The South Pacific objective now achieved, the offensive drive across the Central Pacific began. The first of a series of amphibious operations was to re-capture the Gilbert Islands, which had been invaded early in the war. The Japanese had established a seaplane base at Makin Atoll and built an airfield on Tarawa. Their defenses had been greatly strengthened, particularly at Tarawa, following a diversionary commando raid by marines landed from the large sub-marines *Nautilus* and *Argonaut* in August 1942.

As covering forces for the assaults that began on November 20, 1943, the powerful Fifth Fleet had two fast carrier task groups from Pearl Harbor in addi-tion to the two returning after the Rabaul raids, augmented by five fast battle-ships that were transferred from the Third Fleet. These groups were deployed north of the Gilberts where they intercepted Japanese planes heading down from the Marshalls. Added to their screens were fast battleships whose powerful anti-aircraft armaments included ten 5"/38 twin mounts and 16 40-mm quadruple mounts, all radar controlled, and numerous 20 mms. The effectiveness of these batteries was vividly demonstrated in the destruction of Betty torpedo planes skimming the water while attempting night attacks. Thereafter, the demands for employing battleships for antiaircraft protection of fast carriers was so great that their full potential for other missions was not exploited, a prime example being the Leyte operation.

The landing of an army regimental combat team at lightly defended Makin posed few problems. It was far different at Betio Island, Tarawa where the air-field had been constructed. The defenses there were truly formidable and well designed to resist bombing, naval gunfire, and amphibious assault. Furthermore, the reef inside the atoll over which the assault waves proceeded proved to be so shallow that landing craft grounded far from the beach.

The desperate marines fought with extreme valor. After suffering many casualties, they finally succeeded in capturing the island on the third day. Later operations would benefit from the costly lessons learned there.

On their way back to Halsey's Third Fleet, the fast battleships bombarded Nauru.

While carrying out support operations for many actions of the Pacific Fleet, submarines had the strategic mission of cutting off the Japanese flow of oil and other supplies upon which that nation vitally depended. Even a partial cut off would weaken its ability to wage war and could conceivably be decisive. Impos-ing a conventional close blockade was manifestly impossible until the war's final stages. But by the end of 1943 Japan's stocks of petroleum and a number of other strategic materials had been reduced by more than 50 percent.

THE MEDITERRANEAN

In the war against the Axis powers, the Allies had achieved victory in North Africa by the spring of 1943. The amphibious assault at Sicily in July, which included airborne landings, was soon followed by the far more costly operations to establish beachheads on the Italian coast. The situation ashore for a time was desperate. Continuing air and naval gunfire support and the delivery of crucial supplies by sea were essential to the success of the bitter fighting ashore. Defense of ships off the coast was complicated by determined German air attacks, including the use of guided bombs. The Italians surrendered that September, but more fighting against German forces on the peninsula was still required.

Support of the war in that theater and the buildup for a campaign in northern Europe now was benefitting from the progress in the Battle of the Atlantic. For example, the monthly average tonnage sunk during the last five months of 1943 was but a half of that lost during the preceding seven months.

20

World War II:
The Final Phases

Still further success was being achieved in the Battle of the Atlantic during the third year since Pearl Harbor. The sinkings by U-boats in terms of average monthly tonnages for 1944 were down yet another 50 percent from those in the latter part of 1943. Cross-ocean deliveries to support the Allied war efforts were further increased by the mass production of cargo vessels in the United States.

In June 1944, supported by air strikes and naval gunfire, the massive combined British-U.S. amphibious operations across the British Channel and onto French beaches commenced with landings in southern France in August.

By now the Germans had resumed the Battle of Britain, this time employing guided missiles—the winged, jet-propelled V-1. One of the measures that helped blunt the damaging attacks by this new weapon was to provide U.S. proximity fuzes and advanced fire control for Britain's antiaircraft batteries. Then, late in the war, Germany introduced the ballistic V-2 missile.

Meanwhile, their country was suffering more and more from the cumulative effects of its inability to receive materials from abroad. With the attrition of its fighter planes, German strength and morale were being further weakened by the mass bombing by British and U.S. aircraft. The Soviet Army was advancing, and on the western front the Allies crossed the Rhine in March 1945.

German armies began surrendering on May 4. The unconditional surrender was signed three days later and in Berlin the following day. The European war was over.

THE CENTRAL PACIFIC

On the other side of the globe, the recapture of the Gilbert Islands, located on the western side of the date line, had set the stage for the Central Pacific forces to advance across the Pacific Ocean. In January 1944 Admiral Nimitz decided to occupy undefended Majuro Atoll in the western Marshalls chain and then, bypassing Japanese bases, move against Kwajalein, some 2,500 miles west of Pearl Harbor. The Marshall Islands operations were conducted, as was the Gilbert operation, by the Fifth Fleet under the command of Vice Admiral R. A. Spruance.

Kwajalein, the world's largest atoll, was captured the first week in February. The assault of Eniwetok soon followed, as carrier aircraft struck powerful Truk and Ponape, exacting a heavy toll of enemy aircraft and ships. At its army's insistence, Japan diverted some of its best submarines to resupply forces on the isolated islands bypassed by U.S. forces. This significantly reduced the contributions of its submarines to the war at sea.

The advance across the broad Pacific demonstrated the extreme importance of the capabilities for refueling at sea developed by the U.S. Navy. The contribution of underway replenishment would become ever greater as the scene of action moved west and the size and tempo of operations increased. As the war went on, improvements in equipment, rigs, and techniques greatly increased transfer rates of black oil, aviation gasoline, and diesel oil. Multiproduct fuelings to ships steaming on both sides of a fleet oiler were becoming common.

Other types of auxiliary ships, including vessels carrying provisions and other supplies, were being equipped with transfer rigs, while a special development program provided ammunition ships with underway replenishment capabilities. In later stages of the war entire task groups would rendezvous with underway replenishment groups in forward areas. This allowed maximizing the effective number of combatant ships in a high state of readiness at the scene of action.

Sustained combat operations in areas thousands of miles away from the nearest naval base in Hawaii were made possible not only by service squadron replenishments but also by another type of service squadron composed of a variety of logistics ships and craft, such as floating drydocks, repair ships, supply ships, and many other specialized types. Deployed and redeployed as the war progressed, these squadrons, with compositions determined by the tasks at hand, provided floating bases at forward anchorages.

The capture of the Marianas, over 1,000 miles further west, began with carrier aircraft strikes followed by the amphibious assault of Tinian in June 1944. The Japanese fleet attempted to intervene and suffered heavy losses of experienced pilots, most of whom were shot down by U.S. carrier fighter planes in the Battle of the Philippine Sea. U.S. carrier aircraft and submarines sank three carriers. Meanwhile, the Japanese Navy was being further weakened by the increasing numbers of other types of warships being sunk or damaged by submarine attacks.

By the end of July Saipan, Tinian, and Guam had been captured. The army air forces now had fields from which heavy bombers could attack Japan's home islands. Retaking Guam provided a support base for fleet operations, and Admiral Nimitz moved there with key members of his staff. Advances across the Central Pacific and up from the Southwest Pacific continued.

What was known as the Fifth Fleet had alternating commanders, Spruance and Halsey. While one was at sea, the other and his staff were in Pearl Harbor planning subsequent operations. When Halsey commanded, the forces were designated the Third Fleet.

According to the JCS plan, the next major objective was Leyte, to be followed by securing Manila or landings on Formosa and at Amoy, China. During the first phase Central Pacific forces were to capture Ulithi Atoll, Yap, and the Palau Islands southwest of Guam and only 300 miles from Mindanao. The Southwest Pacific command was to capture Morotai, south of Mindanao, and then occupy an island further north in October, land on Mindanao a month later, and conduct an amphibious assault at Leyte in December.

The plan was changed, intermediate steps to Leyte were canceled, and the schedule was advanced as a result of a Third Fleet operation in which Halsey headed west from Eniwetok with his fast carrier force for diversionary strikes including some against the Philippines. When strikes at Mindanao received no opposition, he went north to the Visayas where Leyte is located. Sorties on two days eliminated about 200 Japanese planes, sank many ships, and inflicted destruction on installations in the area.

The amphibious assault at the Palaus, where heavy opposition was overcome by the marines, and the landing on Morotai were carried out as scheduled. Orders were issued to seize Ulithi promptly to serve as an advance fleet base.

The flexibility of naval operations was again demonstrated. The Yap Attack Force, together with its landing force, all shipping employed in the Palaus operation after unloading, and the fire support warships and escort carriers of that assault were assigned to the Seventh Fleet.

The amphibious operation at Leyte was preceded by air strikes by the fast carrier force of the Third Fleet against the Ryukus and the Formosan airfields. The latter lasted three days, during which some U.S. ships were damaged by Japanese air attacks. Assault landings by the two amphibious forces attached to the Seventh Fleet began on October 20, 1944.

The naval battles associated with the Allied return to the Philippines deserve some mention. Japan set in motion a plan to attack naval forces in Leyte Gulf by surface warships in a pincer-type operation from the South China Sea with one strike force coming through Surigao Strait, the other via San Bernadino Strait. During the approach of the latter, more powerful force it was detected on October 23 by a pair of well-placed U.S. submarines. One heavy cruiser was so badly damaged by torpedoes that she had to retire under destroyer escort. Two others were sunk, one being the flagship of Admiral Kurito, who transferred to super battleship *Yamato.* Both forces were detected the next day by air searches. Planes from carriers of the Third Fleet, which was commanded by Admiral Halsey, hit four battleships and inflicted such damage on a heavy cruiser that it was forced to retire. The second of the super battleships, *Musashi,* was sunk after being hit by many torpedoes and bombs.

The ships of the Third Fleet (nine large carriers, seven light carriers, six new battleships, cruisers and destroyers) were operating as Task Force 38, which comprised four carrier groups. On the afternoon of October 24 Halsey issued a battle plan that stated four battleships, three heavy cruisers, three light cruisers, and 14 destroyers "WILL BE FORMED AS TF [Task Force] 34."[1] Admiral Kinkaid, who was Seventh Fleet commander and commanded the amphibious force at Leyte, was not an addressee since he was part of General MacArthur's command and General MacArthur did not allow direct communications between the two fleets. However, the message was intercepted by his command; Admiral Thomas C. Kinkaid, who was Seventh Fleet commander and commanded the amphibious force at Leyte, was not an addressee since he was part of General MacArthur's command and General MacArthur did not allow direct communications between the two fleets. However, the message was intercepted by his command; Admiral Kinkaid read the message and concluded that this surface force would cover the San Bernardino Strait.

There was yet another naval force in the *Sho-Go* plan of the Japanese—the mobile force. It had a heavy carrier, three light carriers, and two battleships with flight decks aft, while six carriers including four large new ones remained in Japan. The force was successful in carrying out its mission, which was to lure Halsey's force away from the scene of action.

Having located the mobile force, Halsey ordered three task groups north and the fourth to join them at high speed. The message to commander, Seventh Fleet—"Am proceeding north with three groups to attack enemy carrier force at dawn"[2]—reinforced Kinkaid's belief that the strait north of Samar was covered. In any case, Kurita's presence was not revealed until, nearing Leyte Gulf, he opened fire shortly before 0700 hours on the 25th on the slow, small carriers (CVEs) of one of the three escort carrier groups of the Seventh Fleet. The Japanese force should have reached its objective—the transports off Leyte—but instead the battle was fought against the escort carrier groups. The battleships, cruisers, and destroyers failed to carry out their mission for several reasons, including a belief that one of Halsey's task groups was engaged in the morning haze, the attacks of CVE planes, and the heroic and professional performance of destroyers and destroyer escorts from the carrier group screens, which continued their attacks even after expending all their torpedoes. In any case, Kurita decided later that morning to retire.

Not only had the *Sho-Go* operation failed to achieve its objective, but, together with the sinking of the four carriers of the decoy force that day by Task Force 38, the Japanese Navy's losses were such that it fought no more fleet actions.

To provide a location for airfields to support operations against Luzon, landings on Mindoro began on December 15.

By this time the Japanese had introduced guided missiles in the form of airplanes loaded with explosives employing sight as a sensor, the brain as a computer, and servo systems comprised of nerves and muscles for guidance to impact on a ship—the suicide Kamikazes. The United States was to introduce another form of guided antiship weapon toward the end of the war, the Bat, a radar-homing glider bomb.

The sinkings and damaging of ships during the advance operations and the amphibious landings at Ligayen, Luzon in January 1945 proved the extreme seriousness of the Kamikaze threat. The assault, however, was successful. Many more operations involving Admiral Kinkaid's Seventh Fleet forces were required over the next several months before the Philippines were retaken.

Meanwhile, a carrier task force sortie into the South China Sea added to the heavy toll on Japanese shipping being extracted by U.S. submarines.

Late in January the Third Fleet became once again the Fifth Fleet as Spruance, who had been at Pearl Harbor planning forthcoming operations, took over command from Halsey.

The next objective of the Central Pacific command was the capture of heavily-defended Iwo Jima. Only 660 miles from Tokyo, the island was to provide the army air force with a base for medium bombers and fighters. The preliminary operations included an air strike against targets in the Tokyo area on February 16 by Task Force 58, now comprising 13 large carriers and five light carriers plus fast battleships, cruisers, and destroyers. Iwo Jima was taken after a bloody assault beginning on the 19th followed by valiant actions ashore by the marines.

Admiral Nimitz had also been assigned the objective of capturing the Ryukyus to provide airfields for tactical aircraft and a location for advanced bases during military operations against Japan. Admiral Spruance issued his operation plan in January 1945.

Very little opposition was encountered in gaining control of the islands of Kerama Retto, the sheltered anchorages of which were desired for replenishment of ammunition and fuel to the many navy ships and craft that would be operating in nearby waters.

The major amphibious landing on Okinawa on April 1 went smoothly but the U.S. ground forces found operations ashore extraordinarily difficult. The time it took to eliminate numerous well dug-in Japanese troops required the continuing presence of the large gunfire and covering force, the support carrier group, and amphibious and logistics ships. In addition, the fast carrier force remained in the vicinity for three months opposing the Japanese air effort, providing fighter cover over the island, and providing additional close air support. Further south, a British force, including four carriers with planes provided by the United States, neutralized airfields on islands between Formosa and Okinawa except for periods of refueling, when a U.S. group of escort carriers fulfilled the mission.

Japanese air attacks, mainly by suicide planes, sank 15 naval vessels during the Okinawa campaign. As the Kamikaze hits were above the waterline, none of the warships sunk was larger than a destroyer. One destroyer, *Laffey*, suffered severe damage and heavy casualties when hit by five suicide planes and four bombs, yet it somehow survived. All in all, more than 200 ships, including merchantmen, were damaged by Kamikazes—some beyond repair. Hits on carriers resulted in the loss of many aircraft and lives. To cope with this ominous threat, new defensive tactics were devised, including the use of radar picket destroyers to detect low-flying attackers and to guide interceptions by carrier fighters.

Meanwhile, MacArthur's command began operations to gain control of Borneo, where the Seventh Fleet conducted preparatory bombings and landed an Australian force on May 1, 1945. Other landings were planned for June 10 and July 1.

SUBMARINE WARFARE

Throughout this period Pacific Fleet submarines were taking an ever-increasing toll on Japanese shipping. In June the undersea campaign was finally extended into the Japan Sea to sever the flow of strategic materials from Korea. The noose was being tightened. With the help of the army air force, influence mines were planted in Japanese waters.

All in all, almost 9 million tons of Nippon's merchantmen were sunk during the war. The majority were sent to the bottom by submarines. Carrier aircraft accounted for 16 percent, mines 9 percent. Others were lost to naval gunfire and to land-based navy, marine, and army planes.

Confronted by U.S. control of the sea, a total blockade, and the build-up of forces for an amphibious invasion, the Japanese faced a hopeless situation. In June their government decided to seek peace through the offices of the Soviet Union. The United States learned of the move by breaking coded diplomatic messages. The Soviets had agreed to enter the war and wished to share in the spoils. So, without informing the Allies, they temporized.

THE ATOMIC BOMB

In 1939 physicists had started to discuss the possibilities of obtaining vast releases of energy of a gradual or explosive nature through chain reaction fission of uranium atoms. Problems, including the extraction of usable quantities of sufficiently enriched fissionable material, were so imposing that the practicality was long in doubt. Nevertheless, publication of U.S. professional papers on this subject was brought under control the next year.

Theoretical and experimental efforts expanded and the highly secret Manhattan Project began in June 1942. There was still no certainty that the objective could be achieved, and, even if it could, the accomplishment would undoubtably take a very long time. Nevertheless, methods for manufacturing significant quantities of fissionable materials were devised, plants were built, and fission bombs were developed in a remarkably short time. A warhead was tested on July 16, 1945 at Alamogordo, New Mexico. It worked.

Ten days later, at the Potsdam Conference, the United States, Great Britain, and China issued a surprise declaration calling for the "unconditional surrender of all Japanese armed forces." If such action was not taken immediately the consequences would be "prompt and utter destruction."[3]

This time when W. S. Parsons, now a captain, went west he was accompanied by fissionable material. As weaponeer, he completed the assembly of the atomic bomb and during the flight loaded the gun-type bomb (Little Boy) that fired fissionable material into the main bomb causing its detonation. On August 6 the air force B-29 took off from Tinian and dropped the uranium bomb on Hiroshima. Two days later the Soviet Union declared war on Japan and invaded Manchuria. On August 9 another B-29, piloted by an air force officer but commanded by Commander F. L. Ashworth, a naval aviator, dropped a plutonium implosion bomb on Nagasaki. Japan began its negotiations with the United States the next day. Under the peace agreement reached on August 14, the imperial system of Japan continued, initially subject to the authority of a supreme allied commander. The terms of surrender were signed on board USS *Missouri* on September 2, 1945.

As demonstrated by World War II, warfare at sea had become vastly more complex. But its main roles, the importance of those roles, and the determinants of effectiveness were basically the same as in prior conflicts. The outcome of the war against the Axis powers, as in World War I, had hinged on progress in the Battle of the Atlantic. The war on the other side of the globe against Japan had been primarily a naval war.

The advent of nuclear weapons of mass destruction led many to assume, however, that the nature of warfare was radically changed. The need for traditional naval power would be questioned. A campaign would be mounted to revise radically the organization for national defense and the command relationships that had proven to be effective and efficient in the immense global war just completed. This would lead in time to an additional layer of control and a vast bureaucratic overhead structure imposed over the military departments, tendencies to disregard fundamental differences between naval power and other forms of military power, diffusion of responsibility, reductions in the command authority of the chief of naval operations, and less flexible direction of naval operating forces.

Part V

The Nuclear Age

The Cold War

World War II was hardly over before the nation's need for naval power was being deprecated and even ridiculed. Moreover, a move was underway to take actions contrary to lessons of history, such as had been pointed out by Mahan, in which countries had suffered from directing naval affairs and employing naval forces as if their primary purpose was to contribute to land warfare. The proposal was to do away with the Navy Department; to assign authority over all armed services to a single military commander and his staff; to transfer responsibilities for naval aviation to an air force, as had been done with such adverse effects in Britain and Italy; and to make the navy dependent upon support and services provided by a separate logistics organization.

Less than a year after the attack on Pearl Harbor, General George C. Marshall, chief of staff of the army, had recommended to the Joint Chiefs of Staff that a plan be prepared for shifting to a single military department after the war. Meanwhile, he formed a special planning division within the War Department and charged it with the task of formulating plans for the size, composition, and organization of the entire postwar military establishment.

Shortly thereafter the divison came up with a plan advocating, not surprisingly, one military department with an organization similar to that adopted by the War Department soon after entry into World War II, when three commands (army ground forces, army air forces, and a service of supply) were formed under the general staff. The main difference was that there would be four instead of three commands: "Ground Forces," into which the marines would be merged with the army; "Air Forces," including naval aviation; "Sea Forces"; and a "General Supply Department," later described as a "Common Supply and Service Force."[1]

A plan along these lines was unveiled by the army during the spring 1944 hearings of the Congressional Select Committee on Postwar Policy and laid groundwork for an intense prosecution of a campaign for such a reorganization following the war.

When peace finally came, the power of the secretly developed atomic bomb had been revealed and was being billed as "the Absolute Weapon."[2] The United States now possessed a device capable of inflicting vast damage and mass casualties by a release of energy in the form of blast, heat, and radiation that, even in the initial versions, was four orders of magnitude (that is, about 10,000 times) greater than that attained by chemical explosives. Obviously, these new weapons had the potential to decide a war by themselves. It was little wonder that the implications of this awesome means of destruction occupied much attention on the part of policymakers, scholars, military strategists, and self-appointed experts. The continuing relevance of lessons of the past came under widespread questioning, at least concerning the composition of military forces and the nature of future wars.

Some of those attempting to forecast the future consequences believed that atomic bombs would soon make conventional weapons obsolete, that the relative importance of armies and navies was drastically reduced, that principles of warfare had been nullified or radically changed, that the very nature of war was altered completely, and that prior concepts would have to be revised. Views were influenced to some extent by all-out actions in the war just concluded. One feature had been the resort on both sides to mass destruction, including bombing cities and other acts contrary to previously recognized international rules of warfare. Views being expressed were in contrast to earlier concepts advanced by Mahan when he wrote, "War now is never waged for the sake of mere fighting, simply to see who is the better at killing people. The warfare of civilized nations is for the purpose of accomplishing an object, obtaining a concession of alleged right from an enemy who has proven implacable to argument."[3] In any case, the possibilities of U.S. involvement in limited wars were largely ignored.

While giving some recognition to the continuing value of submarines, some commentators went to the extreme of contending that it was ridiculous to assume that there would be fighting on the oceans in the future. A few questioned the need for any kind of a navy.

THE SOVIET UNION

A tendency to assume that conflicting interests would be resolved by the United Nations was wishful thinking, at least insofar as the Soviet Bloc was concerned. The concept of a United Nations organization had been expressed in an Inter-Allied Declaration in June 1941. It envisioned that "free peoples" working in peace as in war should have a good chance of achieving an "enduring peace."[4] The statement was issued ten days before the Soviet Union, upon invasion by the German Army, had joined the Allies. The charter of October 1945 included compromises. Among the original 51 members were a number of countries whose peoples could hardly be classified as free.

Instabilities on the international scene had been exploited to advance goals of the communist movement since a Marxist regime became firmly established in Russia. Formed in the aftermath of World War II, the Third International (Comintern) embraced the cause of world revolution, espoused the ideal of a socialist world order, and extended activities to colonies and semicolonial countries.

Hitler's actions in 1939 and the signing of the German-Soviet Union non-aggression treaty set the stage for the Soviet Union's war against Finland, a portion of which was annexed, and for the seizure of Lithuania, Latvia, and Estonia.

When the end of the European war was in sight in February 1945, Josef Stalin installed a Marxist government in Romania. Communists seized power in Poland. After the Allies became victorious, the Soviet Army was stationed in other Eastern European countries and occupied much of Germany. The departure of troops from northern Iran was delayed. Soviet diplomatic efforts to establish a base in the Turkish Straits were accompanied by the threat of Soviet forces in Bulgaria, where a communist government was installed.

In China there were two armies—that of the Nationalist government, which had suffered heavy losses, and that of the communists, which held portions of the north. Prior to its last-minute entry into the war against Japan, the Soviet Union gained concessions from the Chinese that set the stage for a communist takeover in Outer Mongolia.

When the Soviets declared war against Japan, their army invaded Manchuria. Arms and ammunition captured there were transferred to the forces of Mao Tse-tung. The two Chinese factions were soon fighting one another. As soon as Japan announced its willingness to accept the terms of surrender, the Vietnamese Communist party set in motion its "August Uprising."[5] Viet Minh armed forces gained some control over the capitals of Tonkin, Annam, and Cochin China by the time the peace treaty was signed. Their revolutionary government was announced as established over all of Vietnam, which throughout history had always been a divided land. The Soviet Army entered northern portions of Korea.

DEMOBILIZATION

The days of employing a navy to influence events in critical areas of the globe were far from over. Nevertheless, a precipitous demobilization began as soon as victory was achieved, and the U.S. Navy had tremendous difficulty in fulfilling its commitments. It was fortunate that, although President Harry Truman abolished the position of commander in chief, United States Fleet, the latter's responsibilities were transferred, along with the staff, to the chief of naval operations. Command over the operating forces thus continued to be exercised by the senior officer of the navy. He still had authority over the bureaus and offices of the Navy Department to fulfill the requirements of those forces.

There could be no certainty as to the extent to which Japanese forces on the Asian mainland would comply with the terms of surrender. To deter adverse actions, the Seventh Fleet was employed in a show of force. Carriers in the Yellow Sea launched powerful air displays over key locations in China and over Dairen, Manchuria. Prepared for possible opposition, the Third Fleet landed combat troops, logistics forces, and administrative units in Japan. Marines were landed at three points in China. The Seventh Fleet's amphibious force delivered army forces to southern Korea in September and, in an operation that included minesweeping, withdrew Chinese occupation troops from Tonkin (northern Vietnam) that fall and transported them north.

Throughout this period U.S. Navy ships brought forces of all the services back across the Pacific and until April 1946 provided transportation for repatriating Japanese troops and Koreans. Minesweeping forces were engaged in the difficult and dangerous task of clearing U.S. influence mines from coastal waters of Japan. When it was discovered that communist troops were being infiltrated into southern Korea from the north, the U.S. Navy established patrols along the coast.

A continuing U.S. presence was required in the Mediterranean. Countries bordering the sea were being threatened by the superimposition of communist control over additional countries due to the influence of the powerful Soviet Army. Tito gained control of Yugoslavia. Albania adopted a constitution based on that of the Soviet Union. Communists were making a strong bid for power in the coming Italian elections. Confrontations at Trieste between Yugoslavia and Italy produced a series of crises. Moscow sought the secession of certain Turkish territories, joint control of the straits, and a new convention governing their passage, the parties to which would be limited to Black Sea powers. Political unrest erupted in Algiers.

The communist-controlled National Liberation Front attempted to seize power in Greece. Laying claim to the Greek province of Thrace, Bulgaria applied pressure along the border, as did Yugoslavia. Threats against Turkey continued. When the United States sent the mighty battleship *Missouri*, a cruiser, and destroyers to return the remains of the Turkish ambassador, the reception was enthusiastic. Turkey refused to yield to Soviet demands.

No longer could reliance be placed on the stabilizing influence of the British Navy. Britain had accepted responsibility for the eastern Mediterranean but, having financial difficulties in maintaining sufficient naval forces, it sought increasing U.S. involvement. As a consequence, the operational area of U.S. Naval Forces, North African waters was extended to include the eastern Mediterranean and the Red and Black seas.

At British urging the United States activated a new Eighth Fleet with a carrier striking force in the spring of 1946. Naval visits were made to Greece during the tense period of guerrilla actions and frontier incidents that summer. The new attack carrier *Franklin D. Roosevelt* conducted an impressive air demonstration prior to the plebiscite on retention of the Greek monarchy. Visits to Trieste and the assignment of task groups to the Adriatic helped stabilize the situation there. Port calls were made to the troubled French colony of Algeria.

Carrier *Leyte* and nine other warships were sent to Greece in the spring of 1947. President Truman viewed this "as a token of our intention, hoping to persuade the British to stay on, at least until our aid to Greece became effective."[6] Meanwhile, Italy's strong Communist party was making an all-out effort to gain control over the government. U.S. Navy visits were scheduled. In requesting the aid grant to Greece and Turkey, approved by Congress, Truman announced a policy interpreted as a decision to prevent further communist advances through U.S. containment actions. Many naval operations lay ahead in the Cold War.

Ironically, this was a time of serious reductions in the naval operating forces of the United States. As a result, it was becoming ever more difficult to maintain a well-balanced fleet. Not only had the transition to peacetime levels proceeded rapidly, but further cut-backs were being imposed to the point that Navy Department expenditures in the coming fiscal year would be only a third of those in the previous year.

As subsequent events would reveal, it was fortunate that the navy following the war had retained and preserved a number of decommissioned ships and craft in an inactive status in a Reserve Fleet. It was fortunate also that so many experienced personnel after their active duty had joined the naval reserve, ready to return if needed in an emergency.

While the chief of naval operations made full use of the flexibility and mobility of naval units in meeting demands in widely separated areas of the world, the army continued to press for unity of command over land and sea forces. Truman directed the implementation of a plan whereby the surface of the globe would be divided into geographic areas in which all of the armed forces, other than strategic forces, would be under a unified commander. The navy felt that joint commands were warranted to meet specific situations, such as in a war, but that overall responsiveness, preparedness, efficiency, and effectiveness of the fleet depended upon it remaining under a naval chain of command.

A compromise solution was reached whereby the Atlantic and Pacific unified commands were assigned to the officers who commanded the Atlantic and Pacific Fleets. Rather than placing naval forces under the commander of units within Europe, a specified command was created for U.S. Naval Forces, Eastern Atlantic and Mediterranean, which consisted of units of the Atlantic Fleet when deployed to those areas. Overall naval operational command for the two unified and one specified commands was maintained by the designation of the chief of naval operations as the Joint Chiefs of Staff's "executive agent."[7]

One source of uncertainty concerning the future of U.S. naval power was the campaign to change the responsibilities and authority of the military departments.

Erosion

The campaign to establish a single military department had been launched as soon as World War II was over. The Senate Military Affairs Committee, the cognizance of which did not extend to naval matters, held sympathetic hearings in the fall of 1945 on two bills closely aligned with War Department proposals.

That December President Truman, who had served in the army in World War I and then in the national guard, sent a message to Congress recommending a Department of Defense organized basically along the same lines as the War Department. He based his rationale to a large extent on assumptions about the nature of future wars. If there was another, it would "strike directly at the United States. . . . The boundaries that once separated the Army's battlefield from the Navy's . . . have been virtually erased."[1]

Yet the physical boundaries separating land and sea were still important. Those defining the limits of territorial waters continued to be recognized. Whereas navies were free to operate over the wide expanses of international waters without violating sovereign rights, this was not true with regard to stationing troops or basing aircraft on foreign soil. There were still fundamental differences between the exercise of naval power and the employment of armies. The overlapping capabilities of land-based weapons and those employed by warships had been greatly extended by aircraft developments; but there were still limitations, such as the limited operational ranges of tactical aircraft and fighter planes.

The Senate Military Affairs Committee drafted a bill along the lines proposed by the president. After differing views were expressed in hearings before the Naval Affairs Committee, a legislative Reorganization Act merged the committees into the Senate and House Armed Services Committees.

THE NATIONAL SECURITY ACT

Under presidential pressure, the secretaries of war and navy reached compromises on a number of issues in January 1947. Hearings by the Senate Armed

Services Committee and the House Committee on Expenditures were followed later that year by passage of the National Security Act. In providing for the common defense, the United States had depended for a century and a half on two military departments, war and navy, each directly under the president. Now three departments were established within the newly created National Military Establishment: the army, navy, and air force.

The army was to be "organized, trained, and equipped primarily for prompt and sustained combat incident to operations on land." It included "land combat and service forces and such aviation and water transport as may be organic therein."[2]

The "entire operating forces of the United States Navy, including naval aviation, and . . . the United States Marine Corps," were retained in the Department of the Navy, as was the coast guard when operating as a part of the navy. "Organized, trained, and equipped primarily for prompt and sustained combat incident to operations at sea," the navy was "generally responsible for naval reconnaissance, antisubmarine warfare, and protection of shipping." All naval aviation, including "land-based naval aviation, air transport essential for naval operations," was to be "integrated with the naval service as part thereof within the Department of the Navy." The marine corps was to be "organized, trained, and equipped to provide fleet marine forces of combined arms, together with supporting air components, for service with the fleet in the seizure . . . of advanced naval bases and for the conduct of such land operations as may be essential to the prosecution of a naval campaign." It was also to "provide detachments and organizations for service on armed vessels of the Navy." There were to be "detachments for the protection of naval property at naval stations and bases."[3]

Within the newly established Department of the Air Force, the air force (formerly the U.S. Army Air Forces; the Air Corps, U.S. Army; and the Air Force Combat Command) was to be "organized, trained, and equipped primarily for prompt and sustained offensive and defensive air operations."[4]

While specifying that the secretary of defense was to be "the principal assistant to the President in all matters relating to the national security," the act placed limitations on his powers, particularly with regard to decisions considered to be prerogatives of Congress. There were limitations as well on the size of his staff. He could "appoint from civilian life not to exceed three special assistants to advise and assist him in the performance of his duties." Officers of the armed services could be detailed "as assistants and personal aides"[5] but the establishment of a military staff was prohibited.

The secretary would be responsible for performing certain duties under the direction of the president. One was to "establish general policies and programs" for the National Military Establishment, its departments and agencies. Another was to "exercise general direction, authority, and control" over these. He was also to "take appropriate steps to eliminate unnecessary duplication or overlapping in the fields of procurement, supply, transportation, storage, health, and research."[6] Duties of the secretary that would prove especially difficult in those days of severe reductions in military funding were supervising and coordinating budget estimates of the departments and agencies, formulating budget estimates, and supervising budget programs.

The Departments of Army, Navy, and Air Force were to be "administered as individual executive departments." Their secretaries retained "all powers and duties . . . not specifically conferred upon the Secretary of Defense." They were not to be prevented "from presenting to the President or to the Director of the Budget, after first so informing the Secretary of Defense, any report or recommendation relating to his department which he may deem necessary."[7]

The National Security Act provided for the formation of a "War Council" to "advise the Secretary . . . on matters of broad policy relating to the armed forces" and "consider and report on such other matters as"[8] he might direct. He would be chairman of the council. Other members were the secretaries of the military departments, the chiefs of staff of the army and the air force, and the chief of naval operations.

The Joint Chiefs of Staff became a statutory body "subject to the authority and direction"[9] of the secretary of defense as well as the president. Assigned specific duties, they were authorized a joint staff not to exceed 100 officers.

Also included within the National Military Establishment were the Munitions Board and the Research and Development Board.

With the purpose of coordination for "national security," the National Security Council was formed and under it the Central Intelligence Agency. The council would "advise the President with respect to the integration of domestic, foreign, and military policies relating to the national security so as to enable the military services and the other departments and agencies of the Government to cooperate more effectively in matters involving national security."[10] It would be composed of the president; secretary of state; secretary of defense; secretaries of the military departments; chairman of the National Security Resources Board, which the act established; and, as the president might designate from time to time, chairmen of the Munitions Board and the Research and Development Board. No others could be designated without the advice and consent of the Senate.

Although the final version of the National Security Act had been based on very extensive consideration of many complex issues, many who had favored a single military department, including Truman, viewed the law as but the initial move toward their ultimate goal of a much more centralized organization. Steps to bring about further changes began shortly after James Forrestal was sworn in on September 17, 1947 as secretary of defense, long before the new system could receive a full test.

In January 1948 a presidential commission headed by Thomas K. Finletter issued a report entitled "Survival in the Air Age," which concluded that the nation's military security must be based on "mass-destruction weapons."[11]

Whereas the budget request about to be submitted to Congress provided for an air force of 48 groups, the commission urged an increase to 70, a number the force had previously expressed as a goal. For the navy, new replacement aircraft were recommended but no increase in numbers. Reducing its procurement of other types of aircraft, the air force reallocated funds to produce substantial additional numbers of B-36 strategic bombers.

The National Security Act had been in effect for only seven months when groundwork began to be laid for changes that would depart from some of the basic principles adopted after prolonged consideration by Congress. After a Truman conference with Forrestal, the Hoover Commission on Organization of the Executive Branch of the Government (one of the members of which was the secretary of defense) formed the Committee on National Security Organization. It was headed by Ferdinand Eberstadt, whose report prepared at Forrestal's request in 1945 had made major contributions to the subsequent act. The commission's recommendations were submitted in February 1949 and were similar to the new Everstadt committee report.

On May 1, 1949, shortly after taking the oath of office, this time as the elected president, Truman asked Forrestal to submit his resignation. Louis A. Johnson, a former American Legion commander who had served for a time as assistant secretary of the army, was nominated to become the second secretary of defense.

On May 7 the president submitted his proposal for changes in the National Security Act. While phrased along the lines of the Hoover report, his recommendations on centralization of authority went further than the commission's.

In the hearings of the Senate Armed Services Committee one senator expressed fear that if "there is perhaps an unwise appointment of a Secretary of Defense, . . . this bill will give him very substantial and arbitrary power."[12] Forrestal, although supporting the bill, concurred that there was such a risk.

Eberstadt, who chose to testify as an individual rather than on behalf of his committee, urged caution with regard to the temptation to cure defects in policies and personnel through "organizational expedients." He warned that "the attempt . . . will not only fail of its purpose, but may injure a sound organization." He suggested, prophetically, "that great care be exercised lest the Office of the Secretary of Defense, instead of being a small and efficient unit which determines the policies of the Military Establishment and controls and directs the departments, feeding on its own growth, becomes a separate empire."[13] He also expressed specific reservations.

Although it was almost two months before the Senate committee came up with its recommendations, testimony totaled only eight days, during which a few selected witnesses were queried on a limited range of issues. The Senate passed the bill on May 26, four days after the tragic death of Forrestal.

Despite the declining budget, the Navy Department was placing unprecedented peace-time emphasis on research and development. One important achievement was a twin-engine carrier plane redesigned so that it could deliver the plutonium implosion-type bomb, now being produced, that was five feet in diameter and weighed 10,000 pounds. The navy was urging the development, as of then opposed by the air force, of smaller types, including those that could be employed in warfare at sea.

Shortly after taking office Secretary Johnson had asked the Joint Chiefs of Staff for their opinions on the advisability of continuing the construction of a new and larger carrier. It was scarcely surprising that the chief of naval operations favored completion and the air force and army chiefs recommended cancellation. In ordering stoppage of work on the carrier, Johnson went well beyond the intent of the 1947 act. Secretary of the Navy John L. Sullivan resigned in protest.

The administration endorsed an expansion of the air force to 55 groups. Congress went further by adding funds for an increase to 70. These actions, coupled with the cancellation of the carrier, stimulated counterattacks in the media, particularly by certain naval aviators. Not only was the number of land-based strategic bombers questioned, but claims were made that the performance of the newly-developed B-36 was inadequate to fulfill its mission effectively. The so-called carrier–B-36 controversy at times became acrimonious.

The prospect of providing and maintaining a navy adequate to meet the nation's needs was growing ever dimmer. The level of national defense funding for the coming fiscal year was to be the lowest since World War II. The percentage cut for the navy was about ten times that for the air force.

The number of attack carriers had already been reduced to 8. Secretary Johnson planned to bring the number down to 6 or 4. Carrier air groups were to be cut from 14 to 6 and marine air squadrons from 32 to 11 or 12.

When the House Armed Services Committee held its hearings on reorganization, members expressed concern that the president had recommended the secretary of defense be given authority to reassign, abolish, or consolidate the combat functions of the armed services. Consequently, the amendment passed by Congress included the following safeguard: "Notwithstanding any other provision of this Act, the combatant functions assigned to the military services . . . shall not be transferred, reassigned, abolished, or consolidated."[14]

The National Military Establishment became the Department of Defense, over which the secretary was to have "direction, authority, and control." Although still "separately administered," the Departments of Army, Navy, and Air Force would no longer be executive departments. Not only were their secretaries denied membership in the cabinet and the National Security Council, but they were subordinate to an under secretary of defense, a position added in April, who was to "perform such duties . . . as the Secretary of Defense may prescribe." The act authorized three assistant secretaries to whom powers could also be delegated. Another center of authority was the chairman of the Research and Development Board who, subject to the authority of the secretary and in respect to such matters authorized by him, was to "have the power of decision on matters falling within the jurisdiction of the Board."[15]

Whereas the original act specified that if there was a chief of staff to the president he would be a member of the Joint Chiefs of Staff (as Admiral William D. Leahy had been in World War II), the amendment established the position of chairman of the Joint Chiefs of Staff to take precedence over all officers of the armed services. Congress added the proviso that he was not to "exercise military command over the Joint Chiefs of Staff or over any of the military services."[16]

The provision that the chairman would provide a link between the armed forces and the president and secretary of defense raised the possibility of compromising the direct relationship of the army chief of staff and chief of naval operations with the commander in chief, which was so successful in the last war. Another duty of the chairman was to furnish the Joint Chiefs of Staff with agendas for their meetings.

In August 1949, the same month that the act was signed, the United States learned that the Soviets had tested an atomic device. It had been recognized that the USSR in time would acquire such a bomb, but officials assumed that the date would be much later. As subsequently learned, traitorous actions by British citizens and at least one American had provided extensive information on scientific details and achievements of the Manhattan Project.

In testimony during House hearings that fall on the "National Defense Program—Unification and Strategy" most air force and army witnesses portrayed the next war as a total one employing atomic weapons. On the other hand, Fleet Admiral King observed that "a likely possibility now is that there will be some kind of a stalemate unless both sides expect to destroy each other."[17]

JCS Chairman General Omar M. Bradley was sarcastically critical of navy witnesses and the cases they had presented. He stressed the high priority of strategic bombing and minimized, among other things, the need for amphibious warfare capabilities.

The opening statement of Admiral Louis E. Denfeld, chief of naval operations, expressed concern over "reductions in the fleet and its functions which are being imposed by arbitrary decision." In strongly worded testimony, he asserted that the "Navy is not accepted in full partnership in the national defense structure." He asserted that "there is a steady campaign to relegate the Navy to convoy and antisubmarine service."[18] Truman relieved him of his responsibilities despite the fact that Denfeld had not completed his statutory term of service as CNO.

In his end-of-year report Secretary Johnson stated he was exercising "greater control" over the affairs of the military departments and placing emphasis on "the responsibilities of staff agencies."[19] He had issued new charters giving the authority of decision to the chairmen of the Research and Development Board and of the Munitions Board and brought certain joint boards under the control of staff assistants. In addition to the three assistant secretaries of defense now permitted, Johnson created the new position of assistant to the secretary for foreign military affairs and military assistance.

EXPANSION OF COMMUNIST CONTROL

As for the continuing cold war, in September 1947 the Cominform (Bureau of Information of the Communist Workers' Parties) was organized with participants from the Soviet Union, Poland, Czechoslovakia, Hungary, Yugoslavia, Bulgaria, Romania, Italy, and France.

Following the Italian Peace Treaty signed that month, Yugoslavia threatened to invade Trieste. A continuing U.S. naval presence was maintained in the Adriatic.

Elections were held in Poland. Despite a Soviet agreement with the United States and Britain, international supervision was denied. After two years the communist takeover there was essentially complete. In Romania, the National Democratic Front headed by the Communist party displaced the National Peasant party and proclaimed the People's Republic. Soviet troops threatened an invasion of Czechoslovakia and applied heavy political pressures. After the mysterious death of Foreign Minister Jan Masaryk, President Eduard Benes yielded and the communists were soon in control of the government. Following a meeting of Soviet and Southeast Asian communist leaders in Calcutta, insurgents launched campaigns almost simultaneously in Malaya, the Philippines, Indonesia, and Burma.

Expressing concern over the growing imbalance between commitments and capabilities, the Joint Chiefs of Staff recommended increases in force levels. Greece, Italy, Palestine, and Korea were identified as explosive points. Some additional military manpower was authorized.

A temporary commission sent to Korea by the United Nations was unable to get cooperation from North Korea. In March 1948 the communists began the construction of fortifications north of the 38th parallel. In what appeared an effort to influence elections scheduled for the south, the north conducted firing exercises.

In Eastern Europe the Soviets sealed off all contact between the zones they occupied and those occupied by the United States, Britain, and France.

Within the United States military appropriations for the coming fiscal year were increased to somewhat higher levels. However, the navy was to receive only a minor share.

In March 1949 the United States joined ten European nations and Canada in signing the North Atlantic Treaty whereby an attack on one or more of the signatories would be considered an attack against all of them. Thereafter, top military priority, after America's own defense, was assigned to the security of Europe. Although the ability of the United States to fulfill this commitment would depend on its use of the sea, naval requirements continued to be minimized by claims that a war involving Europe would be decided in a very short time.

When the Soviets imposed a land blockade that June on routes into the Allied sectors of Berlin, U.S. naval aircraft participated in the determined air delivery of essential supplies until the blockade was lifted in late September, although harassment continued.

The situation in the Far East was deteriorating. The last troops had been withdrawn from Korea in June. Following the visit of the Marshall mission to China, Mao Tse-tung proclaimed establishment of the People's Republic of China on October 1. The Nationalist government withdrew to Formosa. Later in the year CNO Admiral Forrest Sherman ordered that an attack carrier be deployed continuously to the Far East.

Early in January 1950 President Truman declared that the United States would not furnish military aid and advice to the Chinese Nationalists. In a speech defending U.S. policy during the struggle in China, the secretary of state defined the "defense perimeter"[20] as running along the Aleutians to Japan and then down to the Ryukyus and the Philippines. In case of an attack beyond that perimeter, initial reliance would be placed on resistance by the people attacked and on the United Nations.

In Southeast Asia naval forces had been playing key roles in the French-Viet Minh War, now underway for three years. Operations of sea-going and riverine units of the French Navy included interception of movements by sea along the coast, and on and across rivers; troop transportation; amphibious landings; support of forces ashore by naval gunfire and carrier aircraft; provision of waterborne logistics support; and patrol of critical stretches of inland waters. Major progress had been made in establishing and consolidating important areas of control along the coast and in the populous deltas of the Red and Mekong rivers. Naval actions had helped defeat Viet Minh attacks launched from the undeveloped interior.

The war in Indochina, however, was entering another phase. The communists, now in control of mainland China, were providing safe haven for Viet Minh forces and furnishing them with military supplies.

That spring the Seventh Fleet, which was operating in the Philippines area, had in addition to the recently deployed carrier merely one heavy cruiser, eight destroyers, four submarines, two squadrons of patrol planes, and two underway replenishment vessels (a fleet oiler and a refrigerated stores ship). An antiaircraft cruiser, four destroyers, and ten minesweepers (three of which were not in service) were under the operational control of Commander Naval Forces, Far East, Vice Admiral C. Turner Joy, the naval component commander in Japan under General MacArthur. The entire Pacific Fleet had but one remaining ammunition ship, then located at San Francisco. Its last stores issue ship had been decommissioned.

Further reductions in U.S. naval operating forces were in prospect as a result of budget cuts for the fiscal year about to begin.

23

Limited War

Before dawn on Sunday, June 25, 1950, the Army of the People's Republic of Korea launched an attack south across the 38th parallel.

In the land war that followed the value of naval power would once again be demonstrated. Almost all of the logistics support of South Korea and ground forces from outside the country would have to come by sea. The scene of action was a peninsula south of communist Manchuria that is 400 to 500 miles long and throughout most of its length only 100 to 200 miles wide. The eastern coast extended close to the Soviet port and naval base at Vladivostok.

Surface warships, carriers, amphibious forces, and minesweeping forces of the U.S. Navy had important and sometimes pivotal roles to play.

It was extremely unlikely that the war on land would be accompanied by warfare at sea. On the other hand, it would be foolhardy to be unprepared. Taking advantage of German experience and technology, the Soviets had embarked upon a program to create a large, modern submarine force. The program initially produced small types suitable mainly for coastal operations, but these were soon followed by larger and more advanced types of capable of offensive actions on the high seas. By now their navy possessed at least 370 submarines.

In a crucial naval engagement on the first evening, a South Korean patrol craft (PC) intercepted and sank an armed ship headed for Pusan on the southern tip of the peninsula with 600 North Korean troops embarked. If this had not happened the invaders would undoubtably have gained control of that key port across Tsushima Strait from Japan. Not only would Pusan be the point of entry for the first U.S. forces and for reinforcements during the desperate first phase of the war, but it was to serve as the main logistics port for the U.S. Army thereafter.

Vice Admiral Joy sent two of his destroyers to furnish protection for the sea portion of the evacuation of U.S. citizens from Seoul, the South Korean capital.

As the North Korean Army advanced toward that city, a separate division headed down the east coast of the peninsula. Here, the thrust by land was

Map 23.1
East Asian Waters

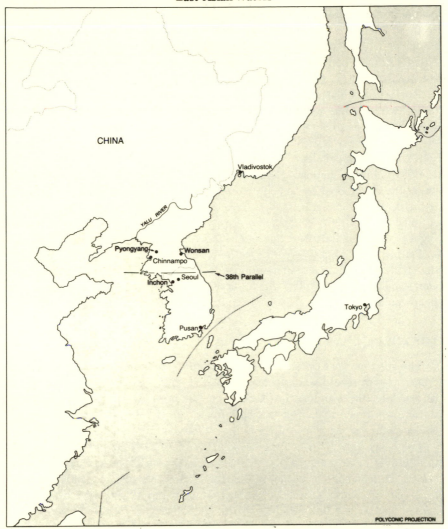

Source: Drawn for the editors by the University of Maryland Geography Department, Cartography Service Laboratory, 1987.

accompanied by amphibious movements that bypassed defenses near the 38th parallel and landed some 10,000 troops at locations further south. A number of North Korean supply missions also went by sea. The only South Korean naval vessel that could have provided even token opposition was the one PC.

A resolution calling upon North Korea to stop its aggression and withdraw, which would have undoubtably been vetoed except for the Soviet boycott of meetings, was approved by the United Nations Security Council.

In addition to authorizing air and naval force support south of the parallel, President Truman assigned a sea control mission to the Seventh Fleet to prevent either a Chinese communist invasion of Formosa or a Nationalist attack against the mainland.

Rumors of landings caused Admiral Joy to dispatch an antiaircraft cruiser to check two locations near Pusan. The cruiser and a destroyer were then sent into the Sea of Japan to bombard concentrations of North Korean forces and to conduct patrols. Two destroyers were sent into the Yellow Sea to patrol stations south of the 38th parallel.

CNO Admiral Sherman placed the Seventh Fleet, then on its way north, under the operational control of commander of naval forces, Far East. Assigned the task of conducting air and surface operations to neutralize Formosa, Vice Admiral A. D. Struble conducted a show of force in the form of a concentrated flight of carrier aircraft from one end of the strait to the other on June 27.

Patrol planes of the Seventh Fleet soon began to maintain surveillance over the strait. After the arrival of additional destroyers from across the Pacific, some were employed in patrolling waters between the island and the mainland. The fleet would continue to carry out this mission of deterrence throughout the war.

THE KOREAN WAR

The situation in Korea became ever more desperate. The lightly-weaponed South Korean troops were no match for the large well-armed army of North Korea. After the withdrawal of U.S. forces the previous year, the U.S. administration, concerned that Syngman Rhee might launch his own attack, had not included tanks and medium artillery in the military aid furnished.

Following passage of a second resolution of the UN Security Council, this time calling upon members to assist the Republic of Korea in repelling the invasion, Truman approved sending U.S. forces from occupied Japan and a naval blockade of North Korea. He authorized bombing as governed by military necessity above the 38th parallel.

The Seventh Fleet's striking force, joined by a British Commonwealth slow, light carrier group with a cruiser and three destroyers, steamed into the Yellow Sea. There the planes of the U.S. attack carrier, well beyond the range of the aircraft in Japan, struck airfields and railroad marshalling yards near Pyongyang, the North Korean capital. Further south, the British light carrier attacked an airport.

The first U.S. Army contingent to arrive was an advance force of two companies airlifted from Japan to Pusan. Moving north, they contacted a vastly larger enemy force.

The remainder of the infantry division was transported by sea from nearby Sasebo. Commander of naval forces, Far East was able to provide the lift promptly since he had 39 landing ship tanks (LSTs) and 12 freighters with Japanese crews. Organized as Task Group 96.3, they had been engaged in returning prisoners of war from the Asian mainland and providing logistics services for U.S. forces occupying Japan.

The movement of a second division was accomplished by the Military Transportation Service of the navy. It will be recalled that the navy had assumed ocean transportation responsibilities at the army's request in World War I. This time, however logical the recently established Military Sea Transportation Service (MSTS) may have been, the purpose had been functional unification, an objective that seems all too often pursued as an end in itself in recent years.

In any case, the navy was now responsible for the sealift of personnel and cargoes for all the military services. Under the chief of naval operations, commander MSTS operated commissioned ships, U.S. naval supply ships manned by civil service crews, and private ones under time charter. For the delivery of petroleum products such as fuel oil, gasoline, and diesel oil, he controlled oil company tankers under contract. He also chartered space for cargoes and individuals in merchantmen on their normal routes.

The next division sent to Korea was the First Cavalry. Rather than being delivered to the port of Pusan, it was landed by a makeshift amphibious force further north on the east coast at Pohang.

None of the fleet's amphibious units was normally deployed to the western Pacific. It was by coincidence that Commander, Amphibious Group 1 Rear Admiral James H. Doyle was conducting training exercises with units of the Eighth Army in Tokyo Bay. Having only an attack transport, an attack cargo ship, and a fleet tug in addition to his command ship (AGC), he was assigned Japanese-manned LSTs, landing craft (LCUs) that were activated at the Yokosuka naval base, and MSTS ships. Two of the latter had been attack transports but to prepare them for the forthcoming operation they had to be outfitted and manned by qualified crews and have boat fittings and other equipment installed.

The admiral's preparations and operation order provided for an assault landing because of the possibility that rapidly advancing North Korean forces would reach the area first. Thus his attack force included minesweepers, an underwater demolition team, and a naval gunfire support group. Provisions were made for close air support by the Seventh Fleet.

As it was, the July landing encountered no enemy opposition. In the subsequent fighting on land in the Pohang region, however, naval gunfire was a decisive factor.

Because of advances in carrier aviation, the need for naval gunnery had been subject to considerable questioning. Its value, however, was once again demonstrated during the Korean War. Warships so armed were required for bombardments preparatory to amphibious assaults and accurate close support of the landing force, especially under conditions of low visibility. They were ideally suited for patrols to intercept coastal traffic.

Moreover, it was once again proven that within their range, naval guns had capabilities against targets ashore that were in some respects unique. Contributing factors were high velocity and accuracy; effectiveness of the armor-piercing projectiles of large caliber guns in penetrating hard targets, including vertical faces when the range was short; the ability to engage when visibility was low; and the ability of warships to remain on station for prolonged periods of time. These capabilities were especially valuable along the east coast of Korea where, because of terrain, the roads and railroad were often near the sea.

Additional ships of the Pacific Fleet and from the Atlantic were on their way west. Back in the United States, rapid progress was being made in reactivating warships and auxiliaries of the Reserve Fleet.

By the end of July the U.S. troops who had proceeded north were withdrawn, along with South Korean forces, to within a defensive perimeter formed around Pusan. In addition to conducting air strikes against enemy lines of communications, the Seventh Fleet augmented the close air support being provided by U.S. Air Force planes from nearby fields in Japan.

A task group arrived from the eastern Pacific with a provisional marine brigade combat-loaded in amphibious ships and an escort carrier with part of a marine air wing. Instead of conducting a counter-offensive operation near Seoul, as had been planned, the situation was so precarious that MacArthur had the brigade landed at Pusan.

Conducting strikes from the CVE carrier, the marine aircraft supported the brigade's operations ashore. Bitter combat in the area was to continue into September.

By then the number of deployed warships was greatly increased and they were being supported by a service squadron composed of a full range of underway replenishment and other types of support ships.

What reversed the tide of war was an amphibious assault at Inchon. Not only was this the port that served Seoul, but also forces landed there would be in position to sever the main route on land over which supplies flowed to the bulk of North Korean forces operating in the south.

The joint task force formed under the command of Vice Admiral Struble included the fast carrier task group, patrol and reconnaissance planes, and blockade and escort forces; the service squadron; a blockade and covering force comprised of the British Commonwealth ships; and an attack force with landing forces composed of the marine brigade backloaded from Pusan, the army's Seventh Infantry Division, corps troops, and the First Marine Division and Air Wing in an amphibious group from the Atlantic Fleet.

Doyle's attack force totaled about 180 ships. At the time of the Pohang operation there had been no landing ship docks (LSDs). Now there were five plus a landing craft repair ship and a hospital ship. Also assigned to his force were 2 heavy cruisers, 3 light cruisers, 12 destroyers, 3 rocket ships [LSM(R)] for preparatory bombardments and gunfire support, and 2 escort carriers with the marine aircraft.

On September 12, 1950, planes of Task Force 77's two attack carriers, soon joined by a third that had just arrived, conducted fighter sweeps of airfields and strikes to seal off the objective area as those from the British light carrier hit selected targets further north. Two days of intense naval gunfire preceded the landing of marines on September 15 with close support provided from the escort carriers.

The landing force was soon in possession of Kimpo airfield where, after repair of damage, the first air force planes arrived from Japan. Marines were nearing Seoul when, on the 24th, Admiral Struble passed command of the landing force to the commanding general of X Corps.

U.S. and Republic of Korea (ROK) troops at the southern tip of the Korean peninsula had begun an offensive on September 16. The only significant progress was the advance of ROK forces, aided by naval gunfire including that by the 16-inch guns of USS *Missouri,* the only battleship in commission at the start of the war. Then, faced with logistics difficulties, the North Koreans began to pull back from the northern sector of the perimeter around Pusan on September 20 and ordered a general withdrawal five days later. Soon the allied armies were in control of almost all of southern Korea.

Secretary of Defense Johnson was replaced by George C. Marshall. Although, as a general of the army, he had not been retired, Truman appointed him "from civilian life." Congress granted an exception to the law's provision that "a person who has within ten years been on active duty as a commissioned officer in a Regular component of the armed services"[1] was not eligible for appointment as secretary of defense.

On September 27, 1950, Marshall sent MacArthur a message authorizing operations above the 38th parallel to destroy the armed forces of the People's Republic of Korea. The war was now entering a new phase.

MINE WARFARE

The consequences of reductions in mine warfare readiness during the past three years, in which severe ceilings had been imposed on the Navy Department's budget, were about to be experienced. The potential of mine fields had been appreciated but, as so often happens in times of low funding, the need to set sequential priorities prevented maintaining a balanced navy. Even though the mine forces absorbed but a tiny proportion of the budget, very few minesweepers were retained in service. The Mine Force, Pacific Fleet had been disestablished. The degaussing of ships had not been updated. There now was no degaussing station west of Pearl Harbor.

Soon after the Korean War began, work had begun on the reactivation of the small minesweepers (AMs) that had been placed in reserve in Japan. However, when Admiral Joy requested more in August, he had been advised that other types had higher priorities.

There was, as of then, no knowledge that the Soviets had already sent mines, along with experts, down the railroad from Vladivostok to lay fields at Wonson and Chinnampo. Early in September the South Koreans reported that floating mines had been sighted, an enemy mine craft had been sunk, and one field of enemy mines had been laid. Later in the month a few mines were exposed by low tides at Inchon. A U.S. minesweeper sank after striking a mine, and two destroyers and two ROK auxiliary motor minesweepers were damaged.

MacArthur's plan called for a two-pronged attack. As the Eighth Army attacked north after gaining control of the Seoul area, X Corps was to be withdrawn and landed at Wonsan on the east coast. Its port was to become a base for an advance across the peninsula to the North Korean capital.

The Wonsan operation, for which Joint Task Force 7 was reestablished, was scheduled for October 20. At busy Inchon landing craft returned the marine division, with its arms and equipment, to amphibious ships, the last of which put to sea on the 17th. The army's Seventh Division made its way to Pusan while LSTs brought its tanks and heavy equipment.

Sweeping off Wonsan started ten days before the first landings were scheduled. That day 18 mines were destroyed in clearing a ten mile-long channel to the 30-fathom curve. The intended route south of islands off the harbor was abandoned when helicopters reported five fields ahead.

In clearing a lane to within four miles of the north channel on the following day, two of the three small AMs in the group were sunk by mines. A countermining effort employing delayed-action 1,000-pound bombs achieved no apparent successes. Despite magnetic sweeping, a Korean YMS-class minesweeper was sent to the bottom by an influence mine on October 18. Not until a week later was the route deemed safe for deep-draft ships.

By now Admiral Sherman had assigned overriding priority to the reactivation of nine small AMs and four large AMs. Many crucial operations, such as those associated with clearing additional ports and amphibious landings, lay ahead for the Minesweeping Force, Western Pacific activated under the command of a rear admiral in early November.

The ROK Army, which encountered little opposition in its progress north, occupied Wonsan on October 11. The landings of marines onto the beach began on the 26th.

In view of the rapid progress of the South Korean Army, Commander Amphibious Group 3, Rear Admiral Lyman A. Thackrey was assigned the task of landing the U.S. Army's Seventh Division at Iwon, 100 miles further north. Since no mines were discovered there, the ship-to-shore movement began on the 29th.

Lieutenant General Walton H. Walker sought to use Chinnampo, the port in the Korean Gulf that served Pyongnang, for logistics support of the advancing Eighth Army. There a specially-formed task element consisting of newly-arrived U.S. minesweepers, some Japanese sweepers, and supporting vessels cleared two channels. Tug-towed barges and shallow-draft vessels began delivering cargoes on November 6. Then the more heavily mined deep-draft channel was cleared. There had been no losses or damages, despite the fact that some 217 moored and 25 magnetic mines had been planted by the enemy.

NAVAL AIR SUPPORT

By now the tide of war was again shifting and the situation ashore was creating a desperate need for carrier operations. MacArthur had ordered the rapid advance north of all forces. U.S. and ROK troops heading up roads through narrow passages toward the Yalu River had become overextended by the time it was learned that the first units of a Chinese Army had made their way undetected across the river. Chinese aircraft, including high performance MIG-15 jet fighters provided from the Soviet Union, began operations from airfields in Manchuria.

The mission of employing naval forces in a "maximum air effort . . . in close support of ground units and interdiction of enemy communications, assembly areas and troop columns" was assigned Admiral Joy on November 4, while the Far East Air Force was directed to conduct an all-out two-week effort "to destroy every means of communications and every installation, factory, city and village"[2] below the Yalu. The Fast Carrier Task Force of the Seventh Fleet was in the Sea of Japan carrying out its mission two days later.

An urgent request from the Far East Air Force commander for jet fighters resulted in some being taken on board a light carrier and an escort carrier for delivery across the Pacific.

In authorizing air attacks against bridges over the Yalu, Washington placed severe restrictions on flight paths. Assigned the upstream bridges, the navy demonstrated the superior accuracy of dive bombers. As it was, bridges did not provide the sole routes across the river, for it was now frozen.

One of the tasks of carrier aircraft was to escort heavy bombers beyond the range of land-based fighters, which became ever more important as airfields were abandoned during the retreat south.

A notable amphibious operation in December 1950 was the withdrawal of marine and army forces and equipment from Hungnam, which was followed by their reinsertion into southern Korea. On the other coast, units were brought out of Chinnampo by sealift. Amphibious ships extracted some troops and equipment from Inchon as Seoul was abandoned soon after the beginning of the new year.

The UN forces established a line further south and then fought their way back. Seoul was recaptured in mid-March 1951. Early the next month Truman had

MacArthur relieved by General Matthew B. Ridgway, who had commanded the Eighth Army after the death of General Walker.

The president had by now decided that the United Nations should seek a settlement whereby the war would be ended with establishment of a boundary between the two Koreas near the one recognized before the invasion.

Evidence of a buildup of Chinese forces across from Formosa drew the carrier task force to the area for a show of force. It then steamed back to Korean waters to help repel another offensive from the north. After it was repulsed and the UN forces began a campaign north, the president banned ground operations further into North Korea.

The communists launched another offensive in May 1951. It had been turned back and a counter-offensive was making progress when the Soviet Union proposed a cease fire. The prolonged negotiations that commenced on July 10 would be exasperating for the UN negotiators. The enemy coupled the process with military actions and, by cleverly exploiting opportunities for propaganda, raised hopes of peace and eroded the resolve of Americans and allies.

The Republic of Korea had been saved, but combat and supporting operations would be required for another two years.

When the UN negotiators offered a compromise in the spring of 1952, it was rejected by the communists who, rather than discussing issues, turned the talks into propaganda sessions. The lack of progress toward constructive meetings led that summer to the launching of air strikes against hydroelectric plants and other installations in the north, including those by carriers in the Sea of Japan against targets in the northeast.

After the passage of another winter, the United States had growing expectations of reaching agreement on the terms of an armistice. Playing on such hopes, the communists once again artfully orchestrated propaganda and military actions with negotiations. Time and again, issues appeared to be resolved only to have the enemies insist on renegotiations in efforts to gain further concessions.

The enemy launched a major attack on June 10, 1953 against a sector being defended by a ROK Army corps. The front was stabilized ten days later after the loss of some ground.

The frustrating Panmunjon talks continued. Starting on July 13, a heavier communist attack, which was accompanied by applying pressure on the east coast, achieved an ominous breakthrough. There were urgent demands for close air support by the air force and by carrier aircraft, and for naval gunfire. In a counterattack begun four days later, some of the lost terrain was recovered. The amphibious force was kept busy throughout this period by a series of emergency movements of troops from one area to another.

The uncertain armistice was signed on July 27, 1953.

It is worth noting that the use of atomic bombs was advocated by some U.S. authorities during the desperate time when the overextended troops were under attack by the major Chinese force that made its way across the Yalu. Authority was denied, but only after serious consideration.

In this war, at least, nuclear strike capabilities had not reduced the requirements for conventional forces.

24

The New Look

Insofar as U.S. naval power was concerned, it had been fortunate that shifts in authority permitted by the 1949 amendment to the National Security Act had not taken full effect when the Korean War began. Further, during the critical year he served as secretary of defense, Marshall carried out his responsibilities at the policy level without attempting to master-mind actions of the military departments, as would be done with adverse effects in a later war.

As it was, the Navy Department functioned essentially as it had in World War II. Under the secretary of the navy the bureaus exercised initiative in anticipating needs and were fully responsive to requirements determined by the chief of naval operations. The Joint Chiefs of Staff (JCS) also functioned much as it had during the war. The flexibility and effectiveness with which naval operating forces were employed were in large measure due to the authority vested in the CNO.

In any case, the promptness with which units were redeployed from other areas of the globe, the amazing speed with which combat and auxiliary ships were reactivated from the Reserve Fleet and a high state of operational readiness achieved, and the rapidity of crucial logistical actions were nothing short of remarkable. Yet, once the most critical phases of the conflict were over, the processes of changes away from assignments of authority that had proven so successful in the past were resumed.

Robert A. Lovett, who had been assistant secretary of war at the time of the 1944 hearings, had succeeded General Marshall as secretary of defense in September 1951. The process of superimposing centers of functional authority over the military was resumed when the Defense Supply Management Agency and the post of director of installations were established in the summer of 1952.

During the presidential campaign that year, Dwight D. Eisenhower advocated setting up a commission to study the operations, functions, and actions of the Department of Defense. In testifying on the proposed National Security Act in 1947, the general had viewed the bill as a start, or to "constitute the most feasible effective step." In his opinion, this was not the time "to prepare a detailed legislative pattern for unification." He believed in a single chief of staff but felt that, because of fears, it "would be wrong for the moment."[1]

Truman, who was seeking reelection, asked for Lovett's opinion on what was wrong with the National Defense Organization. The request was made in August but it was not until after the November election that the secretary responded with a letter expressing views and recommendations.

Considering "unification" as being "evolutionary" and deploring the fact that, while allowing officers as assistants and aides, the law banned a military staff for the secretary of defense, he recommended that the JCS be confined to "planning functions and the review of war plans." "The balance of the military staff functions" should be transferred to the secretary of defense who would control "efficiency ratings and promotions" of the officers on his "combined military-civilian staff." The secretary would "in effect, be the Deputy of the Commander-in-Chief." The JCS would "not 'operate' or 'command' except in time of war and then 'by direction.' " The secretary of defense should assign unified commands to a military department as his "agent, if necessary." The chairman of the JCS should be allowed a vote. Lovett also discussed "a more radical, long-term possibility"[2] that would amount in essence to an armed forces general staff, even though that type of organization was prohibited by law.

Another recommendation was that the Munitions Board be abolished, with its functions transferred to an additional assistant secretary of defense.

Lovett also proposed a "functional and organizational study of the three Military Departments," which following "a pre-unification pattern,"[3] were all different. After being sworn in as president, Eisenhower appointed a Committee on Department of Defense (Rockefeller Committee). Its members included Lovett; General Bradley; David Sarnoff, a reserve officer of the air force who had been an advisor to General Eisenhower in World War II; and the president's brother. There were no members with experience in naval operations or the Navy Department.

It was scarcely surprising that the committee's report in April 1953 was closely aligned with the recommendations recently submitted by the outgoing secretary. One comment clearly aimed at the navy was that "it is essential to have a single chain of command or line of administrative responsibility within the Department of Defense and each of the military departments."[4]

Going beyond the contents of Lovett's letter, committee recommendations included abolishing certain boards established by acts of Congress and a tripling of the number of assistant secretaries of defense. A legal opinion by counsel expressed the belief that the secretary possessed the authority to take such actions.

Stating "as a former soldier who has experienced modern war at first hand, and now as President and Commander in Chief of the Armed Forces of the United States, . . . our Defense Establishment is in need of immediate improvement."[5] Eisenhower advised Congress of those portions of his plan that he considered were required by law to report prior to implementation. Despite the fact that a majority of the Committee on Government Operations opposed Reorganization Plan No. 6, the House of Representatives voted otherwise. The Senate took no opposing action within the required 60 days.

And so it was that as the fighting in Korea ended, the Department of Defense that was superimposed over the military department had, in addition to the secretary and under secretary, nine assistant secretaries, each with his own functional area of authority. Civilians were to be included in the process of strategic planning.

The JCS now had a chairman empowered to conduct, guide, and administer the work of the joint staff; select the individuals to serve on it; and determine their tenure. Moreover, he was to participate fully as a member of the JCS and submit his own "views, advice, and recommendations"[6] when he disagreed with the collective judgment of the JCS.

An interesting proviso was that "for the strategic direction and operations of forces and for the conduct of combat operations, . . . [the] military chief [of the designated department] would be authorized by the Secretary of Defense to receive and transmit reports and orders to act for such department in its executive agency capacity. . . . This arrangement will make it always possible to deal promptly with an emergency or wartime situation."[7] The role of the chief of naval operations would thus continue much as before for the next few years with beneficial results. But changes in command authority and organizational proliferation were far from over.

STRATEGY

Upon becoming president, Eisenhower followed a campaign theme in announcing there was to be a "New Look"[8] strategy whereby nuclear war capabilities would take precedence over conventional forces. Once the war was over, the expenditures of the air force continued to rise, reaching 50 percent of the total for the entire Department of Defense.

Meanwhile, the navy was gaining additional capabilities of its own to aid in deterrence and, if need be, to carry out nuclear weapon strikes. The development of smaller and lighter atomic bombs meant that carrier aircraft other than the large AJ could now be used. Fission warheads were soon augmented by those that, through nuclear fusion, would release vastly greater explosive power.

The first test of such a U.S. nuclear device was followed by a similar Soviet test eight months later. One consequence was the initiation of steps to provide a system to aid in the defense of North America. The navy provided extended warning coverage by employing specially equipped radar ships on station in the Atlantic.

SOUTHEAST ASIA

Despite the priority accorded nuclear warfare capabilities, Korean War experiences and an awareness of the possible effects of continuing communist aggression in its various forms caused the United States to maintain carrier, surface, and service force strengths of the navy at considerably higher levels than before the war. The reemphasis on mine warfare and mine countermeasures continued for a time. Another area receiving renewed attention was amphibious warfare. Fast merchantmen were being converted into attack transports and attack cargo ships for employment in amphibious ready groups. Helicopters had now been developed to the point where, operating from carriers, they could complement the main assaults over the beach. A specialized type of amphibious carrier, LPH, was being constructed.

The western Pacific was one of the areas in which naval operations might be required on short notice. As for sea control missions, the U.S. Navy was continuing warship and air patrols off Korea, above as well as below the line of demarcation, to prevent communist infiltration by sea and to provide support to ROC forces in case of an offensive along the coast by North Korea. The Seventh Fleet still had responsibility for guarding the Formosa Strait. The Soviet Union had refused to join in the signing of the September 1951 peace treaty with Japan. Meanwhile, the United States had a continuing commitment to defend the defeated nation. The communist-led insurgency in the Philippines, to which the United States was linked by a defense treaty, was not yet fully under control. Actions by guerrillas in Malaya continued.

As for the struggle in Indochina, the United States had decided in the spring of 1950 to grant military aid to the French. The navy members of a joint state-defense mission sent there judged that the objectives for seagoing forces should be to prevent delivery by sea of foreign supplies and ammunition to the Viet Minh, to carry out combined operations against enemy-held coastal regions, and to ensure the flow of supplies to French forces. Riverine naval forces were required to deny Viet Minh use of waterways, prevent arms traffic, protect French use of rivers and deltas, and conduct combined operations. The French desired that the U.S. Navy "block off Tonkin Gulf and South China Sea to enemy forces which might attempt landings."[9]

The transfer of U.S. landing craft and amphibious ships proved to be timely. When the Viet Minh launched major attacks early the next year into the Red River Delta, riverine forces played indispensable roles in the operations that inflicted heavy losses on General Giap's troops and repulsed the offensive. Other French successes were achieved as the result of three amphibious operations on the coast of Annam (a kingdom with Hue as its capital, which is now part of Vietnam).

In talks held by the United States, France, and Britain in December 1951 consideration was given to warning communist China that aggression in Indochina would result in retaliation "not necessarily limited to the area of aggression."[10] A committee, which included Australia and New Zealand, agreed that the best prospects for halting intervention would be a combination of sea blockade and air action against China.

Three months later Truman assigned responsibilities for the Marianas, Formosa, and Southeast Asian areas to Commander in Chief, Pacific, Admiral Arthur W. Radford who also commanded the Pacific Fleet, as did Nimitz in World War II. Radford, under the direction of the chief of naval operations, established procedures for control of aircraft over Indochina in case carrier air support was ordered.

The death of Stalin in March 1953 and Soviet preoccupation with internal problems brought about an easing of Cold War tensions in many parts of the world. Communist revolutionary action in the Far East and threats of further aggression, however, had not abated in the Far East.

Responding to Viet Minh actions, the French Army withdrew some of its troops that spring from the Red River Delta where, enjoying the support and combat actions of naval forces, they had been increasingly successful. These troops were then deployed to isolated strong points in Laos.

There were signs that in the seventh year of frustrating warfare in remote Southeast Asia, the resolve of many French people was weakening. Adverse news reporting and propaganda were accelerating the process. Soon after the Korean armistice that July, which was not followed by a peace treaty, the Soviet Union and the People's Republic of China called for a settlement of the French-Viet Minh War. In September John Foster Dulles warned China of the consequences of aggression in Indochina.

Supported by naval riverine forces, the French Army inflicted heavy casualties on a Viet Minh division. According to *Khrushchev Remembers,* Ho Chi Minh, in seeking Chinese intervention about this time, described the Viet's situation as hopeless unless there was a cease fire soon. Under pressure from Parliament, the French premier agreed to try to achieve peace through negotiations. Ho indicated his willingness on November 20 to examine French proposals.

Ironically, that was the same day that two French paratroop battalions captured the valley post at Dien Bien Phu in the remote highlands next to the Laotian border only 100 miles south of China. The decision to continue to hold this position, far from the sea and dependent on airlifts to its runway for supplies and reinforcements, was to prove fateful.

In announcing a progressive reduction of ground forces in Korea, Eisenhower stated that U.S. military forces in the Far East would now feature "highly mobile naval, air and amphibious units."[11] Earlier, as the probability of a renewal of fighting in Korea receded, it had been planned to make a major reduction of naval forces deployed to the western Pacific. When the time came, the situation was such that the cut was restricted to the return to the Atlantic Fleet of a battleship and a division of destroyers.

Secretary John Foster Dulles delivered what has been called his Massive Retaliation Address in January 1954. He announced that the president, with the advice of the National Security Council, had made a major policy decision. Placing more reliance "on deterrent power and less dependence on local defensive power," the United States was to "depend primarily upon a great capacity to retaliate, instantly, by means and at places of our choosing." He warned that open Chinese aggression in the French-Viet Minh War would result in "grave consequences which might not be confined to Indochina."[12]

CNO Admiral Robert B. Carney, with the approval of the joint chiefs, ordered two attack carriers south to the Subic Bay area where they were soon joined by a third carrier, a squadron of destroyers, and underway replenishment ships. There they were placed under commander, First Fleet, who had been flown across the Pacific with some of his staff for the announced purpose of training in the fair weather conditions of that season in the South China Sea. Hopefully, the force's presence might have a deterrent effect on Chinese aggressive actions in Southeast Asia. Prepared to take prompt actions in case of concurrent emergencies, commander, Seventh Fleet, operated in the vicinity of Formosa and elsewhere in the northeast with the remainder of his fleet, which included two other attack carriers.

As the Viet Minh committed the majority of their regular forces to the siege of Dien Bien Phu, China not only supplied and helped deliver weapons and support down jungle-shrouded roads and trails from Yunan Province, but it also provided advisors and technical help as the Viet Minh positioned themselves on the ridges, where artillery pieces were dug in and hidden in locations overlooking the French stronghold. Monsoon weather was hindering air operations when the Viet Minh began their attack with a heavy artillery barrage on March 13. Three outposts were soon captured.

France asked the United States to respond in case of Chinese air intervention and to provide air support to Dien Bien Phu in case of no such intervention. A U.S. task force sent to the entrance of Tonkin Gulf on March 22 was prepared to furnish combat support if required. A week later carrier aircraft began reconnaissance of Chinese airfields, assembly points for shipments south, and supply routes.

In early April the French government sought immediate employment of U.S. aircraft against enemy forces attacking Dien Bien Phu. The request was not granted, and the carrier task force was returned to the Philippines.

In the meantime, a light carrier of the Seventh Fleet brought 25 marine aircraft from Japan, flew them into Tourane (Danang), and transferred them to the French Navy to restore the depleted squadron of their carrier *Arromanches*. A second French carrier was on station by the end of the month. General Henri Navarre was later to praise the naval air arm as the only military service that met and surpassed its obligations at Dien Bien Phu.

As the situation became ever more desperate, France again made a plea for U.S. help. There was some advocacy of the use of an atomic bomb. An air burst over the ridge would hardly have been suitable because of effects on the defenders. Consideration was given to employing a penetrating weapon developed jointly by the Bureau of Ordnance and Los Alamos and now available to the fleet, which could have been delivered accurately on the other side of the ridge.

Repeated requests for U.S. air strikes were not approved. Dien Bien Phu fell on May 7, 1954.

Soon thereafter expanding Chinese military activity across the mainland from Formosa brought Seventh Fleet carrier task forces to the area. Naval patrols on and over the strait were increased. On one occasion a communist fighter plane unsuccessfully attacked a U.S. Navy patrol plane.

When Chinese fighters shot down a British Air Cathay passenger plane southeast of Hainan Island that July, ships of the First Fleet commander's "Fair Weather Training Force"[13] reacted promptly to the distress call and rescued nine survivors. As the search continued, two Chinese planes attacked three carrier aircraft. Both of the attackers were shot down.

At Geneva, France and the Viet Minh had just concluded their three agreements on cessation of hostilities. One of the provisions in the one dealing with Vietnam called for the country's division by a demarcation, and French forces were to withdraw from the northern section. The state of Vietnam, which had been formed five years before by France's merging of Cochin China, Annam, and Tonkin, was not a party to the agreement. The other agreements were for Laos and Cambodia.

The day on which a phased French withdrawal of troops, military equipment, and refugees south from the Hanoi-Haiphong area by air and sea began, Ngo Dinh Diem, president of the Republic of Vietnam, sent a personal message to President Eisenhower asking for help in moving a million refugees from North to South Vietnam.

When Admiral Carney assigned the mission to the Pacific command, commander in chief, Pacific Fleet was responsible for the "Passage to Freedom"[14] operation and for providing overall support. Command of the sea evacuation was assigned to commander, Amphibious Group One, who was authorized to employ elements of the Western Pacific Amphibious Force and Military Sea Transportation Service. Commander, Service Squadron Three provided mobile logistics support along the Indochinese coast.

TAIWAN

When forces of the People's Republic of China threatened to invade the Nationalist-held Tachen Islands north of Taiwan (Formosa), other Seventh Fleet forces were positioned nearby as destroyers visited the islands on August 19. The "Fair Weather"[15] command was dissolved and assigned ships were returned to the Seventh Fleet.

On the 26th Communist China tested the defenses of Nationalist-occupied Quemoy on the mainland side of the Formosa Strait. When heavy bombardment began on September 3, Seventh Fleet forces, including attack carriers, were on the scene until the crisis ended.

Heavy bombings by aircraft from the mainland of the Tachens, further north and beyond the distance for continuous coverage by the Nationalist Air Force, began on January 10, 1955. Ichiang Island, within artillery range of the Tachens, was captured by the communists on the 20th.

Congress authorized the president to employ forces as he deemed necessary for defense of Taiwan and the Pescadores, including securing or protecting positions in friendly hands if he judged it necessary or appropriate. Five attack carriers were retained in the western Pacific by delaying the departure of one that was completing its tour.

In response to a Republic of China request for help in removing civilians and military forces from the Tachens, the Seventh Fleet amphibious force assisted the Chinese Navy in the successful evacuation while protection was provided by surface action and carrier striking forces. Similar cover was provided for evacuations from two other islands.

The year and a half since the signing of the Korean armistice had placed continuing demands on the U.S. Navy. In meeting these demands full advantage was taken of the quick responsiveness and flexibility of naval forces that were possible when they were properly and efficiently commanded and when naval forces are not unnecessarily diverted to peripheral operations. The peacetime importance of naval power's influence and its capability to deter war were again being demonstrated.

Valuable lessons were taught by the French-Viet Minh War. Regrettably, later events would reveal that some of the basic lessons were not recognized by the United States or were not properly interpreted.

Two months after the Geneva Accords on Indochina, the United States, Australia, New Zealand, the Philippines, Thailand, Pakistan, the United Kingdom, and France established the Southeast Asia Treaty Organization (SEATO). In the months to come U.S. naval forces participated in a series of exercises with other SEATO nations, thereby strengthening their resolve and providing valuable training in operations at sea and in amphibious warfare.

In accordance with President Eisenhower's policy, U.S. military contributions in opposing acts of aggression in the area were to consist of applying naval and air power in support of the ground forces of other countries. As long as such a policy was being followed, the nation could avoid the adverse consequences that might result from employing U.S. forces on foreign soil and becoming committed to fighting a land campaign.

The policy was revised early in 1955 when, on the urging of General Maxwell D. Taylor, army chief of staff, the concept became "readiness to retaliate promptly with attacks by the most effective combination of U.S. armed forces."[16]

With further centralization of authority in the secretary of defense following yet another reorganization act, including assigning him direct command authority over unified commanders, there would be an increasing tendency to involve all the military services, whether or not necessary and appropriate in each and every situation.

Naval Influence

The following period saw an intensification of the Cold War and a series of scattered crises. It was one in which the soundness of the existing system of command and control continued to be demonstrated by prompt deployments and redeployments of U.S. naval forces, often in anticipation of developing requirements, and their effective employment in the exercise of peacetime naval influence. Nevertheless, the period witnessed a radical departure from the alignment of responsibilities and authority that had proven so successful concerning the naval element of national power.

This was also a time in which new capabilities of great importance to the future of U.S. naval power were beginning to be introduced. The rapidity of the advances was in large measure due to the fact that, despite the seriously declining budget of the Navy Department following World War II, emphasis had been placed on research and development to a degree unprecedented in peacetime. Important programs started during that war were continued. Through an expanded system of naval laboratories and contracts, a technological base was being laid for the design and engineering of new and significantly improved weapons and weapon systems as sufficient funds became available. The Office of Naval Research, established soon after the war, provided support for the purer forms of research that might have pay-offs in the more distant future.

A breakthrough of profound implications was demonstrated when USS *Nautilus* first got underway on nuclear power on January 17, 1955. Not only would the nuclear submarines' ability to operate at high as well as slow speeds without surfacing be of immense value in carrying out conventional naval missions, but further advances were to provide the nation with nuclear warfare deterrence capabilities critical to the future national security.

On the other hand, problems of antisubmarine warfare were becoming ever more difficult, for sooner or later navies of other foreign powers would acquire their own nuclear propulsion plants. The nature of the operating medium was such that no single means would prove sufficient to counter the increasing underseas threat. As in the two world wars, offensive and defensive naval capabilities on, over, and under the surface of the ocean would be required in wartime to minimize the probability of enemy submarines reaching the high seas, to seek out and destroy as many as possible, and to protect naval forces and shipping. Continuing advances were needed in detection, weapon systems, and countermeasures. Helicopters of improved performance, and operating from small carriers and from platforms on other types of ships, would have important roles to play in antisubmarine warfare.

Anti-air warfare was another area in which spectacular progress was being achieved by the U.S. Navy. The world's first guided-missile ship, modernized heavy cruiser USS *Boston* with a Terrier missile system, joined the fleet in November 1956. By then navy air-launched anti-air missiles were in an advanced state of development. Together with higher performance carrier aircraft, this greatly enhanced the naval forces' ability to carry out their missions in advanced areas.

BALLISTIC MISSILE SUBMARINES

As for nuclear weapon capabilities, the army and air force were developing ballistic missiles for delivery of thermonuclear warheads. Early in 1955 a study entitled "Meeting the Threat of a Surprise Attack," prepared by a group headed by James R. Killian, recommended that such missiles be developed for launching from sea-going vessels, including submarines.

Despite considerable opposition within the Department of Defense, CNO Admiral Arleigh Burke succeeded that fall in getting Secretary of Defense C. E. Wilson's permission to begin a program to achieve such a capability. Although some additional funding was expected, none was provided. Nevertheless, Burke established the Special Project Office, attached to and supported by the Bureau of Ordnance, to develop a fleet ballistic missile system. Within the Navy Department the project was given overriding priority for funds and personnel.

Ostensibly, the plan was to adapt the missile being developed by the army. Yet, from the very start the navy knew that the liquid propellants of that missile were unsuited for shipboard employment and that missile acceleration would be insufficient to launch it from a vessel subject to sea motions. Instead, a solid-propellant, inertially guided missile with a radically smaller warhead, capable of being launched from underwater, was developed together with a shipboard fire control and launching system. In addition, the design of a class of nuclear-powered submarines then under construction was changed to incorporate the system. The first ballistic missile submarine was brought into service in less than five years.

The ability of these submarines to lie hidden beneath the sea ready to launch missiles would in the following years provide the keystone to U.S. nuclear warfare deterrence.

THE SUEZ WAR

Once again, the Cold War was intensifying. By 1956 Nikita S. Khrushchev and his associates were securely in power in the Soviet Union. In Poland, an uprising of workers at Pozan resulted in 44 deaths and hundreds of wounded. A Hungarian revolt against the communist regime was crushed ruthlessly by the army of the Soviet Union in October.

Britain had completed its troop withdrawals from the Suez area in June and the USSR was now delivering arms to Egypt. When U.S. oil interests in Saudi Arabia were threatened, two destroyers were deployed to the scene. When Egypt delayed their passage through the canal, Admiral Burke placed the Sixth Fleet on alert.

Nationalization of the canal set in motion a series of events culminating in the October Suez War. The Sixth Fleet, then operating in the Ionian Sea, was again alerted on June 28, the day before Israel began its attack into the Sinai.

As it turned out, Egypt's action had led Britain and France, in conjunction with Israel, to conduct an invasion. The fleet's amphibious force evacuated Americans and others from Haifa and Alexandria. A task force from the Seventh Fleet was sent from the western Pacific into the Indian Ocean with a battalion of marines embarked. A hunter-killer antisubmarine force proceeded from northern Europe to the Mediterranean.

If there had been any doubts about the influence of U.S. naval power in that region of the world, they should have been dispelled by subsequent events. The Egyptian government requested Sixth Fleet intervention. Germany sought protection for its evacuation ship. France desired offshore security for Port Lyautey. Both Greece and Turkey made inquiries concerning protection by the fleet.

A British-French ultimatum for each side, Egypt and Israel, to withdraw ten miles from the canal and resolve not to use force was rejected. Following this, British planes from Cyprus attacked targets in Egypt. When the UN General Assembly passed a U.S. cease fire resolution, Egypt sought the presence of the Sixth Fleet to enforce it.

By now, a combined British-French amphibious force was headed for the area. A helicopter delivery of troops to Port Said was followed by the landing of forces on beaches as two French aircraft carriers provided combat support.

The Soviet Union asked for a Sixth Fleet cooperative effort to end the war. The United States did not agree. Meanwhile, the presence of that fleet was playing a key role in influencing Britain and France to end hostilities.

When the Soviets began to recruit "volunteers"[1] for service in the Middle East, U.S. Air Force strategic forces were placed on alert, the Atlantic Fleet was readied for a possible general war, and a two-carrier task force was ordered to proceed to the eastern Atlantic. The danger of Soviet action eased.

As the Suez War came to an end the Sixth Fleet had yet another role—providing logistics support to UN forces supervising the disengagement. Britain and France completed troop withdrawals in December 1956.

DETERRENCE

The development of long-range ballistic missiles with fusion warheads was accompanied by another change in national policy. In September 1957, a month after the Soviets tested the first such missile, the U.S. secretary of state announced a new approach to countering the threat of aggression. Highlighting the strategic air force and stock of nuclear weapons, Dulles stated that "the military strategy of the free-world allies [since 1950] has been largely based upon our great capacity to retaliate should the Soviet Union launch a war of aggression" and that this had "contributed decisively to the security of the free world." Now such a strategy was considered acceptable only as a last resort. With the view that destruction and radiation effects of nuclear weapons could be confined to predetermined targets and their immediate surroundings, less reliance was placed upon the "deterrance of vast retaliatory power" and more was placed on limited use of nuclear weapons. The present emphasis was on collective security and military and economic aid. Noting that the United States had entered into collective security treaties with 42 other nations since 1945 and had less formal arrangements with several more, the secretary asserted that the "nearly worldwide system of regional collective security" had "deterred aggression and given much needed assurance to peoples who are specially exposed to attack."[2] He made no reference to the pivotal roles played by naval power.

The launching of satellite Sputnik I in the following month gave spectacular evidence of Soviet progress in missile technology. Before the end of the year the United States tested an Atlas missile. A U.S. satellite was sent into orbit in January 1958.

A significant portion of the defense budget by now was being absorbed by ballistic missile programs. Yet, once again, the introduction of a new mode of warfare had not reduced the worldwide demands on the U.S. Navy. Before the year was out operations of the fleet made crucial contributions to resolving overlapping crises in the Mediterranean and the Far East.

THE MIDDLE EAST

The situation in the troubled Middle East, where the Syrian government had been overthrown, became increasingly tense that spring. Admiral Burke delayed the scheduled detachment from the Sixth Fleet of an amphibious squadron and its marine battalion landing team, both about to be relieved by a similar force. A third squadron and landing team were deployed from the United States.

Upon signs of an impending crisis that summer, the chief of naval operations stationed the Sixth Fleet over the horizon from Lebanon. A coup in Iraq in July 1958 and the continuing expansion of rioting in Lebanon led to concern that a Soviet-supported attempt might be made to overthrow the government there. In response to a decision by President Eisenhower to grant a request for assistance from Lebanese President Camille Chamoun, Admiral Burke set in motion the operation that landed marines on the following morning. After a delay required to obtain permission from countries to be overflown, U.S. Army troops from Europe began to arrive by air five days later.

The threats to the Lebanese government soon declined, and U.S. troops were soon withdrawn.

THE FAR EAST

As for the situation in the Far East, there was evidence of a concentration of Communist Chinese military forces on the mainland across from Taiwan. There were two airfields in the area. A third was placed in operation on August 6 and a fourth two days later. Heavy shelling of Quemoy Island began on the 23rd.

Admiral Burke immediately ordered that the Seventh Fleet be sent to the vicinity. Four days later, when radio broadcasts from the Peoples Republic of China referred to an imminent invasion of Quemoy and a determination to liberate Taiwan, additional warships, including a carrier, were deployed west from the eastern Pacific. A Sixth Fleet carrier task group was sent through the Suez Canal. Carrier aircraft began supersonic flights over the strait between Taiwan and the mainland. While carrier planes provided coverage overhead, U.S. destroyers helped escort Nationalist resupply missions to Quemoy. On the diplomatic front, the secretary of state associated the defense of Quemoy and the Matsus with the defense of Taiwan.

One of the highlights of this confrontation was the decision early in September to provide the Chinese Nationalists with Sidewinder guided missiles recently developed by the Bureau of Ordnance's Naval Ordnance Test Station at China Lake, California. By September 15, 20 planes were equipped to fire the simple missile and eight pilots had been trained. Within a week all the squadron pilots were qualified. On the 25th four Sidewinder-armed fighters engaged high-performance Soviet-built MIG-17s. Four out of the six missiles fired hit and each destroyed a MIG.

The rapid deployment to the western Pacific increased the strength of the Seventh Fleet to the point that it had six attack carriers with screening forces and other types. The communists gradually eased their siege of Quemoy.

REORGANIZATION

It was ironic that even as U.S. naval power was making such key contributions to resolving concurrent crises in widely separated areas of the globe, steps were once again being taken to revise the alignment of responsibilities and authority that had contributed so much to anticipating needs and providing appropriate responses before situations deteriorated to a serious extent.

President Eisenhower, in his State of the Union Address of January 1958, listed defense reorganization as the first of eight priority tasks. Prior to submitting a draft of proposed legislation in April, he sent a message to Congress discussing changes he considered "essential to the effective direction of the entire defense establishment." He asserted, as a first principle, that "separate ground, sea, and air warfare is gone forever. If ever again we should be involved in war, we will fight it in all elements." The president added that "strategic and tactical planning must be completely unified," and that "combat forces organized into unified commands . . . [must be] singly led and prepared to fight as one, regardless of service."[3]

In the Reorganization Act, passed in August 1958, Congress went along with most of the president's recommendations. The chief of naval operations was no longer charged by law "with the operations of the fleet, and with the preparations and readiness of plans for its use in war." Instead, he was to "exercise supervision over such of the members and organizations of the Navy and Marine Corps as the Secretary of the Navy determines."[4] He would not be in the chain of command over the Pacific and Atlantic unified commands or the eastern Atlantic and Mediterranean specified commands, the three to which the vast majority of naval combat forces were assigned. Although still designated principal naval advisor to the president on the conduct of war, his direct input into decisions at the national level would inevitably decrease.

The unified and specified commands now would report directly to the secretary of defense as well as the president. Reorganized as directed by Eisenhower along the lines of a conventional military staff, the Joint Chiefs of Staff would be considered as the immediate military staff of the secretary. The chairman of the joint chiefs gained increased authority over the staff. He was now permitted to vote on decisions of the JCS. Whenever the commandant of the Marine Corps considered a matter before the joint chiefs to be of direct concern he would now meet with them as a co-equal.

Other provisions of the act resulted in extensive transfers of authority from the secretaries of the military departments to the secretary of defense, his assistants, and agencies. Instead of being "separately administered," the military departments were now "separately organized." The secretary of defense could "assign or reassign, to one or more departments or services, the development and operational use of new weapons or weapon systems."[5] One case of further functional centralization was the act's creation of a director of defense research and engineering to whom extraordinary powers were granted. Although the stated purpose was to eliminate duplication, the new director extended his activities even into programs and projects that involved only one of the military departments. A case in point was his establishing the position of assistant director for underseas warfare.

Far-reaching changes were to result from the act's provision that directed the secretary of defense to "take appropriate steps (including the transfer, reassignment, abolition, and consolidation of functions) to provide in the Department of Defense for more effective, efficient, and economical administration and operation and to eliminate duplication."[6] Despite the requirement that Congress be notified 30 days before implementing such steps, the potential consequences, such as on the readiness and responsiveness to the needs of the operating forces, only rarely received any significant congressional attention. The elimination of duplication tended to become an end in itself. Whether or not the steps taken did in fact result in more effective, efficient, and economical administration and operation was all too often not critically evaluated. Some of the results would be the progressive fragmentation of the military departments' authority over the means required to fulfill their responsibilities, further growth in the overhead structure imposed over those departments, and increasing tendencies to deal with functional matters as if they were primary goals.

A further complicating factor was the office of the secretary of defense's superimposition of four "force" categories over the budget for the coming fiscal year. The categories were strategic forces, air defense forces, sea control forces, and tactical forces. Although this artificial breakdown for the time being recognized the most basic naval mission, it reflected a lack of understanding of the multimission capabilities of warships and other naval units, and the versatility and flexibility with which they are so often regrouped in response to changing situations, needs, and opportunities. Incongruities resulted, such as including amphibious warfare, naval support of operations on land, and carrier forces under "sea control forces," while placing carrier aircraft and sea transportation under "tactical forces."[7] Such forced fits and administrative actions were but a part of the continuing process of fragmentation. The budgetary processes were becoming ever more complex and time consuming, the criteria for program justification more diverse and confusing.

THE COLD WAR CONTINUES

Meanwhile, communist aggression was continuing. They had shown over the years that they were not preoccupied with any single type of conflict. Step by step, they had sought progress toward long-range goals on the world scene by preparing the way and selecting the time, place, means, and degree of boldness deemed most likely to succeed in exploiting opportunities. The fact that the international movement was not truly monolithic added to the variety of actions that might be undertaken.

As 1958 came to a close, the North Vietnamese Army seized positions in Laos just below the 17th parallel on the main road into Quang Tri, the northern province of South Vietnam. The Laotian government asked the United States to influence the Democratic Republic of Vietnam to withdraw its troops, but there they would remain.

Communist attacks the next summer led Laos to inform the UN of violations of the Geneva agreement of 1954 and a North Vietnamese pledge not to interfere in Laotian internal affairs. The Seventh Fleet prepared to execute a contingency plan whereby the fleet marine force would employ their new C-130 aircraft to insert advance units in Thailand. That step was to be followed by the landing of the main body of marines and heavy equipment by the fleet's amphibious force. Meanwhile, carrier planes of the strike force, operating off the Vietnamese coast, would provide fighter protection and other support, if required. If the plan was implemented the landing force would proceed north to the vicinity of the Laotian border.

In August the Seventh Fleet was alerted when actions in Laos resulted in a request for a UN force.

In the western hemisphere, the United States, influenced by anti-Batista propaganda, a minimizing of Fidel Castro's communist connections, and a lack of appreciation of the consequences, had failed to take timely actions that might have prevented the overthrow of the Cuban government. By the end of the year Castro was in control. He would soon install a government controlled by the Communist party aligned with the Soviet Union. Efforts to expand the revolution to nearby countries began.

Because of its vital canal, Panama was a prime target. The landing of about 90 men there led to assigning the Second Fleet to establish surveillance off the Caribbean coast of that country. The day after the patrol started the landing party, mostly Cubans, surrendered. Other Cubans were inserted into Haiti where 30 were killed or captured. In July 1959 the Dominican Republic announced that a Cuban-supported incursion of 86 men had been defeated.

In the following year the premier of the Soviet Union threatened to retaliate with a nuclear rocket attack if the United States intervened in Cuba. President Eisenhower responded by warning that the United States would never permit establishment of a regime dominated by international communism in the western hemisphere.

This was a troubled time in Europe as the Soviets threatened Western power rights in Berlin. A U.S. RB-47 reconnaissance photographic plane was downed.

There was trouble also in Africa where Belgium had agreed to the establishment of an independent Congolese state by June 30, 1960. Within a week after Patrice Lumumba came to power, Congolese soldiers mutinied against their Belgian officers. There were acts of violence against European civilians. Belgium flew in paratroopers. The United Nations sent a force to help stabilize the situation.

Over the next two years the U.S. Navy transported personnel and equipment to the UN contingent. The conflict might have been resolved far more rapidly if, under UN sponsorship, the United States and others had instituted a selective blockade to sever the flow of military supplies being delivered by sea to Lumumba's forces.

Nicaragua invaded Costa Rica. Troops in Guatemala revolted. After Castro threatened to intervene in Central America, Eisenhower ordered a naval patrol into the area.

Despite increasing signs of competition for leadership and disagreements between the Peoples Republic of China and the Soviet Union, accord was reached by the leaders of 81 Communist parties on a long statement on the "further struggle" and for the "triumph of socialism and communism on a world wide scale." The all-encompassing and variegated strategies woven into the rhetoric ranged across the full continuum of political, economic, propaganda, disarmament, and military actions. The declaration's coverage of the uses of force spanned the spectrum from acts of terrorism to the application of military force in "just struggles."[8]

In November 1960 John F. Kennedy was elected president of the United States.

Flexible Response

The incoming administration proclaimed its adoption of another new strategy, one of "Flexible Response,"[1] Used in campaign rhetoric, the phrase was from a book published during the election year written by General Maxwell Taylor in retirement after his tour as army chief of staff. A Kennedy advisor who was returned to active duty early in 1961 to serve on the White House staff, the general was to have a major influence on the military policies of the new regime.

Taylor's book, *The Uncertain Trumpet*, advocated abolishing the Joint Chiefs of Staff, its replacement by a single chief of staff, and "functional budget-making" rather than by military services. He recommended a "new Military Program" based on five kinds of forces: "atomic deterrent forces, both their offensive and defensive components; . . . continental air defense forces; . . . overseas deployments; . . . strategic reserve forces; . . . [and] air and sea forces necessary to give strategic mobility to the U.S. reserves and to maintain air and sea lines of communications."[2]

He placed major emphasis on providing "strategic air and sea lift" for the army, coupled with "stockage of forward depots in overseas areas."[3] No recognition was given to the possible need for assault over the beaches in the objective area by landing forces put ashore from combat-loaded amphibious ships and for the kinds of naval preparatory and supporting actions that had proven crucial so often in the past.

What was stressed was a rapid deployment force, the bulk of the weapons, ammunition, equipment, vehicles, and combat supplies of which would be positioned somewhere overseas. Major reliance on such a concept continued to be advocated by Taylor and by others in the years to follow. Attention was not always drawn to the requisites of effectiveness in any given situation, such as whether the prepositioned stocks would be at the right place at the right time; whether the weapons, ammunition, and vehicles would be safely protected, well maintained, and in a high state of readiness; whether secure fields for landing airborne forces would be convenient to the scene of the crisis; and whether joining troops and prepositioned stocks would always result in an operational force prepared for immediate combat.

Passing judgment on naval requirements, the general noted the importance of antisubmarine capabilities but was critical of the carrier program. Stating that aircraft for combat support of forces ashore could operate from antisubmarine carriers, he ignored requirements for high-performance naval aircraft for this and other tasks, offensive and defensive.

While accepting "the apparent advantages of the Polaris submarine-missile combination," he was "skeptical as to its time of availability."[4] Ironically, a ballistic missile submarine, complete with missile system and weapons, conducted an operational mission the year the book was published.

The first months of the new administration were extremely hectic for the military departments. As later actions would reveal, the incoming secretary of defense, Robert S. McNamara, a seeker of personal and bureaucratic power, was skeptical and even distrustful of military professionals and the judgments of those who had preceded his reign. He brought in as key assistants and staff members a number of academic theoreticians on whom he placed great reliance.

In his annual report, which covered the first half year in office, McNamara informed Congress that "numerous steps were taken to make the existing organization as well as procedures and practices more responsive to the staff requirements of the President and Secretary of Defense." As Arthur M. Schlessinger, Jr. phrased it in his book, *A Thousand Days,* the new secretary "was absorbed in the endless task of trying to seize control of the Pentagon, firing a March 1, 1961, "McNamara mounted his first assault on the Pentagon, firing a fusillade of ninty-six questions, each aimed at a specific area, directed to a specific man and requiring a specific answer by a specific time."[5] As a consequence, key officers, civilian officials, and staffs of the three military departments were heavily preoccupied with preparing, revising, and providing, as adequately as the deadlines allowed, written answers to the questions—many of which were on complex issues with profound implications for the future.

From the start of his term Kennedy placed major emphasis on counterinsurgency, on increased training in paramilitary warfare, and on expansion of guerrilla units. His first budget provided for a doubling of the army's counterinsurgency forces and for a substantial increase in capabilities for airlifting ground forces.

THE BAY OF PIGS

One of the early decisions of the new president, who in his campaign had criticized U.S. complacency on Cuba, was to approve the landing of a force of Cuban exiles to take actions against the Castro regime, an operation proposed by the Central Intelligence Agency (CIA), which had been created under the National Security Council by the National Security Act of 1947. These exiles had been in training under CIA auspices. The landing was supposed to be covert, but specific information on what was planned seems to have been concealed more from U.S. military commanders than from Castro.

The responsibility for planning and directing the projection of the quasi-military force onto the island fell to a marine officer assigned to the CIA. He had landing force experience, but no one with the experience of a navy amphibious force commander was involved. Due allowance was not made for the possibility of opposition by Cuban troops and aircraft during the landing phase. The miscellaneous ships were poorly organized and not properly loaded.

Commander in chief, Atlantic and U.S. Atlantic Fleet received his information belatedly and through abnormal channels. Naval air support and other fleet actions that might have altered the final outcome were not approved by the president.

In the eyes of the world, the disastrous Bay of Pigs effort in April 1961 was a U.S. defeat in the Cold War—and indeed it was. More than that, it raised questions about the resolve and determination of the nation.

VIETNAM: THE BEGINNING OF U.S. INVOLVEMENT

A few days after the frustrating fiasco, Kennedy announced that consideration was being given to the use of U.S. force, if necessary, to help the Republic of Vietnam to resist pressure. The Taylor-Rostow mission to Saigon in October recommended increased U.S. military involvement, including basing planes in the country to provide airlift for South Vietnamese troops and air reconnaissance. Also recommended was a 10,000-man U.S. force for self defense and security.

A detachment of an air force combat training squadron was deployed the next month. Its crews and planes with Republic of Vietnam markings soon were engaged in paramilitary combat operations. Two army helicopter companies arrived by ship. Other forces followed. With the basing of U.S. military units on foreign soil and their use in combat, a step-by-step process of commitment to warfare in that distant land was underway.

No such commitment was involved in tasks assigned to the Seventh Fleet. To aid in detecting vessels that might be transporting personnnel or supplies from North to South Vietnam, minesweepers of the fleet patrolled a line extending 30 nautical miles to sea from the three-mile limit off the Demilitarized Zone.

In February 1962 coverage was extended in random fashion by navy patrol planes as far as the Paracel Islands. Destroyer escorts were employed in the Gulf of Thailand to assist in detecting movements through the passage inside Phu Quoc Island from Cambodia.

A marine helicopter squadron flew off the USS *Princeton* of the Seventh Fleet's amphibious force to an airfield in the Mekong Delta. The ship provided an example of adaptation to changing requirements. Originally an attack carrier constructed during World War II, she had been decommissioned in 1949 and placed in the Reserve Fleet and then reactivated to meet the needs of the Korean War. She had served after that war as an antisubmarine carrier and been converted five years later into an amphibious assault carrier.

The situation in Laos was becoming more tense. In May 1962 the amphibious force put its marine landing force ashore in Thailand. The situation eased and most were withdrawn in July.

CUBAN MISSILE CRISIS

Before long there was a confrontation of Soviet and U.S. forces on the other side of the globe, one in which naval power played the key role. In addition to increasing its military aid to Cuba, the USSR had sent some 20,000 armed forces to that island. By October 1962 there was positive evidence of sites being built preparatory to the introduction of ballistic missiles capable of nuclear strikes against the United States.

On October 22 the president announced a quarantine of Cuba—actually a conditional naval blockade—to prevent the delivery of offensive weapons. He indicated that readiness steps were being taken to apply measures of increasing severity. These might involve a full blockade, air attacks, or invasion. Strategic air forces and all available Polaris submarines were placed in a high state of alert.

The United States was now involved in a grave emergency requiring local control of the sea. The Joint Chiefs of Staff wisely fixed responsibilities along the lines that had proven so successful in World War II. They designated the chief of naval operations to act for them on quarantine matters. The air force chief of staff was assigned similar responsibilities for air reconnaissance over Cuba.

Under the commander in chief, U.S. Atlantic Fleet, the commander, Second Fleet conducted the blockading operation with a force of 48 ships and 240 naval aircraft. Vessels heading to or from Cuba were located. Twenty destroyers formed on a distant line in the Atlantic and Caribbean kept the vessels under surveillance. The Soviets had six submarines in the area. All were detected and trailed; they surfaced. All suspect ships had been turned back. Other stopped or slowed until they received orders from Moscow.

The lesson was not lost on the Soviet Union, which, as later became evident, stepped up its construction program of modern surface warships.

Despite this latest demonstration of the fundamental importance of the ability to control uses of the seas, Secretary McNamara eliminated the sea control forces from the budget prepared for submission to Congress. Expressing concern that he must ensure that the navy be well balanced to the requirements of the army, he superimposed "program packages" over the military departments: general warfare offensive forces, general warfare defensive forces, general purpose forces, airlift and sealift, civil defense, research and development, general support, and military assistance. The introduction of these "packages"[6] was accompanied by a multiplication of centers of authority within the office of the secretary of defense. Two new defense agencies were created—intelligence and supply.

COUNTERINSURGENCY

In the continuing struggle in Southeast Asia, increasing pressure was applied to get the Republic of Vietnam to adopt U.S. theories of counterinsurgency. The U.S. government and the numerous advisors it sent to the area repeatedly tried to tell the South Vietnamese, both broadly and in great detail, the military, para-military, economic, and political actions they should take. U.S. expressions of dissatisfaction with the current leadership preceded the November 1963 coup in which President Diem was murdered.

One of the prescribed communist routes of take-overs of former colonies was by a war of national liberation followed by consolidation of control and establishment of a socialist system under the Communist party. The overthrow of the Diem government and the instabilities that followed, with something like nine successors in two years, helped set the stage for such a war.

Under Lyndon B. Johnson, who succeeded to the presidency upon the assassination of Kennedy later that month, decisions concerning the conflict were heavily influenced by recommendations of the National Security Council, which had been created by the 1947 act to "advise the President with respect to the integration of domestic, foreign, and military policies relating to the national security."[7] At times the council's advice would go well beyond that and extend into detailed matters—even to those of a purely military nature. Studies by an ever-growing staff and inevitable tendencies toward committee-type solutions would lead to never ending reexaminations of decisions during the forthcoming Vietnam War. One consequence was the adoption of many transient courses of action by the United States.

Making full use of the powers now permitted the secretary of defense under the president, McNamara masterminded strategy. Underestimating enemy resolve and failing to follow proven principles regarding the application of military force, he adopted a theoretically derived strategy of gradualism and measured response. One of the new positions soon created was assistant secretary of defense (systems analysis), the purpose of which was to apply "methods of quantitative economic analysis and scientific method" to the "choice of weapon systems and strategy."[8]

Meanwhile, the exercise of controls had already gone beyond decisions on strategy and extended to detailed tactical directions. For instance, when in May 1964 it was decided to conduct carrier air reconnaissance over the Ho Chi Minh trail, commander, Seventh Fleet was not permitted to exercise authority commensurate with his responsibilities and in accordance with his professional judgment on the scene of action almost halfway around the world from Washington.

Instead, the secretary of defense insisted on determining the number, size, and timing of missions, and on prescribing flight paths and their altitudes. Two of the planes were shot down.

THE VIETNAM WAR

Destroyer *Maddox*, in international waters in the Gulf of Tonkin on a mission to acquire "hydrographic" and "intelligence"[9] information, was attacked by North Vietnamese torpedo boats on August 2, 1964. One boat was sunk and the other damaged by the destroyer's gunfire and by carrier aircraft. After evidence of another attack two days later, a carrier air strike was ordered against naval targets in North Vietnam.

Congress passed the Southeast Asia Resolution authorizing the president to repel any attack against U.S. armed forces and to prevent further communist aggression. On November 1, just prior to the presidential election, the Viet Cong conducted a mortar attack that destroyed air force bombers and killed some Americans at the Bien Hoa Air Base. Recommendations that air strikes be launched against targets in North Vietnam were not approved.

Following the election, an interagency group of the National Security Council recommended continuing the broad policy that had as its goal an independent, noncommunist Vietnamese republic and then examined specific programs for action, including those for the U.S. armed forces.

In December 1964 President Johnson authorized "armed reconnaissance"[10] by U.S. planes over the Laotian panhandle, the land route for movements of supplies and personnel in support of communist actions in South Vietnam. The flights were limited by McNamara to only a couple four-plane missions each week.

The North Vietnamese were heavily dependent upon receipt of shipments by sea for their support of the Viet Cong, for one of their army regiments that had been inserted into South Vietnam, and for antiaircraft defenses.

Premier Alexi N. Kosygin's state visit to Hanoi in February 1965 resulted in greatly increased deliveries of Soviet military weapons, equipment, and munitions by sea. The deliveries included MIG-15, -17, and -21 aircraft; new antiaircraft batteries; and surface-to-air missiles. This was one of those times when U.S. naval power conceivably might have been employed to impose a conditional blockade to stem the flow of such cargoes, as in the Cuban crisis. One of the recommendations made by Admiral U. S. G. Sharp, commander in chief, Pacific, was mining the approaches to Haiphong and other key ports and establishing a blockade.

Throughout the duration of the Vietnam War, all the oil and more than 85 percent of the military supplies for the communists were delivered by sea to Haiphong. Yet it was not until 1972, after the U.S. withdrawal had begun, that mines were employed to close the port.

As of 1965 the sea control tasks of the U.S. Navy were limited to operations along the coast of South Vietnam, with the purpose to intercept communist craft attempting deliveries from the north. By now the North Vietnamese had formed the 603rd Battalion for the infiltration by sea of cells and delivery of supplies to their bases. The capabilities of the Republic of Vietnam Navy were improving but it was still unable to provide the necessary coverage, which was complicated by the great length of the coastline and the myriad of fishing craft that often blanketed large areas of coastal waters.

Early in 1965 Seventh Fleet carrier task forces, sustained on station by underway replenishment ships of the Service Force, were maintaining a presence off Tonkin Gulf (Yankee Station) and off the middle region of South Vietnam (Dixie Station). In the months that followed, their ability to operate in international waters that were within easy tactical range of their fighters and accurate dive bombers provided unique capabilities in both North and South Vietnam. These strikes included some against targets in the northern part of North Vietnam, which were more difficult to reach from air bases in South Vietnam or Thailand.

After a communist attack against a U.S. advisors' compound at Pleiku and U.S. barracks at Qui Nhon in February 1965, Washington ordered two raids by carrier planes against groups of barracks in North Vietnam.

Later in February the president authorized the second phase of the program recommended by the National Security Council, which was a gradual escalation of air strikes in North Vietnam. Office of the secretary of defense and State Department representatives in the working group conceived such graduated action as ultimately bringing Hanoi into negotiations favorable to the United States.

The first carrier air strikes against targets in South Vietnam were in April 1965. The ability of land-based squadrons to carry out operations in support of troops was very limited prior to the strengthening and lengthening of existing runways and the construction of additional airfields and airstrips. Beginning in July the Seventh Fleet maintained an attack carrier off the southern portion of the republic, where its planes conducted close support and strike operations for the Military Assistance Command. Carriers further north carried out similar operations in addition to their missions north of the Demilitarized Zone (DMZ). The gunfire support of operations ashore by Seventh Fleet destroyers, cruisers, and later by a recommissioned battleship was at times crucial.

One of the fields within Vietnam to which air force planes were deployed was at Danang, only about 75 miles south of the Demilitarized Zone. To help provide protection, marines were landed there by the Seventh Fleet's amphibious force in March 1965. During the following month President Johnson approved more active use of the marines. He also authorized sending additional battalions and a marine air squadron. Soon thereafter, more air force planes and army troops were being deployed.

The amphibious force was involved in a number of operations. Most met little or no opposition. One that did was in August when intelligence was gained of a Viet Cong regiment of some 2,000 men in the area of Van Tuong peninsula south of an airstrip built at Chu Lai. Supported by naval gunfire and carrier planes, an assault landing was made while amphibious vehicles brought others from Chu Lai by water. Helicopters landed some inland. Catching the enemy by surprise, victory was complete, with a body count of almost 1,000.

Some of the extraordinary tasks assigned to the navy in this strangely conducted war were of a logistical nature. Earlier, the concept of common supplies had been embraced, which led to designating the navy as "Administrative Agent" for the Pacific area. Thus, naval logistics support was being provided to the Military Assistance and Advisory Group when the buildup of U.S. forces within Vietnam began. The responsibility was not altered when a U.S. Military Assistance Command, with a majority of army forces, was established. To meet the rapidly expanding needs of General Paul D. Harkins' command, the navy formed the Headquarters Support Activity, Saigon in July 1962 to furnish "administrative and logistic support to the . . . Military Advisor Group, . . . and other activities and units designated by the Chief of Naval Operations."[11]

While each of the military departments was responsible for providing service-peculiar items, the navy furnished common supplies and services and carried out other logistics tasks for which arrangements had not been made. As the build-up continued, support was extended to some remote locations. The expanding scope resulted in the support activity being assigned to commander, service force, Pacific Fleet.

Army units required for some logistics support functions were in the reserves. In the absence of national mobilization, they were not called to active duty. One of the deficiencies was the lack of army engineer battalions, as a consequence of which Naval Mobile Construction Battalions (Seabees) of the service force were deployed to perform duties beyond those for the support of navy and marine forces. Earlier contributions had been made by Seabee Technical Assistance Teams, the first of which had been sent in July 1962 to serve with army special forces.

Once landed, the logistics support of marine operations ashore in the I Corps Zone posed problems. Because of the army's low state of readiness for operational logistics support of deployed forces, the navy was required to provide it. Since there was only one shallow draft pier at Danang, the Seventh Fleet's amphibious force retained a task organization on the scene for off-loading ships and transferring cargoes over the beach by landing craft. The navy's headquarters support activity was doing its best to meet the extraordinary demands for common support and services in that area as well as elsewhere. As result of the failure of the chief of naval operations to have the army carry out such responsibilities, following the March landing by the marines, in July the navy established the Naval Support Activity, Danang under commander, Service force, Pacific Fleet.

The rapid buildup of capabilities was made possible by Navy's Advanced Base Functional Component System, which had been developed in World War II and wisely maintained with its equipment, vehicles, structural components, et cetera, and by transfers of key personnel from all over the world.

Additional marine troops and aircraft were brought in. Support was needed for operations soon to be undertaken in other regions of I Corps and for new airstrips. The nature of the terrain, the low capacity of roads and trails, and the vulnerability of bridges across numerous rivers meant that the bulk of ammunition and supplies were transshipped from Danang by sea and sometimes up rivers, at times encountering mines, to island-like areas employing amphibious-type ships and craft.

The substantial buildup of army advisors in Vietnam, their deployment to remote locations, and the piecemeal introduction of combat units were not accompanied by balanced provisions for logistical organizations. When the Department of the Army wished to form an army logistical command, the Department of Defense required justification. Gaining approval took considerable time and then authorization was incremental. As a consequence, the transfer of responsibilities for logistics support in II, III, and IV Corps Tactical Zones from the navy to the army begun in September 1965 was not completed until the following May. During this period the service force formed Naval Support Activity, Saigon to carry out logistical responsibilities with regard to naval forces operating out of scattered small bases along the coast and on inland waters of these zones.

One case of functional centralization directed in great detail by the office of the secretary of defense was construction. A 1963 directive signed by a deputy assistant secretary of defense designated the navy's Bureau of Yards and Docks "Department of Defense Construction Agent in Southeast Asia." The rationale was that this was one of the "areas in the Far East where the current and projected workload for design and construction does not warrant the continuation of several construction agencies."[12] Yet by 1965 the bureau had two officers in charge of construction, one for Vietnam, the other for Thailand.

The Department of Defense imposed a single set of priorities over all Vietnam, even though needs varied greatly from one region to another. For a long time airfields were accorded first priority. As it was, the foremost cause of the clogging of Danang and other ports was vast quantities of incoming shipments of construction materials ordered by contractors, much of it prematurely. It was not until the situation at Danang became desperate that deep-draft piers were authorized. None was available until the fall of 1966.

Four days after the marines landed at Danang in the spring of 1965, Seventh Fleet destroyers began a surveillance patrol off the coast of South Vietnam. A decision to include operations within the three-mile limit was followed by the establishment of a coastal surveillance force composed of coast guard cutters and specially designed naval craft. Since close coordination with the Vietnamese

Map 26.1
Southeast Asia

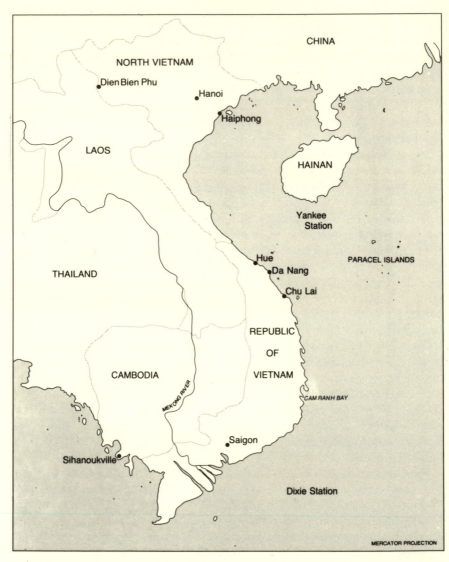

Source: Drawn for the editors by the University of Maryland Geography Department, Cartography Services Laboratory, 1987.

Navy was required, command was assigned to the chief of the U.S. Naval Advisory Group, later designated Commander, Naval Forces, Vietnam. The Republic of Vietnam authorized stopping, searching, and seizing vessels within territorial waters.

Augmenting the riverine capabilities of the small Vietnamese Navy, U.S. naval forces played important roles on inland waters. After shallow-draft river patrol boats were constructed, the U.S. River Patrol Force began operations in the approaches to Saigon and on the complex waterways of the vast Mekong Delta in April 1966.

Effectiveness was later enhanced by helicopters attached to the force. Early in 1967, following the building and conversion of craft in the United States and training, a mobile riverine force and its riverine assault flotilla commenced operations, providing what amounted to an amphibious force on inland waters for landing and for gunfire and logistics support of army troops. The force included barracks ships and craft, landing craft, and other types to provide highly mobile capabilities.

Throughout this period Seventh Fleet carrier and air force planes conducted armed reconnaissance along the Ho Chi Minh Trail and struck targets in North Vietnam. Progress toward the objective of causing the Democratic Republic of Vietnam to cease its direction of, participation in, and support of war in the south was hindered by ever-changing restrictions placed on targeting and on areas in which bombing was permitted. Strikes were suspended just when there was evidence of significant cumulative effects. August 1967 was such a period. A ten-day cessation of attacks of the Hanoi area was ordered while the United States attempted to get the North Vietnamese leaders to agree to negotiate. Although they did not, two months passed before such strikes were resumed.

Mining of deep-water ports and extensions of surface warship patrols further up the enemy coast were among the recommendations of the Joint Chiefs of Staff that were not approved.

With the beginning of the northeast monsoon in the fall, aircraft interdiction of inland supply movements east of the Laotian ridge of the Annam mountains was periodically hindered by low clouds and poor visibility. The enemy took advantage of these conditions and of the U.S. announcement of stand-downs over the Christmas and New Year's Day holidays.

Hanoi indicated that the National Liberation Front would suspend military attacks from January 26 to February 2, 1968 for the Tet religious holiday. Except in I Corps, where there was evidence of a heavy buildup, the South Vietnamese began their leaves and cease-fire observations of the holiday on January 29. Within the next two days, the North Vietnamese and Viet Cong launched attacks in one form or another against provincial capitals, many district capitals, and military installations throughout South Vietnam.

Although for a time the communists gained control of the traditional capital, Hue, they were defeated there and suffered extremely severe losses in a month's fighting. Nevertheless, the events, made to appear especially grim by the media's sensational coverage, shocked some of the decision makers in Washington and triggered peace demonstrations accompanied by negative propaganda.

McNamara resigned his position as secretary of defense and was succeeded by Clark Clifford on March 1. Soon thereafter, President Johnson, once again hoping to get Hanoi to participate in peace negotiations, restricted bombings to the southern portion of North Vietnam where the authorized strikes were mostly against roads and trails used to move forces and supplies destined for below the DMZ.

An offensive that fall by the mobile riverine force, the river patrol force, and task groups of the coastal surveillance force achieved notable results. The suspension of all strikes against North Vietnam on November 1 gained no concessions from the communists.

Richard Nixon became president in 1969. Gradual withdrawal of U.S. troops began in July. Nixon announced the Vietnamization policy that November.

CAMBODIA

Fighting within South Vietnam continued, as opposition in the United States to the remote, prolonged war mounted. By 1970 the port of Sihanoukville, Cambodia was being used for the delivery of military supplies and munitions to North Vietnamese troops utilizing that country as a base of operations across the border. Information now indicates that Chinese shipments of such cargoes to that port had begun in 1965. Thereafter, something like 95 percent of the ordnance for Viet Cong and North Vietnam troops in the southern region, the location of Saigon and the Mekong Delta, came by sea through Cambodia. Evidence of such deliveries had been ignored or discounted. In any case, there appears to have been no consideration given to imposing a selective or conditional blockade that by visit and search might have turned back the ships or resulted in the seizure of cargoes of munitions destined for the enemy—a traditional use of naval power.

President Nixon's authorization in the spring of 1970 of an incursion by U.S. forces into Cambodia to destroy base areas across the border resulted in strong antiwar reactions in the United Staes. A congressional amendment later in the year prohibited such actions.

Free from bombing, North Vietnam staged forces in the southern portion of their country and in Laos in 1972. The offensive started with the movement of a well-armored division across the DMZ on March 30. Aided by the gunfire support of U.S. warships, South Vietnam troops arrested the advance. A one-time strike against specified targets in the Hanoi-Haiphong area was authorized.

The failure of peace negotiations that May led the president to order the mining with sophisticated influence mines of entrances to Haiphong and other North Vietnamese ports to prevent ship movements. He ordered the interdiction of movements of supplies on claimed territorial and inland waters and a resumption of air and naval gunfire attacks against land communications systems and military targets. The last U.S. combat forces were withdrawn from South Vietnam in August. A compromise peace agreement was reached in January 1973. The mines blocking North Vietnamese harbors were then removed by U.S. minesweepers.

Despite violations of the treaty by North Vietnam, Congress withdrew funds for combat activities in, over, or off the shores of Cambodia, Laos, or North and South Vietnam; restricted the president's authority to use armed forces in combat; and in 1974 cut military aid funds.

When the Republic of Vietnam fell in 1975, the victors acquired great quantities of materials, supplies, weapons, military equipment, and vehicles left behind by the Americans. The communists could now benefit from the many installations, including airfields, built by the vast construction program. Major facilities, including deep-draft piers constructed primarily for the army and air force at Camranh Bay, would provide the Soviet Navy with a ideally located base alongside the dense shipping route of the South China Sea.

The Shifting Balance
of Sea Power

Since World War II the United States has tended to take for granted the peacetime and wartime benefits of sea power supremacy. Now, in the final quarter of
the twentieth century, the nation's ability to use the seas and exert naval influence faced ever increasing challenges.

The withdrawal of U.S. forces from Vietnam that had begun in 1969 was
accompanied by cutbacks, not only in specialized ships and craft employed in
Southeast Asia, but also in the warships and auxiliaries in active service in the
seagoing fleets deployed throughout the world. Furthermore, a large portion of
U.S. Navy ships were of World War II vintage. Despite some modernization of
systems, many had reached the point of block obsolescence in terms of modern
warfare capabilities. They had been aging and nearing the end of their useful lives.

Various factors had combined to limit severely the construction of replacements to meet future needs Among these were preconceptions about the nature
of future wars, the priority of the Vietnam effort, overly optimistic fiscal
budgets that failed to provide adequate margins to meet the needs resulting from
surges and escalations of the fighting, and the inflationary stimulus of supple-
mental budgets. The requirements of the conflict, as in the Korean War, had
demanded the reactivation of many ships and craft from the Reserve Fleet,
which diminished in size.

Military operations overseas continued to depend upon prompt and adequate
ship deliveries of cargoes. During the Vietnam War tonnages per U.S. man greatly
exceeded the requirements of previous wars. Very nearly maximum use was
made of air transportation, but this accounted for only a tiny portion of the
total tonnage and bulk. Ships delivered all the bulk fuel and over 96 percent of
the dry cargoes. Failures to authorize adequate quantities for surges in requirements resulted in airlifting unprecedented amounts of ammunition. Nevertheless,
over 99 percent went by sea. The navy's Military Sea Transportation Service was
augmented by reactivations from the reserve fleet of merchantmen. Foreign as
well as U.S. vessels were placed under charter. With the passage of time, fewer
and fewer of the merchant ships in world trade flew the U.S. flag.

THE DEFENSE ESTABLISHMENT

There had been increasing tendencies to accept the assumption that all future wars would be fought by combinations of land- and sea-based forces. Within the Department of Defense, unification and the elimination of duplication were tending to be pursued as primary objectives. Additional layers of overall, functional, and program reviews and controls had been superimposed over the military departments. Such actions had led to similar changes within the Navy Department, which tended to fragment the authority and accountability for providing and maintaining a navy, for achieving and sustaining high states of readiness and effectiveness, and for developing and acquiring new and approved means for exercising naval power in the future.

The centers of authority within the expanded office of the secretary of defense reached the point where there were a deputy secretary of defense, 12 assistant secretaries of defense, 9 deputy under secretaries, 22 deputy assistant secretaries, and 3 assistants to the secretary. Over 100 members of the staff had the title of director of one function or another. Many others were deputy directors.

Time lags in the approval process were greatly prolonged, and instabilities were created by such procedures as a highly involved system of program and budget planning and justification, imposition of an extensive process of program definition as a prerequisite to the design and building of ships, weapons, and aircraft, increased demands for time and effort consuming studies in ever-continuing analyses with theoretical and sometimes changing assumptions, and the introduction of scenarios that postulated specific warfare situations as criteria for decision makers. Concerning continuity and consistency, the department of defense program-budget system did include five-year programs. These, however, were restudied and revised annually and portions were often set aside for further justification.

The Department of the Navy was now classified as a defense component along with nine defense agencies and the other two military departments. Pressures from the Department of Defense led to abandoning the lean, highly decentralized, efficient bilinear system of the Navy Department. Material bureaus were fragmented and replaced by system commands. These were now at a lower echelon, being under a chief of naval material and an increasingly large staff. Project officers were designated who reported directly to the chief of naval material, the chief of naval operations, or the secretary of the navy. Laboratories were detached from bureaus (system commands) and reported to a director of laboratories, who was on the staff of the assistant secretary of the navy (research and development) and had another title under the chief of naval material. There was now an Electronic Systems Command but no longer a Bureau of Ordnance or Ordnance Systems Command. Many who had exercised line authority in the bureaus were now coordinators.

Chart 27.1
Department of Defense Organization Chart, 1986

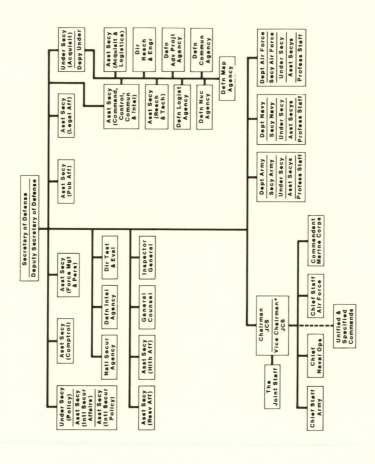

*The position of vice chairman of Joint Chiefs of Staff was added by the Goldwater-Nichols Reorganization Act of 1986.   - - - Normally, orders to Unified and Specified Commands are transmitted through the Chairman of the Joint Chiefs of Staff.

Source: Based in part on the January 1987 Department of Defense Key Personnel Locator.

Problems were further compounded by a tremendous growth in the staffs of congressional committees involved in military affairs and the formation of defense budgets. This was accompanied by increasing demands for detailed justifications of individual line items, small as well as large.

THE SOVIET NAVY

Meanwhile, the Soviet Union had been expanding and modernizing its navy and employing it increasingly to exert influence in various regions of the world. Traditionally, the USSR had subordinated the conduct of naval affairs and the employment of naval forces to the army and its policies. This was no longer the case, or at least not to the same degree. Nor were the composition and employment of the navy so overwhelmingly committed to missions in support of land operations and coastal defense.

Following the Cuban Missile Crisis, increasing numbers of warships, including destroyers and cruisers, had begun to come off the ways. U.S. Navy projects for developing surface-to-surface guided missiles after World War II had been terminated. Thus, the Soviets were the first to arm warships with such weapons. Three guided missiles fired by a Soviet patrol boat on loan to Egypt sank an Israeli destroyer in 1967.

As has been noted, the Soviet Union, with the aid of German engineers, initiated a major submarine construction program after World War II that not only augmented coastal types but also provided for longer-range actions against warships and shipping. In the continuing program, submarines were built that were armed with antiship guided missiles. Nuclear-powered as well as diesel types were introduced, some with ballistic missiles.

In a nonnaval element of sea power, the Soviet Union from 1950 to 1973 had raised the standing of its increasingly modern merchant fleet from twelfth to sixth among the world powers. In the next five years its tonnage was increased by more than a third and that of the Eastern Bloc by two-thirds. Although the Soviet percentage of the total global tonnages of all types of cargoes was still relatively small, a European Market estimate indicated that 28 percent of the freight between Europe and North America, 35 percent of the traffic between northern Europe and Mediterranean destinations, 25 percent between Europe and the west coast of South America, and more than 20 percent between the Mediterranean and the Gulf of Mexico went in Soviet bottoms.

In contrast, the merchantmen flying the U.S. flag, which in 1950 carried almost 50 percent of the nation's foreign trade, in the mid-1970s transported only about 5 percent. U.S. companies owned a number of foreign-flag ships, such as those of Liberian or Panamanian registry, but their availability in some possible warfare situations was uncertain. Furthermore, features desirable in case of war had not been incorporated into their designs.

SOVIET STRATEGY

Soviet actions during this period and prospects for the future warrant evaluations in light of Admiral of the Fleet Sergei G. Gorshkov's work, *The Sea Power of the State,* first published in 1976.

With a considerable portion devoted to drawing lessons from naval history, the basic principles derived in that book coincide with or are similar to those set forth by Mahan a century earlier. Among these are the far reaching consequences of maritime supremacy; the importance of exercising sea control, though not as an end in itself; the profound influence of sea commerce; effects produced by a naval presence; and fundamental differences between warfare at sea and on land.

Gorschkov's concept of sea power is essentially that of Mahan, who defined it as "embracing in its broad sweep all that tends to make a people great upon the sea or by the sea." While stressing "the dominant importance of the navy," the Soviet admiral describes "the sea power of the state as a system characterised not only by the presence of links between its components (military, merchant, fishing, scientific research fleet, etc.) but also by the inseparable union with the environment."[1]

Stressing "all modern great powers are maritime countries," he stated that the Soviet Union had become a maritime power. "Possessing sea power and tirelessly expanding it," it was increasing the employment of that power "to make effective use of the World Ocean in the interests of communist construction."[2]

The effectiveness of a navy as an instrument of foreign policy stems from "constant high combat readiness, mobility and ability in a short time to concentrate its forces in selected areas of the ocean," and the neutrality of the sea, which permits these to be "moved forward and concentrated . . . without providing the other side with formal grounds for protests or other forms of counteraction."[3]

In contrast with earlier years when the nation's naval forces had been designed and employed for operations to defend the homeland, "with the emergence of her navy on the ocean expanses, the Soviet Union has gained new and wider possibilities for its use in peacetime to ensure her state interest." Reference is made to "consolidating the economic, political, cultural and scientific links of the Soviet people with the peoples and countries friendly to it;" tasks of a military-diplomatic nature; the value of a fleet presence to negotiating parties; and the substantial contributions made by port visits and naval demonstrations to the "enhancement of the international authority of the Soviet Union."[4]

According to Admiral Gorshkov, "demonstrative actions by the fleet . . . have made it possible to achieve political ends without . . . armed struggle."[5] The enormous role played by the navy in local wars is stressed.

The USSR had indeed been employing naval power on an ever expanding basis since the end of the Vietnam War. A case in point was the Angolan civil war, during which Soviet merchantmen delivered large quantities of military supplies to the insurgents. A naval quarantine might have prevented the communist takeover in 1975 but no such action was taken. As it was, the Soviet Navy maintained a strong presence in the area when Cuban troops were inserted to augment the rebels.

Ethiopia was another country in which the delivery of munitions by sea and the deployment of Cuban forces gave crucial assistance to the establishment of a communist-controlled regime.

At the same time, the Soviets were maintaining a significant naval presence in the Indian Ocean. Following the Vietnamese invasion of Cambodia, Chinese troops took actions south of their border with Vietnam, and Soviet naval forces were deployed to the vicinity. Another show of Soviet naval force demonstrated support of South Yemen in its conflict with North Yemen.

As for a possible major war, the admiral of the fleet considered the Soviet Navy a "potent means of achieving the political ends of armed struggle in wartime." He refuted the argument (similar to that so often advanced in the United States in recent years) that since combat activities have become so swift and productive there is now no need to gain dominance at sea. Navies have been brought "into the first rank" for modern warfare by "their high manoeuvrability, ability to concentrate covertly and to form unexpectedly for the enemy, powerful groupings and better resistance than the land forces to the actions of nuclear weapons." His conclusion is that "not only the absolute, but also the relative importance of armed struggle at sea has indisputably grown."[6]

Regarding basic differences between warfare at sea and on land, Mahan had noted "that at sea there was no field of battle to be held, nor places to be won." As expressed by Gorshkov, the tasks and modes of operations of navies and land forces, being "determined by the medium and means of struggle, substantially differ."[7]

One section of his work is devoted to "dominance at sea, . . . a special category particular solely to the armed conflict in marine theaters." An important feature is the relatively greater importance of naval operations against an enemy fleet than against the shore. "Any fleet always seeks to create in a particular area of the sea the regime necessary for it, for example, to gain control of shipping and ensuring its safety, freedom to deploy one's forces, etc."[8] The admiral identifies three maritime areas as especially important—the Arctic Ocean, the Mediterranean, and the Indian Ocean. He calls attention to the significance of key straits.

Repeatedly emphasizing the importance of a versatile fleet, Gorshkov states that "one of the main qualities of modern naval forces is their universality . . . expressed in the ability . . . to solve multiple tasks." While attaching prime importance to "multipurpose atomic submarines" and submarine missile systems, he points out the necessity of constructing "surface warships, without which the solution of a number of tasks facing the fleet is impossible." He highlights the crucial value of shore- and ship-based naval aviation and expresses the need for "seaworthy oceanic supply vessels, floating shops and floating bases."[9]

He discusses effects of blockades and mining. Noting how near the German campaign against shipping came to success in two world wars, he points out that U-boat effectiveness could have been enhanced by "backing them up with other kinds of forces, especially aircraft."[10]

The links connecting the various elements of sea power were far tighter in the Soviet Union than in the United States. In routine peacetime operations, in exercises, and in times of conflict and emergencies, naval controls were being employed to a degree that has been approached by the United States only in special warfare situations.

The merchant fleet is described as "a universal component of the sea power of a country which has a most important role in war and peacetime." Stressing the "tremendous economic and political importance" of shipping, Gorshkov asserts that "the development and use of merchant fleets of various countries in peacetime are constantly in the sphere of the economic and political struggle in the international arena which continues to remain an unchanged accompaniment of antagonistic social systems."[11]

The current "transport significance of the ocean"[12] is due to the increasing dependence of countries on the receipt of overseas cargoes and the extent to which worldwide tonnage demands had multiplied over the past couple of decades. Military sea lanes of communication are crucial.

As a "reserve of the navy," the Soviet merchant fleet was used for "material and technical supply of fighting ships, . . . cargo transfers at sea, . . . the re-fuelling of ships and vessels underway, . . . [and] the transports of large contingents of troops, their arms and supplies."[13] At one time during this period, something like one-fourth of Soviet-bloc merchantmen were providing support in one form or another.

As for his third component of sea power, Gorshkov highlights the ocean's food resources as "one of the main sources for solving the food problem of the growing world population"[14] and as a supply of nutrition for his own country. Fish provided about one-fifth of the animal protein consumed in the Soviet Union and were an important fertilizer source. The Soviets had the world's largest fishing fleet of technologically advanced vessels, including factory ships, that were engaged in extracting catches from all over the globe. According to the admiral, they would perform naval tasks in time of war.

Concerning the scientific research fleet, the study of the world ocean is "an important factor influencing the status of the sea power of the state." It was opening up new possibilities "for satisfying the rapidly-growing requirements of our country for energy and fuel, useful minerals and foodstuffs."[15] In addition to an extensive oceanographic program, vessels attached to it were engaged in intelligence work, such as monitoring U.S. weapons tests and naval operations, tailing U.S. Navy task forces, and occasionally interfering with their movements.

Taking full advantage of international laws and customs insofar as their own ships were concerned, and insisting on a right of immunity of state merchant ships, the Soviets sought to restrict some of the freedom-of-the-seas rights of others. They laid claim to closed seas around their country, referred to historic internal waters regarding the Arctic Ocean north of their borders, denied the right of innocent passage of warships through what it claimed to be territorial waters unless prior permission had been obtained, and maintained that within regional seas such as the Black and Baltic seas only states bordering them had rights within them. Two icebreakers of the U.S. Coast Guard proceeding outside the 12-mile limit along the Arctic shipping route north of the Soviet Union were turned back at Vilkitskogo Strait.

The extent to which the Politburo heeded the advice of its admiral of the fleet was reflected by the continuing program of modernization and expansion. This was in sharp contrast to what had been happening in the United States, where the number of ships in the active fleet in 1979 was less than half of those in commission ten years earlier.

THE U.S. NAVY

As for total numbers of warships, the active fleet of the United States was down to fewer than two-thirds of that of the Soviets. It was also a less versatile fleet. For instance, the few vessels being built as replacements for over-aged general purpose destroyers and cruisers were essentially screening and escort types, designed primarily for antiaircraft or antisubmarine warfare, or both. Priorities assigned to defensive tasks, such the protection of carrier task forces, and the increasing complexity of the systems resulted in neglecting offensive capabilities such as needed in certain kinds of control missions. The ability to carry out gunfire support and shore bombardment tasks had been seriously degraded. Surface combatant types lacked armaments adequate to ensure success against well-armed opponents, although some surface-to-surface capabilities were being developed belatedly.

Once again, mine warfare was being accorded a very low priority, at least insofar as minesweepers were concerned. Considering the situations and conditions that might be encountered, there were dangers of placing over-reliance on potential developments in helicopter mine-sweeping devices. In contrast with ten years before, when the active fleet had 74 mine vessels and the reserve fleet 14. The numbers were now 3 and 22, The Soviet Navy had 147.

As for submarines of all types, the United States had 123, the Soviets 355. Advances in the ability of U.S. nuclear-powered boats to operate undetected were enhancing their capabilities for deterrence and for a variety of other missions. Specialized types had been designed, equipped, and armed for actions against enemy submarines. However, the total number of U.S. submarines was not only far fewer than the Soviets' but also the rate of construction was much slower. They too were making significant advances in speed, noise reduction, and the ability to operate at deeper depths.

There was a great disparity in the numbers of patrol vessels. The Soviet Navy had 129, the U.S. Navy 3.

The ability of the Soviet Navy to conduct distant operations had been enhanced by major increases in logistics ships, which now totaled 147. The U.S. Navy had 61, down from 112 a decade earlier. The reduction had been accompanied by a familiar theme, that of replacing some with civilian-manned merchantmen modified for the task.

Another factor was the increased number of strategically located ports available for Soviet use as naval bases. These included the Congo on the west coast of Africa, Mozambique on the east coast, Madagascar in the Indian Ocean, Aden near the entrance to the Red Sea, and Camranh Bay on the South China Sea.

In the United States, as prior to the Korean War, the requirements for amphibious assault capabilities were being depreciated.

The Department of Defense had become increasingly enchanted with concepts of a rapid deployment force. The troops and some of the lighter arms, vehicles, and equipment of such a force were to be transported overseas by air where there would be prepositioned stocks, including the heavier tanks, weapons, and equipment. A proposal concerning the formation of a group of fast deployment logistics ships for prepositioning failed to get congressional approval in 1967, but a similar concept was later implemented. This resulted in the formation of the Rapid Deployment Joint Task Force. Seventeen merchant ships chartered by the Military Sealift Command were loaded with equipment, vehicles, weapons, ammunitions and other supplies and stationed in the Indian Ocean near Diego Garcia.

The fact that the initial joint task force commander was a marine and the plan was for him later to be designated commander in chief of a united command for Southeast Asia raised questions as to whether the lessons so painfully learned about command relations regarding seaborne movements and amphibious operations had been abandoned.

In many respects there were limits to the overseas power projection potential of a string of aircraft flying detachments of troops and limited supplies across the ocean to land on foreign airfields, there to attain prompt readiness for sustained operations by utilizing cargoes delivered by civilian-manned ships conveniently prepositioned. It would be naive to consider such a concept a substitution for naval readiness for amphibious operations. To the extent demanded by the specific situation, naval forces are able to provide secure movements to the objective area; diversions and deception as to landing sites; preparatory actions such as clearance of mines and obstacles, carrier air strikes, and bombardments by surface warships; over-the-beach and helicopter landings of troops with organic arms munitions, vehicles, equipment, and appropriate supplies from combat-loaded amphibious ships; fighter air support; fire support; logistics support; and, if necessary, the capabilities for withdrawal.

In any event, the number of amphibious ships had been reduced and was now only two-thirds of that of the Soviet Navy.

In the modern world, evaluations of comparative naval strengths are difficult and uncertain. Not only are there differing types of warships, but also within each category there are differences in size, performance, and weaponry. Much depends on the ability to make prompt and full use of the mobility, flexibility, and combat potential of the fleet as a whole; on the effectiveness with which various types are combined to fulfill changing missions and tasks; on strategy and tactics; and on professional competence. Whereas care should be taken not to over-evaluate the importance of superior numbers of the several types of warships, it would be naive to under-assess the advantages. There are many potentially significant operating areas in widely separated regions. Concurrent trouble spots and multi-crises have become more the rule than the exception. Moreover, there have been instances in history when powerful warships have been defeated by coordinated attacks of lesser men-of-war.

Attack carriers, a type not yet included in the Soviet Navy, provided the United States a means of mobile, concentrated striking power against forces at sea and targets ashore. The number, however, was limited. More than one is needed for sustained combat operations by a task group. Other types of warships can employ aircraft, including vertical takeoff fixed-wing planes and helicopters, but they are inadequate substitutes for attack carrier aircraft for some important missions. Moreover, limitations imposed by the effects of weather and sea states are more severe on smaller ships trying to launch and land aircraft. These conditions might restrict or completely halt aircraft operations on smaller ships, while larger attack carriers could still operate their aircraft.

In any case, the United States could no longer take for granted the sea power supremacy that it had enjoyed since World War II.

Part VI

The Future

The Past Is Prologue

Surrounded by the sea except for its borders with Canada and Mexico, the United States throughout its history has been a maritime nation. Naval power has been a primary determinant of the course of that history since colonial days up to the present. The significance of this, however, rarely has been fully understood or appreciated. More often than not, national policies have failed to appreciate the roles of that power other than those connected with wars on land.

There has been a tendency to focus on battles to the neglect of the more subtle roles of naval forces. In the Revolutionary War, for instance, the contribution of the French Navy resulting from the Battle of the Virginia Capes was recognized, but not the cumulative effect on the outcome of the war and peace treaty of the many actions by the small Continental Navy, the many privateers, and vessels with letters of marque.

After the war, this lack of recognition, along with the state of finances, prevented the country from providing for a navy until the young country suffered from the depredations of Barbary powers, the humiliation and cost of paying tribute, and a disregard for the rights of our shipping by other countries. When Congress belatedly authorized construction of warships, it failed to understand the deterring influence of a strong navy and added a proviso to stop contruction if the United States was at peace with Algiers. Ideally, our naval power could have deterred acts that might start a war, while advancing the nation's goals in peacetime, and without infringing upon the sovereign rights of others.

The inadequacy of the U.S. Navy was one of the causes leading to French actions against American shipping and undeclared warfare at sea. It was fortunate that President Washington was permitted to complete three frigates, that the Department of the Navy was established in 1798, and that a more adequate construction program was authorized.

The lesson, however, had not been learned. For, once the Quasi-War was over, Congress reduced the program and suspended work on naval facilities. Shortly thereafter, a squadron deployed to the Mediterranean learned on its arrival that Tripoli had declared war on the United States. The war might have been over soon if an effective blockade had been maintained, but too few warships were deployed. When Morocco took piratical actions against U.S. commerce, the squadron was able, through a show of force, to get reaffirmation of a former treaty. Only after the Mediterranean Squadron had been greatly strengthened and vigorous action was taken did Tripoli agree to peace.

Nevertheless, Jefferson's administration reduced the fleet drastically and placed undue reliance on small, inexpensive gunboats. Had a strong naval presence been maintained in the Mediterranean, the Barbary wars might have been over. But this was not to be the case until the deployment of an adequate naval force following the War of 1812.

That war had been preceded by further neglect of the navy and a concept that major warships should be either laid up or employed in defense of harbors. Although President Madison's war message cited British acts infringing on the maritime rights of the United States, there were no plans for naval operations. On the assumption that the war would soon be won by land campaigns, prompt measures were not taken to increase the readiness and strength of the navy. Yet, once again, the cumulative effect of naval actions, including those by private vessels with letters of marque, had a major and perhaps controlling influence on the outcome.

The need to maintain a strong peacetime navy in order to avoid wars was regretfully one of those lessons that would have to be learned again and again through bitter experiences. The naval disarmament in the decades prior to the Japanese attack on Pearl Harbor provides a most severe example. While the United States sought to save money by deferring naval construction programs, Japan was altering the balance of power in the Pacific by modernizing and increasing the strength of its navy. In the decades following World War II we have once again witnessed a shift in naval power. This time the shift involves Soviet and U.S. sea power.

The early years provided basic lessons that were to be confirmed time and again: Naval affairs should be managed separately from army affairs, officers experienced in sea command should be assigned to authoritative positions in the Navy Department, and the nation should draw upon its experience when determining national policy.

Recognizing the need for experienced naval officers participating in the direction of naval affairs, the first secretary of the navy recommended in 1801 the formation of a board of such officers. This was during the interregnum period between two administrations and no action was taken.

In the War of 1812 the need for experienced naval officers to provide advice and guidance was fully revealed. The creation of the Board of Navy Commissioners at the end of the war marked the coming of age of the U.S. Navy and brought greater efficiency to naval affairs management.

The board was assigned ministerial duties relating to the employment of vessels of war. Logical as this was, the incoming secretary insisted on retaining that authority and refused to provide the board with information on ship movements. The president supported his policy. This would not be the last time that an appointed civilian official insisted on exercising direct command over military forces. In the twentieth century, orders issued by a secretary of defense during the Vietnam conflict provide another prime example.

Fortunately, the advice of commissioners was heeded by later incumbents and the board acted for secretaries when they were absent, which was often the case.

In this earlier era the United States and its interests benefited greatly from deploying ships and squadrons to many areas of the globe. Since this was a time of major instabilities and revolutionary actions in the western hemisphere, operations in the Caribbean and off Central and South America were especially important. Concern over possible intervention by European powers led to announcement of the Monroe Doctrine in 1823.

In our era there would be many times when the U.S. Navy was called upon to carry out missions in the Caribbean basin. In the latter part of the twentieth century the Soviet Union supported terrorist and revolutionary actions. Communist control was established in Cuba and then Nicaragua. Ships delivering Soviet ballistic missiles to Cuba were turned back by a naval quarantine. The communist actions in Grenada, including the building of a major airfield, led to an amphibious operation. To stem the supply by sea of weapons for the support of guerrilla actions in neighboring Central American countries and for possible use in invasions, it might have been far better to impose overtly a conditional naval blockade. Instead, mines were furnished covertly by the Central Intelligence Agency to opponents of the communist regime in Nicaragua, the explosion of one of which brought international criticism of the United States.

The era of the commissioners saw the beginning of technological changes that were to provide naval power with new dimensions. One was the introduction of steam propulsion. Warships would no longer be dependent on the wind's speed and direction. As demonstrated in operations against pirates in the Caribbean, the Mexican War, and then more extensively in the Civil War, benefits from steam propulsion would be realized in coastal and restricted waters. Endurance, however, was extremely limited and frequent refuelings were necessary. It would be many years before the efficiency of this means of propulsion permitted complete elimination of sails. A related development of great importance was the introduction of the screw propeller.

The introduction of rifled guns provided another breakthrough, allowing guns to operate at longer ranges with higher accuracy against other vessels and shore facilities. It would not, however, alter the basic missions and tasks of naval power.

A new, although restricted, mode of warfare resulted from major advances in mine warfare. There had been earlier cases of employing primitive mines weapons, with but few successes. Hereafter, it would be possible to lay highly destructive minefields.

Contact and controlled mines of ever increasing effectiveness were to become a major threat to vessels of the Union Navy operating in restricted waters during the Civil War, requiring minesweeping and other countermeasures. In World War I mining was a key factor in preventing passage of the Turkish Straits by British and French vessels for delivery of military supplies to Russia, and thus undoubtably played a major role in altering the course of world history.

U.S. developments in moored mines toward the end of that war led to laying the North Sea barrage. Although it was only in the process of being completed when the war ended and had not yet achieved its full effects, it revealed how mining could prevent enemy submarines from reaching the high seas. In World War II the planting of influence mines by U-boats off England posed a grave threat until effective countermeasures were developed. Mines played important defensive and offensive roles in the Pacific. For example, those dropped by aircraft off Japan at the end of the war were highly effective against shipping and warships.

Although readiness to conduct mine warfare, including mine clearance operations, would often be neglected, it was to play important roles in future wars. The belatedly approved mining of the port of Haiphong late in the Vietnam War provides a recent example.

As the direction and management of naval affairs became increasingly complex, the Board of Navy Commissioners recommended delegation of specific responsibilities to individual members, while continuing the board for overall direction and coordination. Yet, when the bureau system was later adopted, the board was terminated, on the recommendation of a secretary of the navy. Since members became the first bureau chiefs, actions for a time were well coordinated. But with the expansion to meet the Civil War needs, bureau chiefs, who were specialists, took actions in areas where seagoing officers have experience without conferring with them. After heated debate, some corrective measures were instituted; but it was not to be until World War II that an ideal system would finally evolve.

In the Mexican War the Pacific Squadron carried out operations paving the way for California's acquisition. When the army campaign in the east toward Mexico City bogged down, troop movements by sea and an amphibious assault made the successful land campaign possible. The skillfully conducted amphibious operation demonstrated the importance of naval command in such operations. Regrettably, this lesson was not learned and a number of operations in the Civil War suffered the consequences. The lesson that movements by sea and amphibious operations should be under naval command was still not learned. This principle was again violated during the campaign to take Santiago in the Spanish-American War.

Prior to the entry of the United States into World War I, the Gallipoli disaster demonstrated the consequences of faulty command relationships. One result was a widely adopted conclusion that major amphibious assaults were not practicable in the modern world. Studies by the U.S. Navy and Marine Corps were a major factor in developing the policies and procedures, later adopted by the army, which proved to be so extraordinarily successful in the Pacific during World War II.

Nevertheless, in recent years there have been tendencies to compromise these basic command relationships.

Returning to the nineteenth century, the beginning of the Civil War was yet another of those times when the nation would have benefited from more adequate naval operating forces. A much larger home squadron properly employed might have been very beneficial when the first of the southern states began to secede.

The navy suffered as well from a serious deficiency, since the department lacked a board of officers charged with responsibility for employing naval operating forces, and a chief of naval operations who could provide advice to the secretary and the president. That officer also could have coordinated the planning and conduct of joint operations with the army's commander in chief. Such an operation might have succeeded in providing relief to Fort Sumter shortly after South Carolina seceded, whereas the army effort by sea failed. The subsequent abortive operation, proposed to General Scott by former naval Lieutenant Fox who later exercised command under War Department direction, and conflicting orders issued separately by the president and navy secretary bring to mind unsuccessful ad hoc operations of recent years.

After becoming the first assistant secretary of the navy, Gustavus Fox fulfilled some of the functions of a chief of naval operations, although not all. In any case, after the war was over he was absent from Washington for a long time and resigned upon his return.

The third quarter of the nineteenth century witnessed the coming of the new navy. Efficiencies of steam engines now allowed the elimination of sails. Steel construction made larger warships practicable. Major caliber guns were mounted in turrets.

The truly major breakthrough during this period was the development of an effective self-propelled torpedo. It was one of those times when advances in weaponry caused claims that capital ships were no longer needed. Instead, as so often the case, a new means of sinking and damaging ships had been introduced without reducing the requirements for existing capabilities. Naval warfare was becoming ever more complex.

Meanwhile, progress in communications had major implications for fleet operations. The laying of transoceanic cables meant that, although dispatch boats were still needed, information and orders could now be transmitted speedily to key ports in distant areas. It was fortunate that Secretary Chandler took long overdue action by assigning responsibility for the direction of ship movements to the chief of the Bureau of Navigation, who also became a member of the Naval War Board formed shortly before the start of the Spanish-American War.

The prompt receipt of a message by cable to Hong Kong in 1898 set in motion actions that resulted in the victory in Manila Bay. This and the subsequent Battle of Santiago determined the outcome of the war in a remarkably short time, thus confirming precepts of Mahan.

Experiences in the Spanish-American War led to the secretary's order establishing the General Board. This board of senior naval officers provided important planning and advice until it was disestablished years later following the superimposing of the ever-increasing authority of the Department of Defense.

Another lesson at long last learned was the need for a body of army and navy officers to coordinate planning. The Joint Board of the Army and Navy served the nation well in peace and war until the beginnings of the Joint Chiefs of Staff.

Among the important advances at the turn of the century was the development of radio communications. And the developments in submarines and aircraft, of course, would have profound significance in the future. Whereas changes in naval capabilities meant that the potentials of cruising warfare as exercised in the past were greatly reduced, the introduction of U-boat warfare had ominous implications. It was fortunate that the position of chief of naval operations was created in 1915 and that his authority was increased the following year.

World War I illustrates why the navy must exercise suitable control over shipping during a maritime war, particularly when convoys are required. The War Department recognized this and requested naval manning and control of transports and ships carrying cargoes and munitions for the army. After World War II, when the secretary of defense assigned the Navy Department responsibility for the Military Sea Transportation Service, his purpose was to provide a common service. Then, in 1971 there was a defense directive that the secretaries of the army and navy submit a joint plan to consolidate activities of the Military Sealift Command (formerly MSTS) and the more recently established Military Traffic Management and Terminal Service in a single new jointly-staffed agency. Despite the experiences of two World Wars, this new agency was to report to the secretary of defense through the secretary of the army, who would be "the single manager for DoD surface transportation, worldwide."[1] Congress, although focusing also on management and not wartime implications, required some sensible modifications of this plan.

The rapid progress being made in military aviation led air power enthusiasts to insist, once World War I was over, that a major navy was no longer needed because of the vulnerability of warships to air attack. In addition, they insisted that bombings of the enemy's homeland meant the next war would be far too short for the effective application of sea power. Yet, World War II was a prolonged conflict in which the outcome in Europe hinged on the Battle of the Atlantic, and the Pacific war was decided primarily by naval forces.

Contrasting experiences of the British and U.S. navies during World War II revealed how extremely fortunate was the failure of the strong campaign in America for a separate department or agency with authority over all military aviation.

Command relations were an important factor in the war. The command authority exercised by Admiral King, including his role as the JCS's executive agent for the Pacific area, ensured that sea power objectives were not neglected and that full use could be made of the mobility and flexibility of the naval operating forces. His designation as both commander in chief, United States Fleet and chief of naval operations, coupled with the high degree of authority delegated to the bureaus, minimized the staffs and maximized efficiency in the conduct of naval affairs.

Yet, the United States had just entered the war as a belligerent when the War Department proposed a single military department with a chief of staff and a general staff superimposed over ground forces into which the marines were merged, air forces including naval aviation, naval forces, and a general supply organization. The campaign for a single department and a general staff continued at the end of the war. Compromises were necessary to get passage of an act, but there were those who continued to pursue their initial goals. The result was step-by-step increases in centralization of controls over the military departments, fragmentation of authority, and bureaucratic expansion.

Although a general staff was forbidden by Congress, efforts in that direction did not cease. The 1949 amendment to the National Security Act established the position of chairman of the Joint Chiefs of Staff who would take precedence over all officers of the armed services. The authorized size of the joint staff was more than doubled. Eisenhower's reorganization after the Korean War gave the chairman authority to conduct, guide, and administer the work of the joint staff; select the individuals to serve on it; determine their tenure; participate fully as a member of the JCS; and submit his own views, advice, and recommendations. Under the 1958 Reorganization Act the chairman gained further authority over the staff and could now vote on JCS decisions. Again, an approximate doubling of the joint staff was authorized. The latest major move toward an armed forces chief of staff was a campaign launched in 1982 to strengthen the role of the chairman of the JCS, provide a "Vice Chairman,"[2] remove the JCS as a body from addressing matters in the joint arena, limit service staff involvement in the joint process, and remove statutory restrictions on service on the JCS. Many of these objectives were met in the Defense Reorganization Act of 1986.

After World War II the continuing requirements for naval power were questioned and the probability of conventional wars in the era of atomic bombs was minimized; however, our post-war experiences have shown the need for naval forces with both conventional and nuclear capabilities. Despite the difficulties arising from the precipitous demobilization and severe reductions in the size of the fleet, the U.S. Navy exerted a powerful influence on the many conflict situations occurring in the period of instability that followed World War II. Many examples can be cited during this period of Cold War situations that threatened countries in the Mediterranean area. The crucial contributions of the tiny Seventh Fleet during the desperate early days of the Korean War were followed by the highly successful amphibious assault on Inchon, which reversed the tide of the war. The diverse and continuing need for naval power was shown also by the essential sealifting of logistics support for land forces; crucial combat support from carrier aircraft, particularly after the crossing of the Yalu River by Chinese troops; and demand for naval gunfire support.

After the Korean armistice, the U.S. Navy, which was maintained at a considerably greater strength than before the war, carried out peacetime operations. While not infringing on the sovereign rights of others, the navy acted as a stabilizing influence in troubled areas and provided a principal means of defusing some serious confrontations. The high states of readiness in fulfillment of national policy decisions, particularly in times of multi-crises in different areas of the world, resulted from anticipatory orders to the fleet by the chief of naval operations, including shifts of operating forces from one area to another. It was more than ironic that after the Reorganization Act of 1958 the chief of naval operations no longer had the statutory responsibilities for fleet operations and for the preparation and readiness of fleet wartime plans.

The disastrous Bay of Pigs fiasco three years later demonstrated, among other things, the need for sound planning and command of an amphibious operation involving sea movement, landing of forces and supplies, and a possibility of military opposition.

At the time of the 1962 Cuban Missile Crisis, the Joint Chiefs of Staff wisely designated the chief of naval operations to act for them in quarantine matters.

Soon thereafter General Maxwell Taylor, an advocate of the single chief of staff, was assigned the duties of chairman of the JCS. He had been returned to active duty to serve as military advisor to President Kennedy, and it had been on his recommendation that a squadron of aircraft, which soon became engaged in paramilitary combat operations, and an army self-defense and security force were introduced into South Vietnam. This was merely the start of an increasing involvement leading to the Vietnam War—a war greatly influenced by the transient strategies of theoreticians and the over-control in matters large and small by the Defense Department in Washington half way around the world from Vietnam. It was a war in which the enemy achieved their objectives.

The abortive 1980 effort to rescue captives held by Iran provides a more recent example that violated basic principles of planning and control. The rescue mission failed in its initial phases when the helicopters encountered a desert dust storm. Such conditions were discussed in the mission's background reports on Iran's meteorology, but the planners had not prepared for them.

As for changes in naval capabilities since World War II, none was more significant than the enhanced performance of submarines. While not supplanting the need for surface warships, the introduction of nuclear propulsion greatly increased the ability to carry out a full range of offensive and defensive underseas tasks. And with the development of underwater-launched fusion warheaded missiles, the navy now had the additional mission of providing the nation with a survivable nuclear warfare deterrence.

After the Korean War, major advances in naval capabilities occurred, such as the introduction of anti-air-guided missiles and the improvement of anti-submarine warfare sensors and weapons. This rapid progress, to a large extent, resulted from the ability of the Navy Department promptly to initiate research and development programs. In recent years project and program initiation has been impeded by an increasingly prolonged and repetitive approval process involving a multitude of reviewers who are not accountable for results.

The remarkable progress of Soviet sea power in all its dimensions poses serious threats. This makes it ever more important that the policies for the future be shaped by reexamining the suitability and adequacy of U.S. naval power to meet future challenges, the requisites of that power, and the relationships of naval power with other forms of national power in light of both historical experience and continuing changes in naval power.

Requisites

Despite expanding capabilities, such as in carrier aircraft over land and in ballistic missile submarines, traditional naval missions remain as important as in earlier years.

No longer does the United States possess the overwhelming naval power advantages enjoyed since the end of World War II. It would be foolhardy to assume, as some have in recent years, that the days of a war at sea separate from one on land are over. The possibilities of naval confrontations have been increasing.

Once again, the nation needs a versatile fleet with a full range of capabilities, one capable of meeting challenges across the spectrum of conflict and warfare situations. It has become ever more important that full advantage be taken of the navy's unique abilities to achieve national objectives without resorting to war or infringing on the rights of others.

The most pervasive and basic naval capabilities continue to be those required to carry out what has been labeled "control of the sea." Through the fulfillment of such a role, locally or on a wider scope, the nonmilitary and military uses of the oceans in the nation's interests can be safeguarded, and controls may be exercised over uses contrary to those interests. Local control, for instance, is involved in the objective area of an amphibious operation and in invoking a selective or conditional blockade.

Since the United States has become ever more dependent upon the delivery by sea of critical raw materials, it would be dangerously naive to assume that future wars, whether limited or not, will be of short duration. Moreover, there have been cases in the past when pacific blockading-type actions, or the threat of such actions, have caused nations with lesser navies to accede to demands rather than escalate the conflict.

While military preparations must take into account the possibilities of a general war, limited wars are more probable. Maritime warfare unaccompanied by war on land is still possible and, as in the past, there may be cases of concurrent warfare on land and sea. In the event of a naval war, the ultimate goal will still be the elimination of enemy opposition, whether by denying them access to the high seas or by battles on and below the sea surface.

Extensive scientific and technological advances over the years have resulted in a progressive expansion of the range of capabilities required to cope with challenges that will confront naval power in the future. All too often budgetary restrictions have led to the neglect of some capabilities later found to be urgently needed. Such neglect has been frequently rationalized by faulty assumptions, and at times the maintenance of a well-balanced fleet has suffered from focusing on a narrow range of capabilities in setting priorities. Such problems have been compounded in recent years by the imposition of additional layers in the program decision-making processes of the Department of Defense, by prolonging the time involved in the formulation of fiscal year budgets, and by bureaucratic measures that have greatly increased lead times to attain new capabilities.

In the future, as in the past, it is crucial that basic and subtle differences between naval operations and those of other military forces be fully recognized and their significance appreciated. Some of the differences are derived from the great percentage of the earth's surface covered by navigable waters; from the high mobility, flexibility, operational endurance, and self-sufficiency of naval forces; and from the versatile capabilities of some types of warships. Others result from fluid properties and the dynamic nature of the seas upon which surface ships operate, and from the complex and varying underseas environment. Still others stem from the nature of key sea power missions. These and other differences become a source of concern when personnel in the unified commands do not understand these differences and exercise unnecessary control over fleet operations.

Only through an understanding of past experiences in a wide variety of situations can one gain a full appreciation of fundamental principles concerning the naval power needs of the nation; the provision, maintenance, and support of a navy well suited to those needs; and the optimum employment of the fleet in fulfilling sea-power roles and contributing to the achievements of other military objectives.

Alterations in the organization and direction of national defense have had an adverse effect on U.S. naval power and other elements of military power. The creation of the Department of Defense was followed by the accumulation of an enormous staff within the office of the secretary of defense. A staff was superimposed over the military departments. The secretary has gained extraordinary authority, in some cases involving matters that formerly required decisions by the president or Congress.

The authority of the heads of the military departments is no longer commensurate with their responsibilities. Accountability for results has become diffuse and uncertain. In the drive for uniformity, organizational and procedural changes have been more or less forced upon the military departments, often without recognizing valid reasons for differences between the departments.

The military departments have lost control of some capabilities required for effective and efficient mission achievement. The meeting of some operational forces' needs is now dependent on defense agencies that report to assistant secretaries of defense. Bypassing established chains of command, secretaries at times have issued orders directly to commanders of operating forces at the scene of action. There have even been occasions, while forces were fulfilling warfare missions in dynamically changing situations, that orders were issued specifying in detail how the operations were to be conducted.

Another consequence of the tremendous growth of the office of the secretary of defense has been the increased overhead and its associated costs. In addition to direct costs such as the pay of the many appointed officials, high-ranking civil service executives, their assistants, and of a number of military officers in the inflated structure, there are indirect costs. Ironically much of the growth was justified on the basis of predicted savings. This author is convinced that the functional centralization imposed over the military departments and the spawning of defense agencies have resulted in greater rather than lower expenditures. In any case, a critical examination of direct and indirect expenditures is long overdue.

The command authority of the chief of naval operations, which was exercised so successfully in peace and war, has been diluted since the World War II victory. Furthermore, the Joint Chiefs of Staff no longer functions as it did during that war nor do the members have the same relationship with the commander in chief, the president. Civilian control and unification have all too often been pursued as if they were ends in themselves.

The consequences of the many changes influencing the U.S. military preparedness and effectiveness must be assessed to identify corrective measures that may prove essential in coming years.

Notes

CHAPTER 2

Naval Power and Winning Independence

1. Treaty of Paris, 15 February 1763, in William M. James, *The British Navy in Adversity: A Study of the War of American Independence* (London: Longmans, Green, 1926), p. 19.
2. V Adm Graves, 1 September 1775, 23 November 1775, *Naval Documents of the American Revolution,* ed. William B. Clark and William J. Morgan, vol. 1, p. 1282, vol. 2, p. 1106.
3. Instructions to Captain Whipple, 13 June 1775, ibib., vol. 1, p. 670.
4. Journal of the Continental Congress, 18 July 1775, ibib., p. 916.
5. George Washington's Instructions to Captain Nicholson Broughton, 2 September 1775, ibid., pp. 1287–88.
6. *Providence Gazette,* 10 December 1774, ibid., p. 9.
7. Journal of the Continental Congress, 13 October 1775, ibid., vol. 2, pp. 441–42; ibid.; Estimates For Fitting Out Warships, 30 October 1775, ibid., pp. 649–51.
8. Journal of the Continental Congress, 11 December 1775, ibid., vol. 3, p. 59.
9. Journal of the Continental Congress, 6 November 1776, ibid., vol. 7, p. 66.
10. Massachusetts Act Authorizing Privateers and Creating Courts of Admiralty, 1 November 1775, ibid., vol. 2, p. 835.
11. Alfred T. Mahan, *The Influence of Sea Power upon History 1660-1783* (Boston: Little, Brown, 1890), p. 134.
12. Continental Congress, 7 September 1781, Charles O. Paullin, *Paullin's History of Naval Administration, 1775-1911: A Collection of Articles from the U.S. Naval Institute Proceedings* (Annapolis, MD: U.S. Naval Institute, 1968), p. 44.
13. James, *The British Navy in Adversity,* p. vi.

CHAPTER 3

Consequences of Neglect

1. Jefferson to Adams, 11 July 1786, *Naval Documents Related to the United States Wars with the Barbary Powers,* ed. Dudley W. Knox (New York: G. P. Putnam, 1948), vol. 1, p. 10. Hereafter cited as *Barbary Wars.*
2. Senate Committee, 6 January 1791, ibid., p. 26.
3. U.S., *Statutes at Large,* 29 March 1794, vol. 1, p. 351; Knox to House of Representatives, 29 December 1794, *American State Papers,* Class VI, *Naval Affairs,* vol. 1, p. 6.
4. Treaty of Amity and Commerce, 6 February 1778, *The Treaties of 1778,* ed. Chinard, p. 40.
5. McHenry to House of Representatives, 22 March 1798, *American State Papers,* vol. 1, p. 39.
6. Congress, 30 April 1798, *Naval Documents Related to the Quasi-War between United States and France,* ed. Dudley W. Knox (Washington, DC: GPO, 1935–38), vol. 1. pp. 59–60.
7. Instructions to commanders of armed vessels, 28 May 1798, Knox, *Quasi-War,* vol. 1, p. 88.
8. U.S., *Statutes at Large,* 30 June 1798, vol. 1, p. 575.
9. Stoddert to House of Representatives, 15 January 1801, *American State Papers,* vol. 1, p. 75.
10. Jefferson to Albert Gallatin, 13 September 1802, *In Peace and War, Interpretations of American Naval History, 1775–1984,* ed. Kenneth J. Hagan (Westport, CT: Greenwood, 1978), pp. 38–39; U.S., *Statutes at Large,* 3 March 1801, vol. 2, p. 110.
11. Dale to secretary of the navy, 25 September 1801, *Barbary Wars,* vol. 1, p. 580.
12. Preble to secretary of the navy, 23 October 1803, ibid., vol. 3, p. 161.
13. U.S. Squadron Mediterranean, 10 September 1804, *Barbary Wars,* vol. 5, p. 8.
14. Hamilton to Joseph Anderson, 6 June 1809, *American State Papers,* vol. 1, p. 194.
15. U.S., *Statutes at Large,* 30 March 1812, vol. 2, p. 699.

CHAPTER 4

Coming of Age

1. Madison to Congress, 1 June 1812, *The Naval War of 1812: A Documentary History,* ed. William S. Dudley (Washington, DC: GPO, 1985), pp. 73–75.
2. Hamilton to Rodgers, 21 May 1812, ibid., p. 118.
3. Rodgers to Hamilton, 3 June 1812, ibid., p. 119.
4. Decatur to Hamilton, 8 June 1812, ibid., p. 123.
5. Jones, 1814, in John D. Long, *The New American Navy* (New York: Outlook, 1903), vol. 1, p. 101; Junes, 1814, ibid.; Jones to Senate, 16 November 1814, *American State Papers,* vol. 1, pp. 322–23.

6. 7 February 1815, *Statutes at Large,* vol. 3, pp. 202–3.
7. Ibid.
8. Porter and Rogers, "Conditions and Needs of Our Navy, 1815," reprinted in *United States Naval Institute Proceedings* 53 (December 1927):1309–15.
9. Ibid.
10. Ibid.
11. Ibid.

CHAPTER 5

Advancing Technology

1. Commissoners to secretary of the navy, 13 November 1829, *Annual Report of Secretary of Navy,* 1 December 1829, pp. 299–310.
2. Ibid.
3. Ibid.
4. Ibid.
5. Ibid.
6. Commissioners to secretary of the navy, 30 December 1835, Frank M. Bennett, *The Steam Navy of the United States: A History of the Growth of the Steam Vessel of War in the U.S. Navy, and of the Naval Engineer Corps* (Pittsburgh: Warren, 1896, reprinted 1970, Greenwood), p. 18.
7. 30 December 1835, ibid.; January 1836, ibid.
8. Rodgers, 1836, in Paolo E. Coletta, *American Secretaries of the Navy,* vol. 1, p. 158.
9. *Annual Report of the Secretary of the Navy,* 5 December 1835, p. 331.
10. Upshur to Henry A. Wise, chairman of the Committee on Naval Affairs, 7 March 1842, in Hooper, *The Navy Department: Evolution and Fragmentation;* U.S. Congress, House, Doc. No. 167, p. 7.
11. *Annual Report of the Secretary of the Navy,* 5 December 1853, p. 310.

CHAPTER 6

The Role of Naval Power in Preserving the Union

1. Memo by Fox, March 1861, in Fox, *Confidential Correspondence of Gustavus V. Fox,* ed. M. Thompson and Richard Wainwright, vol. 1, p. 8.
2. Fox to Blair, 31 March 1861, ibid., p. 12.
3. Lincoln to Wells, 29 March 1861, U.S. Office of Naval Records and Library, *Official Records of Union and Confederate Navies,* vol. 4, Series 1, p. 227 (hereafter cited as *Official Records*); Cameron to Fox, 4 April 1861, ibid., p. 232.
4. Wells to Mercer, 5 April 1861, ibid., p. 235.
5. Robert D. Powers, Jr., "Blockade: For Winning without Killing," *United States Naval Institute Proceedings* 84 (August 1958):63.
6. *Annual Report of the Secretary of the Navy,* 2 December 1861, pp. 4, 15.
7 *Annual Report of the Secretary of the Navy,* 1 December 1862, p. 44; *Annual Report of the Chief of Bureau of Ordnance,* 20 December 1863, p. 4.

8. Ibid.
9. Report by Du Pont, Bernard, Bache, and Davis to Wells, 16 July 1861, *Official Records,* vol. 12, series 1, p. 199.
10. Du Pont, 3 March 1862, U.S. Naval History Division, *Civil War Chronology,* part II, p. 28.
11. Du Pont to Wells, 9 February 1863, *Official Records,* vol. 13, series 1, p. 655.

CHAPTER 7

Inland Waters

1. Wells to Farragut, 20 January 1862, *Official Records,* vol. 18, series 1, p. 8.
2. Dahlgren, 11 February 1861, *Civil War Chronology,* part I, p. 5; Mallory, 18 July 1861; ibid., part I, p. 19.
3. Report of the board to examine plans of iron-clad vessels, under act of 3 August, 1861, 16 September 1861, *Report of the Secretary of the Navy in Relation to Armored Vessels,* p. 5.
4. McClellan to E. M. Stanton, 19 March 1862, U.S. War Department, *Official Record of the Armies,* ed. Rush, vol. 5, series 1, p. 58.
5. McClellan to Goldsborough, 26 June 1862, *Official Record,* vol. 7, series 1, p. 510; McClellan, 30 June 1862, *Civil War Chronology.* part II, p. 74.
6. Lee to Davis, 4 July 1862, *Lee's Dispatches,* ed. Douglas S. Freeman, p. 26; Lee to Davis, 6 July 1862, *Official Record of the Armies,* vol. 11, series 1, part III, p. 635.

CHAPTER 8

Concluding Phases of Warfare between the States

1. Wells, *Civil War Chronology,* part II, p. 105.
2. Confidential orders by Stanton, 21 October 1862, *Official Record of the Armies,* vol. 17, series 1, part II, p. 282.
3. Porter to Fox, 3 March 1863, in Fox, *Confidential Correspondence of Fox,* vol. 2, p. 161.
4. 12 May 1864, *Civil War Chronology,* part IV, p. 59.
5. Wells to Thatcher, 24 February 1865, *Official Records,* vol. 22, series 1, p. 48.

CHAPTER 9

The Postwar Period

1. *Annual Report of Secretary of the Navy,* 3 December 1866, p. 25.
2. *Annual Report of Secretary of the Navy,* 2 December 1867, p. 30.
3. J. Q. A. Ziegler, 27 June 1866, *Annual Report of the Secretary of the Navy,* 3 December 1866, pp. 68–69.
4. A. Murray to Wells, 16 June 1866, ibid., p. 72.

5. Report of Board on Steam Machinery Afloat, 29 September 1869, *Annual Report of the Secretary of the Navy*, 1 December 1869, p. 142.
6. Ibid., p. 149.
7. *Annual Report of the Secretary of the Navy*, 2 December 1867, p. 24.
8. Borie, 12 March 1869, in Coletta, *American Secretaries of the Navy*, vol. 1, p. 364.
9. Ibid., p. 383.

CHAPTER 10

Beginnings of the New Navy

1. Porter, 19 June 1881, *Annual Report of Secretary of the Navy*, 28 November 1881, p. 100.
2. Coletta, *American Secretaries of the Navy*, vol. 1, p. 393; 5 August 1882, U.S., *Statutes at Large*, vol. 22, p. 291.
3. Mahan, *Influence of Sea Power upon History*, p. vi.
4. Ibid., p. 11; Mahan to Samuel A. Ashe, 2 February 1880, *Letters of Alfred Thayer Mahan*, ed. Robert Seagen II and Doris D. Maguire (hereafter cited as *Mahan Letters*), vol. 1, p. 625; Mahan, *Influence of Sea Power upon History*, pp. 2, 9.
5. Mahan, *Influence of Sea Power upon History*, p. 138; Mahan, *Sea Power in Its Relations to the War of 1812*, vol. 2, p. 301.
6. Mahan, *Influence of Sea Power upon History*, pp. 1, 507, 522.
7. Ibid., p. 209.
8. Ibid., p. 288.
9. Mahan, *The Influence of Sea Power upon the French Revolution and Empire 1793-1812*, vol. 1, p. 335.
10. Mahan, *Influence of Sea Power upon History*, p. 136.
11. Alfred T. Mahan, *Sea Power in Its Relations to the War of 1812*, vol. 1, p. 288.

CHAPTER 11

Warfare against a European Power

1. 3 March 1893, U.S., *Statutes at Large*, vol. 27, p. 718.
2. 3 August 1886, U.S., *Statutes at Large*, vol. 24, p. 215; 30 June 1890, U.S., *Statutes at Large*, vol. 26, p. 205.
3. Long to Dewey, 24 April 1898, *Annual Report of the Secretary of Navy*, 15 November 1898, vol. 1, p. 6.
4. Mahan to Montgomery Sicard, 19 May 1898, Navy War Board, *Mahan Letters*, vol. 2, p. 554.
5. Ibid.
6. H. C. Corbin to Shafter, 30 May 1898 (sent in cipher 31 May 1898), U.S. Adjutant General's Office, *Correspondence relating to the War with Spain*, vol. 1, pp. 18-19.
7. Ibid.

8. Shafter to Sampson, 1 July 1898, *Report of the Secretary of the Navy,* 15 November 1898, vol. 2, p. 617.

CHAPTER 12

Prelude to Another War

1. Mahan, *Sea Power in Its Relations to the War of 1812,* vol. 1, pp. 293–94.
2. Julius A. Furer, *Administration in World War II,* p. 108.

CHAPTER 13

The Great War

1. Maurice F. Parmelle, *Blockade and Sea Power,* pp. 29–31.
2. 18 October 1907, *The Hague Conventions and Declarations,* ed. James B. Scott, p. 220.
3. 28 January 1915, U.S., *Statutes at Large,* vol. 38, pp. 800–1.
4. 3 March 1915, U.S., *Statutes at Large,* vol. 38, p. 929.
5. Ibid.
6. 29 August 1916, U.S., *Statutes at Large,* vol. 39, p. 558.

CHAPTER 14

America Enters the War

1. Baker to Edward N. Hurley, 17 December 1917, Lewis P. Clephane, *History of Naval Overseas Transportation in World War I,* p. 62.
2. Mahan, *Influence of Sea Power upon the French Revolution,* vol. 1, p. 203.

CHAPTER 15

Between Wars

1. Morison, *History of United States Naval Operations in World War II,* vol. 1, pp. xlvii–xlviii.
2. General Board, June 1919, ibid., p. xlviii.
3. U.S., *Statutes at Large,* 11 July 1919, vol. 41, p. 133.
4. The Hague Rules of Air Warfare, December 1922–February 1923, *The Law of War: A Documentary History,* ed. Friedman, vol. 1, p. 440.
5. William Mitchell, *Winged Defense,* pp. 4, 5, 17, 18, 109.
6. Ibid., pp. xvii, 4, 12.
7. Ibid., pp. 11–12, 102, 125–26.
8. Ibid., pp. 5, 101–2, 126, 127.
9. Morison, *Naval Operations in World War II,* vol. 3, p. 14.

CHAPTER 16

Another Global War Begins

1. Adolf Hitler, *Mein Kampf,* p. 892.
2. Ibid., pp. 899, 950, 978–79.
3. Morison, *Naval Operations in World War II,* vol. 1, p. 14.
4. Londonderry to Simon, 5 February 1932, Stephen Roskill, *Naval Policy between the Wars,* vol. 2, pp. 143, 198.
5. Chatfield to Hoare, 14 December 1936, ibid., p. 399.
6. Inskip, 21 July 1937, ibid., p. 403.

CHAPTER 17

The Crucial War at Sea

1. Antiaircraft Defense Board, 26 December 1940, Furer, *Administration of the Navy Department in World War II,* p. 343. (Hereafter cited as *Administration in World War II.*)
2. Morison, *Naval Operations in World War II,* vol. 3, p. 36.

CHAPTER 18

A Two-Ocean War

1. Morison, *Naval Operations in World War II,* vol. 3, p. 101.
2. Ibid., p. 36.
3. Organization Chart, *Annual Report of the Secretary of the Navy,* 10 June 1946, p. 43a.
4. Ibid.
5. Ibid.
6. Ibid.
7. Ibid.
8. President Roosevelt, Executive Order 9096, 12 March 1942, *Administration in World War II,* p. 133.
9. Ibid., pp. 132–33.
10. 11 February 1925, U.S., *Statutes at Large,* vol. 43, p. 881; ibid, 28 May 1924, vol. 43, part I, p. 204.
11. Morison, *Naval Operations in World War II,* vol. 4, p. 190.
12. Mahan, *Influence of Sea Power upon the French Revolution,* vol. 1, p. 335.
13. Churchill to Roosevelt, 14 March 1942, *Churchill and Roosevelt: The Complete Correspondence,* ed. Warren K. Kimball, vol. 1, p. 404.

CHAPTER 19

Turning the Tide

1. Executive Order 9096, 12 March 1942, Furer, *Administration in World War II,* p. 133.

2. Ibid., pp. 132–34.
3. 3 March 1915, U.S., *Statutes at Large,* vol. 38, part I, p. 930.
4. Admiral King to Joint Chiefs of Staff, 1 May 1943, Morison, *Naval Operations of World War II,* vol. 10, p. 22.
5. Ibid., p. 317.

CHAPTER 20

World War II: The Final Phases

1. Halsey, 24 October 1944, Halsey and Bryan, *Halsey's Story,* p. 214.
2. Halsey to Kincaid, 24 October 1944, E. B. Potter, *Bull Halsey,* p. 296.
3. Morison, *Naval Operations in World War II,* vol. 14, p. 342.

CHAPTER 21

The Cold War

1. Edwin B. Hooper, *The Navy Department: Evolution and Fragmentation,* p. 21.
2. Bernard Brodie, *The Absolute Weapon.*
3. Mahan, *Sea Power in Relationship to the War of 1812,* vol. 1, p. 293–94.
4. Resolution of the Governments Engaged in the Fight against Aggression, London, 12 June 1941, U.S. State Department, *Documents on American Foreign Relations,* vol. 3, p. 444.
5. Hooper, Allard, and Fitzgerald, *The United States Navy and the Vietnam Conflict: The Setting of the Stage to 1959,* p. 82.
6. Truman, *Memoirs,* vol. 2, p. 107.
7. C. W. Nimitz, 18 October 1947, *Annual Report of the Secretary of the Navy,* 31 December 1947, p. 4.

CHAPTER 22

Erosion

1. Truman's message to Congress, 19 December 1945, *The Department of Defense,* ed. Alice C. Cole et al., p. 10.
2. The National Security Act of 1947, 26 July 1947, Public Law 253, 80th Congress, 1st Session, chapter 343, ibid., p. 41.
3. Ibid., p. 42.
4. Ibid., p. 45.
5. Ibid., pp. 40–41.
6. Ibid.
7. Ibid.
8. Ibid., p. 45.
9. Ibid.
10. Ibid., p. 36.
11. Thomas K. Finletter, 1 January 1958, *Survival in the Air Age,* p. 15.

12. Senator Saltonstall, 24 March 1947, *Hearing on National Security Act, Senate*, p. 17.
13. Eberstadt, 29 March 1947, ibid., p. 49.
14. Public Law 216, 10 August 1949, *The Department of Defense,* p. 88.
15. Ibid., pp. 88–89, 97.
16. Ibid., p. 95.
17. King, 12 October 1949, Hearing before the Committee on Armed Services, House of Representatives, *National Defense Program—Unification and Strategy,* p. 250.
18. Denfeld, 13 October 1949, ibid., pp. 350–52.
19. Johnson, 31 December 1949, *Semi-Annual Report of the Secretary of Defense,* p. 29.
20. Dean Acheson, "Crisis in Asia—An Examination of U.S. Policy," *The State Department Bulletin* 22 (23 January 1950):116.

CHAPTER 23

Limited War

1. The National Security Act of 1947, 26 July 1947, *The Department of Defense,* p. 40.
2. James A. Field, *United States Naval Operations-Korea,* p. 256.

CHAPTER 24

The New Look

1. Eisenhower, 7–8 May 1947, Hearing before Committee on Executive Department, House of Representatives, pp. 272–73, 291.
2. Kovett to Truman, 18 November 1952, *The Department of Defense,* pp. 117–24.
3. Ibid.
4. Report of the Rockefeller Committee on Department of Defense Organization, 11 April 1953, ibid., p. 130.
5. Eisenhower to Congress, 30 April 1953, ibid., p. 149.
6. Secretary of Defense Wilson's directive, July 1954, "Major Changes in Joint Chiefs of Staff 1942-1969," Historical Division Joint Secretariat, Joint Chiefs of Staff (Washington, DC: U.S. Naval Historical Center), 23 January 1970, p. 34.
7. Ibid., p. 31.
8. Eisenhower, January 1953, Edwin B. Hooper, Dean C. Allard, and Oscar P. Fitzgerald, *Navy and the Vietnam Conflict,* p. 210.
9. Ibid., p. 183.
10. Ibid., p. 189.
11. Eisenhower, 26 December 1953, ibid., p. 235.
12. John F. Dulles, 12 January 1954, "The Evolution of Foreign Policy," *The Department of State Bulletin* 30 (25 January 1954):108.

13. Hooper, Allard, and Fitzgerald, *Navy and the Vietnam Conflict,* p. 236.
14. Ibid., p. 273.
15. Ibid., p. 348.
16. *United States–Vietnam Relations, 1945–1967,* vol. 2, part IV. A. 4, p. 11.

CHAPTER 25

Naval Influence

1. Press Release, in *New York Times,* 7 November 1957, p. 1.
2. Dulles, 7 October 1957, *The Department of State Bulletin* 37:572.
3. Eisenhower, 3 April 1958, *The Department of Defense,* p. 175.
4. 3 March 1915, U.S., *Statutes at Large,* vol. 38, part I, p. 929; Department of Defense Reorganization Act of 1958, 85th Congress, 6 August 1958, The Department of Defense, p. 210.
5. Public Law 216, 10 August 1949, *The Department of Defense,* p. 88; Department of Defense Act of 1958, 6 August 1958, ibid., pp. 198, 199.
6. Ibid., p. 197.
7. *Semi-Annual Report of the Secretary of Defense,* June 1959, pp. 7–8.
8. "Meeting of Communist Leaders, Moscow," *New York Times,* 7 December 1960, pp. 14–17.

CHAPTER 26

Flexible Response

1. Maxwell D. Taylor, *The Uncertain Trumpet,* p. 98.
2. Ibid., pp. 147–48, 158, 178.
3. Ibid., pp. 98, 143.
4. Ibid., p. 100.
5. *Semi-Annual Report of the Secretary of Defense,* 11 October 1961, p. 22; Arthur M. Schlesinger, Jr., *A Thousand Days: John F. Kennedy in the White House,* pp. 250, 317–18.
6. *Semi-Annual Report of the Secretary of Defense,* 11 December 1961, p. 25.
7. National Security Act of 1947, 26 July 1947, *The Department of Defense,* p. 36.
8. Dr. Alain C. Enthoven, U.S. Navy Department, *Navy R&D Management 1946–1973* (Booz, Allen and Hamilton), p. 68.
9. Edward J. Marolda and Oscar P. Fitzgerald, *The United States Navy and the Vietnam Conflict, from Military Assistance to Conflict, 1959–1965,* p. 395.
10. Ibid., p. 479.
11. Hooper, *Mobility, Support, Endurance,* p. 14.
12. Deputy Assistant Secretary of Defense, 8 March 1963, *Mobility, Support, Endurance,* pp. 180–81.

CHAPTER 27

The Shifting Balance of Sea Power

1. Mahan, *Influence of Sea Power upon History,* p. 1; Gorshkov, *The Sea Power of the State,* p. ix.
2. Gorshkov, *The Sea Power of the State,* pp. 57, 60, 278.
3. Ibid., p. 248.
4. Ibid., pp. 2, 251, 252.
5. Ibid., pp. 247–48.
6. Ibid., pp. 152–54, 211.
7. Mahan, *Influence of Sea Power upon History,* p. 288; Gorshkov, *The Sea Power of the State,* p. 213.
8. Ibid., p. 229.
9. Ibid., pp. xiii, 276, 281.
10. Ibid., p. 118.
11. Ibid., pp. 28–29.
12. Ibid., p. 9.
13. Ibid., pp. 28–29.
14. Ibid., p. 6.
15. Ibid., p. 278.

CHAPTER 28

The Past Is Prologue

1. News Release for Office of Assistant Secretary of Defense (Public Affairs) number 169–71, 26 February 1971.
2. Goldwater–Nichols Department of Defense Reorganization Act of 1986, 1 October 1986, U.S., *Statutes at Large,* Public Law 99–433, sec. 201.

Bibliography

EDITOR'S NOTE

Bibliographical material in Admiral Hooper's working files was divided by subject. While we are not certain of his intent for the final bibliography, we have split the bibliography into six sections: general works and the five historical divisions of the book. Clearly, these divisons are not hard and fast but describe general areas into which we arbitrarily divided the reference material. For example, material from the War of 1812 is placed in "The Early Years," while the book discusses the war in "The Transitional Period."

GENERAL

American State Papers, Class VI, *Naval Affairs*, vol. 1. Washington, DC: Gales and Seaton, 1834.

Coletta, Paolo E., ed. *American Secretaries of the Navy*. Annapolis, MD: U.S. Naval Institute, 1980. 2 vols.

Furer, Julius A. *Administration of the Navy Department in World War II*. Washington, DC: Government Printing Office (hereinafter, GPO), 1959.

Hagan, Kenneth J., ed. *In Peace and War: Interpretations of American Naval History, 1775-1984*. Contributions in Military History. Westport, CT: Greenwood, 1984.

Knox, Dudley W. *A History of the United States Navy*. New York: G. P. Putnam's Sons, 1948.

Paullin, Charles O. *Paullin's History of Naval Administration, 1775-1911: A Collection of Articles from the U.S. Naval Institute Proceedings*. Annapolis, MD: U.S. Naval Institute, 1968.

Potter, E. B., and Chester W. Nimitz, eds. *Sea Power: A Naval History*. Englewood Cliffs, NJ: Prentice-Hall, 1960.

Sprout, Harold, and Margaret Sprout. *The Rise of American Naval Power, 1776-1918*. Princeton: Princeton Univ. Press, 1939.

U.S. Department of Defense. *Semi-Annual Report of the Secretary of Defense*. Washington, DC: GPO, 1947/48-1986.

U.S. Department of the Navy. *Annual Report of the Secretary of the Navy.* Washington, DC: GPO, various publishers, 1821–1948.

U.S. Department of State. *State Department Bulletin.*

Weigley, Russel F. *The American Way of War.* New York: Macmillan, 1973.

EARLY YEARS:

Chapters 2–3 (1774–1815)

Allen, Gardner W. *A Naval History of the American Revolution.* Boston: Houghton Mifflin, 1913.

Bird, Harrison. *Battle for a Continent.* New York: Oxford Univ. Press, 1965.

Bowler, R. Arthur. *Logistics and the Failure of the British Army in America 1775–1783.* Princeton: Princeton Univ. Press, 1975.

Bradford, James C. "The Navies of the American Revolution." In *Peace and War: Interpretations of American Naval History, 1775–1984.* Contributions in Military History 41, Westport, CT: Greenwood, 1978.

Broomfield, J. H. "The Keppel-Palliser Affair, 1778–1779." *Mariner's Mirror* 47 (August 1961):195–207.

Chinard, Gilbert. *Honest John Adams.* Boston: Little Brown, 1933.

————, ed. *The Treaties of 1778 and Allied Documents.* Baltimore, MD: Johns Hopkins University Press, 1928.

————. *George Washington's Navy; Being an Account of His Excellency's Fleet in New England Waters.* Baton Rouge: Louisiana State Univ. Press, 1960.

Clark, William B., and William J. Morgan, eds. *Naval Documents of the American Revolution.* Washington, DC: GPO, 1964–76. 7 vols.

Dudley, William S., ed. *The Naval War of 1812: A Documentary History.* Washington, DC: GPO, 1985.

James, William M. *The British Navy in Adversity; A Study of the War of American Independence.* London: Longmans, Green, 1926.

Knox, Dudley W. *The Naval Genius of George Washington.* Boston: Houghton Mifflin, 1932.

————, ed. *Naval Documents Related to the Quasi-War between United States and France; Naval Operations from February 1797 to December 1801.* Washington, DC: GPO, 1935–38. 7 vols.

————, ed. *Naval Documents Related to the United States Wars with the Barbary Powers: Naval Operations Including Diplomatic Background from 1785 through 1807.* Washington, DC: GPO, 1939–44, 6 vols.

Leiner, Frederick C. "The 'Whimsical Phylosophic President' and His Gunboats." *American Neptune* 43 (October 1983):245–66.

Mackesy, Piers. *The War for America 1775–1783.* Cambridge, MA: Harvard Univ. Press, 1964.

Maclay, Edgar S. *A History of American Privateers.* New York: D. Appleton, 1899.

Mahan, Alfred Thayer. *The Influence of Sea Power upon History, 1660–1783.* Boston: Little, Brown, 1890.

Morgan, William J. *Captains to the Northward: The New England Captains in the Continental Navy.* Barre, MA: Barre Gazette, 1959.

Murray, Oswyn A. R. "The Admiralty, VI," *Mariner's Mirror* 24 (July 1938): 329–52.

Peckham, Howard H. *The War for Independence, a Military History*. Chicago: Univ. of Chicago Press, 1958.

Syrett, David. *Shipping and the American War 1775-1783: A Study of British Transport Operation*. London: Univ. of London, Athlone, 1970.

TRANSITIONAL PERIOD:

Chapters 4–9 (1816–1881)

Albion, Robert G. "Distant Stations." *U.S. Naval Institute Proceedings* 80 (March 1954):265–73.

Bauer, Karl J. *The Mexican War 1846-1848*. New York: Macmillan, 1974.

_____. *Surfboats and Horse Marines: U. S. Naval Operations in the Mexican War, 1846-1848*. Annapolis, MD: U.S. Naval Institute, 1969.

Bennett, Frank M. *The Steam Navy of the United States: A History of the Growth of the Steam Vessel of War in the U.S. Navy, and of the Naval Engineer Corps*. Pittsburgh: Warren, 1896. Reprinted 1970 by Greenwood.

Bradford, James C., ed. *Captains of the Old Steam Navy: Makers of the American Naval Tradition 1840-1880*. Annapolis, MD: Naval Institute Press, 1986.

Chapelle, Howard I. *History of the American Sailing Navy*. New York: Bonanza Books, 1949.

Fox, Gustavus V. *Confidential Correspondence of Gustavus V. Fox*. Richard M. Thompson and Richard Wainwright, eds. New York: De Vinne, 1918–19. 2 vols.

Gerson, Noel B. *Yankee Admiral*. New York: David McKay, 1968.

Hooper Edwin B. "Developing Naval Concepts: The Early Years." *Defense Management Journal* 12 (July 1976):19–24.

Howe, M. A. Dewolfe. *Life and Letters of George Bancroft*, 2 vols. New York: C. Scribner's Sons, 1908.

Lee, Robert E. *Lee's Despatches, Unpublished Letters of General Robert E. Lee, CSA, to Jefferson Davis and the War Department of the Confederate States of America, 1862-1865*. Douglas S. Freeman, ed. New York: G. P. Putnam's Sons, 1915.

Mahan, Alfred T. *The Navy in the Civil War: The Gulf and Inland Waters*. New York: Charles Scribner's Sons, 1883. Reprinted 1959 by Blue and Gray; 1968 by B. Franklin.

Meader, Equen B. "Birth of the Amphibian: Navy-Marine Operations in the Mexican Gulf, 1846-1848." *Shipmate* 44 (November 1981):28–31.

Milligan, John D., compiler. *From the Fresh Water Navy: 1861-64; The Letters of Acting Master's Mate Henry R. Browne and Acting Ensign Symmes E. Browne*. Annapolis, MD: U.S. Naval Institute, 1970.

Morison, Samuel E. *"Old Bruin"; Commodore Matthew C. Perry, 1794-1858; The American Naval Officer Who Helped Found Liberia*. Boston: Little, Brown, 1967.

O'Connor, Raymond G. "The Navy on the Frontier." In *Proceedings of the Seventh Military History Symposium,* James P. Tate, ed. Pp. 37–49. Washington, DC: GPO, 1976.

Offutt, Milton. *The Protection of Citizens Abroad by the Armed Forces of the United States.* Baltimore: The Johns Hopkins Univ. Press, 1928.

Parmelle, Maurice F. *Blockade and Sea Power.* New York: Thomas Y. Crowell, 1924.

Paullin, Charles O. *Commodore John Rodgers, Captain, Commodore, and Senior Officer of the American Navy, 1773-1838.* Cleveland: Arthur H. Clark Co., 1910. Reprinted 1967 by the U.S. Naval Institute.

Porter, David, and John Rogers. "Condition and Needs of our Navy, 1815." Reprinted in *United States Naval Institute Proceedings* 53 (December 1927): 1309–15.

Powers, Robert D., Jr. "Blockade: for Winning without Killing." *United States Naval Institute Proceedings* 84 (August 1958):61–66.

Riesenburg, Felix. *The Pacific Ocean.* New York: McGraw-Hill, 1940.

Soley, James R. *Admiral Porter.* New York: D. Appleton, 1903.

Symonds, Craig L. *Navalists and Antinavalists: The Navy Policy Debate in the United States, 1785-1827.* Newark: Univ. of Delaware Press, 1980.

U.S. Navy Department. *Report of the Secretary of the Navy in Relation to Armored Vessels.* Washington, DC: GPO, 1864.

U.S. Navy Department. *Annual Report of the Chief of Bureau of Ordnance.* Washington, DC: GPO, December 20, 1863.

U.S. Navy Department. *Report of Board on Steam Machinery Afloat.* Washington, DC: GPO, September 29, 1869.

U.S. Naval Department, History Division. *Civil War Chronology, 1861-1865.* Washington, DC: GPO, 1971.

U.S. Office of Naval Records and Library. *Official Records of the Union and Confederate Navies in the War of the Rebellion.* Washington, DC: GPO, 1894–1922. Series I, 27 vols.; Series II, 3 vols.

U.S. War Department. *The War of the Rebellion: A Compilation of the Official Records of the Union and Confederate Armies.* Washington, DC: GPO, 1884–1903. Series I, 53 vols.

West, Richard S. *Mr. Lincoln's Navy.* New York: Longmans, Green, 1957.

White, Leonard. *The Jeffersonians: A Study in Administrative History, 1801-1829.* New York: Macmillan, 1951.

THE NEW NAVY:

Chapters 10-12 (1881-1913)

Allin, Lawrence C. "The First Unification Crisis: Chandler, Dingley, Folger, and the Bureau of Navigation, 1879–1884." *Military Affairs* 47 (October 1983): 133–40.

Bennett, Frank M. *Steam Navy of the United States: A History of the Growth of the Steam Vessel of War in the U.S. Navy, and of the Naval Engineer Corps.* Pittsburgh: Warren, 1896. Reprinted 1972 by Greenwood.

Coletta, Paolo E. "The Perils of Invention: Bradley A. Fiske and the Torpedo Plane." *American Neptune* 37 (April 1977):111–24.

_____. "The 'Nerves' of the New Navy." *American Neptune* 38 (April 1978): 122–30.

Fisk, Bradley A. "American Naval Policy." *U.S. Naval Institute* 31 (March 1905):1–80.

Holbrook, Francis X., and John Nikol. "The Chilean Crisis of 1891–1892." *American Neptune* 38 (October 1978):291–300.

Hone, Thomas, and Norman Friedman. "Innovation and Administration in the Navy Department: The Case of the Nevada Design." *Military Affairs* 45 (April 1981):57–61.

Hourihan, William F. "The Fleet That Never Was: Commodore John Crittenden Watson and the Eastern Squadron." *American Neptune* 41 (April 1981):93–109.

Karsten, Peter. *The Naval Aristocracy: The Golden Age of Annapolis and the Emergence of Modern American Navalism*. New York: The Free Press, 1972.

Long, John D. *The New American Navy*. New York: Outlook, 1903. 2 vols.

Mahan, Alfred T. *The Influence of Sea Power upon History 1660–1783*. Boston: Little, Brown, 1890.

_____. *The Influence of Sea Power upon the French Revolution and Empire 1793–1812*. Boston: Little, Brown, 2d ed., 1893. 2 vols.

_____. *Sea Power in Its Relations to the War of 1812*. Boston: Little, Brown, 1905. 2 vols. Reprinted 1968 by Greenwood; 1970 by Haskell.

_____. *The Major Operations of the Navies in the War of American Independence*. Boston: Little, Brown, 1913. Reprinted 1968 by Greenwood.

_____. *Letters of Alfred Thayer Mahan*. Robert Seager II and Doris D. Maguire, eds. Annapolis, MD: U.S. Naval Institute Press, 1975. 3 vols.

Seager, Robert. *Alfred Thayer Mahan: The Man and His Letters*. Annapolis, MD: U.S. Naval Institute Press, 1977.

Schurman, Donald M. *The Education of a Navy: The Development of British Naval Strategic Thought, 1867–1914*. Chicago: Univ. of Chicago Press, 1965.

U.S. Adjutant General's Office. *Correspondence relating to the War with Spain and Conditions growing out of the same, including the insurrection in the Philippine Islands and the China Relief Expedition between the Adjutant-General of the Army and Military Commander in the United States, Cuba, Porto Rico, China, and the Philippine Islands from April 15, 1898 to July 30, 1902*. Washington, DC: GPO 1902. 2 vols.

Wheeler, Gerald E. *Admiral William Veazie Pratt, U.S. Navy: A Sailor's Life*. Washington, DC: GPO, 1974.

TWO WORLD WARS:

Chapters 13–20 (1914–1945)

Allard, Dean C. "Admiral William S. Sims and United States Naval Policy in World War I." *American Neptune* 35 (February 1975):97–110.

_____. "Anglo-American Differences During World War I." *Military Affairs* 44 (April 1980):75–81.

Allison, David K. "The Origins of the Naval Research Laboratory." *United States Naval Institute Proceedings* 105 (July 1979):62–69.

Andrade, Ernest. "The Battle Cruiser in the United States Navy." *Military Affairs* 44 (February 1980):18–23.

Booth, Ken. *Navies and Foreign Policy.* New York: Crane Russak, 1977.

Churchill, Winston, and Franklin D. Roosevelt. *Churchill and Roosevelt: The Complete Correspondence.* Vol. 1. Warren K. Kimball, ed. Princeton: Princeton Univ. Press, 1984.

Clephane, Lewis P. *History of the Naval Oversea Transportation Service in World War I.* Washington, DC: GPO, 1969.

Cooke, A. P. "Naval Reorganization." *United States Naval Institute Proceedings* 12 (October 13, 1886):491–505.

Corbett, Julian S. *Some Principles of Maritime Strategy.* Rev. ed. London: Longmans, Green, 1918.

Davis, George T. *A Navy Second to None: The Development of Modern Naval Policy.* New York: Harcourt, Brace, 1940.

Dyer, George C. *The Amphibians Came to Conquer: the Story of Admiral Richmond Kelly Turner.* Washington, DC: GPO, 1972. 2 vols.

Friedman, Leon, ed. *The Law of War: A Documentary History.* Vol. 1. New York: Random House, 1972.

Furer, Julius A. *Administration of the Navy Department in World War II.* Washington, DC: GPO, 1959.

Graham, Gerald S. *Empire of the North Atlantic, the Maritime Struggle for North America.* Toronto: Univ. of Toronto Press, 1950.

Grenfell, Russell. *The Art of the Admiral.* London: Faber and Faber, 1937.

Halsey, William F., and J. Bryan III. *Admiral Halsey's Story.* New York: Whittlesey House, 1947.

Hezlet, Arthur R. *Aircraft and Sea Power.* London: P. Davies, 1970.

Hitler, Adolf. *Mein Kampf.* New York: Raynal & Hitchcock, 1941.

Holmes, W. J. *Undersea Victory: The Influence of Submarine Operations on the War in the Pacific.* Garden City, NY: Doubleday, 1966.

Jones, S. Shepard, and Denys P. Myer. *Documents on American Foreign Relations.* Vol. 3. Boston: World Peace Foundation, 1941.

King, Ernest J., and Walter M. Whitehill. *Fleet Admiral King, a Naval Record.* New York: W. W. Norton, 1952.

Klachko, Mary, and David F. Trask. *Admiral William Shepherd Benson: First Chief of Naval Operations.* Annapolis, MD: Naval Institute Press, 1986.

Martin, Laurence W. *The Sea in Modern Strategy.* New York: Praeger, 1967.

Mitchell, William. *Winged Defense: The Development and Possibilities of Modern Air Power-Economic and Military.* New York: G. P. Putnam's Sons, 1925.

Morison, Samuel E. *History of United States Naval Operations in World War II.* Boston: Little, Brown, 1947–62. 15 vols.

Nimitz, Chester W. "The Navy's Secret Weapon." *Petroleum Today.* (Spring 1961.)

Parmelle, Maurice F. *Blockade and Sea Power: The Blockade 1914-1919, and Its Significance for a World State*. New York: Thomas Y. Crowell, 1924.

Playfair, I. S. O. *The Mediterranean and Middle East*. Vol. 1. *The Germans come to the help of their Allies*. Vol. 2. London: Her Majesty's Stationery Office, 1954.

Potter, E. B. *Bull Halsey*. Annapolis, MD: U.S. Naval Institute Press, 1985.

Roberts, Stephen S. "The Decline of the Overseas Station Fleets: The United States Asiatic Fleet and the Shanghai Crisis, 1932." *American Neptune* 37 (July 1977):185-202.

Roskill, Stephen W. *Naval Policy Between the Wars*. New York: Walker, 1968-76. 2 vols.

———. *White Ensign; The British Navy at War, 1939-1945*. Annapolis, MD: U.S. Naval Institute, 1960.

Scott, James B., ed. *The Hague Conventions and Declarations of 1899 and 1907: accompanied by tables of signatures, ratifications and adhesions of the various powers, and text of reservations*. New York: Oxford Univ. Press, 1915.

Sigaud, Louis A. *Douhet and Aerial Warfare*. New York: G. P. Putnam's Sons, 1941.

Sprout, Harold, and Margaret Sprout. *Toward a New Order of Sea Power: American Naval Policy and the World Scene, 1918-1922*. 2nd ed. Princeton: Princeton University Press, 1946. Reprinted 1969 by Greenwood.

Trask, David D. *Captains and Cabinets: Anglo-American Relations 1917-1918*. Columbia: Univ. of Missouri, 1972.

Trimble, William F. "Admiral Hilary P. Jones and the 1927 Geneva Naval Conference." *Military Affairs* 43 (February 1979):1-4.

U.S. Office of Naval Record and Library. *The Northern Barrage and Other Mining Activities*. Washington, DC: GPO, 1920.

U.S. Strategic Bombing Survey. *Summary Report (European War)*. Washington, DC: GPO, September 30, 1945.

Wilson, Henry B. *An Account of the Operations of the American Navy in France During the War With Germany*. U.S.S. *Pennsylvania*: July 1, 1919.

THE NUCLEAR AGE:

Chapters 21-27 (1946-1987)

Acheson, Dean G. *Present at the Creation: My Years in the State Department*. New York: W. W. Norton, 1969.

Aliano, Richard A. *American Defense Policy from Eisenhower to Kennedy: The Political Changing Military Requirements, 1957-1961*. Athens, Ohio: Ohio Univ. Press, 1975.

Anderson, George W., Jr. "The Cuban Crisis." *United States Institute Proceedings*, Naval History Symposium. Arnold R. Skapack, ed. Annapolis, MD: U.S. Naval Academy, 1973.

Brodie, Bernard, ed. *The Absolute Weapon: Atomic Power and World Order*. New York: Harcourt, Brace, 1946.

———. *The Atomic Bomb and American Security*. New Haven, CT: Yale Institute of International Studies, 1945.

———. *A Guide to Naval Strategy*. 5th ed. New York: Praeger, 1965.

Burke, Arleigh A. "The Lebanon Crisis." *Proceedings, Naval History Symposium*. Annapolis, MD: U.S. Naval Academy, 1973.

Cagle, Macolm W., and Frank A. Manson. *The Sea War in Korea*. Annapolis, MD: U.S. Naval Institute, 1957.

Cole, Alice C., Alfred Goldberg, Samuel A. Tucker, and Rudolph A. Winnacker, eds. *The Department of Defense: Documents on Establishment and Organization, 1944-1978*. Washington, DC: GPO, 1978.

Field, James A. *History of United States Naval Operations–Korea*. Washington, DC: GPO, 1962.

Finletter, Thomas K. "Survival in the Air Age." Washington, DC: GPO, U.S. President's Air Policy Commission, 1948.

Forrestal, James V. *The Forrestal Diaries*. Walter Millis, ed., with collaboration by E. S. Duffield. New York: Viking, 1951. Reprinted 1966 by Viking.

George, Alexander L., and Richard Smoke. *Deterrence in American Foreign Policy: Theory and Practice*. New York: Columbia Univ. Press, 1974.

Gorshkov, Sergei G. *The Sea Power of the State*. Annapolis, MD: U.S. Naval Institute Press, 1979.

Hewes, James E., Jr. *From Root to McNamara: Army Organization and Administration, 1900-1963*. Washington, DC: GPO, 1975.

Ho Chi Minh. *Against U.S. Aggression for National Salvation*. Hanoi: Foreign Language Publishing House, 1967.

———. *On Revolution: Selected Writings*. 1920–66, Bernard B. Fall, ed. New York: Praeger, 1967.

Hooper, Edwin B. *Mobility, Support, Endurance: A Story of Naval Operational Logistics in the Vietnam War, 1965-1968*. Washington, DC: GPO, 1972.

———. *The Navy Department: Evolution and Fragmentation*. Naval Historical Foundation, 1978.

Hooper, Edwin B., Dean C. Allard, and Oscar P. Fitzgerald. *The United States Navy and the Vietnam Conflict: The Setting of the Stage to 1959*. Washington, DC: GPO, 1976.

Huntington, S. P. *The Common Defense*. New York: Columbia Univ. Press, 1961.

Kaufmann, William W. *The McNamara Strategy*. New York: Harper & Row, 1964.

Khrushchev, Nikita S. *Khrushchev Remembers*. Strobe Talbott, transl. and ed. Boston: Little, Brown, 1970.

McNamara, Robert S. *The Essence of Security: Reflections in Office*. New York: Harper & Row, 1968.

Marolda, Edward J., and Oscar P. Fitzgerald. *The United States and the Vietnam Conflict: From Military Assistance to Combat 1959-1965*. Washington, DC: GPO, 1986.

Ries, John C. *The Management of Defense: Organization and Control of the U.S. Armed Services*. Baltimore: The Johns Hopkins Univ. Press, 1964.

Ryan, Paul B. *Iran Rescue Mission: Why It Failed.* Annapolis, MD: Naval Institute Press, 1985.

Schlesinger, Arthur M., Jr. *A Thousand Days: John F. Kennedy in the White House.* Boston: Houghton Mifflin, 1965.

Taylor, Maxwell D. *The Uncertain Trumpet.* New York: Harper & Row, 1960.
   . *Responsibility and Response.* New York: Harper & Row, 1967.

Truman, Harry S. *Memoirs.* Garden City, NY: Doubleday, 1955–56. 2 vols.

U.S. Defense Department Study. *United States-Vietnam Relations: 1945–1967.* Washington, DC: GPO, 1971. 12 vols.

U.S. Joint Logistics Review Board. *Logistics Support in the Vietnam Era; A Report.* Washington, DC: GPO, 1970.

U.S. Navy Department. *Review of Navy R&D Management, 1946–1973.* Contract No. N00014-74-C-0251.. Prepared by Booz, Allen and Hamilton, Inc., June 1, 1976.
   . *Review of the Management of the Department of the Navy.* Navexos P-2422A. Washington, DC: Department of the Navy, 1962.

Vo Nguyen Giap. *Banner of People's War, the Party's Military Line.* New York: Praeger, 1970.
   . "The Military Art of People's War." Russel Stetler, ed. New York: Monthly Review Press, 1970.
   . *People's War, People's Army: The Viet Cong Insurrection Manual for Underdeveloped Countries.* New York: Praeger, 1962.

Yarmolinsky, Adam. *The Military Establishment: Its Impacts on American Society.* New York: Harper & Row, 1971.

Xydis, Stephen G. "The Genesis of the Sixth Fleet." *United States Naval Institute Proceedings* 84 (August 1958):41–50.

Index

accountability: diffusion by staffs, 97;
diffusion in Defense Department, 261;
in Navy Department, 36. *See also*
authority
Adams, President John, 20, 22, 24
advisory council to secretary of navy, 124
air force, established, 191
aircraft carrier: B36 debate, 194; British,
WWII, 146; capabilities, 138; escort,
169–70; first, 134
aircraft: development of sea operations,
138; air-cooled engines, 138; liquid-
cooled engines, 166. *See also* aviation
Alabama, CSS sloop, 61
Albemarle, CSS iron-clad, 72
Alert, HMS sloop, 32
Aleutians, U.S. campaign in WWII, 172–73
Alliance, Continental Navy frigate, 19
American Expeditionary Force to France,
WWI, 130
Ammonoosuc, USS steamer, 78
Amphibious Force: following Vietnam
War, 246–47; Vietnam War, 232
amphibious operations: Bay of Pigs, 226–
27, 258; British during War of 1812, 33–
34; Civil War, 58–60; command rela-
tions, 47, 141, 254–55; development of
modern technology, 211; Gallipoli, 121;
Japanese at start of WWII, 161; Korean
War [Hungnam] 205, [Inchon] 202–3,
258, [Pohang] 201, [Wosan, Iwon] 204;
Lebanon, 220; Mexican War, 47; North
Vietnam evacuation in 1954, 214;
planning before WWII, 141; Spanish-
American War, 94–95; WWII, 167,

172–74, 176–78, 180, [German against
Norway], 147
Anson, Admiral George (Great Britain), 9
Antiaircraft Defense Board, 153
antiaircraft: protection by battleships, 174;
technology, 171–72; U.S. lack in 1940,
153
antisubmarine: destroyers [WWI], 128,
[WWII], 149; development, 216–17;
mines, 130–31; technology, 171; WWII,
169–71
Argonaut, USS submarine, 174
Argus, USS, 27
army-navy joint operations: *see* amphibious
operations, riverine forces
Arnold, Brigadier General Benedict, 16
Arnold, General H. H., 164
Arromanches, French carrier, 213
Ashworth, Commander, F. L., 182
assistant secretary of navy, first, 58
atomic bomb: against Japan, 181–82; effect
on military planning, 186; stalemate
predicted, 195; tested by USSR, 195
Augusta, USS, 77
authority: centralization under secretary of
defense, 193, 208, 215; delegation of,
158; fragmentation and centers in
Defense Department, 221–22, 228–29,
239, 257; and responsibility, 22, 42,
158, 168. *See also* accountability
auxiliary ships: *see* stores ships
aviation: advances in 1930s, 138; agreements limiting use, 101, 136; arguments
for, 136–37; attack on Tokyo, 164;
beginning of naval, 99; British naval in

WWII, 145–46; 166; following WWI, 133-34; Japanese naval, 156-57; lack of Italian naval in WWII, 151; naval command, 133-34; haval flying corps established, 124; U.S. naval in Korean War, 205; U.S. naval in Vietnam, 231; U.S. naval in WWII, 163-65, 173-74, 177-80; WWI, 123, 128, 132. *See also* aircraft, aircraft carrier, antiaircraft, dive bombers, overflight, seaplane

Badger, Secretary of Navy George E., 49
Bainbridge, Captain William, 34
Banks, Major General Nathaniel P., 74-75
Barbary States: conclusion of war, 34-35; conflicts before 1800, 19-21; war with, 24-27
Barney, Commodore Joshua, 33
Barras, Commodore Count de Saint-Laurent, 17
Barron, Commodore James, 28
Barron, Captain Samuel, 27
bat glider bomb, 180
battleships, modern, 101-2
Bay of Pigs, failure of invasion, 226-27
Benes, President Eduard (Czechoslovakia), 196
Benson, Captain William S., 124; Admiral, 130
Biddle, Captain James, 38
Blair, Montgomery, 51-52
blockade: British in War of 1812, 33; British in WWI, 119-20; conditional [of Cuba] 228, [of Mexico] 45-46, [possible in Congo] 224, [possible of Nicaragua] 253; effects in WWI, 131; legal, 55, 101; of Barbary States, 24-27; of Confederacy, 53, 55-56, 71; of North Korea, 200; of North Vietnam recommended, 230; of Venezuela, 103; Spanish-American War, 91
Board of Admiralty, Continental, 17
Board of Commissioners, 42-43
Boggs, Commodore C. S., 78
bombs, tests against ships, 135-36
Bonaparte, Secretary of Navy C. J., 97
Borie, Secretary of Navy A. E., 79
Boston, USS heavy cruiser, 217
Bradley, General Omar M., 195, 209
Branch, Secretary of Navy John, 42
Broughton, Nicholson, 14
Brown, Vice Admiral Wilson, 164

Buchanan, President James, 51
bureau system: *see* Navy Department
Bureau: Aeronautics, 134; Construction and Repair, 45, 73; Equipment, 103; Medicine and Surgery, 45; Navigation, 56, 96, 124; Ordnance and Hydrography, 45, 48, 63-64; Ordnance, 56, 131, 140; Provisions and Clothing, 45; Steam Engineering, 56, 73; Yards and Docks, 45
Burke, Admiral Arleigh A., 217-20
Burnside, Brigadier General A. E., 67
Bushnell, David, 48
Butler, Major General Benjamin F., 59, 65-66

Cairo, USS, 72-73
Cambodia, North Vietnamese logistics through ports, 236
Cameron, Secretary of War Simon, 52
Canonius, USS class of monitor, 72
Caribbean Sea, naval mission in, 253
Carney, Admiral Robert B., 213-14
Castro, Fidel, 223-24, 226
Cervera y Topete, Admiral Pascual, 92, 94-95
Chamoun, President Camille (Lebanon), 220
Chandler, Secretary of Navy W. E., 86, 256
Chauncey, Commodore Issac, 33
Chesapeake, USS, 28
chief of naval operations: after Defense Reorganization Act, 221; authority, 158, [in WWII] 168-69; established, 124; need for, 98; powers strengthened, 125
Choiseul, Duc de, 10
Churchill, Winston, 166
Clifford, Secretary of Defense Clark, 236
coal: consumption by iron-clads, 77; lack on Mississippi, 66; refueling needed, 46; remote fueling, 103; ship capacity specified by Congress, 91; station at Midway Island, 81
coast guard, established, 123
codes: British convoys' broken, 154; German broken, 170; U-boat broken, 154
Colt, Samuel, 48-49
command: masterminded by government leaders, 11-13, 71, 229-30; problems in Civil War riverine forces, 64; unified following WWII, 189. *See also* leadership
commodore, rank established, 66
communications advances, 98. *See also*

radio, codes
communist expansion during cold war, 196
congressional acts and authorizations:
armored vessels 1886, 91; construction
[1881] 85–86, [1934] 142, [1940]
148; Embargo Act, 28; Flag rank, 66;
gunboats, 27–28, 66; lend-lease 1941,
150; National Industrial Recovery 1933,
139; navy established, 21–22; reorganization [1842] 44–45, [1862] 56; ship
building 1847–58, 49; submarine [1893]
91, [1924–25] 161, [pre-WWII] 123,
125
Connor, Commodore David, 46–47
Constellation, USS frigate, 22
Constitution, USS frigate, 32
constitution, army and navy, 20
construction, Continental Navy, 14–15
construction, naval responsibility in Vietnam, 233
constructor, chief, 41
Continental Congress: Committee of Three,
14; Marine Committee, 14–15
convoys: Mediterranean, 38; Murmansk,
166; WWI, 128–30; WWII, 157
Conyngham, Gustavus, 16
Coral Sea, Battle of, 164
Cork and Orrey, Admiral of the Fleet
Lord, 148
Cornwallis, General Charles, 17
Crane, Commodore W. M., 45, 48
Crowninshield, Secretary of Navy Benjamin
W., 36–37
cruisers: Confederate, 53, 61; limited by
radio, 98, 122; limits, 89; Revolutionary
War, 15; steam, 80; War of 1812, 32–33.
See also submarines
Cuba: Bay of Pigs, 226–27; Castro, 223–24;
missile crisis, 228; Spanish-American
War, 93–94
Curtiss, Glenn H., 99
Cushing, Lieutenant William Barker, 72

Dahlgren, Lieutenant John A., 48; Com-
mander, 67; Rear Admiral, 75
Dale, Commodore Richard, 24–26
Danang: logistics port, 232; protection by
marines, 231
Daniels, Secretary of Navy Josephus, 124
David, CSS gunboat, 72
Davis, Captain Charles H., 65–66
Davis, President Jefferson (CSA), 52, 70

Davis, Charles H., 73
Decatur, Commodore Stephan, 32, 34–35
Defense Department: authority in, 209–10,
261; established, 194; following Vietnamese War, 239–41; proposed, 190;
recommended, 136–37. *See also* authority
Defense Reorganization Act, 1958, 220–22
defense secretary: after Defense Reorganization Act, 221; established, 191–92
Delano, B. F., 77
Denfeld, Admiral Louis E., 195
depth charge, developed, 171
destroyers, antisubmarine, 169
Dewey, Commodore George, 92; Admiral
of the Navy, 96, 98, 103
dey of Tripoli, 35
Dickerson, Secretary of Navy Mahlon, 42–
43
Diem, President Ngo Dinh (Republic of
Vietnam), 214, 229
Dien Bien Phu: capture by French, 212;
siege and fall, 213–14
dive bombers: development, 138; German,
152–53; Japanese, 157
Dobbin, Secretary of Navy, 49
Doolittle, Lieutenant Colonel James H., 164
Doorman, Admiral K. W. F. M. (Dutch),
163
Douhet, Colonel Guilo, 136
Doyle, Rear Admiral James H., 201–2
Dreadnought, HMS battleship, 101
Du Pont, Captain Samuel F., 56–57; Flag
Officer, 59–60, 68; Rear Admiral, 71–72
Dulles, Secretary of State John Foster, 212,
219
Dunkirk, 147–48

Eaton, Navy Agent William, 27
Ebertstadt, Ferdinand, 193
Eisenhower, President Dwight D., 208–10,
212, 214–15, 220–21, 223–24, 257
Electra, USS, ordnance ship, 46
Ellis, Lieutenant Earl H., 141
Engineering Corps: established, 45; merged
into line, 102
engineers, qualifications of naval, 43
Enterprise, USS, schooner, 24–26; aircraft
carrier, 146, 163–64
Ericsson, John, 67–68, 73
Essex, USS, 32
Estaing, Vice Admiral Comte d', 16

exploratory expedition, U.S. 1838–42, 44

Farragut, Flag Officer David D., 60, 64–66; Rear Admiral, 74, 80
Farragut, USS class destroyers, 139
Faxon, Assistant Secretary of Navy William, 79
Ferdinand, Archduke Franz (Austria), 104
Finletter, Thomas K., 192
fishing rights, 3; USSR, 244
Fiske, Lieutenant Bradley A., 99; Rear Admiral, 124
Fleming, George, 48
Fletcher, Rear Admiral F. J., 164
Florida, USS steamer, 78
Foote, Captain Andrew H., 63–65
Formosa: see Taiwan
Forrestal, Secretary of Defense James, 192–93
Fox, Lieutenant Gustavus Vasa, 51–52; Assistant Secretary of Navy, 58, 71–74, 77, 79, 255
France: naval support in Revolutionary War, 16–18; Quasi-War, 22–24. *See also* Dien Bien Phu, Indochina
Franklin D. Roosevelt, USS carrier, 188
Fredonia, USS, stores ship, 46
Fremont, Major General John C., 63
Frolic, HMS, 32
Fubaki class destroyers, Japan, 139
Fulton, Robert, 40, 48
Fulton (Demologos), USS, first steam-powered warship, 40
Fulton (second), USS, 43–44
funding, effects of limits, 17, 19, 32, 43, 86–87, 138–39, 194
fuze, VT (radar proximity), 140, 171

Galena, USS iron-clad, 67, 69–70
Gallipoli, amphibious operation, 121
General Board: see Navy Department
general orders, Porter's following Civil War, 79–80
General Staff, recommended for navy, 97
George III, King (Great Britain), 11
Giap, General, 211
Gilmer, Secretary of Navy Thomas W., 45
Glorious, HMS carrier, 147
Gneisenau, German battle cruiser, 147
Goff, Secretary of Navy Nathan, 81
Goldsborough, Flag Officer Louis M., 67,

69–70; Rear Admiral, 78
Goodrich, Lieutenant C. F., 86
Gorshkov, Admiral of the Fleet Sergei G. (USSR), 242–45
Grant, General Ulysses S., 63–64, 73–75; President, 79–81
Grasse, Rear Admiral Count de, 17
Graves, Vice Admiral Samuel (Great Britain), 10–11
Graves, Admiral Thomas (Great Britain), 17
Great White Fleet, 103
Greece: following WWII, 188–89; WWII, 152–53
Greer, USS, 154
Guadalcanal, Battle of, 167
Guerriere, HMS, 32
gunboats: in Barbary Wars, 27; inland waters in Civil War, 62–63; Jeffersonian, 27–28, 33, 252; on rivers in Civil War, 69–70; USS *Panay* sunk by Japanese, 142
gunnery: analog computer, 100; antiaircraft, 139–40; Dahlgren gun, 48, 67; explosive shell [Stevenes'], 44; fire control, 100, 139, [radar] 140; gyroscopic stabilization, 139; lack of antiaircraft guns in 1940, 153; naval during Korean War, 201–3; Paixhaus gun, 44; proximity fuze, 140; rangefinder, 99; servos, 139; standardization of guns, 48
gyroscopic: compass tested, 99; gun stabilization, 139; steering of torpedoes, 90

Hague Peace Conference, 1907, 101, 123
Halleck, Major General H. H., 63, 66, 73
Halsey, Rear Admiral W. F., Jr., 163–64, 173–74, 178–79
Hamet, Caramanli, 27
Hamilton, Secretary of Navy Paul, 28, 31–32, 34
Hampton Roads, in Civil War, 66–67
Hannah, Continental schooner, 14
Harkins, General Paul D., 232
Harriet Lane, USS cutter, 52
Hartford, USS screw-sloop, 66, 74
Haswell, C. H., 42–43
Hayes, President Rutherford, 81
Herbert, Secretary of Navy H. A., 91
Hitler, Adolf, 142–44, 147–49, 152–55, 187
Ho Chi Minh, 212
Hobson, Congressman Raymond P., 124

Hopkins, Commodore Ezek, 14
Hornet, USS carrier, 164
Housatonic, USS, 72, 127
Howe, General Sir William, 16
Hull, Commodore Isaac, 35
Hull, General William, 32
hull: damage due to tamping effect of
   water, 48; design against torpedoes and
   mines, 133; design improvements, 100
H. L. Hunley, CSS submarine, 72
Hunt, Secretary of Navy William H., 85–86

Illustrious, HMS carrier, 146
Indochina, French-Viet Minh War, 197,
   211–14. *See also* Dien Bien Phu, Vietnam, Vietnam War
inland waters: Revolutionary War, 15–16;
   War of 1812, 33. *See also* riverine forces
Insurgente, French frigate, 23
intelligence, gathering assigned to Bureau of
   Navigation, 86
international law, naval, 101. *See also*
   blockade, Hague, London, Washington
iron-clad monitors: Civil War, 67–68; 71–73;
   following Civil War, 76–78
iron-hulled steamer, first, 49
Isherwood, Chief Engineer Benjamin F., 73,
   77–79, 85
Iwo Jima, assault on, 180

Jackson, Andrew, 34
Japan: "New Order", 155; Marshall,
   Caroline, and Mariana islands, 121; sur-
   render on mainland, 187–88. *See also*
   Pacific Ocean
Jay, John, 21
Jefferson, President Thomas, 20, 24, 28,
   252
Jeffersonian gunboats, 27–28, 33, 252
John Adams, USS, stores ship, 26
Johnson, President Lyndon B., 229–31,
   236
Johnson, Secretary of Defense Louis A.,
   193–96, 203
Joint Army-Navy Board: established, 96–97;
   WWI, 124
Joint Chiefs of Staff: 1947, 192; abolish-
   ment advocated, 225; after Defense Re-
   organization Act, 221; chairman, 257;
   coordinated planning, 256; in Defense
   Department, 195, 209; WWII, 160
Jones, Captain John Paul, 16

Jones, Secretary of Navy William, 34
Joy, Admiral C. Turner, 197, 198–200,
   204–5
Jupiter (*Langley*), USS collier, 134

kamikaze attacks, 179–81
Kearney, Commodore Lawrence, 44
Kearsage, USS, 61
Kennedy, President John F., 224–27, 229,
   258
Khrushchev, Nikita S., 218
Killian, James R., 217
Kimmel, Admiral H. E., 160
King, Admiral Ernest J., 160, 163–66,
   168, 172–73, 195, 257
Kinkaid, Admiral Thomas C., 179–80
Knox, Secretary of War Henry, 20
Korea, communist fortifications in North,
   196
Korean War: 200–7, armistice, 206; start,
   198
Kosygin, Premier Alexi N. (USSR), 230
Kurita, Vice Admiral Takeo (Japan), 173,
   178–79

Laffey, USS, first "aeroplane carrier", 134
Laos, North Vietnamese aggression, 222–23
leadership: lack of naval experience, 9–10,
   15, 31, 37–38, 45, 80–81, 222; need for
   naval officer in naval affairs, 24, 35, 51,
   56, 78–79. *See also* command
Leahy, Admiral William D., 195
Leary, Vice Admiral H. F., 164
Lebanon, amphibious operation, 220
Lee, General Robert E., 70, 75
Lee, Rear Admiral S. F., 71
Lee, Continental, 14
lendlease, to Britain and USSR, 154
Lenthall, Chief Constructor John, 73, 78,
   85
Leopold, HMS, 28
Lexington, USS carrier, 135, 138, 164–65
Leyte Gulf, Battle of, 178–79
Leyte, USS carrier, 189
limited war: Korea, 198–207; possibility
   ignored, 186; Vietnam, 230–36
Lincoln, President Abraham, 51–53, 63, 69,
   74
logistics: Barbary Wars, 24–27; Grant sup-
   port, 75; Great White Fleet, 103; inadequate at start of war, 10, 46, 60; naval
   support during Korean War, 198; on

Mississippi in Civil War, 66; problems with chartered ships, 26; Revolutionary War, 13–14; Spanish-American War, 93; Vietnam War, 232–33; WWII, 161, 177
London Naval Conference of 1909, 101
Long, Secretary of Navy J. D., 91–93, 96
Lovett, Secretary of Defense Robert A., 208–9
Luce, Commodore Stephen, 86
Lumumba, Patrice, 223
Lusitania, British liner, 122

MacArthur, General Douglas, 165, 172–73, 179, 181, 197, 202–6
Macdonough, Lieutenant Thomas, 33
Macedonian, HMS, 32
Maddox, USS destroyer, 230
Madison, President James, 28, 31, 35–36
Mahan, Captain Alfred Thayer, 87–89, 92–93, 100–2, 119, 131, 150, 156, 163, 185–86, 242–43, 256
Maine, USS battleship, 91
Makarov, Vice Admiral Stephen O. (Russia), 100
Manila Bay, Battle of, 92
Mao Tse-Tung, 187, 197
Margaretta, HMS armed schooner, 13
Marianas, capture of in WWII, 177
marine corps: Civil War, 59; purpose, 191; Spanish-American War, 94; WWII, 154, 167, 173–74, 178
Marshall, General George C., 160, 185; Secretary of Defense, 203, 208
Masaryk, Foreign Minister Jan (Czechoslavakia), 196
Maury, Lieutenant Matthew Fontaine, 45, 50
Maximilian, Emperor (Mexico), 76
Mayo, Admiral H. T., 134
McClellan, Major General George B., 59, 68–70
McClernand, Major General John A., 73
McHenry, Secretary of War James, 21
McKinley, President William, 92–93
McNamara, Secretary of Defense Robert S., 226, 228–30, 236
measures and countermeasures: *see* research and development
Mediterranean: communist expansion following WWII, 18–19; following Barbary Wars, 38; Lebanon, 219–20; WWII, 150–

53, 175. *See also* Barbary States
Meig, Captain M. C., 52
Mercer, Captain Samuel, 52
Merrill, Admiral S., 173
Merrimack, USS frigate, 22; screw-frigate [*Virginia*], 67
Metcalf, Secretary of Navy George Von Lengerke, 103
Miantonomoh, USS iron-clad monitor, 73; cruise to Europe, 77
Michigan (Wolverine), USS, first iron-hulled steamer, 49
Middleton, Captain Charles, 16
Midway, Battle of, 164
Miles, Major General N. A., 93
mines: antisubmarine, 130–31, 170; clearing from Japanese waters, 188; Confederate, 53, 72–75; development, 48–49; German in WWII, 144–45; Korean War, 203–5; magnetic, 144–45; Spanish-American War, 94; Suez Canal, 152; use of, 254; WWI, 120–21
mining: of North Vietnam recommended, 235; of North Vietnam, 236
missiles: surface-to-surface, 241; VI and V2, 176
Mississippi River, Civil War, 64–66, 73–75
Missouri, USS battleship, 182, 188, 203
Mitchell, Brigadier General Billy, 136–37
Mobile Bay, Battle of, 74
Monadnock, USS iron-clad monitor, 73, 77
Monitor, USS, 67–68, 70–73
monitors: *Canonius* and *Miantonomoh* class, 72–73; *Passiacs* class, 71. *See also* iron-clad monitors
Monroe, President James, 35, 38
Moody, Secretary of Navy W. H., 97, 102
Moore, Engineer J. W., 78
Morris, Superintendent of Finance Robert, 17
Morton, Secretary of Navy Paul, 102
Musashi, Japan super battleship, 178
Mussolini, Benito, 142, 144, 151

Nagumo, Vice Admiral Chuichi (Japan), 163–64
Nancy, HMS brig, 14
Napoleon III (France), 76
Narvik campaign: 147–48
National Advisory Committee for Aeronautics, 138, 169

National Security Act: 1947, 190–93; amended, 257
National Security Council: and CIA, 226; established, 192; involvement in military matters, 229
Nautilus, USS submarine, 174; nuclear, 365
Naval Academy: established, 45; recommended, 37
Naval Advisory Board, established, 85
Naval Commissioners, Board of, 35–38
naval forces: reduction following war, 24, 27, 81–82, 135, 137–39, 189, 194, 238
Naval Observatory and Hydrographic Office, 84
naval power: differences with army and air force, 190, 260–61; during peace, 19, 38–39, 252; flexibility, 178; Gorshkov's concepts, 242–45; lack of understanding, 222; Mahan's concepts, 87–89; uniqueness, 4–5; USSR, 242–43, 259. *See also* sea control.
Naval Reserve, established, 123
Naval Transport Service, WWII, 130
Naval War Board, planning for Spanish-American War, 92
Naval War College, established, 86
Navarre, General Henri (France), 213
Navy Commissioners, Board of, 252–53
Navy Department: bilinear organization, 168–69, [abandoned] 239; Board of Naval Commissioners, 35–38; bureau system, 44–45, 56, 97–98, 169, 254; Civil War, 55–57; and coast guard, 123; efficiency in WWII, 157–58; established, 22; General Board, 256, [established] 96–97; Korean War, 208; organization of antisubmarine command, 170; proposal to eliminate after WWII, 185; subdivision recommended, 41–42; War of 1812, 34; WWII response, 157–60
navy: organization [Continental] 17, [following constitution] 21, [initial] 22–23; U.S. following Vietnamese War, 245–46
neutrality patrol, 146
New Ironsides, USS, iron-clad, 67, 72
New Orleans: Battle of, 34; capture in Civil War, 64–65
New York, USS, experimental air search radar, 140
Newton, Engineer Issac, 78

Nimitz, Admiral Chester W., 163, 165, 172, 176–77, 180, 212
Nixon, President Richard M., 136
North Atlantic Treaty signed, 196
North Carolina, USS, first ship to launch aircraft, 99
nuclear capability, naval, 210
nuclear deterrence, strategy, 219
nuclear war, stalemate predicted by Admiral King, 195

O'Bannon, Lieutenant Presley, 27
oil, fuel advantages, 78, 100. *See also* refueling at sea
Oldendorf, Admiral Jesse, 179
OpNav: *see* chief of naval operations
ordnance, state in 1835, 44. *See also* specific weapon
Ordnance Department, recommended, 37
overflight, problems in Lebanese operation, 220

Pacific coast, cruises to, 38
Pacific Ocean: naval war against Japan, [central] 174, 176–77; [northern] 172–73; [southern] 173–74
Paixhans, General Henri-Joseph (France), 44
Panay, USS gunboat, 142
Parsons, Commander W. S., 171; Captain, 182
pasha of Tripoli, 24, 26
Passiac, USS class of monitors, 71
Patterson, Commodore Daniel T., 34
Paulding, Secretary of Navy James K., 43
Pawnee, USS, 52, 55, 59
Pearl Harbor, attack on, 156–57
Pennock, Commander Alexander M., 64
Perry, Captain Matthew Calbraith, 43–44; Commodore, 49
Perry, Oliver Hazard, 33
Philippine Sea, Battle of, 177
Philippines: following Spanish-American War, 103; Spanish-American War, 92; WWII, 177–80
Pillow, Fort, Battle of, 65
Pocahontas, USS screw-steamer, 52
Polk, President James K., 45
Pook, Naval Constructor Samuel M., 63
Port Hudson, Battle of, 74
Porter, Commodore David, 35
Porter, Lieutenant David Dixon, 52;

Commander, 65; Rear Admiral, 73-74;
   Vice Admiral, 79; Admiral of the Navy,
   80, 85
Powahatan, USS screw-steamer, 52
Preble, Commodore Edward, 26-27
President, USS frigate, 27
Princeton, USS, first screw-propelled war-
   ship, 43; carrier, 227
privateers, Declaration of Paris 1856, 101.
   See also cruisers
propeller: developed, 43; steam-frigates, 49
Pusan, defense of, 198

Quasi-War with France, 22-24

Rabaul: assault proposed, 165; Japanese
   sieze, 163; base, 173
radar: British use, 152; early development,
   140; magnetron development, 150; surface search on USS Washington, 166-67
Radford, Admiral Arthur W., 212
radio: direction finders, 170; early use, 98;
   WWI warship tracking, 121
Ramsey, Rear Admiral F. A., 91
Ranger, USS carrier, 135
Rapid Deployment Force: Joint, 246;
   limits of, 225-26
rear admiral, rank established, 66
Red River Campaign, 74-75
refueling at sea, WWII, 161, 177
Relief, USS, stores ship, 46
Remey, Commodore G. C., 93
research and development: during depression, 139; during WWII, 169; following
   WWII, 193-94, 216-17; measures and
   countermeasures, 90, 144-45, 168,
   171-72; realistic testing needed, 141;
   value of, 41. See also specific development
resources: from ocean bottom, 3-4; USSR,
   244
responsibility: see accountability, authority
Rhee, Syngman, 200
Richardson, Admiral J. O., 160
Ridgway, General Matthew B., 206
riverine forces: Civil War, 62-70, 73-75;
   during French-Viet Minh War, 197,
   211-12; in Vietnam, 235. See also inland waters
Roach, John, 86
Robeson, Secretary of Navy G. M., 80

Robie, Engineer E. D., 78
Rochambeau, General Comte de, 17
rocket, Hales, 48
Rodgers, Commodore John (father), 31-32,
   35, 43
Rodgers, Commander John (son), 63, 70;
   Rear Admiral, 85
Roosevelt, Assistant Secretary of Navy
   Theodore, 92; President, 97, 102-3
Roosevelt, President Franklin D., 139, 145,
   150, 153-55, 158-60, 166, 168
Root, Secretary of Army Elihu, 97
Russo-Japanese War, 100
Ryukyus, assaults on, 180

Sampson, Commander W. T., 86; Rear Admiral, 91, 93-95, 99
Sandwitch, Earl of, 11
Saratoga, USS carrier, 135, 138, 163
Sarnoff, David, 209
Scharnhorst, German battle cruiser, 147
Schlesinger, Arthur M., Jr., 226
Schley, Commodore Winfield S., 93-94
scientific data: collected for Maury, 49-50;
   survey by Wilkes, 44
Scott, General Winfield, 47, 51, 255
sea control: consequences, 133; importance,
   132-33; Mahan's concepts, 150, 156;
   primary role of navy, 260; Revolutionary War, 11, 15; submarines, 132. See
   also naval power
Sea Gull, USS, first steam-powered warship
   in U.S. service, 40
sea law: see international law
seabees, in Vietnam, 232
sealift, Korean War, 201
seaplane, 99, 134, 138, 147
SEATO, established, 215
service force: 26; Civil War, 60; need for,
   66; WWII, 177
Seward, Secretary of State William H., 52
Shafter, Major General W. R., 94-95
Sharp, Admiral U. S. G., 230
Sherman, Admiral Forrest, 197, 200, 204
Sherman, Brigadier General William T., 59,
   74-75
ship construction: 1940, 148; during depression, 139; during Quasi-War, 22;
   Hitler's plans, 143; long-range planning,
   37
ship: degaussing, 145; design against

torpedoes, 90; limitations after WWI, 135; need for naval officer judgment in design, 78, 102; reactivation in Korean War, 202

Sho-Go plan, Japanese in WWII, 179

shore establishment, in peace, 37, 76

Shufeldt, Commodore R. F., 86

Sicard, Rear Admiral M., 91

Sims, Rear Admiral William S., 127-28

Smith, Brigadier General A. J., 75

Smith, Lieutenant Sidney, 33

Smith, Secretary of Navy Robert, 26

Southard, Senator Samuel L., 48

Soviet: *see* USSR

Spanish-American War, 91-95

Sperry, Elmer A., 99

Spruance, Vice Admiral R. A., 177-78, 180

Squadron: Asiatic, 91; Eastern, 60; European, 91; Far East, 92; Home, 45; Mediterranean, 38; North Atlantic, 58, 62, 71, 91; Pacific, 38, 46; South Atlantic, 59, 68-69, 75; Western Gulf, 60, 64

Stalin, Josef, 187, 212

Stark, Admiral Harold R., 148, 168

steam propulsion: demonstration, 43; progress, 77-78; warship development, 40-43; warships fitted with sails, 80

steel ships, recommended, 86

Stevens brothers, 44

Stimers, Chief Engineer Alban C., 73

Stoddert, Secretary of Navy Benjamin, 22-24, 34

stores ships, Great White Fleet, 103. *See also* logistics

Stringham, Commodore Silas H., 52; Flag Officer, 57

Struble, Vice Admiral A. D., 200, 202

submarines: and cruise warfare, 15; British, 151; capability, 5; early, 48, 72; effects of, 132; fleet, 161; Holland design, 91; increasing capability, 98-99; nuclear, ballistic missile, 216-17; WWI, 120, 122, 126, [British losses to] 127-28; WWII [Battle of the Atlantic] 150, 154, [German] 144, 167, [Japanese oil] 174, [U.S. Asiatic fleet at start] 161-63, [U.S. Pacific] 181. *See also* antisubmarine

subscription warships, Revolutionary War, 22

Suez Canal: control in WWII, 146, 218-19;

WWII mined, 152

Sullivan, Secretary of Navy John L., 194

Sumter, Fort, 51-52

Supply, USS stores ship, 46

Taft, President William Howard, 103

Taiwan: defense, 214-15, 220; sea control in Korean War, 200

Tarawa, assault on, 174

task groups, flexibility of in WWII, 163-64

Taylor, Captain Henry C., 96; Rear Admiral, 103

Taylor, General Maxwell D., 215, 225-26, 258

technology: achieving capabilities of new, 42-43; effects of advances, 253-56. *See also* research and development, specific technologies

Tecumseh, USS monitor, 74

Thackrey, Rear Admiral Lyman A., 204

Thatcher, Rear Admiral, H. K., 75

Thompson, Secretary of Navy R. W., 81

Tito, President (Yugoslavia), 188

Togo, Vice Admiral Heihachiro (Japan), 100

Tonkin Gulf, attack on *Maddox,* 230

Torch, CSS gunboat, 72

torpedoes: acoustic, 171; attack in Russo-Japanese War, 100; development, 90, [mine] 48-49; self-propelled, 81; spar, 72; and submarines, 98; WWII [Japanese] 140-41, 156; [U.S. problems] 140-41, 163. *See also* mines

Tracy, Secretary of Navy Benjamin F., 91

transport, advantages of sealift, 1-3

Truman, President Harry, 187, 189-90, 192-93, 195, 197, 200, 203, 205, 209, 212

Truxtun, Captain Thomas, 22

Tyler, President John, 49

underwater weapons, early development, 48-49

underway replenishment: *see* oil, refueling at sea

United States, USS, 32

Upshur, Secretary of Navy A. P., 45

USSR Navy: expanded, 241; strategy, 242-45

USSR: following WWII, 186-87; territorial waters and regional seas, 245

Van Buren, President Martin, 43
Vicksburg, Civil War, 66, 73–74
Vietnam, support in 1961, 227–28
vVietnam War: control from Washington,
  229–30; naval role, 230–36
Virginia (Merrimack), CSS iron-clad, 67–70
Virginius, US merchant steamer, 81

Walker, Lieutenant General Walton H.,
  205–6
Wampanoag, USS steamer, 77; *(Florida)*,
  78
War of 1812, 31–34
Ward, Lieutenant J. H., 45
Warrington, Commodore Lewis, 45
Washington, General George, 13, 16–17;
  President, 20, 251
Washington Conference, limits warships in
  1921, 135
Washington, USS battleship, 166–67

Wasp, USS, 32–33; carrier, 166–67
Welles, Secretary of Navy Gideon, 52, 55–
  57, 62, 64, 67, 72–73, 75–76, 79
Whipple, Commodore Abraham, 13
Whitney, Secretary of Navy W. C., 86
Wickes, Lambert, 16
Wilkes, Lieutenant Charles, 44
Wilson, President Woodrow, 9, 97, 104,
  124, 127, 130, 134
Wilson, Secretary of Defense C. E., 217
Wilson, Vice Admiral H. B., 128
Wise, Lieutenant H. A., 56, 63
Wolverine (Michigan), USS iron-hulled
  steamer, 49
Worden, Lieutenant John L., 68
Wright, Brigadier General Horatio G., 60
Wright brothers, 99

Yamato, Japanese super battleship, 178
Yorktown, USS carrier, 163, 165

About the Author

Edwin Bickford Hooper (1909–1986) was born and raised in Massachusetts. After graduating from the U.S. Naval Academy in 1931, he had a long career as a naval officer, retiring as a vice admiral in 1970 and then returning to active service as director of naval history and curator for the Navy Department until 1977. He had broad experience in command at sea, amphibious forces, logistics, and research and development. Naval credits included a Bronze Star for his gunnery when the USS *Washington* sank the Japanese battleship *Kirishima* in a night battle at Guadalcanal. He served as commander of the fleet oiler *Waccamaw,* the destroyer tender *Sierra,* Destroyer Squadron Twenty-six, and Amphibious Group One. In 1962 he became commander, Seventh Fleet Amphibious Force in the western Pacific. He was extensively involved in research and development, receiving a Master of Science degree from the Massachusetts Institute of Technology in Electrical Engineering, serving in the Military Applications Division of the then-new Atomic Energy Commission in 1947–49, as assistant chief of the Bureau of Ordnance for R&D in 1955–58, as director of R&D for anti-submarine warfare and as assistant chief of naval operations for research and development in 1965. In 1965 he also took command of the Service Force Pacific Fleet, in 1967 became assistant deputy chief of naval operations for logistics, and in 1969 the senior naval member of the Joint Logistics Review Board.

Vice Admiral Hooper was married to Elizabeth Withers Patrick of Norfolk, Virginia. They raised a family of four sons, all of whom work in science and technology.